Continuing the twenty-eight-gun salute to Billy Porterfield's *Diddy Waw Diddy*:

"Half memoir, half mythic parable, [*Diddy Waw Diddy*] captures a level of American life and presents it in a way few other writers have dared—a parable of stubbornly clung to lost dreams and gathered and regathered hopes."
—A. C. GREENE, AUTHOR OF *A PERSONAL COUNTRY*

"A tour de force of an autobiography. . . . Rich with incident, the memories and yarns here come to suggest that the wild-haired, trip-dancing Porterfield clan may even be the old, antinostalgic spirit of America itself—that complex attitude that has driven more people than we often think to handle their reversals without losing song or spunk."
—JAMES HOGGARD, AUTHOR OF *PLAYING WITH ILLUSION*

"Absolutely compelling. . . . It starts off sounding like a childhood memoir but it gathers momentum, episode by episode, spanning three generations until it becomes an epic—an odyssey of the Southwest, rather than a family saga. It is at the same time racy and poetic, full of humor and wisdom and above all permeated by the author's love of language—by the literary use of words as well as vernacular. As a non-Texan, who, by virtue of being a Texan's biographer, became an adoptive daughter of the state, I was made homesick for the Southwest—by all the rich details of taste and texture and turn of phrase, by the flavor of the region."
—JOAN GIVNER, AUTHOR OF *KATHERINE ANNE PORTER: A LIFE*

"Mr. Porterfield could lay just claim to having given us The True, Unexpurgated Further Adventures of Huck Finn. . . . It's a wild, funny, poignant ride."
—RICHARD C. LYON, PROFESSOR EMERITUS, HUMANITIES, HAMPSHIRE COLLEGE

"Billy Porterfield's book *Diddy Waw Diddy* grabbed my psyche. I became a viewer instead of a reader. It caused me to travel down a road of time in the back seat of a Chevy where at an intersection of life we pulled alongside a Hudson and through the rear window I saw two small boys looking back."
—ANCEL E. NUNN, PAINTER

"Like the legendary writer/historian Frank Dobie, with whom he must be compared, Porterfield sprinkles the hardscrabble language of the range and oil patch with references to the classics, capturing in the process the ambiguity and diversity of Texas culture and heritage. . . . Billy Porterfield is a Texas treasure and *Diddy Waw Diddy* is destined to be a permanent part of our literary map."
—GARY CARTWRIGHT, SENIOR EDITOR, *TEXAS MONTHLY*

"At last the rest of America can rejoice in what Texans have been celebrating for years—the wit, the intellect, the comic insights, and, perhaps best of all, the just plain old down-home crankiness of Billy Porterfield. Now, in this wise, very funny, 100-proof memoir, he tells us just how he got that way."

—MARSHALL DE BRUHL, AUTHOR OF SWORD OF SAN JACINTO:
A LIFE OF SAM HOUSTON

"A poignant, indelible portrait of a family's life on the road, Diddy Waw Diddy begins around the time Jack Kerouac was jumping rope in the schoolyard and ends in the mid-eighties, when the only heroes left were the ones of our own invention. It sparkles with insight, intelligence and innocence. Reading this book is like stumbling upon Tom Joad's secret diaries."

—KINKY FRIEDMAN, AUTHOR OF ELVIS, JESUS & COCA COLA

"Having gone to school in an oilpatch town myself, I well remember the desperate gypsy-style lives of many families who chased transient jobs from one oilfield to another during the Depression. Billy Porterfield regales us with his family saga in language often poetic, occasionally profane. I laughed and cried some. Mostly, I laughed."

—ELMER KELTON, AUTHOR OF SLAUGHTER AND HONOR AT DAYBREAK

"A memoir for all Americans. This book is written with such insight, humor and profound affection, that the characters walk right off the page and live with you like kinfolks."

—MARGARET COUSINS, AUTHOR AND EDITOR

"Billy Porterfield takes us along a virtual reality, E-coupon road trip with his enthralling and rambunctious family across the hardscrabble backroads of depression era Texas. The love and insight and hope of the Porterfield journey has relevance and emotional resonance more than half a century later."

—VAN GORDON SAUTER, PRESIDENT, FOX NEWS

"For those of us who've read Porterfield's columns and essays, this full-length work is a most-welcomed event. For the newly initiated, his writing—evocative and loving, but devoid of sentimentality—will reveal a time and a place full of hardships and optimism. . . . A highly-readable picaresque by a writer whose clearsighted vision is as forgiving as it is truthful."

—ROLANDO HINOJOSA-SMITH, AUTHOR OF PARTNERS IN CRIME

"The Passage itself is memorable: a boy's journey on the dirt roads, told with a boy's big ideas, his chaotic feeling and his overwhelming need to make some sense of things. But what finally won this reader's heart was the storyteller the boy became, with his wry pathos and good humor. There isn't any blame here,

in this book; even the abusive father is forgiven, though he's not excused. There are a few regrets, but not the bitter kind. Mostly, there's a sense of destination, an eye for drama on the way, and in the end, discovery. It seems to me that Billy Porterfield did find Diddy Waw Diddy after all, though of course by then he was too deeply humbled by the searching ever to admit it."
—ELIZABETH CROOK, AUTHOR OF THE RAVEN'S BRIDE AND PROMISED LANDS

"Billy Porterfield is incapable of writing a boring page. Each one is his heart-breaking, heartwarming elegy to a world lost, a world never found, gleams with a singular combination of elegant erudition and tough-knocks experience."
—SARAH BIRD, AUTHOR OF VIRGIN OF THE RODEO

"Few pre-adolescents have befriended so rare a bird as the imaginative Black giant who resurrected and lived a fabricated Egyptian ancestors' theodicy; few adolescents are rescued from stampede by White Bull of Celtic myth; few mature writers had attempted to weave a fabric of simulated reality before the high-tech media invented it. Diddy Waw Diddy is a real place. . . . Porterfield's ligual scope scans all conceivable emotions, from the base to the angelic, with verbal acuity few dare attempt to control. He frames the strangely usual into the strangely unique with this sui generis production."
—CHARLES E. LINCK, JR., PUBLISHER, COW HILL PRESS

"I highly recommend that anyone interested in that mythical place called Texas take Porterfield's enchanting ride to Diddyland."
—TURK PIPKIN, CO-EDITOR OF BARTON SPRINGS ETERNAL

"Billy Porterfield is the product of a fabulous youth in oil-boom Texas and an impressive self-education in our literary and mythic heritage. . . . [His] world is like Texas itself; things you're sure must be creations of fantasy are as likely as not to be cold sober truth."
—DR. JOHN S. MARTIN, UNIVERSITY OF ALBERTA, CANADA

"As a contemporary of Bill Porterfield in place as well as time, I found that reading his memoir stirred up achingly real sights, scenes and wonders. This is an achievement of recollection, entertainingly told."
—BUD SHRAKE, CO-AUTHOR OF HARVEY PENNICK'S LITTLE RED BOOK

"Diddy Waw Diddy is not just a picaresque account of one man's odyssey; not just a window on life in America from the late thirties to the present; not just a life fictionalized by folklore, legend, myth, romance, and flights of fancy; not just the archetypal pursuit of the American Dream; not just an 'on-the-road' narrative. It is all these and more. . . . A galaxy of characters, ancestors, and especially his parents, rove about in the deep well of [Porterfield's] mind, pulling him forward and backward, eventually to enlightenment. . . . The book is, ultimately, about facing one's mortality, and in this respect it reaches out to all humankind."

—ERNESTINE SEWELL LINCK, AUTHOR OF *EATS: A FOLK HISTORY OF TEXAS FOODS*

"Billy Porterfield has written a great, spirited memoir with his frustrating, belligerent, footloose, and fascinating father as the main character. Unlike many modern accounts of childhood, *Diddy Waw Diddy* is not spoiled by either easy sentimentality or revengeful bile. Instead, Porterfield has turned his unusual—to say the least—childhood into an evocation of American life and character that will be read for a long time to come."

—GREGORY CURTIS, EDITOR-IN-CHIEF, *TEXAS MONTHLY*

"Where is Diddy Waw Diddy? Well, it's in Diddyland which is just past Smithville, a dab to the left of Aransas Pass, not more than a hoot & holler from Gladewater, closer than far from Sequin, poquito distante a Los Ovejas, over the horizon and a sunset or two from Shangrila, Oz and the Big Valley. How do you get there? Not in a Hudson automobile with the Porterfield family. It's been tried in an endless trek from a Texas farm to the Texas oil patches. Billy Porterfield's daddy was at the wheel taking the family to where wealth and peace awaited. But it was Billy Porterfield's stubby little pencil and pad that has found it. Diddyland is magical and tragic and juicy and often a puredee, genyew-wine hoot. Readers will find one of the most delicious rides of their lives with an oasis on each rich page. . . . Billy Porterfield's remembrances are a gift to us all."

—CACTUS PRYOR, HOST OF "CACTUS COMMENTS," ON KLBJ IN AUSTIN, TEXAS

DIDDY
WAW
DIDDY

Also by Billy Porterfield

LBJ Country
A Loose Herd of Texans
Texas Rhapsody
The Book of Dallas (with Evelyn Oppenheimer)
The Greatest Honky-Tonks in Texas
Fathers and Daughters

DIDDY WAW DIDDY

★ ★ ★ ★ ★

PASSAGE OF
AN AMERICAN SON

Billy Porterfield

HarperCollins*Publishers*

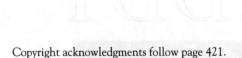

Copyright acknowledgments follow page 421.

HarperCollins books may be purchased for educational, business, or sales
promotional use. For information, please write: Special Markets Department,
HarperCollins Publishers, Inc., 10 East 53rd Street, New York, NY 10022.

FIRST EDITION

Designed by Alma Hochhauser Orenstein

Library of Congress Cataloging-in-Publication Data

Porterfield, Bill.
    Diddy waw diddy : passage of an American son / by Billy Porterfield.
            p.   cm.
    ISBN 0-06-016999-0
    1. Texas—Social life and customs. 2. Porterfield, Bill—Childhood and
youth. 3. Texas—Biography. I. Title.
F391.P83   1994
976.4'06'092—dc20
[B]   93-25301

94 95 96 97 98 ❖/HC 10 9 8 7 6 5 4 3 2 1

Here's to Lucky Pierre
for the good times I shared with
you and Helen
at Barney's wee hotel
north of
the
cemetery
when
we
were
young
and
Room 214
with its Puccini, books and four poster
was
cheap
and even Cold City had a heart

But even if I could sit up all night I don't believe I would choose to be an author. I'm sure it must be lots more fun to do things, than to sit in a room and write about doing them, and there's so many things in this world that a fellow can do, and get such lots of fun out of them. I think the only trouble is to choose which is the most fun to do. And about that I never have been able to make up my mind. Of course the very best way would be to be everything. A little while a pirate, and a little while a cowboy, and so on, and stop being each one when you get tired of it. I wonder if anybody in the world ever managed it so. I think perhaps that is what I shall do myself.

—BILLY, A BOY WHO NEVER WANTED TO GO TO BED
WHEN BEDTIME CAME!
From *The Billy Stories* by Eva Lovett, 1901

It is not just the life that we know. It is not just the life that has been successfully hidden. It is not just the lies about the life, some of which cannot now be disbelieved. It is also the life that was not led.

—GEOFFREY BRAITHWAITE,
From *Flaubert's Parrot* by Julian Barnes, 1984

Contents

Illustrations follow page 202.

Author's Caveat

THIS IS A JOURNEY INTERNAL AS WELL AS EXTERNAL. I'VE TRIED TO keep my muse as true to my total experience as a son as I can without strangling her. That means dream and fantasy play as much a part of my story as the gritty grind of what we take to be everyday reality. And I've worked too long and hard on this without giving imagination and craft their due.

Although I use real family names and follow a trail of actuality, this is in the sum of its evocation my story and no one else's, not even those I portray in my cockeyed way. May the dead forgive me, and the living grin and bear it.

If this that you hold in your hand were my artless life, you would have it, not I. And it would be a handful, a chaotic tub of blood and guts a good deal more expense and trouble to you than the price of a book and the time it takes to read it. If you got bored with me—and you would—you couldn't just lay my life aside on the table with the bills until another day. It would complain, and you would have to pet and feed it and take it to the potty. Good idea to lock up the bourbon too.

So you can thank your lucky stars this is just a representation, like a photograph or a portrait. Of course, retouched and idealized (do you think I'm an idiot?), but I hope not past all resemblance. If it bothers you that I fly only a little better than a dodo bird and commune with ghosts and gods, it means you've been spending too much time at the office. Enjoy.

Postscript: H. L. Mencken called American speech "a flood of racy and unprecedented words and phrases," and I'm afraid you'll hear a touch of that now and then in the mouths of my kin and me, although our expressions were not as unprecedented as they sound. Like the Celts and Elizabethans from which we came, we loved to play with old English words that somehow had stayed alive and growing on our American tongues. I don't overdo it like we did. But if you find my faffling like a tear cat a bit roaky and confusing, you might consult the brief glossary of meanings at the back of the book. I had no idea how to spell the lost words we were regurgitating until I consulted Susan Kelz Sperling's *Poplollies and Bellibones*, published by Clarkson Potter of New York in 1977.

Acknowledgments

Transplanting
> . . . b. concr. That which is transplanted
> 1889 Lancet 20 April 801/1
> . . . Colonies become so intimately fused with others that not seldom the transplanting from them turn out impure.
> —OXFORD ENGLISH DICTIONARY SECOND EDITION

HOW DO YOU CREDIT ANY BUT FAMILY, FRIENDS AND YOURSELF FOR THE life you've led and dreamed as a son? Well, one way is to grow up and become a writer who, from beginning to end, has to have so much help it takes a growing host of boonfellows almost a lifetime to relieve him of his burden.

I thank to the hilt my wife, Diane, who saw only the back of my head—and that in a brown study—for the last half of 1992 and the whole of '93, but like a goddess mad for the muse never wavered in her support. The same goes for my daughter, Oren, all of nine, mine only for summers, come to the mountain to find Daddy transfixed over his book, oblivious to the rapids down in the valley of the Blanco. Now we've got time and the river, my darling.

Diddy began with my life, but it did not manifest into the first draft of a book until the summer of 1967, when I christened it at Paisano, the retreat and goat ranch of the late, great storyteller, J. Frank Dobie. It's been a long haul since Paisano—eight drafts over twenty-six years—and I would have despaired if it had not been for the 132 intimates and colleagues who at one time or another put in their $2.64 worth (that's two cents multiplied 132 times) of encouragement and criticism. The publishers say *bastante*. Enough is enough. I can't name you all. And they are right. You know who you are, so *muchas gracias, especialmente las memorias*.

Another way to pay your dues is to grow up and become a writer who, notwithstanding more objective assignments, finds that he must, out of compulsion or need, sell stories of his personal past. These are not the sort of pieces editors summon from you on command, but rather little midnight pilferings you take from the album of Mother Mnemosyne, whose inspirations you proffer up as a change of pace from your regular rigors in the trenches of the topical, which are always masculine. I always felt I was renting my reminiscences rather than selling them, that once a publisher had his sway with them that they reverted back to me, since I was now the grownup parent of my muse and memories and not some Dickensian waif strapped to the factory floor and the company store. But the establishmentarian law, and lawyers for publishing houses, do not see it that way, and thus the only second-harvest available to a prodigal cognate like me is to gain permission from publishers to return the various shoots and tendrils into the larger family of man tree we had in mind all along. Most permit us that final recovery. And we find ourselves gratefully acknowledging their largess in returning to us our sacred precincts of blood and testament. How Uncle Tomish writers are.

In my case, most of *Diddy Waw Diddy*—save for the aging and death of my parents—had gone through several versions and revisions, and rejections by book publishers, before I robbed Billy to pay Paul and gave up fragments of it over the years to newspaper columns, magazines and that plague of journalists, the collection of miscellanea.

So I am beholden to the *Southwest Review*, *D Magazine*, the late *Dallas Times Herald* and my new benefactor, the *Austin American-Statesman*, for allowing me the embrace and reunion of the orphans of my muse they so kindly took in for one-night stands.

My muse's family, after seven complete transmutations and more transplants than Lamarck would mind, is back home and complete again. And while I never felt like a proper son, I'm beginning to feel like a renewed mother, thanks to my Mystic River agent, Doe Coover, and my editors at HarperCollins, Lawrence Peel Ashmead, Scott Waxman and Charlotte Abbott.

—BMP

DIDDY
WAW
DIDDY

1

★ ★ ★

A Cadenza to the Day

LITTLE EGYPT, OKLAHOMA
Fall 1938

MOST PEOPLE WHO KNEW GRANDPA AT THE END SAID HE HAD gone mad, that the oil boom and all it brought to Little Egypt was too much for him and his old ways. Well I wonder. Because he retreated to the domino bench didn't make him crazy. Isn't that the rural way of growing old? Back to childish games? He grew quieter and was a little queer at times, but I laid that more to senility than insanity. He even seemed happy. When we moved him back to the farm he became a favorite of the children from the oil camps. He would sit on the porch in the rocking chair and entertain them for hours with little stories and songs. Yes he sang! Old Celtic airs we didn't know he knew, said sayings we had never heard before. He continued to dress formally, donning the same dirty black suit each new morning, no matter that ailments kept him bound to the rocker. He hid the sickroom and soil of his clothes behind his old standbys, the fragrance of lilac water and shaving talc.

That last August, when one of the roughneck's wives called him a crazy old coot behind his back, Grandpa turned around and looked into her face. "My dear," he said with dignity, "those who hear not the music, think the dancers mad."

Toward the end, a last vigor seized him, and he was up mornings before the fog in the bottoms had lifted. In our half-sleep we could hear him stirring from the house and making for the woods. His whistling beckoned to us ever so faintly through the mist, lifting in whispy white patches. Sometimes he whistled as if calling someone. I sensed it was his old companion and mine, the mystic Doody Mareain, who had made so good his escape from the county jail that we had not seen him for a year. Alone with me one day, Grandpa confirmed it was Doody who haunted him, and he made me promise that when I reached manhood I would try to track Doody's flight from Little Egypt and determine his fate, at least that which covered his earthly demise, for perhaps by now he was dead, having been a generation older than Grandpa. As for Doody's afterlife, Grandpa said, I needn't bother about that, since shortly he would be privy to such matters. But the air Grandpa mostly whistled was a song of the Hebrides. It was a sweet, gay ditty. Once in a while, rocking on the porch after supper, he would sing the words.

> A . . . far croon-in' is pull-in' me a-way as take I wi' my cromack to the road / The far Coo-lons are put-tin' love on me as I step with the sun-light for my load / Sure my Tum-mel and Loch Ran-noch and Loch-a-ber I will go / By heather tracks wi' heaven in their wiles / If it's think-in' in you in-ner heart the brag-gart's in my step, you've nev-er smelled the tan-gle o' the isles / Oh the far Coo-lins are put-tin' love on me / As step I wi' my cro-mack to the Isles.

It was as if a drum had been beaten, a summons heard. We looked up one evening and the summer was gone. It was after supper and Grandpa had taken his station on the gallery to watch my brother, Bobby, and me pitch horseshoes in the failing light. A breeze built up and blew in from the north, shaking the boughs of the big cedar elm that lorded over us, and in it we could feel the nose of the first frost. Our horses thundered across the pasture, whinnying above the clatter and roar of the lighted drilling rigs at their backs.

Those giant Erector sets and their vampire pumps would become as ubiquitous to Oklahoma and Texas as the cactus, mesquite, rat-tlesnake, Indian and Mexican. Every day and every night for half a century the pumps would suck from the throbbing neck of the earth the dark, incredibly rich blood, the soul sauce of the primordial dead.

And we would burn it, not as incense but as fuel for our gluttonous industry, use it prodigally until the earth itself thirsted. But this was Grandpa's grief, not yet mine, and now he was too old and fey to care. The shadows deepened.

Directly, Grandpa called from the porch. "How can you tow-heads see? By Jess, it's almost dark."

I was aware of a joyous content. All the parts of my world seemed, for a fragile moment, once again in place. Beyond the south corner of the big house I could see the timid cast of light from our kitchen window, and I caught in the frame a silhouette of Mother at the sink. Up on the porch Grandpa's rocker creaked and his pipe glowed like a firefly. He was humming to himself. A horseshoe struck the stake with a clink. Another thudded softly into the dirt, and we called it quits. I could hear Mother calling Daddy. He would be out in the barn milking, two warm, responsive tits in each coaxing hand, drumming the bucket in a creamy cadenza to the day.

As we went up the steps and into the big house I could hear Grandpa singing:

> Row, row, row your boat
> Gently down the stream
> Merilly, merilly
> Merilly, merilly,
> Life is but a dream . . .

When Daddy went to check on him a little later he was dead.

Daddy would wait until morning to tell us kids. As I slipped into sleep that night, I had no way of knowing that the day which had spent itself so sweetly would be the last of its kind for the Porter-fields.

The machine—the drilling rig—was in the garden, making everyone rich but us. Doody, driven from his imitation Egypt and his homemade pyramid by Christian philistines and mummy snatchers, was off in the ether of his dreams, seeking his salvation as an ancient Egyptian in some other part of America. And now Grandpa, the last of my dream fathers, was dead. I felt I was an orphan of the past. The hard stranger who came to steal me away was my direct father, now no longer Grandpa's seed but an oily son of machinery and motion.

We hit the road and struck for the rigs, ever on the runningboard. We went forth in a black Hudson Terraplane. In honor of Doody I dubbed it the Bark of Ra, after the boat of the Egyptian sun god that Doody had carved to take his soul to paradise. And I asked Ra's blessing upon us. I was a foundling among my own people, but I knew I was not alone. The dark angel who was my mother was with me.

Out of Egypt have I called my son
—MATTHEW 2:15

2

★ ★ ★

The Bark of Ra, Its Pilgrims and the First Stage of The Way

DIVIDED VOYAGERS

BEREFT OF GRANDPA, OUR HEARTS BLACK AS THE BARK OF THE Hudson, an heirs' hearse of the darkest reminder, we could not look ahead without looking back at the life and death we were leaving, not to speak of the whereabouts of souls unanswered for, the honorable (if ersatz?) ancient Egyptian Doody Mareain in particular. But beneath that layer of pain, which lay in the cavernous automobile like sour seat covers, was a profounder felt of perfumed memory and talcumed good times which kept Grandpa aromatic and dear to us, even as his thrusting genes propelled us pell-mell into the future.

In the days ahead, Little Egypt and its tombs receded in my father's mind as we sailed south, cresting every cataract, locking their floodgates of nostalgia from our Oklahoman Memphis to our Texan Khartoum. Even into the Sudan, Mother and I would have stayed at the breast of our Nile, white or blue, but my father was done with this nebula of ancient history, this backwoods Thebes conjured by Grandpa and Doody. Wake up, son. Cowboys and Indians were just as dead and a hell of a lot more fittin' subjects for an American boy to dream about than a pyramid full of moth-eaten mummies. He turned in the driver's seat of the Hudson and glared at me. Then he softened. "Son," he said—and he was talking straight and for my own good—"what waits ahead is not the split in the Nile and the Sudan but the Red River and Texas, godblessit! It holds more oil than Oklahoma, and oil is a lot older, and a helluva lot richer, than all the tombs of ever' King Tut, and that's what we're lookin' for. We've no choice. Shit, folks. We're poor asses, our butts skimmin' on bare, and we'd better git while the gittin's good."

Quickly himself, Tice Covey Porterfield was a vital man, irrepressibly American rogue male in his rude get-up-and-go optimism, and he was right. We had no choice but to close ranks behind him that fall as we poked across the Red River landscape of shade and settled lives. Coming out of the ancient mud trough and its trees, the whispering leaves as tawny red and testimonial as the eons of iron ore, Indian blood and buffalo dung that blessed the river, we blinked before the limitless glare, heard our white pagan daddy stomp the gas pedal screaming "Yippee-yay! Here we come-a ki-yi-yippee, yippee-yay," and entered another dimension.

Texas was not new to us. The conflict in Mother's eyes as she reached back and grasped my hand defined her memory of it more than her brave face. We had come this way too many times, for years venturing across the border, through the Grand Prairie and into the gothic gloom and glades of East Texas and its vast stands of pine and oil derrick, where my father had sought work and seeded sons native to the state. And we had suffered the dust storms of its interminable savannah, the once-grassy Panhandle to the west, which in its quoinian grit and heft rose like a wedge out of the Great Plains and lifted the fat ass of Oklahoma, Kansas and Colorado off its butting, jutting head. What I remembered of those forays was rich and wonderful, perhaps because of my newness in the world, but Mother's talk of them was curiously negative. I arch a brow because the trips, at least the first sortie, constituted their honeymoon.

Daddy's telling of their marriage and the first years in Texas was affectionate, and remarkably gusty and rollicking in the face of the fact that they'd set forth in the biting teeth of the Great Depression. I don't want to gainsay the Joads' grief, but let's not make more of that than was the case with us. That the honeymoon was a hunt for work should not have mattered to a migrant girl used to the skinny. Not if she was enchanted with life and her man. Poverty and displacement in America, even during the worst of times—and especially in the light of young love and the serenade of shivaree—is a relative projection of a material society which, in its progressive intent, tends to undervalue the heroic subtleties of common human character, which have nothing to do with dollars and cents and social status. But the poor are branded as insensible cripples, victims of "numbing poverty." The adjective precedes the noun ad infinitum in an impoverishment of syntax, sociology and sensibility, when quite the radiant opposite can be true. It's so evident it seems silly to have to repeat what is a very old saw: The poor can be Saroyan rich, the rich Scrooge poor. We were among the former, at least in my eyes. So Mother's melancholy had to do with something else as we set off again into Texas.

Like Daddy, I hate to backtrack, but if we are to find the answer, damn it, we are going to have to stop, turn the Terraplane around and retreat to 1927 where we erase my brother and me and trade the old sedan for a spiffy Ford V-8 coupe with a rumble seat. My father remains the driver, still a roughneck off hardscrabble, but single. Like many a dude, he blows every dime he makes on his car and girl. Here, upon a lover's lane in the sticks of Oklahoma, I intrude upon my gods—that's what parents are—with dread, employing every beseechment, fingering bead and bending knee. For we are snooping on a couple at the most intimate and seminal turn of their relationship. What they conceived in the rumble seat of Daddy's Ford was both union and division, which held them together and kept them apart for the rest of their lives.

THE HARRELL PASSION

My mother, Janavee Elizabeth Harrell, was used to strong, restless men. Her father, when he wasn't on the bum riding the rails across the continent, pulled his family along behind his roving nature. To the end of her days, Mother yearned to stay in a house that was not towed, rented or shared, a house of her own anchored with an iron-clad title, so pile-deep into its plot of earth that it could not be swayed by the wind of nature or any man's whim. She wanted a house like her abiding soul, which means she dwelled in one but not the other. She never got her dream house. A philosopher would say she settled for the better cave in keeping her soul. But that can't be so if she furnished it with rue and resentment. She drew breath in a house built by her father. The pumpkins were turning a deep orange when Mother was born at Cherry Farm, a mile and a half north of Winslow, deep in the red man's haunts of Indiana. The date was Halloween 1911. William Howard Taft was president of an America as backward as it was forward-looking. Janavee was the third child and second daughter of Bill Harrell and Ora Ann Abell Harrell. Daddy Harrell was a hungry, blue-eyed prodigal in his youth; blunt and burly in his profane age, juicy with life. When he wasn't adventuring across the country—freeloading on the tycoons, thanks to the majority of railroad freight cars over railroad cops—he was a blacksmith. And a bodacious dancer was he, so lyric in his leaps that my last two uncles, now in their nineties, recall him with a respectful awe, even though he was, in their opinion, a possessed character who caroused and cursed too much. He was a Celt. His wife, of English and Black Dutch descent, was as gentle and loyal as he was rash and improvident.

On the surface my mother wore her mother's passive nature. But something else shone in her eyes and heart. Only in her deportment was she an obedient daughter—the opposite of today's feminist, who lets it all hang out. Mother took her father's wild intensity, and, narrowing her black eyes, shoved it down inside her, darkening the cast of her psyche, but electrifying it with the lightning bolts of her intelligence and free will. His turbulent animus both raped and recharged her intuition, which she contained by mainforce, for it could implode with a power equal to that of her father's explosions. The energy in them was good and bad. Even her Eros, as my father would learn, had a stinger in its tail. But then both his sides had horns, a matching set to Daddy Harrell's. This Manichaean duality made father and daughter striking personalities, radiant, repellent. But as I say, the flash of her Logos Mother hid as best she could. And as for Daddy Harrell, why he was so blazing he left no character for his bonny son save that of charm. The Harrell children were handsome Hoosiers. Marguerite, the oldest, was blonde and blue-eyed, wonderfully wicked with her tongue. Glen was tall and too much for the girls of Pike County. Janavee was small, curvy, implosive and mysterious. Oleva came in 1913, a brown-haired beauty of such caressing endearments and magnolia flesh I swooned in her arms as I did Mother's. Oleva and Janavee spoke as much through their refined noses as their cover-girl mouths, and the sounds were sisters in their fetching nasality, which fell on my ears in sweet flats unusually soft and ruffled with inflection. They could call from the grave and I would know them. Mother does. Oleva is alive and well in Arkansas, and Marguerite just died. Mother might still be alive if she had let more of the bile of that brooding sulk out of her.

The family would stay in Indiana until Janavee was nine, and she would never forget those early years at Cherry Farm. They lived in the three-room house Daddy Harrell had built to last, but, typically, refused to paint, and it turned a silvery gray. Mother was not all angst and anger. Janavee the girl loved to hunt rabbits with her dog and roam the woods along the Patoka River. She was fast and fey, a daughter of the rural Middle West, and the Indian sunsets and the Indiana names sang in her until she died, returning on fevered lips to alliterate her last utterance: Tippecanoe and Tyler too, Wabash and Wyandotte.

It was around 1920 that the Harrells moved to Oklahoma, settling for a while in a thirteen-room house on the Dillard Ranch north of Wilson. Daddy Harrell had his blacksmith shop at Rexroat. From the Porterfield place at Little Egypt near Old Hewitt, my father had already begun using Grandpa's mules to haul drilling equipment in and out of the corn patches that were being exploited for oil. He was drawing good money and driving that honky Ford, but when he first came calling at the Harrell house, it was not to court Janavee but Marguerite. The woman who would become his wife was still a kid, and he threw her freshly minted Indian-head pennies to coax her to jig as he waited in the parlor for her sister.

RESOLUTE GROOM, RELUCTANT BRIDE

Within a few years, he was waiting for Janavee.

Impatiently.

She had blossomed.

From the moment he set his sights on her, my father pushed and pulled at my mother—so she said—until he had her so she could not get away. Tantalizing. But no details. He won her parents, especially Daddy Harrell, who saw in the younger man his own muscle and combustive fire, the spark that failed to ignite his strapping son,

Glen. You had to say this about Tice Porterfield, older males snickered: He lit his wick, spun his tool and went at work as he went at play and women: full bore. A fitting son-in-law to Bill Harrell. It was not until after Mother's death that we finally put two and two together and realized I had been hiding in her womb for more than two months when they married.

So that was it?

Not according to Mother. She never spoke of such a thing, although premarital pregnancy has become a family tradition we joke about. All she said was that her parents pushed her to marry Daddy because he had pulled the wool over their eyes. He had a new car, seemed to have money to burn and everyone knew his seminal father and sour but pious mother as pillars not only of a large and hardworking clan, but of the community. Grandpa had seeded a town, a medical practice, named everything around Egyptian at Doody's insistence, seeded almost a dozen kids and set in motion practically all who populate this book. And now that my father had his wife, he wanted to get the hell out of the Dodge City his father had built and make his own way in the world.

Although Mother was vague about other particulars of the advantage she felt our father had taken of her, not even at her blackest did she intimate any sexual trespass on his part.

So, a half-century later, how startling it was, the first time I was alone with my father after Mother's funeral, for him to pull me aside in tears and swear to me he had never forced himself upon her, that he had honored her above all else, reminding me she had been on her deathbed and was out of her mind when she said such a thing. I assured him I had never heard her say that against him, and I did not think she had said it to my brother and sister. It was the last we spoke of it. The only complaint of that nature I remember was her lament that Daddy had not given her enough time to recover from my birth before they started on my brother. His birth ten months after mine had been hard on her. She was perfectly proportioned; and it followed, at least in this case, that her reproductive organs were small. But Daddy and Mother had been light with procreation compared to his parents. Grandmother Alice was a battle-ax, which was why Daddy had none of the feminine in him. If he did, the woman in Daddy was a warrior Mother despised inside and out—the Alice within and the Alice without. But the old Alice without may have to be forgiven. She had eleven children by two husbands. That would sour the sweetest grape. And maybe Alice was armed against Janavee because she could see through the girl's ambivalence about her seventh son.

Within the family, Mother could be almost as bawdy as Marguerite about sex in general. We were too close to the garden and the barnyard to be squeamish about the birds and bees. All of us paraded around the house naked and never thought about it, she and Daddy often taking baths together and sometimes with us. We skinny-dipped in cow ponds and creeks. She handled her children's passage through puberty with common sense, sympathy and humor, befriended unwed mothers cast out by others, and when Bobby and I found condoms in her bedroom dresser, she blushed, laughed and said for us to stay out of her drawers, that that was her territory, and Daddy's.

BOOM, BIRTH AND BUST

They paid off the preacher in Wilson, and in the open-tide of Herbert Hoover's nomination to succeed President Coolidge and carry on Silent Cal's vaunted prosperity, the newlyweds set out for Texas in the Ford of such ill repute for Mother. She hated the car; Daddy loved it, petting it with polish. She thought him a hoddypeak. It seems my father was as unaware of his bride's subterranean tremors as the Republican presidents were of the country's.

The action in the Oklahoma oilfields had just about played out. The boom had shifted to East Texas, where Dad Joiner, the wildcatter, had brought in the biggest field of them all. Tice was by now an experienced hand at every job on a drilling rig, and he was rearing to have a go at lancing that rich Texas crude. He and Janavee spent their honeymoon in a floored tent alongside the asphalt of East Texas between Gladewater and Longview. Was she into it or merely dutiful? I suppose both. She lived fully and passionately in her blooming body, and gave of it to her husband beyond what she could give him of her soul, which was wrapped as tightly as the linen that had held Doody's mummied mother. The damage, if that's what I was, had already been done, and was about to surface.

Born five towns later in a one-room apartment at Henderson, I was walking at nine months and thriving at her breasts when Mother had to give one to Bobby, who came as we returned to Gladewater to rent a ten-dollar-a-month shack on the Superior Oil Company lease. We lived cheap because we had to. The boom was busting. Wall Street collapsed. We kept moving because the jobs kept playing out. Producers couldn't afford to keep their rigs running. So many people were out of work the state voted "bread bonds" to feed the hungry. We would go back to Oklahoma and Little Egypt to take a breather and fatten up on Grandpa's corn and pork. I got so bone deep with Grandpa, and especially Doody, I sometimes stayed behind. President Hoover wheepled and was fired. We had a new president with a jaunty cigarette holder between his teeth promising meat and heat for the snapsaucers and huddled soup lines. Daddy was flag-fallen but he wasn't swerked. He continued to insist his bliss and destiny, his very knighthood, lay ahead in the search for oil, the wine of wages and even riches; we boys his pages, Mother his mattress and, by now, haunted highway woman. During the next years, we moved in Oklahoma from Little Egypt to Graham, to Rexroat to Seminole and back to Little Egypt. Mother and Daddy returned to Texas briefly to work a well at White Deer, in the Panhandle. White Deer was memorable because of the dust storm that blew through on Sunday, April 14, 1935. Daddy was working the evening tour (pronounced *tower*) on a wildcat well three miles northwest of town. "It come up about thirty minutes before sundown," he recalled, "and the way the red sun shined on that black thing scared you to death. When the storm hit the field in front of us, you could see jack rabbits trying to get away by throwing themselves against the hog wire fence. Cows were bawling and dogs were barking. It got so dark we turned on the generator and lit up the rig. Finally, just to breathe, just to stay a' foot, we had to get in the doghouse [iron-sided tool room]. The dust and junk hit the doghouse so hard you'da thought it was a hailstorm."

After White Deer, we returned to Oklahoma and tried to stay close to home. Until now overlooked by the oil craze, Little Egypt was about to try for one last paroxysm of greed and ambition before wasting away into another ghost town of the Old West. It drove everyone crazy, even Grandpa and Granny. Within three years, their deaths would release us from Oklahoma. At least they did Daddy.

A Procession of Exiles and Outlaws

TEXAS
Fall 1938

The Terraplane was big and fast. The hand of its speedometer did not disappear in the right-hand tray until after 120 miles an hour. The heavy sedan was a car fit for my father, who was usually in a hurry. But now, in the fall of 1938, without his disapproving daddy to drive him away, a man on his own in tow with wife and children, our journeys through the Southwest slowed to more than a blur between departure and destination. We often tarried as Grandpa might have, turning the Hudson into a house until we could get one to pull on wheels behind us.

No onlookers broke their necks staring as we passed, this freck-led-necked Okie family quaint or trashy in its white vermin vagabondage, for we were one gypsy band among millions of drifters on the American roads of the thirties, multicolored and eccentric as the hordes Herodotus describes descending upon Greece in the Persian Wars.

We were waging war. It was against poverty and the Republican hangover with its shacktown Hoovervilles of open resistance. But now that Franklin Delano Roosevelt was president things were looking up, in spirit if not everywhere in fact. The Great Turnaround would not be complete until we geared up for war. But FDR's New Deal launched us, and we and the pageant of unemployed marched across the continent confident as never before. Better roads and rural electrification would connect and employ us, and everybody wanted to build up close to the pavement and not back in the ruts of dust and mud. And why not? Grandpa and Grandma had hidden back in the woods or way out on the prairies, but not this crop of comers. The idea was to move and shake among the multitude, who like us had left the played-out farms to follow the map of opportunity the New Deal and Texas oil represented. And when you found your sweet spot you wanted it up on the highway so's not to miss anything. If you had room in your car, you picked up a hitchhiker. And if you had room at the table and a pallet for the floor, you took in strangers. What was there to be afraid of? Some kids might try to Bonnie and Clyde a bank, but shoot, that was cartoon justice as long as you kept your head down and remembered you didn't have a dime on deposit anyway and what a four-flushing fucker the banker was when he foreclosed on your place. The robbers were Robin Hoods to us. Daddy had known Woody Guthrie, the bard of the dispossessed, and Guthrie had reminded Americans that "some rob you with a gun, some with a fountain pen." One of the conceits of my father's eighty-five years was that he was once mistaken for an outlaw. It was a spring night in 1934, when, thirty-two and duded up in a suit and driving his Ford V-8 through Altus, Oklahoma, a dusty outpost just east of the Panhandle, he stopped at a diner for coffee, only to be manacled and led away by marshalls, who mistook him for John Dillinger, the FBI's Public Enemy Number One. Dillinger was on the lam from a jailbreak after a string of bank robberies and killings. Daddy bore a striking resemblance to him, even down to the pencil-thin moustache he was sporting. After his night in jail and sudden celebrity—reporters from everywhere descended upon the court-house—Mother made him shave it off. It was sort of his last strut. As the family grew and the Depression persisted, jobs on the drilling rigs got few and far between. So Daddy, at Mother's urging, traded in his little roadster for the secondhand Hudson, more commodious for traveling in tribe. We camped on the side of the road. It was common in those years to come upon migrant camps where you could rent a cot or bed in an open-air barracks, long as you didn't mind sleeping with a stranger of your own sex, since that was considered safer than opposites. Naive, weren't we? But I never got buggered. People were wonderful to us—and this in a much tighter squeeze than we think we have now, all of a sudden. There was a great differ-ence between the Depression of the late twenties and early thirties and the middle class sag of the late eighties and early nineties. After the rich had taken the lion's share, there was less fat left to the mid-dle, which was not so proportionately large as now, and practically nothing for the multitude of the poor. On the farm, we had eaten well, but on the road it was hard tack—biscuits fit for batting prac-tice, hog hide cut and fried into crackling snacks, and poor-man's pie, which was stale bread dipped in butter and milk, sprinkled with sugar and cinnamon and fried in a skillet over an open fire or baked in an oven. We drank water from streams and rain barrels, coaxed raw milk from the tit—when we settled and could afford a cow—

took doses of castor oil for every internal ailment except earache. The latter Mother treated by having the afflicted pee in a cup, which she quickly poured warm and steaming into the offending ear. It was unpleasant, but it seemed to work. When all our collective ears ached, she made sure that no one's urine but one's own entered one's ear. Hard and angry boils often pused up on our bodies, and Mother lanced them by cutting a tiny hole in a dish towel and pressing it tightly upon the swelling sore until it shot forth its yellow bacteria and corpuscles. Aspirin, alcohol, mercurochrome, certain salves and ointments and the daily dose of castor oil or whiskey were the mainstays of home medicine. We thought of ourselves as sanitary and hygienic as conditions allowed. We brushed our teeth with baking soda morning and night, but I would not discover dental floss or a dentist until I was a young man. The same was true of vitamin pills.

Oh, locals gawked at our gaucherie as people do at first one thing and another, and sometimes pointed, and we did the same right back to them. No one could have been worse at making fun of people in bemusement than we, who, without knowledge of Balzac and Dickens, saw the procession of which we were a part—and the sights in the grandstands—as a human comedy of bizarre and endless fascination. I put myself in the other fellow's eyes, even the Elijahs, to see what he saw, if only to gauge our act from without. So a certain self-consciousness, sometimes a rush of pride, other times a rash of embarrassment, rode with me as we went forth. It appeared to me as we passed in our tinny spangled way that we must have left some laughs, but also an almost poignant sense of groping, since we were literally touching and feeling our way blindly, not knowing where we were going or what we would find. At times we winked into the ribald, for we had wit to whip the running, romping haunch of blood, but even that was tinged with a sadness. Unto weariness, the road can't but go on, like the heart. As Terry Allen says, it is the problem for life. In that sense, we are all gypsies living the Okie life. Oklahoma symphonic composer Roy Harris felt it, and identified it as a pure American folk idiom—this same sweet ache that Woody Guthrie blew from a harmonica.

When families took us in, as the Grishams did one Sunday afternoon when we had a flat in front of their house on U.S. 271 between Deport and Bogota in Northeast Texas, we'd all eat supper outside as much as in, weather permitting, on tables under trees, at twilight and into dusk the voices growing mellow as the meal in our bellies and the last wink of light, Daddy working Floyd Grisham for a reckoning of the work situation around and about, and then just swapping stories and news of the day. Most of the man-talk was about fishing on Cuthand Creek or the Sulphur River, or, more seriously, the optimism that FDR, now into his second term, had spawned, and how it wasn't false. The upturn was real.

And you know what? Over in Germany that new chancellor, Adolph Hitler, is doing his own FDR imitation. Better believe it, brother. The Depression's global, and the Germans, already demoralized by defeat, are worse hit than we are. But now they've got old Adolph, who's lit a shuck under them same as Roosevelt has under us. Krauts've gone back to work, autobahns are being built, cities renewed and business is brisk. Heck, Hitler could beat out Roosevelt for Time's *"Man of the Year."*

By poor-man pie time, talk was sweet and sleepy. Our hosts had offered board and bed and now they gave us their dreams, the Grishams confessing that they too, satisfied as they seemed, were yet exiles and that their hearts would go with us.

The whole world was in flux. Everything that had belonged to the swells was up for grabs, or so we thought, the Republicans on the run. It was exciting, the flip-flop, the arrivals and departures, hellos and goodbyes, the Whitmanesque fraternity of the road. Daddy, epileptic to leave the farm, felt freed. He loved it. He would get so excited about the New Deal he'd get windy and wound up again, trying our yawning hosts. Mother would take away his coffee and ask for milk to calm him, preferably clabber, which was common then. Daddy would reach for a biscuit or corn pone, which he crumbled into the milk and ate with a spoon. Made him sleep like a baby, he said.

Until the crack of dawn.

It was uncanny the way Mother could raise us without an alarm, get dressed and straighten up our mess—folding every blanket and cot—and get us out of there and on the road without waking another person in the house, not even Ruby Grisham, who would find beside a clean sink and a fresh pot of coffee Mother's thank-you note, its sentiment in flowing cursive leaning as expectantly forward as the road we would take.

Before falling to sleep, Daddy had told her that one of the men at supper had given him a lead on a job that seemed like a sure thing, some scratch that would last longer than an itch. And if it worked out, sweetheart, he'd get us a house.

MAJA, THE ALL-MOTHER

At twenty-seven, Janavee Porterfield was still young and expectant. At four feet ten she was an hour-glass of an olive-skinned woman with large black eyes that tapered at both ends, accenting a straight-boned nose over a large curved mouth, the full lips parting to show off a handsome row of perfectly arrayed and perfectly white teeth. Those years she wore her dark curly hair fashionably cropped and oiled, parted on the right side and combed down over the left cheekbone in a tight, rippling swath that ended with a winged flourish short of the corner of her mouth. Rather chic for a country girl. And if it blocked Daddy's view of her face from the driver's side I can't say for certain it was intentional. We can forgive her some reserve. After all, he was pumping her with child after child, not allowing her to catch a breath and rest her womb between Pete and Repeat. And here she was pregnant again. She lived on powdered aspirin, and her makeup hid a worry line that was deepening between her arched (carefully plucked) eyebrows. Yet she seemed happy now, sitting up there on a booster pillow in the deep front seat of the Terraplane beside her husband.

I sat behind Daddy so she could turn and talk to me directly without breaking her neck. I was eager for her favors. I made a funny and she looked around and beamed at me. I asked silently if I could crawl over the seat and sit beside her, and she let me, hushing my father's protest. I sat between them, leaning against her. Everything about her wafted and glowed, the scent of her perfume and powder, the current of her electricity, the sheen of her eyes and hair, the black of her natural beauty mole, the red of her lips and lacquered nails. The knowing eye, dew-lit or damning, the Sybarite lips, the meloned breasts, the swelling belly and figged hips. That autumn in the spring of our family her always-ample breasts were perfumed and bursting with she-wolf milk, so much so that my sister who would emerge shortly from her womb could not contain it all—hellfire, cream's a'wasting—and we males from Daddy on down—my Romulus and Bobby's Remus—helped milk her with our eager mouths. I was glad to be back on the titty. After Bobby's birth, I'd hung on past my father's scorn, until even Mother had had enough.

Quite obviously this abundant young woman was the fount of our family communion, the wafer and wine goddess upon whose bosom we consecrated the fluid, fleshy and emotional needs of man and child. At one time or another, we males would profane her with inconsiderations, outright challenges, even rejection and avoidance. But even mortal maters have the eternal on their side. After each affront we went back to her, even if it took years and the denial of mates, penitent and hungry for the Niagara of her affection and approval, which, for all its Olympian flow, she learned to channel and turn off or on as if by spigot. We were, behind all the masculine buckram and huffty-tuffty, beyond our survival of her death, a matriarchy, if an embattled one, bless her holdout heart and reigning spirit. She was, is, the matrix of my body and soul.

3

★ ★ ★

Gladewater

A JOYCEAN DAWN

BOBBY'S BEAUTIFULLY NAMED BIRTHPLACE IN EAST TEXAS LURED us back again with that job Daddy had been told about, and he got it.

We bartered for a room in back of a widower's farmhouse near the lease. It was cold and filthy but Mother did the best she could. She bought and cooked enough grub for the farmer in feeding us, and that was better'n rent, he said. First time he'd had three squares a day since his wife died. His name was fit for no company—it's a wonder he kept it—so let's call him Mr. Woebegone and say he was a nice man anyway. Daddy was a driller on the graveyard tour of a new rotary rig. That meant he was a shift boss who directed a drilling crew of roughnecks from midnight till noon. The graveyarders were relieved by the daylight crew to keep the rig running around the clock. Twelve hours was a long haul—some producers were cutting tours to eight hours by adding a third crew—but more hours meant more pay and Daddy was hungry to get it. It was the most powerful rig he'd worked on, and they were going deep, more'n ten-thousand feet at a cost of something like forty-thousand dollars. And if they hit pay dirt, there'd be more drilling in the field. The work could last for years. Shoot, we might buy a house!

My father liked graveyard. He said he'd rather wear longhandles in December than strip to the skin and blister in July. Besides, this new rig was powered by old steam, and every time you leaned against something, it was usually a hot pipe, and it got your attention.

He got home in time to eat lunch and get his *zzzzzzzs* and still have a couple of hours to spare. That didn't leave a roughneck time for much of anything, but there was nothing to do in Gladewater if you didn't fish or fight, and there was plenty of that, since the boom-town was wet-eyed with lakes and ladies of the night.

We did go see the cemetery. It was old and said to be the richest and most perpetually caring of the future, thanks to a profitable oilwell amid the tombs that never said die. Daddy fancied himself a rock-hound, which meant in his case a self-taught geologist—he only had a fourth-grade education—and one Sunday he took a kind of creepy conceit in explaining to me why this Golgotha of a gusher was so ever-lastingly effluent. "Whur," said he, "do you think oil comes from?"

"The ground, I guess."

"And what's in the ground?"

"Oil?"

"Yeah," he snorted, "but what makes the oil?"

"Tell me, Daddy."

"Tha dead."

"Grandpa's making oil?"

"Not yet, but he will."

"Tice!" Mother said sharply.

"It's the truth," Daddy said, heh-hehing. I wasn't sure how to take him. But what he said distressed and puzzled me, sounded like a punishment in hell, knowing how Grandpa hated the discovery of oil in Little Egypt and never gave in to its blandishments. I had a pic-ture of Grandpa chained by the devil, forced, by some miscarriage of fate and by some ghastly chemistry I didn't understand, to make the thick, foul-smelling stuff that stained Daddy like a tar man.

"You know what that makes me?" Daddy went on, raising a wicked brow.

Mother and I looked at him stonily.

"A grave robber."

"Stop it, Tice!"

"There's nothin' older'n oil or a better distillation of the dead," he intoned.

"You're horrid, and you're frightening him. He'll have nightmares. He's had enough to dream about without you—"

"Ah, Jennie," he said. "I'm just joshin' the boy. A little lesson in geology won't hurt him none, not if he's gonna end up one of them college-educated rockhounds. Now, Billy Mack, that wouldn't be a bad thing to consider when ye get older. Them pink-faced little graduates come out of school and right on up to the rig floor and tell the big boss what to do. They hate to get the tiniest spot on their white shirts and ties—oh, they're finicky—but they make the dough-re-me, I tell ye. More'n I'll ever hope to make."

"Daddy, you're doing all right," Mother said. "Thank God you're working."

"And we're puttin' away some," he said, grinning, gigging her in the ribs with a big thumb. "Ye'll get'che house, woman."

She shook her head and looked away. "Don't tell me that again, and not mean it."

We saw her shoulders shake. She was crying!

"Well, shit, Jennie," he said, bending down on one knee before her. He got out his bandana and wiped her tears, a bit roughly. His hands were thick and tough as the guy wires anchoring the drilling rig. But his intent was gentle.

That night in bed with Bobby, Doody Mareain appeared in a dream to tell me that my father with his geology had confirmed the power of the dead. I asked Doody if he was dead or alive, and he said that if I still knew my Ba, the bird that flew between the dead and living, I would know. Then Doody withdrew. It was the first I had seen of him since before his arrest, and it frightened me. I shooed Ba away and tried to forget Doody.

The next day was Sunday, and that night after Daddy got up to dress for work, Mr. Woebegone, bundled against the cold, appeared in the doorway. "Porterfields," he said, "have yawl been to the Gladewater Roundup?"

"Nope," Daddy said.

"Well, come on, let's go. The preacher gave me a batch of tickets. He said he preached such a sorry sermon he figured he owed me something, since I was the only man that showed up for the service. Howabout it?"

"Gotta go to work, right here directly," Daddy said.

"I keep forgettin' you don't get a night off," Mr. Woebegone said. "Not even the Lord's day."

"Take the wife and boys," Daddy said. "They could stand some fresh air and manure."

"No, Daddy," Mother said. "I don't feel so good. I've got morning sickness."

"But it's evening."

"I've got that too. Mr. Woebegone, Bobby's over at the McGlintys'. Take Billy and run by and get him. Daddy, give Billy some money for pop and peanuts."

"No you don't," said Mr. Woebegone, "the night's on me. I'm gettin' off light with two whippersnappers."

It was the queerest roundup grounds. Undergrounds was more like it. It had been a salt water pit, now drained and dry, big enough to hold an arena the size of a junior football field. The bulls and horses and cowboys performed down on the sodded floor, well below the level of their heads, while we sat up in airy stands that rose at ground level and looked down on them. They entered the arena through sloping passageways. How they kept it bailed out during the rains was beyond me. I hardly noticed the rodeo. Spent most of my time shivering, helping Bobby shell his goobers and watching the watchers.

My mind was on one thing. What to call Baby Sister when she came? We all wanted a girl to match Mother. We were tired of mostly being boys. Mother giggled and told Bonnie McGlinty that all she saw morning, noon and night were googies, in various stages of repose and erection.

"Let's trade," howled Ms. McGlinty. "All I see are split tails."

"You forget your husband," Mother said.

"Yes," said Ms. McGlinty. "I ain't seen what there is of Clyde's in a month of Sundays."

Mother said Bonnie should thank her lucky stars. "All I can say for myself," Mother added, laughing, "is that if God has any mercy at all, he'll spare me another one."

He did.

She came on a Joycean dawn, Mother babbling in labor like Molly Bloom. The baby had pale yellow hair and green eyes. We called her Joyce Dawn.

Up to Something

But I'm getting ahead of myself.

Some weeks before Joyce's birth, Daddy had gotten very mysterious. Instead of coming home directly from the rig at noon quitting time, he'd drag in at dusk, drop like lead into bed, only to get up after a few winks and head for the rig again.

Mother was beside herself. He wouldn't tell her where he had been or what he was doing. He'd just wink and say he was up to something, awright, but for her not to worry her pretty little head about it, that it would all come out in the end.

Of course, she thought he was running around on her. The doctor had told them to lay off sex until after the baby. The funny thing about it was that he didn't smell of whiskey or strange perfume, had no lipstick on his shirt. In fact, when he came in late he was as iron-toed and oil-rig dirty as he was when he got home at a decent hour. And boy was he tired.

"Ha! It's no wonder," said Ms. McGlinty, narrowing her eyes until they were slits. "He's either being real crafty—you know, cleaning off the evidence and then putting back on his work clothes—or he's messing with some old whore in a hog wallow."

"Well thanks a lot," said Mother, torn between the broad fun Ms. McGlinty was making of her suspicions and her own anxiety.

"I know what's he's doing," Ms. McGlinty said, "and it's something so sweet and husbandly that you oughta be ashamed of yourself, Janavee, having such thoughts. He's sneaking around to surprise you with something. And Clyde's helping him. I shouldn't be telling this much. That's all I'll say. You can eat your heart out and make yourself miserable, or you can take my word and brighten up."

When Mother found wood shavings in his dirty socks she was washing, she started putting an extra sweet in Daddy's lunch pail.

At last, the day came. Not the one with Baby Sister, but the one bearing the surprise. That noon, with great ceremony and style, a showered and shaved Daddy blindfolded Mother with a bandana, and, ordering Bobby and me to keep our traps shut, whisked us off in the Hudson past the woods near the drilling rig and up to a dormant old peach orchard, which we entered by a sandy road. A family of half-grown, half-wild shoats greeted us, running alongside the car with squeals and entreaties for food. Daddy had to kick them away before we could get out of the car. He didn't remove Mother's blindfold until he had her lined up in front of:

Her house—our first.

Mother cried, and kept crying, and Daddy said it was just as well, since the tears magnified the size of the house and made it look like a mansion.

It was tiny—two rooms—but it was ours. If on the shifting sands of another man's land.

Daddy paid forty dollars for it. It had been an unpainted sharecropper's shack, dried and weathered by the years, but intact. Daddy had borrowed a truck from his boss, and, using come-a-longs and boards for rails, he and Clyde McGlinty pulled it up on the bed of the truck and hauled it to the orchard, near the rig. The man who let him put the house on his land said we were welcome to stay as long as we pleased, without rent, so long as we dug him a well. He had thirsty hogs on the place. We could share the water with them. But first, working on the sly, my father and Clyde had renovated the house, replacing rotten piers with new tree stumps they'd cut, repairing floor, walls and roof with sturdy, secondhand lumber and shingles. They washed it with disinfectant inside and out, left the belly of the roof exposed so we could lie in bed on our backs and watch the shafts of sunlight and moonlight streak through the cracks in the shingles. I said we lived in a barn. It was drafty and leaky, a blessing come hot summer when the wind bore rain clouds. Bonnie McGlinty had helped Daddy come up with a few basic pieces of furniture— springs and mattress, cots for us kids, a dresser, a table, icebox and wood cookstove. We already had oil lamps, a radio and such. It was enough for starters. Mother prettied up the place. She hung curtains and covered the kitchen wall behind the cookstove with oilcloth so she could wipe it free of grease. She had Oleva bring from Oklahoma and Arkansas family trunks full of framed pictures and odds and ends. In a week of afternoons, Daddy, red-eyed by now, threw up a screened sleeping porch at the back of the house and a wire-mesh chicken yard with box crates for coops. He even strung chicken wire around the yard to keep the hogs out. Then he had to ease back to the old routine and get his eight zs of an afternoon, lest he fall asleep one night at the bull wheel up on the rig and drop tons of pig iron on himself and the crew. Exhausted, he was in no mood to take on the mankiller: digging a water well by hand in the Texas sun. We prayed for rain and got it, the landlord's hogs drinking from a wet-weather creek and us making do with rainwater hauled from a cistern at a ghostly railroad depot. We filtered it through cotton dish towels.

TATUM AND LARREAUX

But with Joyce dirtying diapers, spring drying into summer and the landlord counting down the days when he was going to see a well, Daddy hired two men to dig for water. They came with spades, picks and grub hoe, windlass, rope and bucket. It was hot and humid, hellish labor, and they went at it in good humor. If we paid forty dollars for a house, I hate to think what we paid them for a well. "Glad to get work," the older one said, watching my face intently.

Their faces were pitch black, glossy in the sun, the whites of their eyes yellow. Thin as wraiths, they looked like brothers of the missing Doody Mareain. This excited me. I asked if by chance they knew Doody. After all, he was a Texan. The older one said no. Well, of course not, silly me. They were Mareains in miniature, barely bigger than boys, and I asked the older one why, telling him Doody was almost taller than God.

"You talk fast for me," he said, bidding me closer with his surprisingly long, tapered fingers, black on the outside, worn tan on the inside grasping part. "Slow down. Say it again, please?"

I did, adding that Doody was seven feet tall.

He chuckled and said a man that high would have to dig a well as big around as a silo or he wouldn't have any working room when he bent over. And you had to bend down to dig a well.

The younger well digger was out of hearing, but the old one must have told him what I said because later I saw them pointing at me and grinning, slapping their thighs and swaying like giants in silent hilarity. We all tiptoed around and spoke in whispers during the afternoons when Daddy was sleeping. I thought they didn't believe any man could be as tall as Doody.

Their names were Tatum and Larreaux, and it became evident how practiced they were at the work for which their size, and tight strength, were so suited. They had to go down about forty feet to strike water in that fruity, ferny oasis. While Tatum and Larreaux took turns digging, tail up, arms constricted the deeper they got, I helped the one on top haul up the dirt the one below had dug. We pulled it up in the bucket attached to rope and windlass. I was in the way, but they indulged me and promised Mother they wouldn't let me fall in the hole. Tatum's only admonition was not to throw or kick anything in the hole when the other fella was down there. Bobby managed to do that very thing and was sent to the McGlintys for the duration of the digging. I was glad to be rid of him, but at the same time sorry for him.

The McGlintys were swell neighbors, but their girls were something else. Older and much taller, their breasts ripe buds and their vulvas swelling, they would slip up behind Bobby and me, lift their skirts and dresses and bring them down on our heads like hoods, holding us tightly as we screamed and struggled. They had Bobby so convinced they were going to smother him in the thrall of puberty that Mother had to coax him from the house.

At the well head, Tatum showed me hand semaphores and how to jerk the rope to signal the ups and downs of the bucket. Each digger went down and came up by the same means, sticking a foot into the bucket, grabbing the rope, jerking it and holding on. On bottom, each was patient and prudent in his shorthanded picking and shoveling, never biting off more than physics allowed, breathing evenly without panic as the air shrank and the sky and the very light retreated from his tunneling descent into damned near darkness. One afternoon, catching Daddy before he went to bed, I got him to let Tatum and Larreaux lower me into the hole. It was like being cast down into the maw of the earth way before your time and far too deeply for mortals to reclaim you. I might've been down there a second before I'd had enough.

It was a day's work to them. Tatum and Larreaux dug shirtless from sunup to sundown, stopping to sit in the shade for sack lunches—usually sausage links soaked in hot sauce on bread, garnished with a ball of raw onion they called the Sabine Sweet, and it was, almost a relief after the peppery sausage.

I savor the tableaux. For all their quiet, contained industry, and because of it, Tatum and Larreaux came up perspiring in the humidity, for this was the tropics. But they did not gulp at the water cooler like me, who did little work and peed every five minutes. They sweated out their water. They drank sparingly at first, then fully as their metabolism slowed. As they sat renewing their efficient and eloquent bodies, drying and eating without speaking, their savanna eyes in Africa as far as I knew, I saw and smelt the salt of their electric sweat skim up in white patches on black. I saw how red and tasted how savory the meat their ivory teeth chewed, how white the bread they passed in hands heavy with earth and hoe.

But how light their fingers! All of a sudden they were fluttering and sailing like manic butterflies. Back and forth at one another these suddenly expressive digits danced, as if freed from the slavery of their masters.

I thought these dark men had gone mad, that, for all their élan, the hole they dug had somehow spooked them into dementia. It had me.

I ran into the house and called Mother. "Tatum and Larreaux have gone crazy," I said. Mother peeped out the porch screen. She turned back to me with a laugh. "Billy, Billy," she said. "They're talking with their hands. Haven't you seen that before?"

"Should I have?"

"Well, come to think of it, I guess not. The deaf in Little Egypt wore hearing horns. Didn't you know Tatum and Larreaux are deaf mutes?"

I was acting a lot younger and stupider since Grandpa and Doody had gone out of my life. Daddy had noticed it, and had put me down a time or two with his timely sneers, calculated to remind me I was falling behind in running my obstacle course to manhood. He was right. I had regressed. In our flight from Little Egypt I seemed to have shrunk back into a thumb-sucking, mother-nuzzling stage which did not sit well with him at all. In hindsight, my retreat was understandable. My play in necropolis with Doody and all his hoary premonishments had made me old before my time, so I was rewinding. But as was typical of me, I had gone too far. My growth was never to be the steady progression to the light it is supposed to be, but a jerky series of reversals and projections that plague the bush-league idiot savant. I was either stupid or bright, immature or on the decaying side of maturity.

"Tatum?" I said to Mother. "He hears and says things. I heard him."

"Tatum reads lips," Mother said, "and he can speak even if he can't hear. So really he's deaf but not mute. But Larreaux is both, and that's why they use sign language."

After that, the first time I said something to Tatum I spoke so slowly that he saw it and hugged me, and he and Larreaux had another of their silent laughs. They bricked the round wall of the well as they went along, and at last they came within striking distance of the water sand. Tatum sent me in the house to fetch Mother. All was needed was a poke and we'd have water. Did she want them to tap it? No, she said, Daddy ought to see. We woke him and all went out to watch. Larreaux showed off by having Tatum and Daddy lower him head-down into the well with a small pick in hand. All we could see were the soles of his feet, and then all we could see was the taut rope. We heard Larreaux's tap, then a gurgle and spurt. And then a gush. Without waiting for a signal, we began pulling to draw up Larreaux, but the line was slack and all we had was a knot in the end.

He had freed himself to ride the rising water, and, light as a water sprite, he rode it to its crest, where we could see him bobbing like a cork. We sent down the line. He came up wet and buoyant, grinning in triumph.

We celebrated. Daddy brought out whiskey, Mother presented iced tea, fried chicken and potato salad, and Tatum and Larreaux had supper with us under the peach trees. The water from the well, while still a bit muddy, was as sweet as the peaches, Daddy said. *But not sweet as Joyce Dawn*, we all said, except Larreaux.

The next afternoon, Daddy popped up off his pillow and said to Mother in alarm, "Jennie, don't ever tell a soul this, but do you realize what we did at supper last night?"

"What, Daddy?"

"We ate with them nigger boys. Somehow, it just didn't register with me."

"So what? Billy's eaten with Doody all his life."

"I know, that was different. Let's just keep this between us, okay?"

"Good Lord, Tice. Go back to sleep."

I know this because my ears heard everything, especially at bed. I listened to everything they said. I wanted things to be right between them, the way it was going.

Daddy's "nigger" thing bothered me. He had been decent to Doody Mareain, and he had been okay with Tatum and Larreaux, but I knew that was because they had kept what he referred to as their place, only eating with us at his invitation, for which he was now sorry. Not long after, he took me to order barbecue in a road-side cafe that had a "Whites Only" sign on the front door. At the back was a "Colored Only" sign over a window with a walk-up counter for orders to go. I asked Daddy what would happen if a black ignored the sign and came inside and sat beside us to order barbecue.

"Why, the owner wouldn't serve him," Daddy said. "He'd tell him to leave and come around to the back, where he belonged."

"But why?" I said. "Why can't they eat with us?"

"Because they're not white folks, son. They're burned blacker than Ham and the Hamites. If the owner here served your nigger, ever' white person in here would get up and walk out, and I'd be among them. They're not supposed to eat with us."

"Daddy," I said. "I thought you said Granny ran out of milk when you were born, and that you suckled at the titty of a black mammy."

"That's right," he said with a grin. "I woulda' died without her. She had me on one tit and her own black baby on the other."

"But if she walked in here and sat beside us to eat, you'd turn and walk away?"

"That's right."

"And if the cook who's got his black hands all over the barbecue we're about to eat did the same, you'd do the same. Right?"

"You got'er right, son. And don't you forget it, either."

Oh, I wouldn't. I had never heard anything so stupid and illogical in my young life.

When we bit into the spicy beef, Daddy looked up at the perspiring black face behind the kitchen counter and said, "Great barbecue, boy."

And the boy, who was old enough to be his father, grinned and said, "Thank you, suh. We aim to please."

Lordy, Lordy. These are the things that make children sad before their time. No wonder Doody was bound and determined to leave this earth, which I was about to embrace for a lifetime.

JUST AS PRETTY AS YOU PLEASE

But it was going right that summer, especially when we got the house and grounds the way we wanted. For the drifters we'd become, we were keen on nesting, even Daddy. And Mother was keen on him. It was clear he meant to make an Eden, if a poor Adam's. Her eyes sparkled and her cheeks glowed when he pined for a garden and boiled okra that slipped down the throat so satisfyingly, even if it was a mite late to seed. Next year, he said. He wanted a milk cow. Next year maybe. He wanted a riding horse. Hell, who could afford a fine one in this day and time? What he got were chickens, young but nubile Plymouth Rock and Rhode Island Red hens ready for a rooster. They were proven brooders, large birds with bloodlines bred for meat and eggs, and Daddy went looking for a flock cock to match his hens.

"Your father is being so good to us I can hardly believe it," she confided to me one Saturday night after Daddy had gone to the rig.

"Has he ever really been bad?"

"He's been hard more than anything else," she said. "And kind of crazy at times when he drinks. I've always known he means well, even if I hate his orders from headquarters way of bossing us around. That's just the Porterfield in him. But, I swear, he's shown less of that since Grandpa passed. It's like he doesn't have to prove himself anymore, and can just be. And when Tice is simply being, you know, just living in the moment the way his Daddy did—or often did, Grandpa had his arrogance too—why he's, well, he's fun."

"Was he fun when you were courting?"

She looked at me oddly. "Yes and no," she said. When I raised an eyebrow she laughed and said, "When Tice tries to be charming, and he was trying very hard with me, he's so transparent it makes him seem silly and insincere—you know, the way he is when he's giggly drunk—and I was not charmed. I hadn't liked him so much when he was calling on Marguerite, and when he turned to me I was both uncomfortable and flattered."

"Why flattered?"

"I was still a girl, really, and he was a prime young man with a reputation for wildness, you know, just enough to make him interesting without turning people off. He was seasoned by life and love and work, and there I was, still self-conscious in lipstick and high heels. Besides, he was the first to ask me out. I had to accept. My parents were practically pushing me."

"I think you need to give him a break," I said in the arrogance of my ten years. "It's about time, after the third kid. Don't you think he's earned it now?"

"Well, Mr. Know-It-All," she said. "That was my point in bringing it up. He's, well, he's been generous, and God knows he works hard, here and out on the rig. I think I'm finally letting my guard down, after all this time."

"Mother, what made you put up your dukes in the first place?"

Her dark eyes flashed and put me back down. I had gone too far. "I'm sorry," I said.

"Let's just be," she said, smiling again. Then she pushed me playfully and said, "See? Don't push, Billy Mack. You're always pushing to know things ahead of your time to know them, just like—"

"Just like you," I said.

"I was going to say just like your father, you little dickens," she laughed, and began chasing me through the house until we collapsed at Daddy's booted feet coming through the front door. He wore his tin work helmet, but he held out to Mother a sack of bourbon.

"Here, woman, pour me a hum and you have one. We're going dancing."

"Dancing? Don't you have to work?"

"The rotary table's cracked, and we can't get one out here until tomorrow. Let's boot scoot while we can. Billy, get'che brother. We'll leave Joyce with the McGlintys and take the peckerwoods."

Roughnecks were expected to root and toot, and that sour mash hydrophobia distilled notoriously with the male sides of the Porterfields and Harrells. But since Daddy was playing it straighter, a once-in-a-blue-moon night off was cause to break the cork and celebrate. We drove alongside the Sabine River to Longview and danced at the new Reo Palm Isle. The old Reo Palm Isle had been a whorehouse. Now that's where Mother and Daddy were perfectly matched: On the dance floor they always took the cake. Square dancing, Texas two-step or Texas swing, the waltz, the Fat Mexican Polka—all of us danced without inhibition.

So Mother and Daddy were doing just as pretty as you please. I hadn't heard a cross word between them. One noon he came from the rig carrying a puppy for us kids. It was a dun-colored little bird dog with a sweet, milky mouth and a soft, milky stomach. Bobby and I couldn't agree what to call him. Joyce was too little to count. Mother said to stop arguing, that the puppy's name would make itself known to us when it was good and ready.

Daddy found his rooster in a strutting Rhode Island Red that had some fighting cock in him—not enough to hurt the hens, Tobin Drexler assured him, but spur enough to send some sass into the meat and eggs he'd sire. Oh, he was a big beauty, yellow-red and majestic, his head crowned with a gold comb that turned red when he was aroused. Daddy didn't even have to pay for him. We could keep him on loan. As a favor from Tobin. He was Daddy's boss, a burly hulk of a tool pusher who not only oversaw the rig we were working but others. In the whole outfit, Daddy liked to say with pride, nobody was a higher bigshot except the superintendent, who was sick and seldom around, and the producer himself.

"The only thing I ask," Tobin said to Daddy when he brought out Big Red and put him in the chicken yard, "is that you take good care of him, Tice, because, as I say, I'll want him back when he's got you a brood a'feathering out good. Feed 'em the best. This cock's my prize. And, say, you know what I'd do if I was you?"

"What?"

"I'd put me a layer of wire over the top of the whole chicken yard, because I don't want you clipping his wings."

"Ye think he might fly out?"

"I know it, Tice. If he sees one of them shoats you got running around the place poking a snout at one of his hens, he'll send that pig squealing. Liable to put his eyes out."

"Heh, heh," Daddy said, showing his even white teeth. "I might like to see that. Except that they're the landlord's lard. And he wouldn't like that. I'll sky hook a mesh roof for Big Red, Tobin. He won't get away. I promise ye that. And I'm much obliged."

"You bet, Tice. Glad to do it. All I ask is that you have that pretty little wife save me a breast or two out of the first batch of fried pullets you get from old Red."

"It's a done deal," Daddy said.

And they shook on it.

"Now idn't that somethin?" Daddy said that night at supper before he left for the rig. "Tobin a'bringin' me his prize rooster."

"You work hard for him, Daddy," Mother said.

"Yeah, and I hope to keep at it," Daddy said. "He's a prime fella if I ever seen one."

Daddy got up early the next afternoon to put that wire atop the chicken yard.

THE EMPRESS OF ROUGHNECKS

We were close enough to the rig that even in our sleep we could hear them drilling. The hoots and growls and grunts of the Waukesha steamers and the clang and ping of pipe became our lullabies. We got so used to the noise we slept soundly until the rig grew quiet— shut down waiting for a parts man, what ever. When the wind was still in those woods and the screens seem lidded like coffins, we boys could come up gasping for air in the torpid dead of night, crying for Mother to come open the windows so we could breathe. We would be wet as eels in our suffocating bed sheets.

"The windows are open," she would say. "I'll let out the screens if you want."

"Why can't we hear the rig?"

"I guess they're stalled. Billy Mack, you and Bobby Lee spend too much time naked and baking in the hot sun. Feel yourselves. You store heat like batteries. Let me get you some cold wet rags for your heads."

"It's creepy."

"You mean the quiet, Brother?" In the moonlight Bobby's eyes got round and bright.

"Well, yeah. That and the fact that something must be wrong. They hardly ever shut down."

"You think Daddy's okay?"

"It's the derrickman. I see him lying all crumpled and everything on the floor of the rig. He's got to be dead, falling from that high up."

"Mother! Billy's trying to scare me."

"I'm not trying. I'm doing it. Bobby is a scaredy cat. Bobby is a scaredy cat."

"You hush, both of you. You'll wake up Joyce. Here, put these rags on your heads and go back to sleep. Good God, it's three in the morning."

Once in a while we could get Mother so stirred up that she couldn't sleep either, and she'd have cookies and milk with us, tickle and pillow-fight or just lie with us, heads in the window, counting stars and telling stories. Once in a great while, when she was really feeling sassy, she'd wake up Joyce, dress us and herself in our Sunday best, and at four in the morning we'd take candles and flashlights and, carrying the baby and a basket of sweets and cakes—which also bore Mother's high heel pumps—set off on foot for the drilling rig. All we had to do was walk twenty minutes through a stand of loblolly pine, which on its floor was clean and clear of underbrush. Out of the woods and into the meadow where the rig stood, Mother would stop and, standing on one foot and then the other, exchange her house shoes for the spiked heels so that we might make our entrance into "tha man's world" with style.

The derrickman would spot us, making our bizarre way across the field with our little pinlights of partial, even peculiar, illumination and he would alert Daddy and the crew below. We would hear Daddy yell "Shut'er down." The great, greasy erector set shuddered and subsided. A hush fell over the works and all the meadow. It was as if we were being filmed without sound, the set lit by hundreds of light bulbs that laced the tower. As we came up out of the grass and crossed the penumbra into their light, Daddy and his dirty roughs snapped to it, turned to us and stood mute at attention, mock Praetorian. The empress of roughnecks was approaching with the royal children.

And as we drew closer they cheered and whistled like sailors and came down to the lazy bench beside the dog house to snack with us, their huge smudgy hands dwarfing the cakes as they reached into the basket. They teased my brother and me, stole adoring looks at Mother while the bravest attempted courtly comments about her sweetbreads. Daddy damned sure didn't want us doing this too often, for he was single-minded in his duties. But Mother timed our visits sparingly, and Daddy, knowing the producer and tool pusher were not likely to appear at such an hour, enjoyed showing us off. Once every crumb had been consumed, it was his crew's time to show off for us.

They clammered back up the steel staircase to the rig floor. Daddy signaled the fireman to give him some steam, and they cranked her up, Daddy in control at the drawworks. The derrickman didn't wait for Daddy to hoist him on the traveling block and tackle; he sprinted up the vertical ladder and was up on the monkey board, strapping on his safety belt and line, before I could count to twenty. When we interrupted them, they were on a run, stringing drill pipe into the hole. Daddy said they were within a hundred and eighty feet of the bottom with a new bit ready to rotate. We could see the last of the drill stem—six of them, four and a half inches in diameter and thirty feet long—stacked standing, from floor to monkey board, within the steel frame of the derrick. There was a rack for them behind the derrickman. Standing on the steel mesh of the monkey board, the derrickman, with one powerful arm, reached back and pulled his end of a threaded and collared drill stem into position before him, its length below swaying like a slightly limber, seven-hundred-pound stick of dry spaghetti. When my father wound the bull wheel cable drum and sent the block flying up, the derrickman with his right hand flung the pipe into the lock at the bottom of the rising block, and with the left hand slammed the lock shut—all this within a split second as the block shot up out of his reach, trailing its new, glistening black tail. Daddy hadn't given the derrickman an inch, and if he had the derrickman would have spit in his eye. As the block approached the crown of the derrick, lifting the bottom of the drill stem from the rig floor, my father eased off, slowing and stopping it so his floor hands could set their end of the pipe into the threaded collar of its underground predecessor, poking up three feet above the hole and held by giant slips. With the rotary table spinning and cat-head chain a'whipping, the three floor men went at the connection with tong and torque, tightening the pipes for the trip down under. At the works my father stopped the rotary, lifted the string of pipe—some one hundred and thirty-three thirty footers, for they were close to four thousand feet deep—just enough for the roughnecks to pull out the slips, and then he lowered the fresh drill stem into the hole, leaving enough above the rotary table to screw another stem on top of it. When the derrickman ran out of drill stem stacked in the derrick—and he would with six thousand feet to go—they fetched more from a horizontal pipe rack that stretched out fifty feet away from an opening in the side of the derrick. The volume and weight of such an operation were staggering, as was the cost to pocketbooks, ranging from twenty-five to fifty thousand dollars, depending upon depth and other factors.

And so the boilers burned and puffed, the red steam engines tooted and roared, the rig groaned and shook and the block went up and down, picking up pipe and putting it into the hole until they reached bottom.

Joyce never woke up. But on the lazy bench the rest of us—even Mother—were all eyes and ears. No matter the times we would watch a crew at work on a rig, we could not help marveling, sometimes with a shudder, at the dangerous and demanding feats these men pulled off so cavalierly with machinery and physics that could remove a finger, an arm or crush them all to Kingdom Come. All this was enacted over a brooding and combustible wound in the earth that was about to burst forth in a hellfire and damnation blowout—if it was a gusher instead of a dry hole—that could be as dangerous, even with blowout preventers, as it was anointing.

Daddy directed the roughnecks to take the swivel and kelly joint out of the mouse hole and screw the unit to the top of the last drill pipe. Then they attached the mud hose—pythons bigger than firehouse hose—to the stationary part of the swivel and opened the jets to the sludge pump, which drew mud from the pits beyond the rig. The mud ran up the hose, through the swivel and kelly and down into the drill pipe to the cutting edge of the bottom. Mud was a godsend. It kept the bit cool and flushed the cuttings out and up between the outer walls of the drill pipe and hole to be hosed into a settling pit. The mud, treated with barite, helped seal the walls of the hole from collapse before casing was inserted. It kept the drill sting from whipping in the hole. It served as flotation, easing the weight— a hundred tons—of what would be two miles of pipe once they hit the oil sand the geologist swore was waiting down there to relieve our thirst.

My father eased off the bull wheel, set the rotary table in motion and let the bit on bottom rotate. Now they were drilling.

I began to put Grandpa behind me and see my father as the cavalier he wanted me to see. It did not take all that much of a stretcher to think of him as a knight who at midnight drew on his armor—

metal-plated boots, thick leather gloves and a tin hat—and went out to slay, or at least harness and ride, this towering steel vampire that screamed and shook in his grip as he made it paw into the earth, made it maw and give suck to the rich fount so treasured there. That was the grail of his quest, the cupping of the lifeblood that fueled our world. It seemed heroic to me, now that Grandpa and Doody were not at my back in derision of the Western exploiter who was my father. He explored for gold just as the conquistadores and miners had, but his was black and liquid, an elixir older—and who's to say less sacred in the measure of primordial earth to Christian myth?—than that of the Holy Grail sought by Parsifal and Galahad, the chalice from which Christ and the disciples drank the blood of the New Testament.

In the spell of such consecration, Bobby and I saw ourselves as our father's acolytes. And when we finally fell asleep back at the house, we dreamed of following in his heavy-booted steps, smelling lavalike of the crust and core of the most ancient and percolating earth brew, of running rigs and talking with other oilmen of spudding in and drilling, of logging and notching, swabbing, coring and perforating. Daddy wanted us on the rig floor and would initiate us, but he saw us wearing soft, expensive loafers instead of steel-toed boots. He saw us as educated men wrestling with seismic graphs and symbols instead of pig iron and mud. He wanted us to have what he had not, yet within the context of his own occupation. It would make him proud, because it would mean that his work was more than drawing wages, that it was, indeed, a saga that sons found irresistible. We would come to speak the same language, seek the same goals, share the same fraternity. Daddy never said it this way. But Bobby and I knew. We knew as well that his father had offered him an even older tradition and investiture on the farm, and that Daddy had finally said no, that he wanted to go his own way in the new world of boomtowns and bonanzas. We told ourselves we would never do to him what he had done to his father. We would strike it rich his way.

LIKE YE THE FALL?

It was getting late, on into fall. The hardwood, which in its deepest stands almost matched that of evergreen pine, was turning its leaves all the colors of last rapture and leave-taking, and it made me think of splendid October, the woman Grandpa illicitly loved and lost—thereby depriving the rest of us of her pleasure. And now that October was gone in the mist that had swallowed up her husband (not to speak of her lover who aced Grandpa), and Doody Mareain and his shadow, Raff Ardmore, one of the ways I had of bringing her back was through the recollections of Aunt Ella, one of her admirers. The subject of October, or anything that had to do with Grandpa and the farm, was verboten around my father. He had been as drawn to October as any man, but she had represented a challenge and a humiliation to his mother, and, ultimately, to his father, whom he both loved and resented, that he could not square. But Mother shared my nostalgia late that October, and even Daddy was wistful. Joyce was growing like a jackrabbit. And here we hadn't taken her to see Uncle Eck and Aunt Ella, only a half day's drive over in Oklahoma Settlement. And for them to see her. Daddy said let's go. Let's just haul off and go. He would ask Tobin Drexler if he'd get a driller to fill in for three days, drawing our pay, so we could have a good visit. But Daddy came home from the rig with worry on his face. "Jennie," he said, "I can't get up the gumption to ask Tobin for time off. We've got some tricky, sticky, shale to work through, and I'm his best driller. Besides that, the man's gone and give me his best rooster, and here I'm turnin' right around and asking him a big favor I just can't bring myself to ask, if you want to know the truth about it. For God's sake, woman, yawl go to Eck and Ella's without me."

"How?" Mother said. "I can't drive the car."

"Well, shit," Daddy said. "I keep forgettin' that. Ye oughta learn. Ye've gotta, Jennie. It's stupid for a grown woman with kids and such not bein' able to drive. Put's a burden on all of us, I tell ye."

"I'll never learn with you in the seat beside me," she said.

"Why, what'che talkin' about, woman? I can teach you in a jiffy."

"I'd sooner walk to hell," she said.

"Well, stay here then. I gotta work."

Mother wasn't about to stay the way he was acting. She understood his need to do right by his boss, but why did he have to take it out on her? She got Bonnie McGlinty to get Clyde to keep their girls, and Ms. McGlinty drove us in the Terraplane to Oklahoma Settlement.

Eck and Ella Adams had been anchored in the earth since the Stone Age. Eck was supposed to be a Choctaw and Ella a Chickasaw, but the reason they were family was because their smaller, darker tribes had mixed so often with our larger, lighter tribe that they looked and acted white, short of hating red men. They would have been salt of the earth in any skin. Exactly how they were kin to us, I've forgotten, if I ever knew. They were simply Uncle Eck and Aunt Ella, essences of the homespun and pastoral, profoundly farmers who had found richer soil and roots away from the reservation.

The lastima we shared had nothing to do with political correctness. We didn't know what that was. Wouldn't have understood it if a spellbinder burned out trying to explain. We knew what our great-granddaddies had done to the Indians, and some of us gloated in it and a few were ashamed. But most said, what the hell, what's done is done. Let's get on with what we've got. Tough titty this time for you Injuns. We ain't giving nothing back. Maybe next time, snort, snort. Maybe this was why Uncle Eck and Aunt Ella had left Oklahoma to fend for themselves in Texas. But this morbific white smugness was everywhere in our scum, evident in the strangely cool clannishness we allowed our hot little selves while walking all over other people. Nothing deadlier than Anglo-Celt trash, the last century or so. It was our Snopseian time and the Faulkners and Sartorises knew it. It's going now, as organisms and fables flash and fade in this amazingly fatal, if scrappy, little soup of a minor planet. But it was our turn. And we knew it in our quadruple-eyed way. In the two apertures above the nose we had planets for perception unlike everybody else. We had black eyes like Mother's and Uncle Eck's, brown eyes like Oleva's and one of Aunt Ella's and one of mine, and hazels like Aunt Ella and I shared in the other eye. But a sea of green and a sky of blue dominated our planets, sometimes one of each in one face, as you've already gathered. That was among our distinctions, these different colors in each eye, and it had its drawbacks. People never knew which eye to address. And this was particularly unnerving when the green eye, say, could not keep from moving over as close as it could to inspect, with love or hate, the blue eye, which fluttered its lids and acquiesced, closing the gap, or darted away to the other side, holding itself there in wall-eyed anxiety. Rudyard Kipling said of the continents that never the twain shall meet. But in our clan they

damned near did. It was the crossing over of people from the opposite side of the street. It was also what Aunt Ella called, in her tickled
way that made Indian lore seem everyday, the big Ma and Pa, meaning the meeting of female and male. And here I paraphrase her simile: an ocean and earth of nurturing lying down with the cold eyes of
stars, who in their unearthly burning are incendiarily attracted to
something so moist and private in its hidden sanctum of life.
Whichever signals first, pouch or expanse, scabbard or sword, the
other reciprocates, because each opposite eyes the other. It was sex
coupling with the confounded abstraction man is, producing his sun-
crazed gibberish and her tropical semaphore. Plato and Paglia. It
becomes Mailer and Steinem—or even Tice and Janavee—when
repugnance drives them apart. But Aunt Ella has pulled me off my
track, which is to tell you that the bluest eyes of the family were in
Uncle Eck's and Aunt Ella's Choctaw-Chicka-Celt son, toward
whom I had a junior awe. It was not because he was older by two
years. It was because Icky could fly, while I just pretended. Well, he
was coming mighty close.

In 1926, when cotton prices went sky-high and Uncle Eck was
feeling expansive, he and Aunt Ella named their late-born son Martin Luther, after the great Protestant reformer whose schism had
made such an impression on them at the mission school back on the
reservation.

By the time of the Depression, cotton was down with everything
else in America, but Martin's name had been elevated, at least aero-
dynamically, to Icarus. Icky for short. As I say, he had a terrible han-
kering to fly, not like Lindbergh but like Leonardo da Vinci.

At three, Icky was complaining he had no wings, just arms. He
would flap them furiously, like an earthbound chicken. He got to taking running starts, leaping off porches, fences and other modest ele-
vations on the farm. I was witness to this because when we made our
quick-money stints into the Texas oilfields, my folks often dropped
me off at Uncle Eck's place, where we had an ark of kin and Icky and
I a great time together.

I helped him make canvas and stick wings. He strapped them to
his arms, climbed the short windmill next to the pig pen and flung
himself into the air. He flapped crazily, sighed, rolled his eyes back into
his head and plummeted to earth, his impact softened by the mud of

the sty. Still, he was in a coma for a couple of days. When he came out of it he seemed fine, as determined as ever to experience the lightness of being a bird. Uncle Eck and Aunt Ella said no, that he was their only child and that they wanted him to lead a normal life on the ground and not up in the air like the bird he clearly was not. But Icky persisted. He did not so much win them over as make them surrender. You had to look up to Icky. The only thing heavy about him was his courage, which outweighed his slight figure. Like a gosling, he had his eye on the wild blue yonder, and, often, while we worked on a new set of wings, he would whisper-sing, "My heart knows what the wild goose knows/ And I must go where the wild goose goes. . . ." My hands helped him in the toolshed. My mind and prayers went with him up into his launches. But vertigo kept me rooted to the ground. The only way I could keep up with Icky was to fly on my imagination. That's how I went with him. He called me his copilot.

Uncle Eck gave up making a farmer out of him.

Our visit that fall fell on the eve of what Icky excitedly confessed, first chance we got away from Bobby, to be the turning point in his life. The next morning, Saturday, Uncle Eck was to take him into the settlement and apprentice him out to Sam Longmeyer.

This was it for Icky. The call from on high. And I would get to tag along for the introduction.

The passing of the son from father to mentor took place in the doorway of the huge Longmeyer barn. It was stacked with more man-sized, Sam-built wings—many broken—than a heavenly hangar. Icky trembled before Sam Longmeyer, a fearsome-eyed, eagle-beaked man who gazed down upon the fledgling with such intensity that later Icky said he felt as if Sam's vision had penetrated past his feathers to gauge the tensile strength of his hollow bones. Sam called himself an aeronaut, a winged gliderman. He was a mythical character in a forest of eccentrics, his crafty deeds of derring-do common in the hyperbole of Piney Woods legend.

In this Daedalus, our Icarus met his true father. Downy-faced Icky had tried to fly from a windmill, but there was not an eyrie the mustachioed Longmeyer had not scaled, not a towering pine or promontory from which he had not propelled himself. He had flown from oil derricks, which were rising in the thicket as fast as the trees were falling to the saws.

Sam came down. He swooped down to Icky's level, placing his horny bill in the boy's face. Sam was as biblically Old Testament as he was Greekly mythological, and he intoned, "So boy, ye say ye want to fly?"

"Yessir."

"Like ye the fall?"

"The fall, sir?"

"The fall. Flapping for men ends mainly in the fall. Can ye take the fall?"

"Yessir. So far, so good."

"Har, har," said Sam. He went back up, puffing his breast in approval, spreading his great wings. He allowed the feather of a wing to grace the cheek of the eaglet. Clearly, it was a benediction. Then Sam grew stern.

"Now, Master Eck," he said. "I will take the little bird as an apprentice on two conditions. The first is that ye understand, the both ye and the boy's mother, that in my passion to fly I have driven away my family. Mad is my wife, gone are my sons, all but Bennie Tom, and, as you know, he's fallen so many times he's dim. So I am a possessed creature, as I am gossiped to be, an eagle in a man's body. And I am devilish to please, a hard master. The second condition is obvious. This is dangerous business, a body heavier than air flapping about. A damned fool could die of it. And only a damned fool would risk it. I've the broken bones and concussions to confirm it. So I enlist no one but myself. I'll teach the boy all I know, but I'll not take responsibility for an act of God, if ye know what I mean?"

"Sam," Uncle Eck said, nudging Icky. "The boy's a damned fool about flying. He's as daft as you are, and he'll be trying to fly whether you take him or not. His mother and I would feel better about his chances with you."

"Yessir," Icky said. "I'd be most proud and humble to be in your service."

"Then so be it."

Icky was to report to the barn for initiation the next Monday morning at sunrise. He was told to bring his own lunch, to stay until dark before heading home and to expect more lecturing from Sam, and more reading and figuring than a boy could stomach, as well as a lot of errand-chasing and carpentry. It would be months, maybe more, before Sam would let him strap on the first wings, and even that would await Sam's final, and most severe, appraisal of his aptitude and progress.

The big day held such excitement for Icky that he could not come down out of the clouds to share himself with me that weekend. I ended up playing with Bobby after all.

But the visit was not entirely a bust.

It gave me some attic time with my notebook. So much was hitting my head about this time, stuff I wanted to remember, that at day's end, or week's end, I'd begun writing notes, on the tiniest scratch pads, to remind myself of what had passed and what I needed to do as a result of it. It wasn't a diary of the mundane like some I've seen. Nor was it confession. It was, as I say, a list of concerns and obligations, ones I owed myself as well as others. Before Bobby would join me for bedtime in the cot he shared with me up in Aunt Ella's floored and windowed attic, I'd slip up there and update my list. One of the things I reminded myself was to include Icky in my nightly prayers for blessings. I didn't want him falling to his death.

That weekend, everyone else got on famously: Uncle Eck showing Bonnie McGlinty the pickled and prodigious penis of his late, great plow horse; Aunt Ella showering Mother with things for Joyce, which included a touching trip to the attic to bring down delicate gowns and dresses she had made years before for their daughter, who had come stillborn. We ate fresh from the garden again, instead of cans; every meal but breakfast Aunt Ella shredding white shoepeg corn from the cob the way I liked it. Her fried chicken and green apple pie won blue ribbons, bellyaches and bicarbonate of soda. After a Sunday supper of pork pie, we settled on chairs in the side yard, watching the last of the harvest moon and listening to the swan song of the last cicada, Uncle Eck reckoned, of a summer chorus of thousands. At dusk, the last of the firefires sparkled and danced. "They always remind me of October," Aunt Ella said, and in her sweet way told a story of our neighbor October Ney that matched a vision of October I'd had in dreams, by morning dismissing them as fancy. Listening to Aunt Ella, I realized Grandpa had told me the story. Over the years it had slipped below my surface until by day I'd forgotten it. Its recall made my weekend.

Back in the Oklahoma springs when they were young and

primping for planting dances, October would send Aunt Ella's younger sisters into the pastures below October and Wit Odin's, Sess-rymmer castle, to capture fireflies. October would make of fine black lace a cage for the fireflies. She'd put as many as she could in it, and place the cage upon a part she combed in the middle of her head, sweeping her abundant red hair up and around the lantern and down her back in a daring way that was fetching of every gaze in the candlelit shadows of arbor dancing. Bugs can be beautiful, erotic ornaments, especially those that flaunt taillights, and October used them as glittering rainment as well as suggestive signals. The radiant nimbus about her pretty head drew boys like moths to flame.

She'd gotten the idea from a book Grandpa kept in his town house office with his medical omnibus and King James Bible. I would thumb through it many times. It was called *Romance of Insect Life*, and the frontispiece was a painting by Lancelot Speed of an Aztec maiden being led to a volcano festival by a warrior. Surely a sacrificial virgin. She wore fireflies in her hair. The effect was that of a halo. In my reveries she became transcendent woman, spiritually superior to the males that murdered her. I found the book recently in the library. It was written by Edward Selous and published by Lippincott in 1906. It tells, as much as Victorians would allow, about the sex life of bugs, particularly lightning bugs. Eighty-five years later, we know a great deal about the chemical properties of bioluminescence in animals and have mountains of data on the firefly's use of it. But we still say the same things, in an objective, scientific way, that the romantics said about these fairy wands—mearth stars, Wordsworth called them. And what they said was that fireflies use their lights to turn each other on. Cool, October.

DADDY'S ASS WAS MUD

We returned to Gladewater to discover Daddy sitting in the dark house dejected, black and blue from a beating Tobin Drexler had given him. All he said was that he had been fired, his reputation for work ruined in that neck of the woods and that we had to leave if we didn't want to starve.

Clyde McGlinty and one of Daddy's roughnecks, who had quit in protest, gave us the real poop. Our puppy had gotten in the chicken yard, was mangled by Big Red and dead by the time Daddy discovered him. When Daddy went in to pick him up, the rooster attacked him, and in a bloody battle Daddy got the best of the bird and, in a rage, threw it against the wall of the chicken house and broke its neck.

Back at the rig, the dead rooster in hand, he had to face Tobin Drexler, who beat him and kicked him off the rig floor. Daddy hadn't offered any resistance, saying to Drexler before the first blow that he guessed he deserved anything Tobin wanted to dish out.

Raising himself from the ground, Daddy had looked up at Drexler leaning over the rail and said, spitting out teeth, "I've still got a job, ain't I?"

And Tobin said no, that his ass was mud and to get off the lease.

We loaded up our things in a trailer behind the Terraplane, said goodbye to the tearful McGlintys, and left our mansion to the land-lord's pigs.

BOTH WAYS AT ONCE

"What kind of life is this?" we cried out to Daddy, he of the once-even pearls now so hideously gap-toothed. Our question was not an indictment of him. He had been Herculean in his effort to make a home and a living in Gladewater. I could even forgive his turning the other cheek to Tobin Drexler's fists in that higher family cause. But now we begged him to take us back to Little Egypt. Mother had always preferred the rhythms of Grandpa's farm to the brawling helter-skelter of oil gypsies, and now Bobby and I were again torn between his world and hers. His liver-colored face convinced us Mother was right. Turn this boat around, Columbus. Let's get out of these godless waters and go back home where the world is flat and stable. I could feel the ghost of Grandpa beckoning, and behind him the phantom of the missing Doody. I felt there were answers to questions still awaiting me in the familiar mystery of Lit-tle Egypt, and I did go back. I did not go home alone. I took every-one in the Bark of Ra with me, Daddy included. It took everything in my power and Mother's to pull it off, but we did it. I'm speaking psychically. I returned to Doody and Grandpa in my daystallions and nightmares. In spite of this, Daddy remained in control of the Hudson Terraplane and our overt lives, and he was not about to let the disaster in Gladewater keep him from following his head. Daddy was a profane Starbuck pushing us on in the Pequod to the task at hand, fishing for oil to light the lamps of the world. But Mother and I were wounded Ahabs with deeper fish to fry. They were Moby-Dicks malevolent and divine, and they tugged us back in reckonings most dreadful and profound. The past, behind Daddy, was hauntingly before us. He put his foot to the gas and sent us sailing south, deeper into Texas, while Mother and I dreamed us north toward home. We were going both ways at the same time.

> Two currents flow through the life of Mark Twain. One flowed away from Hannibal, Missouri; the other, back to Hannibal again.
>
> —JUSTIN KAPLAN,
> *BRIEF LIVES*

4

Father of My Shadows, Grandfather of My Light

Arise, you shall not kneel.
I pray you, rise; rise, Egypt.

—CAESAR TO CLEOPATRA
ANTONY AND CLEOPATRA,
SHAKESPEARE, 1615

LITTLE EGYPT
Spring and Summer, 1935

FINDING THE CHILD'S GRAVE

DOODY AND I MADE AN ODD PAIR. OLD MAN AND BOY. BLACK and white. Giant and runt.

And then there were the graves and the ghosts and the contradiction of those fevered, delirious summers, suddenly shaded and cooled—but not made saner—by thunderheads that appeared out of the west, pelting us with bursts of stinging rain and sometimes hail.

Such a storm sneaked up on us one day in the spring of that portentous year, a stabbing attack of icy shards; then, as if in apology, a shower of soft kisses. Or were they tears? With the weather gods you never knew. At least their display was a dazzler. The aspect of the day, its reality, they had changed, supercharging it with flashing hints of hell and heaven.

The dry old coats of the cattle steamed and the hide of the earth itself sent up a scenty mist of rot and regeneration. An iridescent arc burned in the sky north of town like a branding iron dreamed up by our Zeus, old Zap-A-Long Catastrophe, and mad Doody and I, mule-bound, charged out yonder to seize the rainbow.

That is how we found the baby's grave. It was in a mesquite thicket where we thought the rainbow ended. The headstone was crude and covered with lichen, but when Doody bent to trace the letters with a pocketknife, he could make out the legend:

THIS CHILD DIED AT FOUR MONTHS AND COST US FORTY DOLLARS

Doody was exultant. "Now this grave is old, Billy Mack," he said, slapping his black hat against his thigh.

"It looks old," I agreed. "Where's the name on it?"

"Ain't got one."

"That's funny."

"It is a sin," Doody said passionately.

"No date either?"

"No date."

"This Old Man Bill Connolly's property, ain't it?"

"Could be, could be," Doody said, unbending, rising like some black Lincoln on the prairie. God damn, he was tall. He looked east and said, "Yes. There's his place. Get the mule and let's go see the man."

The big mule went lickety-split through the chaparral, spurred on by my gouging stick. We rode without saddle, Doody up front and me hanging on behind, his long, spidery legs almost dragging the ground, mine barely long enough to get a hold on the brindled belly. A cactus slapped one of his bare ankles and Doody let out a cry and flapped his legs like raven wings.

"Hey!" I yelped. "Be still! You almost made me fall off."

He hunched forward, rejecting the pain in his foot, and goaded the mule on faster.

"The fence, Doody, the fence!"

We came down on it, almost into its barbs, before the mule turned and ran alongside it toward the gate. Sweat on Doody's neck. I thought the old fool acted at times like he wanted to kill himself and take me with him.

Old Man Connolly was on his high rickety porch in the middle of a Mexican breakfast: a piss and a cigarette. He nodded and went on with his business, arching it masterfully over the side and down onto a flock of scratching chickens.

Doody limped up to the porch.

"That's an old grave you got out there," he said, thumbing toward the west.

Old Man Connolly shook his tool and put it back in his pants. "A what, Doody?"

"Old grave out there."

"Grave you say?"

"Yeah."

"Whur?"

"Beyond the limestone ridge."

"Oh, that. Yeah. Why? Somethin' wrong?"

"Nothing's wrong," Doody said. "We just rode up on it a while ago. You know anything about it?"

"Naw. 'Cept that it's been out there since before my daddy bought this place back in . . . well, in 1860, and I know it didn't belong to the people who was here before him."

"Pioneers," Doody said.

"Yeah, I 'spect so."

"You want me to look after it for you?"

"Look after it for me?"

"Yes, sir."

Old Man Connolly wrinkled his nose and scratched it thoughtfully. He looked out at me on the mule and then back at Doody.

"Look after it for me?"

"It's hip-high in rattlesnake grass," Doody said. "I'd like to come out once in a while and clean it up."

"You would?"

"Yeah, out of respect for the dead, Mister Connolly, that's all."

"Oh, well . . . Doody, I can't pay . . . "

"I know that. Don't expect you to. But I'll do it just the same with your permission."

"Oh, in that case, clean 'er, Doody, clean 'er good, and often as you like. Just don't leave any of my gaps open so the cows get out."

We had traveled a piece from the house when I heard Old Man Connolly laughing. I don't think Doody heard him.

DOODY'S OBSESSION WITH THE DEAD

Some people did think it was funny—Doody's interest in the dead, I mean.

You see, after my father took over the farm from Grandpa, Doody became caretaker for the church cemetery, where all the whites but the Porterfields were buried, and later he was given the Negro cemetery to tend. It wasn't in Doody's contract to ride his mule around tending to every outcast grave he came across, but he did. It got to the point where he took a proprietary interest in all our dead, including the Porterfields on the hill (which is how I came to be his junior sexton), and he even began showing what my grandfather thought was a premature interest in his sicker patients.

"God damn it, Doody!" Grandpa would say, "Miz So-and-So is not yet dead. I know that distresses you, but in the interest of science, not to mention the name of humanity, let me have my way with her first. Who knows? I might even break form and save her!"

Doody would, with great solemnity, deny that he was impatient to put Miz So-and-So under. He was only inquiring after her health.

Grandpa would look up at Doody out of the side of his face and declare, "Well, by Jess, Doody, that's very kind of you to ask. But get the hell out of here, will you? You give me the creeps. I liked you better as a farmer."

Everyone said Doody should have been an undertaker, but I don't think he thought so himself, although he always took charge of the bodies until an undertaker from Ardmore City or Punt arrived on the scene. Grandpa joked with the cheerless old Negro, but I felt he had begun to dislike Doody more than a little. There was bite in his jesting, a kind of disapproval that was cutting away at their legendary friendship. I hated it for their sake and mine, since I felt so bound up in their affections. Although Grandpa was not prepared to put it this way, it was evident he thought there was something unhealthy in Doody's fixation for the dead. Since I was his accomplice, so to speak, it put me in a peculiar light as well, in the shadows, as my mother would put it.

I thought then, and still do, that Doody's passion for death was not of a morbid, personal nature, but impersonal and contemplative.

The dead body itself held no fascination for him. It was the spirit and its world that intrigued him, and because he was compelled by that other life, he hung around the spent hulls of this life, hoping that in flight the spirit had, like a comet shedding its incandescent tail, left behind some hint of its direction.

Doody would have been frightening to me if I had not known him before as Grandpa's shadow and our farmer. He was seven-feet high and black as Africa; his head small, bald and oval, with an aquiline nose. The bones of his body were long and refined, and in spite of his age—he was in his eighties—he walked and rode with the fluid agility of a man half his years. Most of the time his countenance was as grave as a death watch. Humor was as foreign to him as soap and water was to Raff Ardmore, the village jomo man and juba dancer. And yet I found Doody a stimulating friend. He had a bizarre, poetic intelligence that most people missed, muted as it was in his role of black with spade and hoe in hand. And he was most wonderfully if oddly educated, in the manner of frontier autodidacts like my paternal grandfather. But where Grandpa could be joyful, Doody was always earnest, even when we chased rainbows. But he was not always solemn. He could get very excited about, well, death and resurrection and rainbows.

Doody Explains the Hereafter

Doody and I kept the child's grave on the Connolly place trimmed and trenched for as long as I was an innocent in Little Egypt. We used to stand over that sad little dump of bones and wonder about the sex of the baby and damn to hell its mean survivors. Doody passionately believed in the afterlife, but he was not sentimental about it.

One day he told me he was sure the child was not in heaven, regardless of its innocence. I was aghast. All children went to heaven!

No, they don't, he said, not without a name.

A name? What did that have to do with it?

"How will God know it without a name?" he asked.

"God knows everything," I insisted.

"Nothing exists without a name," Doody said.

"Oh, Doody! Name or no name, the baby lived! Had to in order to die. Your old mule doesn't have a name but there he is, lookin' right at you."

"Mule is his name."

I was put out with him. "That's a sorry ass name for a mule," I said, hotly. "Who's gonna know your Mule from a hundred other mules?"

"Who's gonna know Billy Porterfield from a hundred other Willies?"

"By the Porterfield."

"Mule Mareain. By the Mareain."

"Okay, Doody," I said, calmer now, giving him my most searching squint, "if this baby here isn't in heaven, where is it?"

"In Nether Land."

"Nether Land?"

"Yes. That's my belief."

"I never heard of it."

"I pray you never will."

"That bad, huh?"

"Don't be sassy, young Mister Porterfield. It is a place between heaven and hell where lost souls wander until they are found and claimed by God or Satan. Some are never claimed. I don't think this child has been claimed and that is a shame, because it was destined for heaven, not hell. It has not been claimed, Billy Porterfield, because it has no name, and when God calls us up for Judgment he calls us by name. Billy Mack Porterfield. Doody Mareain. How will he call this child? The parents may have referred to it as 'Baby,' but they did not record its name, its identity, on the tomb, and therefore God cannot find the tomb to separate the spirit from the body."

Doody spoke with such black, bitter irony, biting off each word, that I was cast down.

"That is a terrible thing to believe," I said wanly, kicking at the dirt.

"It is a terrible truth," he said.

I did not realize it then, but now I know that Doody was the only true ancient Egyptian among us Little Egyptians. All his thoughts were of life beyond the grave, and he was not idle with his thoughts, as I was to learn.

GRANDPA AND THE HERE-AND-NOW—HOW LITTLE EGYPT CAME TO BE—MEDICINE, WHISKEY AND PATRIARCHY

Now Grandpa, he was different from Doody, more in the Western mold in that he was a damn sight more interested in this life than in what death might bring. It was he—Dr. Henry Mack Porterfield—who had founded our village of Little Egypt and had generated its commerce. Without him none of us would have come together in that time at that place. He was as earthy and profane as Doody was austere and mystical. I loved them both their extremes, Grandpa his kingdom on earth and Doody his eternal afterlife.

Grandpa was not without faith. And Lord could he sing hymns. He often said his sovereignty in Little Egypt was due to an Act of God. We may forgive him the conceit of the highly energetic and creative ego. He had come from Tennessee to Carter County, Oklahoma, just before the turn of the century, carrying in his saddlebags a violin that refused to play Beethoven, a scroll that claimed he was a bona fide physician, and a deed that verified he was owner of three hundred acres along Dobie Creek.

To this day I do not know where he got either paper. Perhaps in a poker game. Certainly I saw the most rudimentary science in his attempts to heal his neighbors. In his patients' log he made an entry for March 3, 1899, that declared: "Found patient sicker than hell. I prescribed whiskey and buttermilk." In an entry dated May 29, 1910, he began reporting on the progress of one B. S. Zone, who, he noted, was twenty-four, married, and a laborer. It seems Zone had what my grandfather described as a "gangrenous ulcer" on his left leg. Grandpa records that he prescribed quinine sulphur as an ointment, and told the man to wash the wound four times a day with warm water and whiskey. Well, that sounds fairly reasonable, better than buttermilk. But let us note the progress of the patient, as observed by Grandpa:

May 30—No better.
May 31—Ulcer looks better.
June 1—Same.
June 4—Worse.
June 5—Little Better.

June 8—Worse.
June 9—Amputated leg.
June 27—Stump healing nicely.
July 2—This morning Zone had a chill followed by a fever. He
    died at 4 A.M.

A terrible drought descended on our part of the country. The
fields lay dry and barren, except for a spot in the delta of Dobie
Creek. As God, or Darwin or Adam Smith, would have it, most of
this fertile land belonged to my grandfather. His corn grew thick and
high, so everyone around came to buy it, just as Joseph and his
brethren journeyed to Egypt to buy corn during the famine. The
devout began to speak of Grandpa's cribs and silos as Egypt, properly
humbling it with the diminutive. Dobie Creek became the Little
Nile.

Grandpa did not just sit back and sell corn by the bushel; he
built the saloon and had Hugh Hecker sell it by the bottle. And
knowing the drought would break and reduce the flow of men and
money to Little Egypt, he encouraged others—the Harts, Brautigams,
the Cudes, the Pfeils—to set up places of business around him. It
worked for about a generation. In that time Little Egypt became the
only place of any size worth passing through between Wilson and
Rubottom on the Texas border.

It was a settlement on a square, three stores and a saloon huddled around a patch of a park and its rusty, naked flagpole. All this in
a confused part of Oklahoma, Grandpa said, because it couldn't
decide which it was: plains or hills, red man country, white man
country or bad man country, and so it was all three. Grandpa, half
serious, said Little Egypt's only virtue was that we were close enough
to Texas to skedaddle down there, in times of life-threatening trouble, and never be seen again. Oklahoma was getting so crowded with
outlaws from the Midwest that even Texas seemed safer. The runty
hills were too sorry for growing anything but rocks, rattlesnakes and
cactus. Grandpa said this was meant for goat ranching, though he
never did any of it, and still other sections were flat and loamy
enough to make it a waste just to graze cattle. So farmers settled in
beside the ranchers to grow cotton and maize.

The park in the square, though certainly modest, may have been a little pretentious for a such a wide spot in the rural road. But it was Grandpa's idea and no one was questioning him. His intent was to draw the settlement into itself, to make the place more hospitable, to create an oasis. A flagpole, a symbol of union and communion, marked the heart of it. No one ever raised an Old Glory that I know of after the first one flapped itself to pieces in the gritty wind coming off the plains, although the Thomas boys made nuisances of themselves by drugging skunks and raising them up the pole in the dawn hours of a Saturday, timing it so the critters would awaken and contaminate the air just as the farm and ranch families were converging on the square for their weekly spree of spending in the four business establishments. It gave pungent emphasis to the term *polecat.* Aside from the saloon, which stood alone on the north side of the square, there was Buck and Carrie Cude's general store and post office on the east side, Walter Brautigam's feed store and Hamilton Hart's blacksmith shed and barber shop on the south side. The smithy Hart had laid a floor on the cool side of his forge where he cut hair and whiskers when he could coax a customer into the chair, a tractor seat which quivered and swayed upon a huge spring screwed to the floor. And, alone on the west side, was Grandpa's town house and medical office. That, and the grove of live oaks partially shading the square, the Pfeil cotton gin and dozen or so little houses strung out along the two roads that ran into town and would have crossed but for the hub of the park, the black community in the Froggy Creek bottoms with its progressive academy, and out our farm road the school and the Salt of the Earth Church of the Southwest Oklahoma Primitive Baptist Association of the Absolute Predestinarian Faith and Order, Rev. Samuel J. Reid, pastor, was Little Egypt.

GRANDPA'S COMMAND OF MEN AND HYMNS—MEN WHO DID NOT COUNT FOR MUCH—THE GREAT DRUGSTORE FIGHT

The saloon filled the ground floor of a narrow, two-story frame building that might have borne paint in the beginning but now was naked to the sun and soil of the years. Out front was a gasoline pump, detested by Grandpa but insisted upon by Hecker, who lived upstairs, because he saw the future fueling up at his doorstep. The pump stood like a solitary sentinel, its looped rubber arm in salute. If there was any salutable government in Little Egypt, it emanated from my grandfather, our grand vizier, a man who contained multitudes, a legislature entire unto himself who considered the saloon his senate. He had never wanted for an audience.

Grandpa was one of those men with a speaking voice instantly recognizable, not because he trained it so but because of a natural peculiarity. It was a husky tenor, or, as Daddy described it with a wink, a whiskey tenor. Here is Brother Spinks, one of the deacons, and his lady, Sister Spinks, remembering Henry Porterfield's effect on a congregation a bit more respectful than a saloon:

BROTHER SPINKS: They'd ah, be people that would gather around those old brush arbors. All the seats would be taken up, and the youngsters would sleep on their pallets and the people, well, they were just all over, had come in their wagons and buggies for miles around. And, of course, Doc would always appear. And they had him up there singing half the evening. Just because he was known all over everywhere he went as this wonderful singer. A man to have a voice like that. Why, it sounded like a fiddle string. Now, ah, arrhhggghhh, let me clear my throat and try to give you an idea of Henry's singing. It'll be a poor imitation, you understand, but here goes. Ah, he'd just ah,

> There'll be no dark valley
> When Jesus comes.

Well, shit, Beulah, I forget the words.

SISTER SPINKS: Just go on, dear, it don't make no difference.

BROTHER SPINKS:

> To gather his loved ones home,
> Ones home,
> To gather his loved ones home,
> Oh . . . home . . .

He'd just come down on it that a way. I can see him, the tears rolling down there and dripping off his cheek. That's what made it so impressive, you could just see . . .

SISTER SPINKS: Well, he was living it within him.

BROTHER SPINKS: He was living it within him. As it was coming out. It wasn't some ordinary person up there. It was, if you'll forgive

my candor, a whiskey-breathed old goat, a'full of sin, but transformed, I tell ye, into an angel at that moment. And he was
singing from his heart clear up to the Almighty.

Even after prohibition, Hecker's Saloon was too much of an
establishment to close its doors. The men quit drinking, at least to all
appearances, and went on with their games. There our gentlemen of
substance gathered over sturdy tables and sour spittoons, in winter
over a bulging, baking Great Northern wood stove, to thrash out
common problems and private feuds. It was the scene of the Great
Drugstore Fight that saw Grandpa pitted against Chester Rudel.

Rudel wanted to open a little patent medicine store beside
Cude's General Store and Grandpa, being the only pill pusher within
a day's drive, set about to convince Rudel that he was trespassing, as
a layman, into territory preserved for men of science. Grandpa knew
that country people more often than not considered doctors middle-
men and uselessly expensive when there was a midwife or druggist
around. And by Jess when Grandpa prescribed a medicine, he
expected the patient to buy it from him.

The conflict degenerated into a brawl between the two men one
afternoon in the saloon. Grandpa, being the smaller and getting the
worst of it, grabbed an old beer mallet left over from wet times and
clubbed Rudel on the head. Rudel crumpled to the floor, but as he
went down, he snatched at my grandfather's chin, pulling out a fistful
of hair. The goatee was Grandpa's vanity, and he went about for
weeks with a bald spot on his chin. But this was not the end of it.

The war continued, though on a somewhat higher plane: They
put away fists and mallets and only slandered each other at every
opportunity. Rudel, being a reasonable man, finally grew weary and
threw up his hands in defeat, forsaking his plans for the drugstore. He
confided to my father that he had never met a madder, more obsti-
nate and foul-mouthed man than Doc Porterfield. Daddy, the last of
the long-suffering sons, could only agree. Grandpa and Rudel signed
a peace treaty in the saloon in the presence of witnesses, and because
Grandpa had the habit of jotting down, diary-style, in his patient log
almost everything that happened to him, I am able to transcribe
their agreement. It read: "Each do most solemnly agree not to be the
first to give offense toward the other, and not to resent any trivial

insult from the other, and further not to unnecessarily mention or talk about any differences or difficulties that now exist or have heretofore existed between them."

They remained men of their word.

If you were a man and not a habitue of Hecker's, the attitude, even among the women, was that you were somehow out of things, a neuter in the masculine world. You did not count for much, like the decrepit and childish old men who played dominoes in the park. They were bulls put out to pasture, ignored, outcast.

In the heat of summer and in the warmest days of winter, the nodding gray heads bent over the buckling benches and passed the hours. In the beginning, there were almost a dozen benches under the live oaks, but the old men got in the lazy habit of chopping up the flimsiest for firewood at the first sign of frost. The bench-burning did not create a shortage of seats, as the players seemed to die in proportion to the dwindling facilities. During one year, three regulars suffered strokes while playing. Their cronies carried them to Brautigam's feed store, where two died on beds of sacked grain. The other lingered long enough to be worked over by my grandfather before being cried over by his kin. The games went on for years, fueled by new old blood. As out of it as they were, the old men still had sass enough to tease one another in the rough male way. Still, none seemed interested in setting foot in Hecker's again. Sul Sartain, who had been sheriff and then the highest judge in the county, was content to sit outside with the other debris of manhood. He was a thin, paisley-skinned old gent who wobbled his head on a fragile neck and blinked his rheumy eyes like a sick chicken. I could not imagine him killing thirteen men, but he had. It was as if some rite of natural selection was at work among our men. At a certain point in his life, a man would be drawn, as though by instinct, from Hecker's to the park. Chester Rudel, once so robust, ended up there by the time he was fifty, not long after he and Grandpa stopped fighting. His wife ran off with a woman after their last daughter was old enough to shift for herself, and Rudel seemed to lose interest in everything except eating and playing dominoes. He grew fat and picked at his nose. Brother Reid, the preacher, did not go to Hecker's, but for another reason. The preacher had his place and it was not among the smoking, cursing, dealing men of the weekdays.

He held sway over them from his pulpit one day in the week, and that was enough, all he was allowed. The rest of the time he belonged to the women and their incessant affinity for coffees and teas, temperance lectures and quilting parties—all of which Brother Reid was expected to bless with his Godly presence. Thin-voiced as he was, he was not a delicate sort who liked to sip and trill with the ladies. He had nine delightful children and a relish for politics and horses, and little time to indulge them.

THE FOUR SIDES OF GRANDPA

If the saloon was Grandpa's smoking club and senate, the town house was his mansion and retreat. It was not grand by any scale. It looked much like the saloon—a narrow, plain-faced two stories. Yet it spoke to you with a singular authority appropriate to the man it sheltered. An ornate iron fence protected what little yard there was in front, and always about the eaves was some menial in Grandpa's debt dripping gobs of fresh paint. The fence was shining black, the house stately white. And when Grandpa emerged in the mornings to make his rounds, tapping his gold-headed cane sharply on the stone walks, he turned the women's heads.

I remember hanging at Grandpa's side, hearing him speak and looking up to watch his goatee going one way and his adam's apple the other. He dressed with uncommon flair. His frock-tailed coats were black or white, depending on the season, topped off by a cavalierish felt or Panama straw. And upon his wee feet he paraded elegant slippers, house shoes, the booted roughs called them, which he soiled and discarded as if they were gloves. He smelled of sweat, dust, tobacco and saddle leather, and if he bent down to place a pink, freckled ear at your mouth you caught the faint fragrance of lilac water.

Once his hair had been yellow as sunflowers along a fence, but now it was fading, though not as white as his goatee. I suspect that as a very young man Grandpa had been closer to pretty than handsome. Like a pug-nosed girl. His was not a strong face; the bones were delicate and the nose and mouth small. But the years had roughened and puffed his features and the sun had squinted his eyes to lend him a proper ruggedness. People were drawn to him. And, for the most part, they listened with respect.

I think he was of that strain of men born with an elemental, instinctive hunger for beauty, and that this set him apart from the men of the range. Certainly it divided him and my father, who had known nothing but our prairie. Grandpa found Tice not wanting in the basic things that make a man worthy, solid traits like honesty and industry—the rudder and anchor of a man's character—but in the subtler, sail-shaped nuances of mind and heart that move men to poetry and adventures of the feminine. The only poetry Daddy could see was in the pump of a piston, and the only call to adventure that stirred him was chucking the farm and hiring out at a good hourly wage. His greatest ideal was to work as a mechanic in a new car dealership. Cars were still a novelty, comparable to rocket ships in our time. But this disappointed Grandpa. The last thing he wanted was the damned machine in his garden. He was, after all, a Southerner in the West. Perhaps there was in him a yearning for that storybook aristocracy that was in ruin as he entered the world. He had refinements and perceptions not given to most, and, in seeing more, he wanted more. If his visage had grown crusty on the frontier, so had his will. He could be hard when he had to be, capable of petty meannesses and passionate cruelties. He loved power, and he found it in his saloon wheeling and dealing and his medical practice. He loved homestead and the ties of family as much as he loved hum, and that is why he kept Alice pregnant and at the farm all those years. He saw the need for ethical and moral systems, and that's why he was a progressive in his political views and a deacon in what he called the damned church—damned because of deadly preachers who put a damper on the high of hymn-singing. He was practical as a Jew in his theology, hardly a mystic like Doody, except at the end. And, finally, he loved freedom—his carriage drawn by sleek mules were always within reach—and the room to pursue his quest for the feminine, which Granny had only in the utility of her sexual plumbing, not in heart and the art of loving. Yet I never saw a woman in the town house. It doesn't mean one was never there.

Doody kept the town house clean and Granny kept her place in the big house out on the farm, next to the smaller cottage where my parents and my little brother and I lived when we were not on one of Daddy's road fits. I don't mean to make myself seem apart from my immediate family, because that was hardly the case. But the truth is that during the summer to which I've brought the reader, I preferred the company of Doody and Grandpa, and I spent a good deal of time at the town house. On the farm, Daddy worked me like a hired hand when he could get his hooks into me. Grandpa was less demanding, busy as he was. When I was in his care I was free to roam as I pleased, as everyone was assured that Doody, Grandpa's ghost and now mine, would keep an eye on me. It became, as is by now evident, a magnetic and hypnotic eye that drew me into a world of shadows that not even Mother had known.

Our Mortality

I may have left the impression that Grandpa was an old man but he was not, though he looked like an old gruff with his goatee. He was sixty-three, and, as you may have concluded, admirably robust.

Yet it was our constant concern that he might keel over any moment. There was nothing evident in his physical makeup to cause this fear—he seldom had been ill—but there was plenty of history in our male line to justify it. Grandpa was, at that time, the third oldest male Porterfield in the informal memory of the family. At sixty-three! Imagine. I would prefer to forget it, being older than that, but the fact is we've usually gone before our time. Our record of longevity (for the men, not the women) had been set by Great-Uncle Dub. He was just a dirt-daubing farmer, and not a very good one at that, but he went down in the family Bible as a patriarch to match Methuselah when he turned sixty-seven, outliving his dear, drowned father by one year. Oh, it was quite an event in the family, a cheerful prospect for the rest of the men. His seven sons came all the way from Atlanta. Such was his and our jubilation (I'm speaking now in a family way) that Great-Uncle Dub died ten days after his birthday, presumably from a failing heart overtaxed by too much dancing, drinking and gorging. He had been in good shape, they said, before the party. The seven sons had already returned to Atlanta and they had to turn around and come back for his funeral. So we worried about Grandpa, living the way he did, and if we were Porterfield males we worried about ourselves. Oh, we got on with life. It was our habit to sow our seeds early, to marry young and beget children and get all the gut and grit of it as quick as we could. For it was a misery, I assure you, to be damned with strong bodies over the short pull, to be of such appetite while knowing there lurked within us some mysterious flaw, some grotesque gene or something, that reduced our defenses and killed us in the prime. It was more than blood conspiring against us. It was the fates too. The oddity was that we were seldom sickly until that final, fatal visitation.

With this onus, it seems only natural we were a bunch of hypochondriacs. Lord, there wasn't a one of us, not even blustering Grandpa, who wasn't haunted by the thought of an early death. It loomed in our minds at the slightest head cold. A pain in the back was cause for anxiety. A spider bite was treated as if it were a mortal wound, a scratch from a barbed fence sent us to Grandpa for a tetanus shot. Our women had to become nurses as well as lovers and companions, experts in the psychological art of reassuring their men that death did not lie at the door because of midnight heartburn. We could not have survived without them. There was a saying in Carter County that a girl who married a Porterfield was never in doubt that she had latched onto a man and a damned fool—as long as he lasted.

I Learn About Doody's Past—The Part He Would Have Me Know

So Doody and I did, indeed, make a strange pair. Old man and boy. Black and white. Giant and runt. Immortal and mortal.

There was I, a Porterfield, condemned by the gods, my life ticking away like a time bomb on a short fuse, marveling at how long Doody had lived and at how much he had to go, while he, yearning for the hereafter, seemed to envy us. Doody said he had been born into slavery in Texas about 1849, four years after Texas was admitted to the union—Abraham Lincoln had been a has-been Congressman in Illinois, practicing law without an inkling that he was less than a dozen years from the presidency. Doody had grown up on the prairie, a cowpoke like his father, in the days when a horseman of the Southwest, even in bondage, could ride full swing through miles of stirrup-high grass that was fodder for the Longhorn. He had seen the cattleman harness the prairie with wire, had watched the farmer come to push the plow, and in our time he was seeing the oilman puncture the pasture with pipe. I envied him his age and told him so one day as we rested from our hoeing in the church cemetery.

"Humph," he said, "old is old. The doctor is old to you because he is your grandfather. He's not old to me because he's young enough to be my son. Old to me is my mother."

"Your mother! Is she still alive?"

"Yes, she lives."

"Gosh, Doody, if you're eighty-seven, she must be . . . Doody, you don't mean she's—"

"We say one hundred and seven, thereabouts."

It was too large a sum of years to comprehend. If Doody had told me his mother had been around since Genesis—since the first rock, the first tree, the first minnow in the Little Nile—I would have accepted it. "Golly, Doody, where is she?"

"Home."

"Your house?"

"Yes."

Doody had never mentioned her to me. That was the way it was with black people; they had private sides they kept from you. In all the years I had known Doody—well, I'm sure he was one of the first fellow human beings I ever laid eyes on—I had never been to his house and had only a vague notion about where it was: somewhere in Froggy Bottom, the Negro settlement. He had always come to us; we had never gone to him. Except, of course, Grandpa. Now I was curious. How did he live? What was he like away from us? "Doody," I said, "I'd sure like to meet your mother."

A corona of a smile crossed his dark face. He looked at the sun, past its peak, and then gazed toward Froggy Bottom. He strode up and down, deep in thought, and then picked up a rock and threw it onto the roof of the church. "Let's eat," he said, "and then I'll take you to her." He looked down at me and his eyes were bits boring into me.

"What is it, Doody?" I asked, a sudden uneasiness coming over me.

"Her name is Lonnie," he said, "but you will call her Miz Mareain."

"Sure," I gulped, and for the first time felt a gulf between us. I was wishing I hadn't asked when he picked me up playfully and sat me on his towering shoulders. "Let's eat down there in the Brautigam plot where it's shady," he said, taking a stride that covered three yards.

THE ART OF EATING ON A TOMB

We hunkered down and opened our lunches on Renata Brautigam's headstone, which was as broad and squat as her widower husband, Walter. Brautigam had toted so many sacks of feed he had come to look like one, dumped into denim overalls. He even smelled of crimped oats, and I was sure that if you pulled a certain magic thread in his overalls, the same thread you worked to open the feed sacks, he would come unseamed and spill out on the floor in a cascade of syrupy seed. You could find him in the store sitting on a feed sack, shooting BBs at the rats with a Daisy air rifle. He munched on corn and oats like an old boar, grunting in contentment. *Crack, crack. Crunch. Munch, munch. Oink, oink. Grunt, grunt. Squeeeeeeeal.*

I was hungry and ate my bacon and egg sandwich in about four bites. I looked up to see Doody watching me.

"You're not called on to eat like that," he said.

"I always eat fast."

"Not around me, you don't. You give me indigestion just watching you. You're not going anywhere without me and Mule anyway. See how slow I eat."

He had laid out on the granite two fried pork chops, an onion, and a stack of bread slices soaked in a pungent barbecue sauce. He balanced there on his lean haunches and arranged and rearranged each item until their positions suited him. Doody seemed to like the chops over the date of Miz Brautigam's birth, the onion over her demise. The bread was "Asleep in Jesus." He poked a bony fork of a finger into a chop, lifted it to his mouth and began nibbling around the fatty edge. He took tiny bites and chewed them slowly, savoring each tidbit. He flipped me a slice of the saucy-red bread. It was good but peppery. I washed my food down with drinks from our water can. Doody ate so slowly he didn't need water. I had noticed this before and couldn't help but compare his manner at the table with ours.

At home we would have gagged without liquids, so ferociously did we attack our meat and down it. To the Porterfields, food was fuel, a lump in the belly to ease a hunger pain and not something to savor. We hurried through meals, chomping and slurping, taking time to talk only at the Sunday dinners at Grandma's house. Except for Grandpa, the first Porterfield at table began eating before the others arrived; the first one to fill his belly got up and went about his business. After supper, we went to bed belching and farting and reaching for bicarbonate of soda. Doody would have hated such manners as much as Grandpa did. But Grandpa said nothing because Granny ruled at the table, and if we didn't go hog-wild over her cooking she thought something was wrong.

We did not linger over the essence of a particular vegetable or meat because our women were as primitive in the preparing of a meal as the men were in disposing of it. There was not a good cook in the family. Oklahoma women have always overcooked the finest meats in the world, but Granny went one worse and fried her meat to damned near a cinder. Mother was not much more inventive. Neither had heard of broiling or boiling or baking a steer or pig or chicken. About the only meats they could not ruin were cured from the smokehouse. You would think the flavor of garden vegetables would be retained on any country table, but it was not on the Porterfields'. Granny salted the bounty from the garden until I thought we would all turn into Lot's wife. The old witch boiled vegetables in briny cauldrons until such a simple, evident thing as a stringbean was a mystery to the eye or the tongue. It is a testament to the toughness of man's stomach that we were able to gather hungrily over such slop. Grandpa would ooh and ah at the burnt crust on a drumstick and lap at the salt solutions with such gusto that I have concluded he was either out of his mind or playing a desperate game of domestic diplomacy. Not a bad idea, considering the astonishing freedom he required.

Wise men must find reason to make over their wives, and if Grandpa was straining to enjoy Granny's cooking, it was because he had found nothing else to like about her except her indifference to him, which, conveniently, matched his to her. And yet they kept up appearances, even for the family. For years I pondered without satisfaction over why such mismatched people marry. As soon as I married the answer came to me like a headache that would not go away. I took Mother's powders and I wondered that I had ever asked the question in the first place.

So tedious Doody became a source of revelation. Such a basic drive as hunger could be refined and so civil that there was art in eating a raw onion on a tomb. The sun had moved one hour in the sky before he took out his handkerchief and wiped his mouth and hands and made me to know it was time to see his mother.

THE WAY—DARKTOWN—THE QUEEN

The church and its cemetery were across the creek northwest of town, behind our place, and Froggy Bottom was southwest of town, so we took to the woods along the Little Nile and rode south, past Raff's shack, and then southeast as the creek curved through the mustang arbor below the Odin place, aiming for the road that ran past Froggy Bottom and through Little Egypt, a dark and dignified Quixote and his freckle-faced page, swaying forth on a hybrid and humble steed to pay our respects to a lady of legendary age. It was a lovely May afternoon, the heat not yet hateful and scorching the green that was greenest along the creek. Nothing drooped, not the surging grass, not doleful Doody. The mule, as always, was enduring. In the bottom and on the abutting cliffs we saw beard-tongues and mimosa, cooper mallows and Indian blankets, cliff salvias and bladder pods—a blur of pinks and reds and yellows.

"There's some bluebonnets!" I said.

"*El conejo*," Doody said. "The rabbit."

"A bluebonnet doesn't look like a rabbit."

"No. But it multiplies like rabbits."

Doody, it appears to me now, was a contradiction. For all his philosophical knocking on the doors of heaven and hell, he seemed quite at home on our earth. If he stood out from the rest of us it was because of his height and his mysticism and not because he was a misanthrope. He was a black man, and although I'm sure he had to endure the cruel ironies that went with that particular pox, I think he handled it well. He was his own man and everyone knew it and didn't begrudge him that. He was not sickly and in conflict with nature; like a Mexican he was in tune with it, not trying to stop its clock like Grandpa or trying to hurry it up like Daddy. He got up when the sun got up and he lay down when the sun went down. He planted and harvested in the warm season and hunted in the cold. He grew up in a country where there had been as many Mexicans as Anglos, and he had learned Spanish, which most gringos refused to do. He could speak some of the dialects of the Oklahoma Indian reservations. He knew the land, its strains of soil and its variety of plant life. I could seldom point to a flower or a bush he could not identify in several tongues. It got to be a game. That morning he pointed to a bull nettle. "Mexicans call them *mala mujeres!* Bad women, because of their sting."

"I think I'll start calling them granny weeds," I piped.

"The Mexican has another kind of woman in mind," Doody said.

We came out on the road, crossed the creek bridge, passed the Negro cemetery and rode into Froggy Bottom.

Doody stopped Mule, looked over his shoulder and said to me, "White folks call our side of town Froggy Bottom. That is not its true name. We call it Kushtown. I named it myself, just like I named everything around here after the ancient settlements on the real Nile in Africa. Of course, your grandfather went along with it. I don't know who started this Froggy Bottom business, but I don't like it and neither do my neighbors. So mind your words, you hear?"

"Yessir."

No matter how many times I would come and go in these rural black villages—nearby, but as separate from us as night is to day—they would remain mysterious. No people, not even the Mexicans filtering up from Texas, compelled me more in wonder and empathy. It was not my first time in Froggy Bottom, oops, Kushtown, but it was my first time there with Doody, and I was proud to be his sidekick, puny and washed-out white as I was behind the red freckles. I envied blacks their vivid auras and potent emanations of spirit and flesh. They did not seem to sour up in body and soul the way we white vermin did after the sweat of hell. After love and hate they smelled more strongly of themselves and the prima mater earth, more bound to nature, healthier in every sense. They were beautiful, mysterious; bizarre, surely even to one another. Of course I was impressionable. They were exotics to me, no matter that the Granny Porterfields had been ordering them around for generations. I was both drawn and frightened by them. Even noble Doody could give me a start. As we rode past the shanties my eyes got big thinking of how odd it was that they were on the bottom and we were on the top. There had to be a reason for it, deeper than the machinations of men, and I was uneasy because it seemed to me that whatever it was, it was evil and it had cast us, the whites, as the hit men of its villainy. Our brutality sickened me. And here I was riding on Mule with Doody into a dark-town like nothing was wrong. It appalled me. It enthralled me.

I would have known where we were blindfolded, so strongly did the scent of niggertown strike my nostrils and fill my being. Burnt wood. Barbecue. Boiling clothes. Lye. Starch. Scorched shirts. Shacks. Slat fences. Rusty chicken wire. Singed feathers. Dirt yards.

Dirt so trod upon, so raked and hoed and watered and dried, so sifted and blown, so dug and dumped and packed and pounded and planted, dirt so sweat upon, so pissed upon and bled upon, dirt so used, in toil and tears and creation and destruction, dirt so born in and lived on and died in that it was not just dirt, not just worn-out, dirty dirt, but a higher dust, somehow blessed by the benediction of men simply living and dying on it in a natural way.

In its setting, Doody's house was no more unique than a weed in a ditch, except that it was a taller weed. It was what has come to be known as a shotgun shack. A Klansman could ride up to the front or back, aim a shotgun through the door, and kill or wound everyone within with one blast, so narrow and barrellike was it built. Doody had raised the shack himself. Its only individuality was the height of its ceiling and roof. I marveled as he walked inside. It was the only doorway I had ever seen him enter without ducking. The house was dark inside, the only light from the tiny windows. I stood timidly in the front part while Doody disappeared through a curtain that cut the house in two. As my eyes adjusted to the gloom I could make out the bare board of the walls and floor, a quilt-covered cot beside a wooden box, upon which were stacked tins of food and bottles of medicine and honey with the combs. The cot was obviously Doody's bed because it was not one cot, but two wired together end-to-end and covered with ticking. An Aryan Christ gazed down from a calendar on the wall above the cot, compliments of the Morales Funeral Home in San Antonio, "Where the Sorrow of Parting Is Made Sweeter." Doody came through the curtain whispering, "Come on back here. She's asleep."

"Doody, don't go wakin' her on my account."

"Don't intend to. But you can get a look at her."

"You mean while she's asleep?"

"Yes. Come on. She won't bite."

"I'd just as soon come another time when she's up."

"She don't get up. Her legs are gone."

"You mean cut off?"

"Wore out. Now come on."

The curtain parted. A wood stove and pantry lined the left wall, then there was the back door, and against the right wall was a long narrow bed which held Lonnie Mareain. She lay on her back under a quilted spread, her head and shoulders propped up by feather pillows. Her eyes were closed and she appeared to be sleeping. "She's a fine-lookin' woman, ain't she?" Doody said.

"Yes," I said in a long whisper, meaning it. I had never seen anything like her in my life. She looked, lying there under the cover, as long and thin as her son; certainly she was well over six feet. Her face was like his too—fine-boned and shiny black—but where Doody was bald she was magnificently endowed. Her hair was a frizzy white pyramid a foot high. She might have been an Ethiopian queen laid out in state.

"She ain't got too long," Doody said after I had gazed at her for a while.

"Is she sick?"

"Wore out, that's all."

"Doody, does she talk and everything, or does she just lay there?"

"Oh, she comes and goes. She understands more than she says."

"Well, she sure is striking to look at, Doody. Not common at all."

"No. We're not common."

"Was your Daddy like you and your mother? I mean tall and everything?"

"He was big, but not pretty-made like she is. He was just a plain Negro."

I'm sure I showed my confusion, because Doody said, "My mother is from Ruanda, a place in Africa where there are tribes of giant people called the Watutsi. The Watutsi is not all Negro. He's got some Arab blood in him, which makes him part white man."

"You mean you've got white blood, too?"

"Well, not enough to upset me. Let's you and me keep this between us. Okay?"

"Sure, Doody."

He motioned me into the front part of the house. "How good are you at keeping secrets?"

"I keep them."

"Maybe I'll show it to you," he said, half to himself. "I need some help anyway."

"What, Doody?"

He looked at me oddly. "Our tombs," he said.

"Tombs?"

"Yes," he said, drawing me closer. He was frightfully mysterious. He sat on the cot and put his face into mine and said, "I'm going to show you something I've shown to nobody except my mother. Can I trust you?"

"Doody," I said nervously. "I'd just as soon not see. I mean I wouldn't tell anyway, but I just don't—"

"I want you to see," he said. "Yes, I want you to see." He saw the fear in my face. "It's nothing to be afraid of," he said. "You have your family cemetery on The Hill? Well, I want to take you to mine, only it isn't on a hill, it's in it. That's all it is, Mama's burial place and mine when the time shall come."

"Oh," I said, feigning relief.

THE EGYPTIAN TOMBS—THE GODS AND THE DARK ANGEL BA—MY MOTHER OF SHADOWS

And he took me there, into a deep wood behind the Negro cemetery where I had never been before. We came to a high wire fence that encircled a monumental rock that reached up out of the earth and dwarfed the trees. The fence was as high as Doody's head, but beside the rock it looked low. Doody found a gate and unlocked it with a key and led me and the mule around the rock. "Get down," he said. "We go in here." He removed boulders from a man-sized crack in the limestone and we crawled down into a cavernous room that picked up our footsteps and voices and bounced them back and forth off the walls.

"Doody," I said, "I can't see a thing." I was afraid to reach out, for fear of touching something that might resent it.

"Just stand there," Doody said. "You'll get used to the dark in a minute."

After a while I could see around the room. It was large as a small house with a fairly level floor and a ceiling under which Doody could walk erect. The air smelled dry and stale. My eyes fell on two large, coffin-shaped vaults lying side by side in the center of the room.

"Those," Doody said, "are for Mother and me."

"It's kind of creepy," I said, "to look at your own grave before you're ready for it."

"Don't be silly," he said. "It's important to prepare yourself for what comes after death, and I just don't want to leave it to others, that's all."

"Why'd you pick a cave like this?"

"I prayed for it, and it was given to me," he said. "I was told to seek the bat. One day I came upon the rock, saw bats flying out of it and knew it was the place. I slipped in after the bats were gone. The floor was deep in dung, but I knew that this was our tomb. I cleaned it out, plugged the entrance with rocks to keep the bats from getting back in, and then bought the rock on time from a lawyer in Ardmore who owns all this property back in here. Your grandpa helped me in the transaction."

"You mean Grandpa knows about your tombs?"

"We both know everything about each other," he said, with what I thought was equal parts of pride and irony.

"This is so deep in the woods," he went on to say, "I figured nobody would bother me, but I put up the fence just to make sure."

"Boy, it sure is something."

"I've put almost all my money into this place," Doody said. He ran his hand over one of the vaults. "These are solid granite," he said, "the same red granite in the Texas State Capitol. It cost me some to have them cut and shaped and hauled here. Again, your grandpa helped, but that's just between you and me. I don't want you bringing up to him I've brought you here. That is, unless he gets suspicious and brings it up himself. Then you tell the truth. That's the way I've always done with Henry. I never lie, except, I reckon"—and here he chuckled—"by omission. Say, come and try to lift one of the lids."

I could hardly move it.

"You see, Mother's coffin fits inside, the lid seals on tight-like, and there's no digging to be done."

"Yeah, but how're you gonna keep snoopers, like the Thomas boys, from coming in here and disturbing the body?"

"If they can get over that fence outside, they'll run into one of Raff Ardmore's guard wolves, which we keep inside the fence at night. Raff or I manage to keep an eye on things during the day. Even after Mother dies I'll be back and forth saying prayers and working on my own resting place. And your grandpa's seen to it that we'll both be sealed up nicely and out of harm's way when my time comes. He's made me out a will that leaves instructions and money to have this room sealed off, and the entrance filled in by stonemasons."

"Doody, this is something."

He nodded and displayed a rare grin. "Well, I've been working at it a long time. Now, my idea is not original, you know. The Egyptians have been doing it for six thousand years."

"That's right," I said, lights coming on. "This is like an Egyptian tomb, like the inside of a pyramid!"

"That's the idea," he said. "That's what I'm driving at. Now then, I want you to look around the room, but wait until I light some candles."

I lifted my eyes from the sarcophagi and took in the furnishings of the chamber. Boxes and chests lined the walls, laden with vases, baskets and stands of fantastic figures and statues. Doody lit Mexican witch candles, and in the flickering, sooty light the bizarre images came to life. Exotic green birds, ebony dogs, red serpents and golden lions leapt at me. As I drew closer, I recognized them as cheap wood carvings from the Mexican markets of Texas. One was especially hideous. It was a blue-black dog, devilishly obscene. The scepter in its hand was also its penis. I thought of Raff Ardmore. Doody called the creature Anubis, and said it was the guard dog of the dead. Even the chests were Mexican, but Doody had painted them antique gold and upon that had laid, in vivid colors, panel after panel of Egyptian hieroglyphs. The clay vases were filled with grain and water. Baskets and boxes held a clutter of household and hardware items: pots and pans, soaps and perfumes, trinkets and jewelry—his mother's, Doody said—as well as rakes and hoes and other tools. He opened chests of linen and rolls of wrapping gauze. One drawer contained medicines, drugs and chemicals Doody had filched from my grandfather's apothecary. I noticed in one cabinet a pair of worn boxing gloves, large enough to fit even Doody's long hands. And on a table beneath a set of dominoes was a stack of dusty books. Already a lover of the word, I moved the dominoes aside and opened the first book to the title page. I recognized a passage from the Old Testament, and was impressed because it fit the theme of Doody's repository: "Princes shall come out of Egypt; Ethiopia shall soon stretch out her hand to God." The name of the book, *The Hindered Hand*, stuck in my mind as well, perhaps because I pictured it as a severed hand. I wanted to look at the other books, but Doody, like a tour guide, was moving me on among the treasures. The expressions of sentiment and religion belonged in a bone pit, but the things for work and recreation—garden gadgets? games?—struck me as funny.

"If this is a place for the dead," I said, "why did you haul all this stuff in here for the living? Except for the vaults and carvings, this looks like home to me."

"It is," he said. "This will be our home for eternity, at least one of our homes."

He pulled up a box and bade me sit. And he haunched down beside me in the candlelight and told of the great adventure that awaited the Mareains upon their deaths. Anyone approaching this stone pyramid that hove out of an Oklahoma thicket would never have guessed that inside was a tomb, that inside the tomb sat a boy listening to a man tell of a journey of the dead that began with the death of pharaohs in the deserts of antiquity.

What he told me that day he would repeat, with endless and compelling variation, throughout the summer until I was a true acolyte.

In the beginning, Doody said, there were as many gods and goddesses in the Valley of the Nile as there were congregations of men. The gods presented themselves as beasts and birds and elements of the cosmos, then later as a blend of creature and man and the heavens and hells. The gods, good and bad, came and went as they pleased. Eventually they came down and lived in the bodies of the pharaohs, who ruled for twenty-seven centuries. The kings were destined to live forever, so it was necessary to preserve the human and animal parts of them, their bodies, for the journey through boundless time.

For all the gods, they came to one, the original Tem, the great creator, and beneath him were the lords of regions. Nut was the sky goddess, who every evening swallowed the sun and gave birth to it in the morning. Ra was the sun god, and his dark descent into the belly of Nut became the myth of the soul's journey through the underworld. The dead embarked upon the afterlife in the Bark of Ra, a solar ark which carried the hope of the Egyptian quest for immortality. The scribe of Thoth was pictured as the moon god of enlightenment because he tried to dispel darkness. Sobek the crocodile was the god of waters. Seth the donkey was the god of storms. Osiris was god of the earth and the underworld. It was he who weighed the salvation of souls upon Judgment Day, assisted by Anubis the dark jackal, who operated the scales, and Thoth, who assumed the head of an ibis or baboon as he wrote down the score on each soul. A failing soul had to face a monster known as the Devourer of Souls. If the dragon did not eat you, the frightful boatman Seker, lord of hell, awaited in streams of fire a'boil on the pyres of eternal damnation. It was better to dwell with Osiris.

In Osiris's household were his wife-sister Isis, goddess of magic and protector of children; their falcon-headed son, Horus, who looked after the living; and Nephthys, sister of Osiris and goddess of women. The beautiful cow Hathor was goddess of love; Maat the goddess of truth and uprightness; Ptah the god of stonemasons, craftsmen and also of names.

Now Doody's concern about the dead carrying names made more sense. Ptah called the living into existence by name, and, after death, he beckoned them by name before Osiris for the final roll call. Of course, ordinary people followed the god kings to heaven or hell, and so priests were employed to teach everyone how to get to one and not the other. A life of virtue was the way to paradise, helped by prayers and offerings.

Doody said he and his mother were confident about their chances with Osiris, but that he had a lot of work to do, minor details nonetheless necessary to salvation. I asked what they were.

"I'll show you," he said, rising, striding over to something long and low and covered by canvas. He unveiled a thin canoe he had carved, Karankawa-style, from a palm tree he had trucked in from the Gulf of Mexico. "This is our ship of the dead I mentioned," he said, "the Bark of Ra. It's a light boat and as essential to the mummy as the heavy crypt."

He told me that every being had a natural body, a spirit body (Sahu), a heart (Ab), a miniature double (Ka), a soul (Ba), a shadow (Khaibit), a spirit (Khu) and a name (Ren). All these identities were bound into the character and destiny of a mortal, and they had special powers and roles to play. The mummified body stayed in the tomb as a home to these phantoms. And during the day most of them remained in the body. Birdlike Ba, the soul, was the exception. Restless Ba could not be dead without looking back wistfully at life.

I immediately identified with this dark angel Ba, and felt its soul was one with Mother's and mine, for in our dreams we flew to the dead. Here Doody was saying that Ba fluttered about during the day, often leaving the body and the tomb to haunt the living. Ba could hover sweetly like a hummingbird or swoop fiercely like a falcon, and make life on earth for the survivors pleasant or unpleasant, depending upon its moods and the ghostly premonitions and wisps of the dead it liked to leave about. At sunset Ba had to fly back to the mummy, because after dark it and its companion specters had to board the Boat of the Dead and follow the sun into its descent into the West and the underworld. Below, in the belly of Nut, they passed through the reviewing stand of Osiris and went either into the divine Field of Reeds or into the mouth of the monster or the scalding lakes of Seker. Morning found them up again with the sun, delivered anew by Nut, back in the mummy and the tomb to rest—save for Ba—for the next night's journey. So the boat and the tomb and the provisions were all a part of it, and Doody was providing.

"Of course," he said, "I've got a long way to go yet, all the carving and decorating to be done . . . "

"More carving?"

"Yes, carving messages to God, to Osiris. I'm doing them in wooden blocks and then I'm going to glue the blocks to the vaults, make 'em look real fine and fancy."

"I've never heard of that before."

"Messages. Prayers. Same thing. Except that the messages are in wood and more durable, more lasting. Here, I got some of Mother's already finished. I got 'em inside her vault here."

With a great grunt Doody moved the lid enough to make an

opening. He reached inside and pulled out a block of wood the size and thickness of a pack of cigarettes. On it was carved, in neat, plain letters, "I have not done iniquity."

"Iniquity. That means sin," Doody said.

"Yeah, one of Brother Reid's favorite words. That's a good job of carvin', Doody. How many are you gonna do?"

"Forty-two for each vault, so you see I got my work cut out for me."

"That's a lifetime of carvin'."

"Well, I've got some done and you can help me with the rest if you like."

I could not have been more pleased at Doody's invitation. If it seems strange that a boy would find fascinating secret tombs and incantations to the gods, then I would remind you I was not alone among my peers.

One of the favorite playgrounds in Little Egypt was an ancient and abandoned cotton gin, where boys congregated in gangs and created a kingdom that was as theological as any in the African desert. Armed with willow switch rapiers and rubber guns—our Remingtons of rural warfare—we fought for favor before the gods, the lords being those among our ranks who had been exceptionally brave and just throughout our interminable wars. The battlefield was the second floor of the gin, open enough for traditional column encounters, but harboring as well in its intricate machinery the most ingenious foxholes and tunnels for guerrilla tactics. Those who died in honor went to heaven, marvelous platforms high above the sunlit roof beams, reached by slippery conveyor belts, spindly ladders and the grace of the gods. Those who died in shame went to hell, the dank, dark basement of the gin where great engines and boilers sat silent and foreboding, where snakes and spiders crawled and cobwebbed tramps were known to lie in wait for tender boys. There was not an Ishmael or a Huck among us who did not believe in redemption and resurrection. Each of us was slain and slain again, in glory or gloom, only to be reborn to fight another day. We were enchanted with blood oaths, ritual, secret signs, charms and images and brotherhood with the gods.

And, when we grew up and became merchants and Masons, optometrists and Optimists, ranchers and Rotarians, electricians and Lions—all stolid, solid types, who, if we did not bring fame to Little

Egypt, brought it no shame—we left the cotton gin for the Masonic Hall in other towns, where, like our fathers before us, we filled the temple with less sword work and death scenes but even greater mystery. We donned robes and lit candles and crosses and chanted Christian rites so secret that womenfolk and children could not be told their meanings. This was common as Thursday nights, a fraternal flourish at the end of a workday.

So I was not alone in my mysticism, and did not want to be. And, for that matter, neither did Doody. I accepted his invitation to carve his prayers. It seemed a worthwhile communion, more fun than hoeing in the fields for Daddy.

"Good," Doody said. "You'll catch on. Now come on. I got to get you home before supper."

We started out, but Doody stopped. "Now wait," he said. His face turned hard. "Not a word of this place to anyone, you hear, boy?"

"Yessir."

"Not even your grandpa unless he asks."

"Not even Grandpa unless he asks."

"Not even your mother."

"Not even Mother."

He smiled a half-secret smile, sighed and said—I felt he was addressing himself directly to my mother as well as me—"For all the good our swearing will do. That woman could pick up the soul of a five-hundred-pound pig in Poland or China right out of the air." And he chuckled and asked me if a pig had a soul, and I said yes, liking them. Doody handed me a giant hand to boost me into the passageway.

"It's looks like the Mareains are going to be the first pharaohs of Little Egypt," I said.

"I've not told you this," he said, "because it may be stretching the truth more'n it wants to go, but I like to fancy that maybe some of my own people might have been among the last of the Egyptian pharaohs. Or, if not that, among their subjects."

"How's that?" I said. "I thought you said you all were Watutsi from Ruanda."

"That is so," he said. "But we were not more than a thousand miles south of the White and Blue Niles, where, seven hundred and twenty-four years before Christ, when the prophet Isaiah was in his prime, the black kings of Kush conquered Egypt and ruled as the pharaohs had, restoring the pyramids at Napata, Jebel Barkal, Merowe and El Kurru, and burying their dead according to ancient Egyptian custom. Their power and slave-trading spread deep into East Central Africa, and when I see the prophet Isaiah's descriptions of the Kush as a tall and smooth-skinned people feared far and wide, I can't help myself likening them to my own people. We were all black Africans, whether from the Sudan or Ruanda."

"Good Lord, Doody, where did you learn so much about all that ancient stuff?"

"Mostly from a man named Sutton Griggs, a little on my own from the Hebrew and Christian Bibles," he said. "Mr. Griggs came to me way before your grandpa's time. Someday I might tell you about him. He became what I consider a great man. Course, few have heard of him."

"Does Wit Odin know any of this?" I said.

Odin was October Ney's husband and one of the local school teachers who prided himself on being Little Egypt's Egyptologist. We took a kind of civic pride in Howard Carter's discovery of Tutankhamen's tomb in the real Egypt fourteen summers before.

"Has Mr. Wit mentioned the Nubian pharaohs?" Doody said.

"You mean the black ones?"

"Nubia and the Sudan are the same," Doody said. "They are a part of black Africa. Has he told you of the Pharaohs Piye and Tan-wetamani?"

"Not that I remember. I do know there were black ones. But all he's talked about is Tutankhamen."

"We can forgive him that," Doody said with a royal weariness. "Right now, that Harvard Egyptologist, George Reisner, is finishing up his excavations of the royal burial chambers at El Kurru, and he says he can vouch for a thousand-year line of black pharaohs. But no treasure, after nine years of digging. Thieves took it all. That explains the lack of interest."

As we stepped from the cavern and into the dusk of the fenced area, I looked about, half-expecting one of Raff Ardmore's wild dogs to snarl and make for me with fangs bared. Doody was right. Most any person would back off from a dog like that. But just as quickly I knew that if the Thomas boys wanted something bad enough, they'd go through a mountain of concrete, a ton of granite and a lumber yard of wooden prayers, and no dog, not even Raff's or Anubis himself, would stop them.

Doody paused at the gate and repeated his admonition. "Not a word of this, you hear, boy?"

"Yessir," I said. "Cross my heart and hope to die."

For all my excitement, a cloud passed over me, and I told Doody to take me to the farm and my parents, not to the town house.

I was good at keeping confidences as long as my mother wasn't around. Once in her aura, I had a compulsion to tell her everything. It really didn't matter, my betrayals, because, as Doody suggested, she usually knew what was about to be divulged. Things came to her, without asking. If Doody was the father of my shadows, she was, indeed, the mother.

But I was not about to tell her about Doody's tombs. When I got home I went directly to bed. I dreamt I had taken a boat—it turned into the canoe Doody had carved—to an island in the Little Nile. A sudden rainstorm washed away the boat. The water rose about me. I screamed and Mother came to comfort me. If she sensed my secret of the day, she kept it to herself.

Carving the Prayers—I Learn About the Book of the Dead

The trips to the tomb were the highlight of that summer. We went twice a week, on Thursday afternoons and on Monday mornings. We would sit in the cavern and carve and talk until our laps bore a mountain of shavings. I got to be good at it, almost as deft as Doody, whose patience was infinite. I discovered that the carved prayers were not original with Doody either. He had gotten the idea from some book he had read on Egyptian tombs, and he would allow no departure from the messages described in the book, which I was never privileged to see. All the prayers were negative confessions:

"I have not robbed with violence," "I have not done violence to any man," "I have not committed theft," and so on. The idea, Doody explained, was that these roundabout pronouncements of virtue amounted to a petition on the part of the dead person for acceptance into heaven. God read each of the forty-two statements and so did Satan, and between them they decided on the truth of each carved claim. Then the truths were weighed against the lies, and whichever way the scales tipped was the way the soul went—liars to hell and truthtellers to heaven. The thing to do, Doody advised, was to so live your life that God would win all forty-two rounds with the Devil; otherwise, it would be touch and go and up and down on Judgment Day.

It all sounded quite logical. I could see God and the Devil pulling off the blocks Doody and I glued to the vaults, arguing their merit and raking them into separate corners to be weighed on a scale like Walter Brautigam measured chicken feed. Heaven to me was my granny's white-trash heaven: streets paved with gold; everybody wearing white gowns, sprouting angel wings and halos and flying around with nothing much to do except play harps. Doody's Egyptian afterlife seemed like an ideal farm and ranch community to me, something Grandpa was trying to make right here on earth: a solid home and land that did not fly away; a place with its people for him to love and lead, and they in turn to remember him when he was gone; a son or daughter to hold that for which he had striven, and then to pass it on again to son and daughter and the sons and daughters of that son and daughter everafter.

It was like one of Doody's Egyptian prayers. That summer underground Doody would stop his knife, close his eyes and recite in his stately way:

"Let me eat my food under the sycamore tree of my lady, the goddess Hathor, and let my times be among the divine beings who have alighted thereon. Let me have the power to order my own fields in Tattu, and my own growing crops in Annu. Let me live upon bread made of white grain and let my beer be made from red grain, and may the persons of my father and mother be given unto me guardians of my door and for the ordering of my homestead. Let me be sound and strong, and let me have much room wherein to move and let me be able to sit wheresoever I please."

The first time he recited it, I asked, "Is that from the Bible?"

"The Egyptian Bible, you might say. It is from the Book of the Dead."

"Do you read Egyptian, too?"

"No. I learned that from my mother, who learned it from her mother, and so on back into the earliest times of my people."

"Tell me about your people again," I said.

"Hamites," he said, "descendants of Ham, left the River of the Nile and went down into Ruanda and grew very tall."

"It's funny," I said, "that you would end up in Egypt again, even if it is Little Egypt, Oklahoma."

"Yes," he said.

ELEGY SOSPIRANDO

> You were like the traveler who brings a little box of sand
> From the wastes about the pyramids
> And makes them real and Egypt real.
> You were part of and related to a great past,
> And yet you were so close to many of us.
> You believed in the joy of life.
> You did not seem to be ashamed of the flesh.

That is what Edgar Lee Masters said in the *Spoon River Anthology*, Doody and Grandpa, and if he hadn't been speaking of Father Malloy I would swear he was describing you both. But he also said:

> You faced life as it is,
> And as it changes.

Oh, dear Grandpa, and my dear old dark Doody, my Sherlock of the Stygian, if this too could have been true of you. How haunted is my heart.

TRYING IT ON FOR SIZE

One day in September, just before school started, I helped Doody get his mother out of bed and into a wagon which Mule pulled. We rode into the woods to the tomb. Mrs. Mareain lay on her back in the wagon with her eyes open and a funny little smile on her face, but she never said anything or acted as if she had seen us.

Doody carried her into the cave and lowered her gently into her vault, face up.

"I want to try it on for size," he said. " 'Course she'll be in a coffin. How does she look?"

"Beautiful," I said.

As we drove home a fine mist began to fall, and from the bed of the wagon Mrs. Mareain, without lifting her head, opened her mouth and said in a sweet way, "Son, will you cover my face? I'm getting all wet."

5

★ ★ ★

Music of the Spheres

SEALED IN RED

WE WERE AT THE END OF A LATE HARVEST.

Mornings, Daddy was up earlier than usual to help the Reds pick the last of the cotton. The Reds were a migrant family of nine who camped in a field shack at the edge of the cotton rows. Although the shack belonged to us, the Reds when they used it kept it white-washed and trimmed in bright red. The dirt yard was raked and about it were colorful earthen pots containing Señora Red's well-watered plants and flowers. She hung green chilis to redden in the sun. The Reds were among the few farm workers around who would work for my father.

Tice Porterfield was a slave driver. He drove himself, on the rigs or on the farm he drove his hired hands, and he would have driven us kids that August if Uncle Glen, mother's brother, hadn't arrived to keep us busy at what Daddy called foolishness. It got to the point that help was hard to hire because Daddy demanded a grind few men were up to day after day. It was fortunate we needed help only at harvest. Finally, only Mexicans would work for him. Daddy said it was just as well, observing that the heat and stooping didn't seem to bother them.

But that first day the Big Red got out of his old Model T and waddled up to the door, Daddy took one look and regretted hiring him sight unseen. El Colorado Grande was a very fat brown man with cinnamon hair—a not uncommon sight, thanks to the Latin-loving Irish. How could a man that fat do a nickel's worth of work? But Daddy was committed and at a point where he couldn't be choosy.

"The Big Red will be one of them dictator types," he said to Mother. "You watch. He'll end up sittin' under a shade tree, watchin' his woman and kids work."

But El Colorado Grande surprised, not only keeping up with Daddy but surpassing him in the pounds of cotton picked, the rows of corn pulled. His wife and the sons, each of whom Daddy called "Hey, boy!" were good workers too, as was the daughter, Rosita.

The girl captured Mother's heart the morning Mother saw her put down her hoe, take a rusty tube of lipstick from her shirt pocket and color her lips. Mother thought her pretty. Rosita struck me as a little squat, though her face was fetching and her skin a satiny brown. She could not have been much older than I, at the most twelve or thirteen years to my almost nine. Summers, we sort of grew up together in the fields and developed a good-natured rivalry. She could pick more cotton; I could pull more corn.

Our late corn was for feed and not for the table, so we would not pull the ears until they had grown dry on the stalk. It was hot, dirty work and rough on the hands, even with gloves. Yanking corn was a better word for it than pulling. You grabbed an ear by its end, placed the other hand up under the umbilical stem and popped the ear off by jerking it down upon the web between the thumb and forefinger. The ear was thrown into a wagon by the Reds' younger son, Pepito, and you went on to the next stalk, fighting the bladelike leaves that cut across your face, ignoring the chaff that flew into the nostrils and down the neck. And there were plenty of spiders and hornets, which were best ignored. You just went about your business and they retreated and left you alone. The myth in the fields said if you showed the slightest fear of biters and stingers, they'd be on you like that. After a day of corn-pulling, you came out itching all over and nursing swollen and cracked hands. Rosita's hands would be bleeding through the gloves more than mine. But she would laugh it off and banter about who had covered the most rows.

On the morning I'm telling about, there was only a patch of cotton to be picked, the last of the season. After this, we would not see the Reds until next summer when we would be harvesting wheat, oats and barley. I wasn't needed for the last of the cotton, but since Glen had hit the road, I went out that day to bid the Reds goodbye and wish them a good winter down in Texas near the Mexican border. I meant to stay but a moment, as I wanted to build a self-feeder for the red sow Glen had left me. Daddy and the Reds were out in the cotton, but Rosita was missing. I was surprised at the disappointment that washed over me. In all that bloody corn seed Rosita and I had harvested, something had been planted between us.

I found myself looking for her, a gloom growing in me, when the honking horn of their Model T—*yuga yuga*—spun me around. It was Rosita, waving from their car, parked in a mesquite thicket at the far corner of another field. I trotted toward her.

"Hi," I said, pulling up to stare. She had gotten out of the car and was walking toward me. She wasn't the Rosita of the baggy boy's overalls and bare feet. She wore high-heeled spikes and a red dress that stood out like a flag in the field. Her hair was down instead of up in a bandana, a red ribbon in it. She was shapely instead of squat.

"Hi," she said back.

"Gosh," I said. "You look nice."

"*Bueño*, I did it for you."

"For me?"

"Not for my brothers," she said, laughing.

She led me to the car and showed me a picnic lunch she had prepared. "And this is for us," she said.

I looked toward the cotton field, self-consciously, but she pulled me back. "Mother will keep my brothers from bothering us," she said, spreading a blanket under a mesquite tree.

We munched on tacos and chalupas she had prepared, and sipped the red soda pop they could not do without. We talked pleasantly about the good times we had that summer, even while hard at work. Something that had been stirring in me of late surfaced, and I wanted to kiss her fat little mouth and put my hand down her blouse, but I was afraid. By the precocious standards of the Porterfields, I was almost a pubescent. I knew about sex. All my life I had seen animals do it. Bobby and I had even caught Mother and Daddy doing it. But still, I was not ready, and the circumstances hardly seemed right.

When it was time to go, Rosita pulled me behind the car and gave me a warm and most earnest kiss. I will never forget how sweet it was through the salt. "This is goodbye," she said, tearing up. "My family will be back late next spring, but I won't. *Mi tio* is getting me a job in the five and dime at Eagle Pass. It's an opportunity I can't pass up. It will get me out of the fields."

"Yes," I said, stammering. "That'll be better for you. It won't be so hard on your hands."

"Here," she said, reaching for a mesquite limb and bringing it down between us. "We have to bleed one more time together." She pricked her little finger with a mesquite thorn, pricked mine and when our pinkies were crimson she pressed them together.

"Now, you taste our blood on my finger and I will taste ours on yours," she said, weeping. I did so. She did so. The tang of our blood was a profound communion.

"Now go, Beelly," she cried. "*Adios.*"

I ran all the way to Grandpa's hunting cabin on the Little Nile, and hid out there until my heart stopped hemorrhaging.

RED OCTOBER AND THE ABOMINABLE SNOWMAN

Wit Odin, for all his fine books, art and antiques, was supposed to have been broke when he and October Ney came to Little Egypt from Scandinavia, the Himalayas and Mississippi to live in her late grandfather's country house, Sessrymmer, a rundown palace in miniature that had been hiding out on the howling-wolf prairie long before Grandpa and Doody had drawn others to Little Egypt. But the Odin-Ney duet brought beauty, culture, mind and the mysteries of the rara avis.

Wit, a shambling, loose-skinned polar bear of a Viking, who drank in summer a blue coolant of mysterious elements to keep the white continent of his body from boiling over, taught hot ice music and the cold sciences in the rural school. October tutored a warm and subjective piano in their home. She played for our church services. Reduced circumstances or not, it was said every man in the county envied the ursine professor, not for his knowledge, which was imposing, but for his wife. If, indeed, October was his wife. Even into middle-age, October was breaking necks, even those of the old geezers at the domino tables. If Wit's body was huge and clumsy, October's figure was tall and supple, her face so boldly beautiful it damned the chaste and sent a sweet shiver up the sourest loins of misogyny. Her locks were red curls of rapture, cascading down her back or piled upon her head like a many-tiered crown. She was a sight, and would have made men and women ache in London and Paris as easily as she did in Little Egypt and Oklahoma City.

Mark Twain had been smitten by her beauty and intelligence when she was a child in Florida. Her father, Colonel Mills—one of the Ellis Island Mills; in Sweden he was a Millstrom—sold an orange grove to Twain, and the writer, struck by the girl's beauty, brought her gifts on his winter visits. In 1890, on October's tenth birthday, the much-traveled innocent abroad presented her bottled water he claimed was from the River Jordan. Adding to its mystique was Twain's description of the allogamy of benedictions the water had undergone. It had been blessed by the Pope and by every preacher and prophet he could buttonhole in Europe and the Middle East.

"Christen her with it," Twain instructed the colonel, again emphasizing that the water had been insured by many faiths.

"I'll let her make up her own mind about that," the colonel was said to have replied. Even then, October had a reputation for being independent minded. Why she used her maiden name I can only suppose was dictated by her feminism. She was a strong woman, and she required men whose will matched her own.

October kept the bottle of water, and after she was grown and Twain long dead and his fame firmly established, she would bring it out to show visitors. Anyone could see that the water had not been used, not a sprinkle of it, as it filled the bottle to the tight cork. This caused Granny Porterfield, and her sisters of the Female Auxiliary of the Doctrinal Committee of the Salt of the Earth Church of the Absolute Predestinarian Faith and Order, to reason with some alarm that October Ney, our constant and skilled church pianist, had not made up her mind, after all these years, to accept Christ as her savior and be baptized, else the bottle would show evidence of it. We were Primitive Baptists and we believed in dunking a sinner in the Blood of the Lamb, an act of total immersion, damn near drowning a poor soul, Grandpa complained. Dousing October in the whole bottle of water from that infidel Mr. Twain could hardly have done the trick to suit Grandmother. Sprinkling or pouring, sniff, sniff, was for loose-living Presbyterians. But even a sign of a sprinkle from the bottle would have been better than nothing, if only, sniff, sniff, sniff, it allowed October some brief Purgatorial surcease from the eternal burning that was sure to be her fate. Huff, huff. Puff, puff.

After his own damnable eternity with the prune face, beady eyes and sour soul of Alice Austin, Grandpa may be forgiven the devilment that seized him, for he could not keep a single one of his rekindled senses off October. He took delight in telling me, in a confidential aside, that the Jordan water had long ago evaporated, that October kept it filled with gin, which she uncorked from time to time and shared with him.

Odin himself, so everyone said, did not seem to mind the attention other males paid his lady. Winking, Grandpa said this was because Wit was the very devil himself.

If Wit was a bearish demon—Odin suggests the chilly Norse god—then he was the abominable snowman man of Dante's ninth level of the Inferno that is ice. Beastlike as he was, he seemed to be sheathed in a coat of frigid reserve. When you shook his hand, you came away shivering with a slight sensation of frostbite, and wondered how October warmed to those icicle claws. Daddy said he ought to be drinking antifreeze instead of cooler.

But Odin was more than ice to me. He needn't have been. Though I was too young to take his classes at school—and had no talents for music or science—Wit and October taught me so much of other things that I've always felt beholden to them.

In Wit's wing of the high-ceilinged Sessrymmer were the rooms of a polymath who embraced astrology, alchemy, pagan mythology and the occult, philosophy, religions of the East and West, art, music and world literature, anthropology, genetics, psychology and physics; each room with its alcoved desk given to the tomes, totems and tools of the disciplines that engaged him. Once separated into subjects, randomness seemed to reign in the way Wit used these learned rooms, for each was a chaos of books and papers, charts, maps, arcane instruments, wall hangings and art objects. For several springs, October employed me to help her put them back in order according to subject and period. Wit's study and research seemed to me an unstinting round without end. He remained at his post during our inventories, a great muttering bear devouring the fruit of our labor with such rabid scrutiny, returning their pits to the heaps of helter-skelter with such abandon, that we thought we would never catch up. It was there, sneezing upon leather-backed, gilt-edged treasures laden with calligraphy, the Arabesque and the gothic, that I was cursed not only with an allergy to book dust and beeswax, but damned by an appetite for the rare and esoteric, which I've not had the time or money to satisfy.

The room that drew me into a state approaching hypnosis was devoted to heroes, mostly mythological or representing such early human history that they seemed shrouded in the mists of a time when gods strode the earth. When Wit first caught me gazing from the doorway at the coats of arms, the armor, shields and swords upon the walls, he escorted me through what he explained was his little Valhalla, pointing out the various histories and talismans he had collected from what he called the Ages of Heroes. This was the first of several instructive tours he gave me on the epics of heroes in world mythology, art and politics.

He began by showing me a replica he had acquired of the Spear of Phineas, said to have been forged at the hands of the prophet of God's Chosen People and passed on to Joshua, who shook it at the walls of Jericho. The spear became such a symbol of magical power and destiny that ambitious men, good and evil, seized it. Herod sought to kill the Christ child with it. It found its mark at the Crucifixion in the hands of Gaius Cassius Longinus, the Roman Centurion who thrust it into the side of Christ to try to spare his suffering. Otto the Great carried it against the Mongols. Constantine the Great brandished it at Milvian Bridge. Theodosius humiliated the Goths with it. With it Alaric the Bold sacked Rome. Charlemagne, the first Holy Roman Emperor, slept with it; and thereafter forty-five emperors over a thousand years used it for mostly ill. The spear became the symbol of the Teutonic Knights, who helped the Hohenstauffen Fredericks make Prussia a German state.

After this long litany of the spear's hold on men, Wit brought his replica down from the wall and placed it in my hands. To a boy, it was long and quite heavy.

"See the nail bored into the blade?" he said.

"The one laced by gold and silver?"

"Yes. It is said to be a nail from the cross upon which Christ died," he whispered. And then he corrected himself, explaining that his, of course, was only a copy, but a very exact one in scale and detail.

"Where's the real one now?"

"It is in the Treasure House of the Hapsburgs in Vienna. But I do not expect it to be there long."

"Where will it go?"

"I think Adolph Hitler, the new German president, lusts after it, just as Napoleon did. He is the kind of possessed Teuton who believes in such symbols and knows how to use them. He speaks to the world of peace, but he is oppressing the Jews and building up a monstrous war machine. If I were the Hapsburgs, I would guard the Spear of Phineas with vigilance."

His genius aside, Wit had an almost childlike belief in the efficacy of magical charms and mediums. He wore stones and bones and amulets, was constantly foisting them on me for good luck. Every hero he embraced, light or dark, was successful in his quest only when he carried the enchanted object. And so I got a good grounding in the eternal symbols of redemption. He was my Merlin. He was Poseidon to my Theseus, Cheiron to my Achilles, teaching me that if I would be Orpheus I needed the Lyre, if Jason the Golden Fleece, if Aladdin the Lamp, if Alberich the Rhinegold ring. It strikes me now, in hindsight, that Wit had the grandiosity and high-mindedness of the Teuton and his feeling for myth and transcendant glory. It's a wonder he hadn't turned proto-Nazi, the way he went around with Nietzche's endless melody in his head, as composed by Wagner. No stick-in-the-mud, he saw the gadgetry of modern science as a metaphorical extension of divine or demonic powers. What had been vested in visions and crystal balls was now embodied in the microscope, telescope and X-ray. The magic carpet was the combustion engine with wings, and here Wit was a more complicated version of my father, who, without the mysticism, saw mechanics and the fuel of oil as his ticket to a kingdom on earth. I got to be impatient with them both, believing like Doody and Mother that external rewards weren't worth the effort. I felt power had to come from within rather than from without. But I was an angel without balls, Rosita only a false start. My reckoning as a marauding male would come with pimples and the beard of puberty. First I had to let Grandpa finish with his. That was going to be difficult with October around.

Wit taught his subjects at school like a god, attended Brother Reid's Sunday sermons like a henpecked husband happy to let October take the lead in church activities and everything else that required grace and fellowfeeling. Noting his standoffishness shortly after they arrived in Little Egypt, Granny cornered Wit after the service one Sunday and asked, "Wit Odin, what kind of Christian are you, if at all?"

He looked at her steadily and said, "If you insist on cornering me, Sister Porterfield, I must confess that as a Christian I would have to plead guilty to being a gnostic."

"You mean an agnostic?"

"No, a gnostic, perhaps in the mold of Valentinus, the second-century master of the pneumatic who taught at Rome, was driven from the Christian church and fled to Cyprus, where he founded the Valentinians."

"Is that good or bad?" Granny said, baffled, but suspicious of a term that sounded like a kissing cousin to a doubting Thomas.

"Both," he said, and, with a flourish of his cape, hurried, in his sloth-bearish way that no affectation could hide, past her.

October got a shot at Granny too. It was my grandmother's pleasure to begin the new year's Adult Sunday School Bible Class by teaching the Book of Genesis to the new members. Granny especially loved to work with Chapter 5, which requires no special knowledge or gifts of insight of the teacher-interpreter save the ability to recite, in straightforward, King James fashion, the genealogy of the Patriarchs from Adam to Noah. Granny thought it heroic, and a sign that she was among the elect, because she could recite from memory the thirty-two paragraphs of the lineage out of Adam. Before the course was over, she would require of her brothers and sisters that they do the same.

She was thus engaged one morning with the rote of all this male-begetting, when October raised her hand and said, "Alice Austin, where are the matriarchs in all this? Surely old Enos couldn't beget Cainan without a woman? Who was Cainan's mother?"

"Well, my child, it doesn't say."

"Why doesn't it? It's very careful to list all the fathers. Couldn't the scribes give the mothers a break?"

This struck Amy Reid, the preacher's wife, as a hilariously appropriate question. "My God, October!" she interjected in an outburst of laughter, "I've been thinking the same thing for years, but was afraid to utter it. Now you've just burst the bubble of all this male pomposity. Good for you. Excuse me, Alice, I'm sorry I butted in, but I couldn't resist."

Granny looked at them both as if they were blasphemers. "I don't find it amusing at all that a Christian would question the record of the Holy Bible. If wives are not named it must be because God did not want them named. Perhaps He thought they served His purpose better standing modestly behind their men instead of in front of them, like some I know."

October ignored Granny and turned to Brother Reid, who, like his wife, always sat in on the class. Although doubtless nervous of Alice's growing disapproval, he must have welcomed this departure from her years of unyielding and repetitive recitation by memory. "Brother Reid," October said, "doesn't it make your missing rib cavity ache to discover, as I did the other day while researching my King James, that aside from Eve and her great-great-great-great-grandson Lamech's wives—Adah and Zillah—no woman is mentioned by name in Genesis, for all its begats, until more than two thousand three hundred years have passed, when Abraham and Nahor arrive on the scene and take as their wives Sarai and Milcah? As far as I can tell, Milcah becomes the first woman in the Bible named as the daughter of someone, in this case Haram."

"Why, my goodness, October. You catch me short and quite unprepared to answer you. I . . . ah . . . I guess I just read Genesis and accept it as it is, as Sister Alice says. But no, I didn't realize that what you say is so; still I must admit that my missing rib cavity, as you put it, isn't aching over the loss." He grinned, looked at his wife a bit nervously and added, "But perhaps it should."

More laughter.

Granny was appalled that he had not leapt to a more rigorous defense of the Good Book and her stewardship of the class. This was the first time anyone dared take the discussion away from her. She sat down and became a sphinx. No entreaty would move her. She sat there stonily, dying for a pinch of snuff and wishing down hell stones upon the head of October Ney.

Another woman might have subsided as well. But not October. She turned back to the preacher and said, "Look, I'm not expert on the Bible, and I may be wrong in some of my particulars, although I tried not to be in my research. But I'm sure many women have pondered the question Amy and I raise. Why all this plenty about fathers and sons, leaving only questions about fathers and daughters, much less mothers and daughters?"

"I grant you that the Judeo-Christian tradition is a patriarchy," he said carefully, "just as we speak of God as the Father. We don't speak of Him as the mother."

"The loss of mother is not limited to Jews and Christians," October sighed. "It seems to me the distaff side fares no better when accounts of the rise of man are Egyptian, Persian, Hindu, Greek, Chinese, Mongolian, Tibetan, Teuton or American Indian. Wit and I have discussed this, and he agrees, although he squirms when I point out to him that his beloved pantheon of Norse gods had little use for women either, except as witches and temptresses."

"Then all men must plead guilty," Brother Reid said easily to chuckles. The energy in the room had risen, Amy Reid later recalled, and all but Alice were attentive. Brother Reid paused, raised an eyebrow and asked October, "Must then God plead guilty to this, what? Misogny?"

"You said it," October teased. "But I ask this earnestly. Why is it that when women are remembered, it is as the woeful Eves and Jezebels and Cleopatras? They are enticing, perhaps necessary to the race, but near fatal as black widows."

"But then quite the opposite can be true," Brother Reid said, calling out the Virgin Mary, Mary Magdalene, Ruth.

"Yes, but even these women must be forgiven their sexuality to make the canon of good, even Mary. How could she have been a virgin when there are allusions to other children, at least six, all presumably by Joseph?"

Brother Reid was flabbergasted. My grandmother got up and left the room.

"I don't mean to upset anyone," October went on, "but I feel compelled to say this. If the church loses its women, it loses its men.

That's clearly the case. And I think many women share doubts about their place in the Christian pantheon. Look. If there is a middle current, a fully human woman or even a wagging mermaid in the testaments—and there are, millions of them—they go nameless, a sea of submerged if fruitful wombs, anonymous as jellyfish and squid, these wives and daughters, trailing behind all that begetting by brilliantly bobbing fathers of their flashy, skipjack sons. Even Mary, the mother of Christ, must find her earthly messianic family link through her husband, the divinely cuckolded Joseph's line. Prodigious Solomon himself, who knew more of women than any man, weighs heavily on the carping wife and the unfaithful mate in Proverbs and Ecclesiastes. But then, like any male, he becomes absolutely rapturous over a new bride in his songs. But then Jesus, who seems to atone for the prophets who blamed women for bringing sin into the world, even Jesus and his mother are made into symbols of the sexlessness and purity of—"

"October!" Brother Reid said sharply, raising a foreboding right hand. He repeated her name gently and said that perhaps this subject was one they could pursue alone in his study sometime, since it was a subject of the highest delicacy.

"Oh, rats, Sam!" Amy Reid said. She took October by the hand and said, "Come on. We'll just sit under the oaks and talk girl talk. We've got thirty minutes before Sam starts preaching."

I did not love Wit the way I did October, but I respected him and thought he got a bum deal in Little Egypt, especially from my grandfather, who pretended to be his friend. Hulking as Wit was, his cold hands were as small, pale and tapering as a girl's. He was constantly wringing them, in what I supposed was a perpetual state of anxiety. I thought he loved October more than he let on to us. His manner outside the lecture hall was a polite, timid silence, almost servile. It was as if he was making every effort to shrink down to our level, and even lower. It was impossible for a man of such prodigious and strange appearance, of such odd habit and high intellectuality, to simply subside away, but Wit tried. And, ultimately, he did that very thing. But among friends, he could be himself, at least he could be what he seemed to be to us at the time. And what that was, was a mind chilling in its dimensions, a mind that came and went upon prescription and request in a great, white bear that otherwise was a gentle pet who followed October everywhere—except when she bade him stay at home.

In one of the few rooms of her grandfather's ghostly manse that October and Wit shared—they slept in separate bedrooms—was a studio, the walls of which groaned with less erudition and danced with more warmth, sunshine, art, gay music and conversation than was permitted in the dark, draped, heavily cluttered and chilly rooms Wit had to himself. But he did keep in the studio a shrine—it's the only way I know how to describe it—that struck me, in my childish naivety, as naughty but compelling. Decadence was not yet a part of my vocabulary, but it lurked there in the sensual and morbid beauty of Aubrey Beardsley's drawings and illustrations, which went hand-in-dandy-silk-glove with the writings of Oscar Wilde and the caricatures of Max Beerbohm. One day, when Grandpa caught me turning the pages of Wit's gay dogs, he lifted a Walter Huston eyebrow and asked if they interested me. "Not if Daddy's around," I replied, and that made him hoot with pleasure, for the one thing my father detested was that in affectation of dress, his own father was closer to Wit's flamboyance with cape and glove than Daddy and his he-men would have preferred.

Everyone in Little Egypt seemed to have a secret side, and in this Wit Odin would prove to be as multifarious as Doody Mareain. It was Doody who told me Odin was a master of disguise, that at Halloween he was one of the spooks who ran with the Thomas boys in such destructive devilshine that vigilantes went on patrol against them.

"Why would Wit risk such a thing?" I said. "Our best teacher and all that. Doesn't he know he can't trust the Thomas boys? Eventually, they'll betray him, and that would ruin Wit as far as Little Egypt is concerned, and maybe even ruin October. That is, unless Grandpa raised a hand to save her. She's got to know Wit's doing such as that."

"Not necessarily," Doody said. "Miss October's got her own fish to fry. They each give the other lots of room. Besides, as I say, Mr. Wit's a masquerade man. He's so good at it not even the Thomas boys know who he is when he rides with them."

"Now Doody," I said, "how do you know such things?"

His reply was an enigmatic smile. I figured his source was Raff

Ardmore, who, like a stalking jackal, could have shadowed every move the Thomas caravan made on those devilish Allhallows.

What Doody said about Wit Odin jived with Grandpa's occasional intimations that there was more to Wit than met the eye, that it wasn't all as good as his mind and benevolent pedagogy. Some people stammer before they know it, and can't stop themselves. Wit would erupt with nervous hilarity at the most inopportune times. And these were not bearish guffaws. These were girlish giggles. I remember going with him to Dallas to buy band instruments for the school. Wit had made good purchases and was somewhat full of himself. As we came down from our room in the Adolphus Hotel elevator, he asked the operator, a humped old man, how he was doing. The man replied that he was not doing well at all, that his wife had died the week before. And so help me, Wit laughed. I mean he giggled. And he did not catch himself and offer his condolence. He couldn't. He had gone from possession to being possessed. The giggles tumbled out of him like maniacal little red satans. They swarmed into the face of the poor man, taunting him and his dead wife. And then, flipping their forked tongues and arrowed tails at me, they flew out of the seams of the elevator and shot up the shaft in a munchkin-pitched peal of fiendish laughter that echoed throughout every floor of the hotel. The operator cringed in his corner, horrified. The elevator started to stop at the lobby, but Wit was still in full gale, exhaling his devils. I rushed to the elevator wheel and sent us down into the basement, where I pushed Wit out, who by know was rabid and foaming at the mouth. I found a janitor's closet and a faucet, and washed his dementia away. We left the hotel through the garage, not daring to pay the bill, which the school would cover by mail, and went to the train depot.

All the way to Ardmore, where October would meet us for the ride home, the great white bear sat beside me with his tiny paw in mine, weeping silently. Every once in a while, I would take his monogrammed handkerchief out of his lapel pocket and wipe the tears from his cheeks. Never have I so pitied a creature. I knew he was all right when his hot hand cooled.

This is why, when I balance Odin's heaven and hell, I'm inclined to credit him with what may be called an intent of crystallined perfection. He could be a glacial master of insights into art and science, as everyone with a mind in Little Egypt realized way before my time. If in his ethereal reach for the symmetry and transparency of elements in their most serene and glittering purity, Odin locked himself into the severity of ice, then surely it was because he did not want, in the frost-breathed warmth of biological germination, or in the yawn of fang and the shiver and shake of fur and claw, to contaminate or shatter a single thin shard of paradise. If he backed into hell and madness, by way of its frozen topos, it was because he was a polar Pythagoras, listening for the music of the spheres in the most arctic eyrie of the rational. Inside the white bear was an ermine eagle, a silver Siegfriedian bird that ranged time scales so vast and dilated that Norse gods and Einsteins soared with him on Wagnerian wings.

MADAME SWEELINCK AND BEETHOVEN

On Saturdays, Grandpa rose up out of the routine of home, Hecker's and healing and went forth twenty miles to and twenty miles fro to work at a wondrous, and in our territory, a damned peculiar thing: the playing of the solo passages in Beethoven's Concerto for Violin and Orchestra.

The day was of such importance to him it touches me now to think he went to the trouble to include Bobby and me. Grandpa, who had taught himself to read music, had also taught himself to play the piece, but the results were, even he admitted, an abomination to the ear. This was in no way a reflection on his innate musical gifts when you consider he had never heard the concerto performed. The fact it was the first and only classical piece he had ever tried to play, that it constituted the whole of his repertoire—if such a shaky and single thing can be said to make up a repertoire—that he could not play any better "Turkey in the Straw," upon which he had been sawing most of his life, might also have had something to do with his difficulty in mastering Beethoven.

Grandpa believed in plunging. No timid, tepid approach for him. When at last he did come up for air and an honest accounting of the progress he had made, of the music he was making, he winced, which goes to show that at least his ear was true. He blamed himself and not Beethoven, an unusual modesty. But he was not discouraged.

Perhaps he should have been, but that is beside the point. He sought assistance in the form of a Madame Sweelinck, a music teacher in Ardmore, who said she could receive him on Saturdays. When Granny learned he was about to spend two dollars and a whole Saturday to boot on fiddle lessons with a female in the county seat, she raised such hell that he retreated and called the whole thing off.

He even stopped playing on his own and everyone thought, with relief, that that was the end of it. I think he meant to stop, because he suggested it would be a fine thing if I took up the violin and offered me his. His years of scratching had soured me on the instrument, and I declined. The violin remained in its case in his bedroom closet.

And there it stayed until one evening at the farmhouse, when he brought himself up at the supper table, threw down a charred chicken wing, glared at Alice and said he intended to fiddle until Rome burned, and that there would be no more ifs, ands or buts about it. When Granny started to object, he gave her such a withering look that she fell silent and went to her bedroom behind the kitchen. Grandpa went straight up to his bedroom, brought out the fiddle and returned to the table, tuning it as the rest of us finished the meal in silence.

The news was an aching earful, and I was as dismayed as Mother and Daddy, until Grandpa added that he had just as well carry along Bobby and me to take in next Saturday's movies at Ardmore while he had his lessons under Madame Sweelinck. If we were good boys, he said, it might become a Saturday habit. Daddy didn't think much of the idea, as we had chores around the place on Saturdays, but Bobby and I were ecstatic. We had seen more Christmases than movies, even counting those at Aunt Marguerite's in Marshall, Arkansas, and the thought of a picture show every week had us grinning like cookie thieves.

Grandpa, of course, prevailed over Daddy, with Mother's approval, and that first Saturday finally rolled around after a tortuous tolling of day and night. The sun had no sooner glared over the horizon than Grandpa was parked out front of our door in his much-neglected Model A, honking us to hurry.

"Get out and have some coffee," Mother said, pushing the screen door open with her foot and slinging washpan water into the wisteria, which, in spite of the night's shower, was thirsty. "The kids are just getting dressed."

"No, we're not, Mother," I called from our bedroom, nudging my slowpoke of a brother. "We're ready!"

"No thank you, Jennie, had my cups. Tell the towheads to come on."

"Billy Mack, you and Bobby Lee hurry! Grandpa's got ants in his pants."

"No," he said, heh-hehing. "I just want to get through the rondo, and I won't be able to if I'm late."

"Dang it, Bobby! Bend your fat foot. I can't get your shoe on this a way!"

"The Hondo? You don't mean it's flooded after no more rain than we've had?"

"Comin', Grandpa!"

"Eh, what? Jennie, you'll have to talk a little louder. What's that? The Hondo flooded?"

"Well, I don't know, I thought you—"

"Here we are, Grandpa!"

"Pile in, boys!"

"Billy Mack, now you help take care of Bobby Lee. Grandpa'll be busy. Bobby, mind your brother. Yawl hear?"

"Yes'm, we hear."

"Have you got your money and everything?"

On the running board, we held up our nickels, knotted in handkerchiefs. Grandpa pulled down the throttle. "I think I'll go by way of Brock," he yelled over the noise of the engine. "It's a little longer, but that way I'll avoid the Hondo. Wouldn't want to cross that old bridge at flood stage."

"Kids, your apples!"

We held up our sack of apples and tumbled into the dusty backseat as Grandpa, always insensitive to, yea, confounded by, the accelerator, spurred the flivver to motion in a wobbly, exhaust-snorting lunge, reminiscent of a rickety but resentful bronc hopping from the chute with three busters aboard.

Now the bucking horse became a boat. Across the great ocean of prairie we were propelled, ebbing and flowing, slowing now speeding, stopping now starting until I was seasick and yelling stop.

"Damn, boy. What's the matter?"

I could only gasp greenly.

"He wants to puke, Grandpa," Bobby said, looking at me with interest.

"Carsick, eh? Well, lean out the window and let 'er go."

I did, all over the right rear fender.

"Damn, Billy, couldn't you have aimed it a little farther out? That stink'll stay with us to Ardmore."

"I'm sorry Grandpa. Couldn't help it. Like to not got it out at all."

"Pugh . . . wee," Bobby said, wrinkling his nose.

"Here," Grandpa said, leaning over the seat, offering me his wadded handkerchief and a scent of lilac water. "It'll be all right. We'll just close that window. Bobby, can you wind 'er up, boy? 'At's good. Hey, what's this? Green apples half et? Shit, no wonder you got sick. Your mother ought to know better'n to feed you tart young Eves."

"It wudn't the apples, Grandpa."

"Huh?"

"Wudn't the apples."

"What was it then?"

"Your drivin'."

"My drivin'! What does my drivin' have to do with it?"

"It's jerky, Grandpa. You go up and down on that accelerator like Granny does on her sewing machine pedal. You never just go any- where straight out smooth. You slow down and speed up and lurch along till it makes me dizzy."

He was completely turned around toward us now. His left eye closed to a squint and his goatee danced. He looked at me and then at Bobby. "Have you got any complaints about my drivin' too?"

Bobby lied. "No sir."

"Doesn't make you sick?"

"No siree. I like it."

"Well, your big brother's a mite delicate, so I'll tell you what we'll do, Bob my boy. We'll take him back home and you and me'll go it alone."

That seemed to please Bobby, the little rat, but I was not about to be taken home.

"Grandpa," I said.

"What?" He was letting out the clutch.

"I wuz teasin'."

"Don't say."

"Yessir, I know it was the apples and not your drivin'. I just tacked that on to tease you."

"Why, you don't say?"

"Oh, I do. It was purdee jokin', that's all it was. Now have I ever got sick in your car before? No siree. I have not."

Grandpa laughed. "By Jess," he said, "if you ain't a little humdinger! Throw the rest of them damned apples out, you too, Bobby, and let's get on down the road to Madame Sweelinck's."

Ardmore, once popping at the seams with roughnecks, bootleggers and saloons selling grain beer and malt mead—hard liquor was illegal in the Chickasaw Nation—had seen its boomers move on to other oilfields. You could move through the streets without seeing a fight, although Grandpa did make a detour to the Santa Fe tracks to buy some snorts of Gainesville Shoe to fortify himself for Madame Sweelinck. A Gainesville Shoe was a bottle of black market whiskey hidden in a shoe box brought in from Gainesville, Texas by rail-riding drummers.

Madame Sweelinck lived a block or so off Main Street in a prairie-style house on a tree-shaded street. The house was painted white, with a wraparound porch that showed off the big round window of the parlor where she received her students. The parlor was high-ceilinged and spacious, with sofa and chairs, a grand piano and stands of sheet music about, as well as busts of Bach, Beethoven and Brahms. She was a widow, the wife of some faintly famous violinist from the Old Country (Austria), who had fallen on hard times and been damned by the fates to die adrift in Oklahoma. Madame Sweelinck was the daughter of Germans who had immigrated to the states when she was a girl. She was small and slight, but because she looked and dressed like Mary Baker Eddy, and seemed as forthright, she set us back a bit. That she spoke English with a headstrong German emphasis was to be expected. It even enhanced her reputation as a classical musician and teacher. But her deafness was a stunner to Grandpa. He stared, with mouth agape, at the ear trumpet she shoved into his face.

"Ya," she shouted into the small end of the horn, "yew are de fiddler, Doctor Porterfield. Vell, yewr instrument let me see, und let me hear yew play."

Grandpa, his hands shaking, took his fiddle from its case. Madame Sweelinck snatched it from him with her free hand, gave it a once-over with her bright eyes, plucked the strings loudly into her horn, rolled her eyes contemptuously and said, "Vell, of course, a fake Stradivarius, but vat does it matter in the hands of amateurs? Dr. Porterfield, are yew not a novice?"

"If that," he said wanly.

"Vat? Into my horn, loudly speak, please!"

"YES," he fairly shouted, "A BEGINNER I AM, MADAME. ONE, I'M AFRAID YOU'LL FIND, OF THE MOST ABYSMAL SORT. YOUR TASK MAY BE MADE EASIER, HOWEVER, BY THE FACT THAT I HAVE TAUGHT MYSELF TO READ MUSIC, RUDIMENTARILY, AND TO LEARN THE CORRE-SPONDING NOTES ON THE FIDDLE. AT LEAST, THE NOTES OF THE ONE PIECE I WANT TO LEARN TO PLAY."

"Und dat piece is vat?"

"BEETHOVEN'S CONCERTO FOR VIOLIN, IN D MAJOR."

She lowered her ear trumpet and looked at the three of us as if we had escaped from the asylum. "Boys," she said, looking at my brother and me, "am I my old ears believing, or is my horn deceiv-ing? Did Herr Porterfield say it vas Beethoven he vants to butcher?"

"YES MA'AM," we cried. I raised my hand.

"Speak, young man."

"GRANDPA HAS BEEN TRYING TO PLAY THE BEETHOVEN ON HIS OWN, AT HOME, AND WE WOULD APPRECIATE ANY HELP THAT YOU CAN GIVE HIM."

Grandpa flushed and with a glance told me to go to hell, but Madame Sweelinck was delighted. She chortled and said she could understand our predicament. The Beethoven was the Mt. Everest of violin concertos, she said, and only serious fiddlers should attempt its grandeur, its sweetness, its humor, its mystery. Not even Beethoven himself could play it properly. So our grandfather was a fool facing a hopeless task. Still, she admired such audacity, swing though it must by its own neck. She sent my brother and me to sit on hard seats against the wall, and bade us to be silent or suffer rapped fingers and/or dismissal.

DIDDY WAW DIDDY   103

"I TOLD THEM THEY COULD GO DOWN TO THE PIC-
TURE SHOW AND SEE THE MOVIE," Grandpa said. "WHY
DON'T WE JUST LET THEM RUN ALONG?"

But Bobby and I were not about to miss the torture we could see
Madame Sweelinck was about to put our grandfather through, and
she let us stay over his objections.

She sat at the piano and positioned Grandpa behind her, standing him on an adjustable pedestal so that when he put the fiddle to
his chin it rested lightly on the top of her head.

"Dis vay," she explained, "vit my skull und brain de vibrations I
pick up, vitout de horn. Und now, Herr Porterfield, draw yewr bow
und play. My head don't mind. Around it bend yewr fingering
hand."

"PLAY WHAT, MADAME?"

"De first five notes of de Beethoven concerto."

"BUT THAT'S THE OPENING FOR KETTLE DRUM. THE
SOLO PART FOR VIOLIN DOESN'T COME FOR WHAT . . . ?
SIXTEEN PAGES?"

"Ha! Someting at least yew know, Herr Porterfield. Neverthe-
less, dew as I say." She struck the notes on the piano. "Allegro ma
non troppo. Four-four time, please."

Grandpa scratched the five notes. Madame Sweelinck drew an
elbow up, cocked it and drove it into Grandpa's stomach, catching
him by surprise and almost driving him back off the podium.
"Uhhh . . . " he groaned.

Bobby and I squirmed with silent delight.

"Dat's vat for scratching yew get," she announced firmly. "Bring
firmly de bow across da strings. Don't mince!"

Grandpa repeated, stronger.

"Goot," she said. "Hear da notes, Herr Porterfield? Dese first five
form the pattern for de whole movement. Dey measure square off the
bar. Knock, knock, knock, knock, knock, de say, like raps at de door
of a deaf man, like Beethoven himself. Da master repeats de knock,
knock in de fiddles, de horns und da full orchestra. Herr Porterfield, I
too am deaf, like da master, und from vat I can feel of de vibrations
yewr fiddle is giving me, yew also are deaf, not deaf to the notes but
DEAF TO DE MUSIC, HERR PORTERFIELD! STOP, PLEASE,
OR MAD I VILL GO!"

Grandpa stepped down, red-faced.

"Have ever yew heard the Beethoven played correctly, by a master?" she asked.

"I'VE NEVER EVEN HEARD IT PLAYED INCORRECTLY," he confessed, "EXCEPT FOR MY OWN SAWING, I'VE NEVER HEARD ANYONE PLAY IT."

"But in yewr head, yew hear it, no?"

"YES. SORT OF . . . "

"Yew have a goot soul, Herr Porterfield, if not a goot ear. Und for yew, vill I do dis. An exception, for yew. Dere, vit your grandsons sit, und listen to a master."

She wound up an old gramaphone, and put on it the heavy disc of an old Victor recording of the Beethoven Violin Concerto, performed by Fritz Kreisler with Sir John Barbirolli and the London Philharmonic.

Knock, knock, knock, knock, knock began the kettle drum, and after the long orchestral introduction, Fritz Kreisler and his Guarneri began the solo work with a dominant seven chord, which he broke off into unbearably rich octaves.

"Dolce," Madame Sweelinck whispered, "crescendo," echoing the composer's instructions through the allegro, the largetto and the rondo. During the cadenza, she said to Grandpa, who was transfixed, "Listen to Kreisler. Herr Finck said his cadenza vas to Beethoven's field of flowers und drop of rose attar. Yew see how he embroiders, Herr Porterfield. Ya! Bring oud de D string. Strange und lovely, yew make it, no? Ya, mute de others . . . Oh, glorious!"

It was. It was. And it helped Grandpa's understanding of Beethoven. But it did not help him play any better. In fact, he got worse, the vorst she had ever heard, Madame Sweelinck said. Still, she did not throw him out. Maybe she had grown fond of Grandpa. She probably needed the money. The lessons continued, and we witnessed fewer and fewer as Beethoven became familiar and the movies beckoned. Bobby and I saw more cowboy serials than we would see the rest of our lives.

When the lessons stopped, Grandpa put the fiddle away. Mercifully, he never played again. But Beethoven remained with us. And so did old Tom Mix and Johnny Mack Brown, the new matinee cowpoke.

A Jarring Note, a Wistful Exit

One day I walked in on October and Grandpa in his hunting cabin down on Dobie Creek. I had been shooting at squirrels in the high trees of the bottom, and, feeling hungry, I loped into the one-room shack to get a link of smoked sausage. Grandpa and October were on the floor beside the bed, naked as Adam and Eve. Grandpa was on his back and October was atop him, riding him like a Rhode Island Red hen astraddle a banty rooster. I knew there was no use for me to turn around and dash out as if I hadn't seen them, and they knew it was no use for them to cower for cover and pretend they had just been chatting. The room was too small, my intrusion too headlong and complete. It was regrettable, but irrevocable: I had caught them with their pants down.

October dismounted, as delicately as the circumstances allowed, while I turned to the wall and muttered something like, "My Gawd, Grandpa! I'm . . . well . . . I'm real sorry. I should've knocked."

"Yes, you should have," he said in a flat, bewildered voice.

"Well, I'll leave now," I said, edging for the door.

"Shit," he said, a little fire now in his voice. "It's too late now. The damage has been done. Boy, what in blazes were you—"

"It's not his fault, Henry," I heard October whisper fiercely as Grandpa struggled to his feet. "I told you this was not the place—"

"You're right," he said. "I should've listened—"

"And I could've stopped you, but I didn't, did I?" she said, and I could hear a pout of amusement in her growing and now composed voice, and heard as well what I thought was a comradely smack from her on his cheek. To my surprise, she called me from the door, insisted that I turn around and look at her. I obeyed, expecting her to have covered herself, but October had not. (Grandpa was hopping around the room on one foot, trying desperately to pull his trousers on.) October sat in a chair, her long legs primly together, making no attempt to hide her breasts. I could not blame her. They were gorgeous. It was all I could do to keep my eyes on her face, which was no less beautiful than her breasts, but more familiar to me.

"Billy," she said quietly, looking me in the eye, "I'm not going to be shamed by this if you won't be."

I nodded dumbly.

"This is the way adults love each other," she began, only to laugh and look to the ceiling with an exaggerated sigh. "Well, not always on the floor." (Grandpa moaned and jumped around to stare at her, his right leg in, his left leg out.) "But you know what I mean, being a farmboy?"

She looked at me beseechingly, stuck a long-nailed finger between her teeth and then turned an amused gaze upon my grunting grandfather. "You see," she said, and her eyes seemed to burst with the laughter that was bubbling up out of her, "we are really no better than barnyard animals. Oh, Henry, this is a scream. Look at us. Look at you. And poor Billy." And she fairly howled.

I caught her contagion. Now, it struck me funny too, and I started to laugh but caught myself.

"October!" Grandpa protested, the epitome of dignity, still hopping on one panted leg, the other naked and akimbo.

But she was up now, walking resolutely toward me and the door. I moved to the side. She paused, hugged me as a goddess would a forgiven acolyte who had been caught in her chambers, and then walked through the open door.

Grandpa had hopped up beside me, and neither of us could resist following her with our eyes. She turned in the doorway and said, "I'm going swimming. When I come back to dress, you both had better be gone." She looked back at Grandpa, shook her head, grinned and said, "And, Henry, my dear, ridiculous Henry. When, or if, you ever get your pants on—and if I were you I'd start all over again and put underwear on before the trousers; your shorts are on the floor where you kicked them off—would you please leave my horse so that I may ride out the way I came in? You know, with some carriage and dignity? Do you think I might be able to do that, Henry?"

"Why, of course, my dear," he said earnestly.

And with that, she turned and walked off the porch and strode beneath the naked sycamores toward the cold river, buttocks swinging.

We stared after her.

"Now that is a fine woman," Grandpa said quietly, his voice a reverent whisper as we watched her disappear into the autumnal shadows of the bottom. "More than I deserve, eh?"

"Oh, yessir," I whispered back. Never had we shared a more earnest and truer understanding.

Twilight of the Gods

It was only a few weeks later that we Little Egyptians crowded on a Wednesday night into the Salt of the Earth Church, filling every pew of the small chapel, stacking men and boys with brilliantine cowlicks along the wooden walls front to back, the backs of their heads leaving oily and aromatic stains—stigmatas, Brother Reid called them—that ranged upon the whitewashed walls like notes on a scale of the Hallelujah chorus. But we males, who stood in deference to the sitting females, had come not to sing but to listen to Professor Wit Odin deliver his annual address to the higher minds of the community.

It was an event of great anticipation to no more than a dozen pairs of ears, if that, and had started modestly some years earlier in the saloon of Wit and October's Sessrymmer. But the professor's learned eloquence, and his penchant for failing students who did not show up with parents in tow, conspired to make his lecture as compelling to lamebrains as Brother Reid's spring box supper tent revivals and singings were for sinners. These, along with the Fourth of July, harvest dances, Halloween and Christmas, were the main events of our civic calendar.

Wit Odin took seriously his annual appearance before us, burning midnight oil in the preparation of his oration, which was advertised on handbills posted throughout the county by Doody Mareain, Mule and me. For his part, Doody was allowed to take a chair, once all us whites were assembled inside, in the open doorway of the church, just inches outside on the porch, where he could hear without breaking the line that barred the colored and the pagan. And Doody was certainly both, to a degree that bothered more people than would say, since he was regarded as Doc Porterfield's man. To his grace, Doody saw fit to take this dubious dispensation as an honor, and, dressed in dark suit, tie and top hat, took his chair with dignity and attentiveness. Wit, in his expansive gestures, would often, at a telling point in the development of his theme, seem to direct his remarks to Doody, sometimes openly by name, elevating him as a listener and critic whose consideration and approval he valued above the rest of us. It was not disingenuous. There were cork ears in the house, but they did not belong to Master Mareain. After the lecture, it was Doody's habit to retreat to the side yard of the church until the congratulators were through with Wit, and then he would hitch up with him and October and jaw with them over the salient points of Wit's dissertation as they walked or rode the long way home.

Grandpa compared Wit to Robert Ingersoll, whom he had heard on the Chautauqua. At the podium, Grandpa observed, Wit was larger than the huge Ingersoll, and just as commanding in the sweep of his erudition. Wit did not like the comparison. He said Ingersoll was blind to the metaphysical and damned with a second-rate mind. As odd and uncomfortable as he could be in most social situations, Wit's years of reading, writing, study and teaching had prepared him well for public speaking. On stage, the actor and masquerader whom Doody alluded to transformed our misfit polar bear. Suddenly, for his annual hour, Wit Odin drank the skaldic mead of poetry and made such sound and sense that the dullest awakened. Even his voice, which teetered on the feminine, took on a depth of resonance that was nothing short of metamorphosis. On this night, which fate would have as his last before us, Wit became the hoary-tongued personification of his last name. He was Odin, the great, frosty sky-god of the Norse, Odin in all his manifestations of wonder, delight and dread. But he began as himself, this gentleman of the arcane, or so it seemed to us Little Egyptians. This is my reconstruction of what Wit Odin said:

I spoke last of the theocracy of the Ancient Egyptians, which was of topical interest not only because our local nomenclature recalls the land of the pharaohs, but because of the continuing reports out of Cairo of the enormous scholarly value of the furnishings which Howard Carter found in Tutankhamen's tomb, not to speak of the lessons mortuary scientists are learning from their study of the pharaoh's mummy.

If we Christians can clear our heads of the prejudice we hold toward the pagans, then we may say, without fear of compromising our own beliefs, that, clearly, the ancient tribes of the world had something to teach us. I know that some of you are less enthusiastic about this than others, but the fact that you are here encourages me to suppose that you have come in the spirit of free inquiry, which a healthy skepticism can only complement. I want to thank Brother Reid for allowing us to use his church, which in no way will be profaned by the program. And I particularly want to welcome Sister Alice Porterfield and her contingent from the Female

Auxiliary of the Doctrinal Committee of this church. Sisters, may we all pray for piety, but not at the cost of a concordant edification, which I think you will find a comparative study of man's religions can be. After all, it is not bad that people seek God in divers ways.

And so tonight, I turn from the sun and the sacred geometry of the pyramids and head for the North Sea and icy Scandinavia, whose glacial face and volcanic heart attracted a far different man than the collective and comparatively obedient communioner along the benign Nile. One has only to witness the spectacle of Wagner's allegorical music dramas to realize that these Old Norsemen and their frost maidens were god-crazed in their ferocious blood-lust and romanticism, and, truth to tell, far gloomier than Wagner's nineteenth-century optimism has them in the Nibelungen ring cycle. But how heroic they were.

Oh, my brethren, I am not the only iceman here. The gothic myths of the hero and the grail have become such a part of our own mythology that we forget to thank the Teuton for them. The Teuton is in every Celt and Norman who reddens in the heat of this little house of a gentler God. Even Master Mareain, the blackened desert son of Khen and Ham, cannot go from one work day to the next without uttering the names of these cold, white Norse gods. Tyr was a son of Odin and the god of war, after whom Tuesday is named. Wednesday means Woden's day, Woden being the German translation of the Norse Odin. So it is appropriate that I bade you here this evening on a Wednesday. Thursday is Thor's day, Thor being Odin's mightiest son and protector in his role as the god of thunder. And then we have Friday, named for the lovely love goddess, Freya. More about this enticing sorceress later.

As he mentioned Freya, Wit looked out and found October in the pews, and smiled at her in what appeared to be a fond and teasing suggestion that she was his, and everyone else's, love goddess. She beamed back at him.

And so I invite you tonight to commune with Bragi and drink draughts with me from the wells of Urda, Verdandi, Skuld and Mimir.

In my Norse fatherland, before Christians converted us, a thousand years after Christ, Bragi was the god of poetry. Urda was one of the fates, a Norn who with her sisters guarded the Well of the Past, so holy that none could drink of it. Urda stood for the past, Verdandi for the present and Skuld the future. Their well was near a root of the Yggdrasil tree, which held the universe. This particular root climbed up to Asgard, the lofty and *foreboding ice palaces of the gods. Every day, the gods crossed over the rainbow bridge to look into Urda's well and ponder with the sister fates the deeds of men reflected there, assigning the good-doers to heaven, Valhalla, the hall of the heroes up in Asgard, and the bad-doers to hell, Niflheim, the world of the dead and its snake pit for the wicked guarded by the grim goddess Hel, deep beneath another root of the Yggdrasil tree. Beside still another root of the Yggdrasil was the Well of Knowledge and Wisdom, kept by Mimir the Wise giant.*

Let us go to the Well of Mimir, for there, every Wednesday, we may surely find—quenching his thirst for sagacity and inspiration—Almighty Odin, the greatest of the living gods, the All-Father, creator of the universe, progenitor of the gods beneath him and maker of man and woman. Why, we may wonder, would a powerful and seminal father such as Odin sup so greedily at the Well of Wisdom, even giving up an eye to Mimir as fee for the daily drink?

Here, in a natural blink of the eyes, Wit kept his left eyelid closed for the duration of his talk. It was a minimal pantomime which, initially, many may have missed, but by the end everyone was aware of the one eye and its implication, for it changed the man's whole mien. To this day I think of Wit as one-eyed.

If Odin was the All-Father, the ultimate source of everything in the universe, why would he need to bribe Mimir for a drink of knowledge? If he was absolutely autonomous, autotrophic and self-replicating as his pseudonyms, disguises and forms suggested, why couldn't Odin make his own wisdom, and say to hell with Mimir?

Wit looked from face to face before him, his one eye coming to rest on Brother Reid.

What say ye, Brother Reid?

The good-natured preacher said he had an idea, but didn't want to steal Wit's thunder, causing a murmur of laughter.

Thou art almost as good as Balder, Brother Reid. I should hasten to add that if this comparison to a pagan doeth offend thee, then I remove the name Balder and insert our Lord Jesus Christ. The substitution is easily done either way, and I pray without sacrilege, for to my forefathers Balder, a son of Odin and his wife, Frigg, was our martyred saint, betrayed and killed by Loki, our Lucifer and Judas Iscariot.

Here, I heard the distinctive and disapproving gasp that my grandmother emitted when she thought she heard blasphemy, and I found her sitting behind Grandpa in the row reserved for the wives of deacons. She was staring at Wit Odin with her sour and snuff-stained mouth wide open. Even Grandpa himself, sinfully tolerant as one of the worst of blasphemers, seemed to be nervous, not so much at what Wit had said, but for what he might.

In speaking of Balder, I've given my brethren a clue as to why Odin, for all his mastery, was addicted to the Well of Wisdom. Hast thee picked it up?

Brother Reid, sitting up front, and Doody, out in the doorway, raised their hands, and the preacher, remarking that the rafters were weary with the sound of his voice, gave way to our half-in, half-out guest. And Doody replied that if Balder was born of Odin and Frigg, then he, too, was a god. And if Balder was murdered by the devil Loki, then that meant that the gods of Asgard, even Odin himself, were mortals, same as you and me. And if they were mortals, it meant the gods were flawed as you and me, and needed all the help they could get, even Odin.

Brilliant, Master Mareain. Your induction goes to the heart of the matter and explains Odin's constant vigil for wisdom.

Some of the assembled shifted nervously in their seats, whispering to one another and swiveling their frowning faces to the back, made uncomfortable not only by Doody's acuity, but by Wit's recognition of it. Doody was aware of their discomfort but above it. His slit eyes found me standing along the wall, and when I favored him with a smile, he returned it, ever so slightly, his black mask rigid but recondite with meaning. Wit Odin cleared his throat and continued.

It is a peculiarity, almost singular among men, of the Norseman to make of his gods mortals. It stems from this pessimism I mentioned, a hopelessness not only about human nature and man's condition, but about the intention of creation beyond men. In Iceland, the birthplace of the old Norse gods, even the strongest and most resolutely decent of men found it hard, in the weighing of bright days and dark, to find that good triumphed over evil.

Put thyself in their place, ye inland brethren of the sunny Southwest. Imagine thou art an Icelander of the Neolithic Age, thine vulcan island locked in the teeth and wake of the icy North Sea. How hard life must have been in the interminable and unforgiving winters of darkness. Thou and thy tribe lay low in sod bunkers along a narrow coastline, huddling against the howling tempest of wind and water and snow and sleet blown by the breath of the sea and shrugged down on thee by the quaking, sliding mountains. Instead of being buried alive in ash and lava as in Pompeii, thou wert covered over with a glistening blanket of snow and ice, the better to hide the black molten rock that came down on thee from the boiling heights of the earth's festering sores of thermodynamic damnation. It was nothing to lose fingers and toes and noses to frostbite. Weep that thy clan disappeareth under avalanche! Thou didst shiver before the frost dwarfs and giants that dwelled there in bedevilment. Oh, it was a stern and majestic setting, inhuman in its cold beauty, now serene—the fjords and lakes clear and still as death—now cataclysmic in its eruptions and tides. The cause and effect of such Götterdämmerung was not meteorological. It was theological! And expressed therianthropically! Gods good and bad were behind it, errant man the scapegoat. And mark ye this, brethren: our weatherman is no finer caster of causality than a well-watching witch of the fates. But even the mystic is blinded by biology and culture and the insufferable limitations of man against a deeper understanding. We all must cast about with miserly metaphor. Mystical or scientific, subjective or objective, both are mockups, masks of what might be. The hidden thou felt but so poorly comprehended came to thee behind nature and what thou couldst make out with thy senses. And so it was natural to see the gods as forces of nature, animal or element. Afraid, thou didst wear a helmet of the horns of the bull and the ram, and didst sacrifice a weasel to appease them, and didst pray most pitiably for deliverance. I see thee furrowing a brow at such paganism and the worshipping of images and idols, which thou yet dost in unthinking inheritance while denying it! *Dost thou not understand that the Communion of Eucharist, where thou doth drink the wine of the blood of Christ and partake of the wafer of his body, is a ritual reaching back to the rites of cannibalism? Pagan warriors nibbled not at a slain foe out of gory hunger or contempt. If an acolyte pup did the unspeakable thing in a frisk or frenzy of blood, the elder cuffed him and said look to thine seniors. The veteran warrior ate of his enemy out of respect for the brave fallen, for in consuming a piece of him they not only hoped to gain his courage for themselves, but to extend his life and spirit through their own sustenance. Is this not what ye* do with Christ in communion?

Granny huffed and puffed and fainted, causing such a commotion that Wit Odin stopped his sermon while Grandpa, leaning over the back of his seat, revived her with a slap. She came to, got up and flat walked out, three sisters of the Doctrinal Committee following in her broad-butted wake. Grandpa turned 'round and looked up to the podium, saying he was sorry for the interruption, observing that Wit's interpretation of Communion was a mite strong for Sister Alice, bless her heart, but to keep it up full bore because it damned sure was a breath of fresh air to her husband, and, he hoped, the rest of the congregation. About half applauded, while the other half grabbed their hats and bonnets and filed out after Granny and the sisters of Doctrine. Doody had to scoot his chair aside to let them pass. Brother Reid remained in his seat up front. When everyone who wanted left, the preacher got up and went back to Doody and quietly insisted that he get up and come on inside, which Doody did, taking a place beside me standing along the wall, still crowded with men and boys who weren't about to miss the rest of the show. "Please continue, Brother Odin," Brother Reid said, and Wit, not a whit nonplussed, picked right up where he had left off with a dandy bit of extemporaneous paraphrasing from Will Shakespeare that made us laugh.

We few, we happy few, we band of brothers and sisters; for ye that share thy blood in Communion with me shall be my brother and sister in understanding. Let us then empty the vessel, for it makes the greatest sound. There are occasions and causes why and wherefore in all things. By this leck, I will most horribly revenge. I eat and eat, I swear. All hell shall stir for this.

Grandpa thought it was so funny—and true, all hell would break out at the next deacon's meeting—he was shrieking and snorting, and Hamilton Hart had to hand him a handkerchief to clear his pollen-tortured, runny nose. Wit stopped and looked at Grandpa appraisingly, and continued.

What many a hooded Christian cannot see is that images and symbols of Odin and other heathen gods were used by mine fathers because they dared not name or look upon the true god. That is so in most religions on earth. It is sacrilege for a mortal to contain and restrain a god or goddess by any direct definition or address. In the language of the Elder Edda, one of the two Old Norse testaments, it is said that:

> *The one is born*
> *Greater than all;*
> *He becomes strong*

With the strengths of earth;
The mightiest king
Men call him,
Fast-knit in peace
With all powers.

Then comes another
Yet more mighty;
But him dare I not
Venture to name.
Few farther may look
Than to where Odin
To meet the wolf goes.

Him that mine fathers dared not mention was the unknown God, the very same the Apostle Paul spoke of in Acts Seventeen. Like the pagan magistrate Thorkel Maane, I too ponder on the sublime beauty and mystery of the creation and the uncreation, and suppose a god greater than Odin. But in my abstract way I need not bring him down to earth like the pagan, or to substitute lesser gods for him or her or it or whatever. So Odin and Thor and the others became embodiments of the noblest thoughts and purest feelings the Vikings could conjure up for divinity. A part of them knew that Odin and Thor were only externals, pretends made by men and permitted by God, and thus, out of a piety deeper than our well-meaning Sister Alice, they reduced their gods to almost manlike proportions, even the evil giants, so as not to compare beyond their ken, and thus crippled the Norse gods with mortality. Still, they were frightful a'plenty, as thee can imagine.

But a Norseman paralyzed by stupefaction could freeze to death. Thus, thou didst carry on chopping the firewood and mending the fish nets of summer that would bring thee bounty salted for the winter.

The coming of the sun was what thee prayed for. Sun's day. Sunday. It was the deliverance. The short spring and summer were paradise, and paradise played itself out on the seaboard, the only level belt of green allowed by the great rock plateau that was the island, pocked by one hundred and fifty volcanoes, the mightiest Mount Hecla, whose craggy mass and snowy summits dominated the island. Aye, the summer was heaven-sent. The Nordic sky cleared up in patches, the sun peeped out the best it could and warmed the sea a bit, welcoming men and boys in their boats to net the plenteous schools of fish. Beeves grazed 'round the narrow band of green, goats butted about on the slopes and ridges that lost themselves in the clouds hiding the rimmed crown of molten Mount Hecla. But heaven was not eternal, brief as Sunday is to the week, unless eternity's in the cyclical. And even there in the rotation, my brothers and sisters, the hell of winter came 'round as inexorably as death, its icy grip more insistent than the merciful thaw of spring and summer's fleeting warmth.

Above the civil coast clingers there climbed wilder tribes of men who chose the rocky heights for their hideaways, and they warred amongst themselves and the fisherfolk below. And there came a time, a hundred years before the coming of Celtic Christian missionaries, when this local slaughter and plunder did not sate these men called Vikings. And they didst raid all the islands of Scandinavia and its mainland, thence taking their long boats and warships throughout the British Isles and coasts of Europe, venturing as far west as Greenland and the northern struts of Edenlike America.

Born of ancient Celt, who themselves were sons of German tribes, these red-bearded and flaxen-haired warriors lived and fought to such a close degree the legends of their fearsome gods that in time scribes could not separate men from gods and gods from men. And so, it came to pass that out of the clans upon clans of chieftains, arose the royal households of the kings and queens of Iceland, Finland, Norway, Denmark, Sweden, who trace their blood and right of reign back to the pantheon of Odin himself, and his star-crossed line of heroes.

Ye may not look upon Jehovah and live, but we may look upon Odin. He was a tall, spare, long-bearded man, and when he was on his throne in Gladsheim Palace, or with the heroes in Valhalla, he wore a cloud-gray kirtle and a hood as blue as the sky. On his massive head was a broad-brimmed hat or a helmet of horns. Upon one shoulder was the raven Thought, and upon the other the raven Memory. Each day they flew into the world of men to bring back word. At Odin's feet were the wolves, Hungry and Voracious. Odin was a solemn figure, for the gods and man were fated in every prophecy to be destroyed by the giants of Jotunheim, whom Odin, half-giant himself, had betrayed. The end would come at the day of doom, the battle of Ragnarok, and so Odin did all he could to figure out a way to avoid it. Like Proteus, the Greek god of the sea, he did change his shape and nature at will, a transsexual who roamed the earth in *a thousand disguises to right wrongs and seek wisdom. Even at palace feasts, he ate of nothing. The food placed before him he gave to the pet wolves. As I have said, he did drink, not only at the Well of Wisdom but from the skaldic mead of poetry, which he had stolen from the giants and bestowed upon the gods and man. Odin would go to any length, suffer any pain to make himself a savior of his realm. He crucified himself upon a tree to win the Runes, magical inscriptions of arcane power, which he passed on to men. In the Elder Edda he says that he hung*

> *Know that I hung*
> *On a wind-rocked tree*
> *Nine whole nights*
> *With a spear wounded*
> *And to Odin offered*
> *Myself to myself,*
> *On that tree*
> *Of which no one knows*
> *From what root it springs.*

Here, as we bring Odin down from the tree to slacken his thirst and attend his wound, I beg you to permit me a local aside, which you may find of more than profane interest. In Heavener, Oklahoma, near the Arkansas border, there is a tall and broad stone of inscriptions reaching out of the earth popularly called "Indian Rock." Some of you may have seen it. I too have been to the rock, and what others cannot read of its writing and suppose to be the scratchings of Paleo-Americans, I have read and understood. I have taught myself to read the Runic language of old Scandinavia, and clearly that is the character of what is written on "Indian Rock." I translate it to say, "November 24, 1024." I do not say that it was cut into the stone by a Viking, although Eric the Red had already colonized Greenland, a part of the Canadian shield, forty-two years before the date on "Indian Rock." The likelihood is that some latter-day prank scholar scribbled Runic on Heavener's stone. But we can't dismiss the possibility that Vikings, or even Scandinavian Benedictine monks who came to the New World following the settlement of Greenland, ventured this far down into the continent. Oklahoma is a great distance from Greenland and Iceland, but then, October and I made it.

Grandpa, pleased at Wit's suggestion that there was more to

Oklahoma's history than cowboys, Indians and oilmen, arose and led everyone in a warm round of applause for our Norseman and Norsewoman.

Thank you, Brother Porterfield, thank you all. October and I are grateful for your friendship. And now, if you will permit me, let us return to Old Iceland.

Odin was attended by maidens, the Valkyries, which means choosers of the slain, for their most important task was to witness the battles of men and decided who won and lost and which of the slain had been heroic enough to be sent to Valhalla, where, when Ragnarok came, they were privileged to join the gods in the doomsday fight against the giants. Odin's favorite Valkyrie and lover was the beauty Freya, so favored that half the men slain in battle were hers.

Wit paused and again looked at October. He pointed at her and said:

Is this beauty not our very own Freya, fairest of love and fairest of form?

And everyone who liked October oohed and ahed in approval, which she took grandly like a goddess.

October is not alone in her resemblance to the gods and goddesses of Asgard. Do we not have in Horace Hart the smithy Volund, who made swords for the gods and for heroes like Beowolf? Do we not have in Brother Reid the gods' watchman, Heimdall, lord of the Temple? Is not this church Gimle, hall of the blessed? Do we not have in Raff Ardmore Skoll the wolf who scared the moon? Is not our saloon-keeper, Hugh Hecker, Odin's ale-horn bearers Hrist and Mist, Skegghold and Skogul? Is Gaston's Wood not our Mirkwood? Who, among us, is truly good Balder? It is not for me to say. Who, among us, is bad Loki? The Thomas boys? It is not for me to say, even if my name is Odin.

Wit stopped and let all have a good laugh.

I can, however, say that our wee sprite of a doctor and town founder, Master Porterfield, bears a most startling resemblance to Dain, the elf king.

At this, everyone who had greeted Wit's comparisons with laughter and finger-pointing now joined together in a great, merry guffaw. Grandpa was out of his seat and on his knees in the center aisle, his face red from roaring, pounding the carpet and urging Wit on with his analogies. Wit let everyone settle down before he began anew.

Who, then, am I? And why my godly name? It is written in the sagas that Freya married Oder, a minor character who traveled the world in almost as many masquerades as Odin. It is said that October . . . er . . . Freya . . . missed him so that she wept tears of gold. And when he did not return, she went after him, seeking him in many parts and languages. That is all we know of Oder.

Everyone looked first at Wit and then at October with great tenderness. All save Grandpa. I watched him closely. Already, he was burning up with guilt, and so was October. Beneath her ease and alabaster complexion I saw the red of discomfort and suspicion rise in her neck and cheeks.

But we can intimate more, my friends.

Perhaps Oder fled to wander the world because Freya slept with dwarfs to get a golden necklace. They had to be rich dwarfs, perhaps King Dain and his brothers Durin and Dvalin, because the necklace was so valuable and Odin's jealousy so hot that he sent Loki to steal it from her, and a damnable war resulted.

There was a collective sucking in of breaths as we gasped down what our ears were hearing. Was he actually saying what we thought we heard? All were stunned by this sudden and vicious turn in Wit's revelations. Grandpa and October, rows apart, were so beet red their lantern faces lit up their mortification, bonding and branding them in shame. Brother Reid sprang to his feet and cried out, "No! Brother Odin, stop this, I beg of you, man." But Wit, his face evil as Ahab, went on with his vengeance, a wrathful prophet from every old testament writ by the scribes.

Nay! Hear me out, preacher. I read from the new Norse bible, the Poetic Edda. Loki says to Freya:

> Hush thee, Freya, I full well know thee:
> Thou art not free from fault:
> All aesir and elf within this hall
> Thou hast lured to love with thee.

Again, Loki tells her:

> Hush thee, Freya, a whore thy art,
> And, ay, wast bent on ill;
> In thy brother's bed

The blessed gods caught thee,
When, Freya, thou didst fart.

Hamilton Hart sprang from Grandpa's side and lurched toward
the dais. Doody, leaving me along the wall, was not far behind him.

Oder and Odin were one and the same, ye fools! She has betrayed her
lord not thrice but a thousand times, driving him mad, driving him to
round the horns of earth drinking the bitterest mead, disguising himself in
shame. I curse her. I curse him that lays with her. I curse thee all!

Hamilton Hart and Doody were upon Wit, two giants struggling
with one who was crazed, and it was all they could do to drag him
screaming, making for the back door. Wit broke loose and loomed
before us, more rabid and frothy than he had been that day at the
Adolphus in Dallas. He pointed at Grandpa and cried:

I say to you, dwarf, what Odin said to King Geirrod. Ye art deprived
of my help, of the favor of the fallen, of the favor of Odin. I have told thee
too much, you remember too little. Hostile are the incubi Odin can see
about thee . . . Damn thee, Porterfield, damn thee! Mark my words. She
will weep tears of gold for me, abused and forsaken old Oder, and then she
will follow, never to see thee again on earth.

With great effort, and assisted by more men led by Walter
Brautigam, Hamilton Hart and Doody got Wit out of the church and
into the bed of Hart's truck, where, as the others held him, Hart tore
into Grandpa's omnipresent medical satchel and put Wit to sleep with
a drug, jamming one of Grandpa's hypodermic needles into his thigh.

There was consternation over what to do with him. If they took
him home to Sessrymmer to sleep it off, he might rise in the morning
and kill October. They thought to take him to the county jail, but
for what crime? Wit was mad to the point of violence, but what poor
cuckold wouldn't be if his charges were true? He had committed a
great social blunder in branding his woman's lover before the community, and to have done it in a church, even though the occasion
was supposed to have been secular, was a dreadful thing, what with
women and children among the witnesses. Doody and I stood at the
edge of the circle of men about Wit's slack figure, draped grotesquely
in the rough wooden bed of Hamilton's truck, taking it all in as they
debated about what to do. I was glad Daddy was not among them. He
and Mother and Bobby had missed the whole thing, having been

called to the Texas border to help one of Daddy's brothers move his household to another place. Those who had not fled the church were told to leave, and Grandpa sat alone inside. I had expected him to be ranting and raving that he was ruined in his own town. But he wasn't. Silent, he had not moved from the pew in which he sat. He sat rigidly upright, reminding me of the dressed-to-the-nines mummy of Enid's *The True John Wilkes Booth*, who, seventy years after Lincoln's assassination and a bit threadbare, was still making the rural rounds of carnival freak shows. Grandpa's ghastly face was as blank as a cleaned slate. All the color had drained from him. Brother Reid had said leave him be. I was supposed to spend the night with him at the town house. I would wait and see. And what of October? She too was catatonic. Amy Reid, ever the preacher's wife with a soft heart for outcasts, had taken her to the parsonage and sedated her for the night. The men at Hamilton Hart's truck could not make up their minds what to do with Wit.

At last, the blacksmith threw up his huge arms and in his deep bass said, "To hell with it, gentlemen. This really is none of our business, certainly at this point. I care a damnsight more about October and Doc Porterfield than I do this strange fella, and I'll hate him if he harms them, but the die is cast between them. And it seems to me, just to be flat about it, that Doc and October were asking for whatever Wit's man enough to deal out. Or God. It gives me the shudders to think about all the hellfire and damnation he conjured up in the preacher's stead. Let me put it this way: If it was you or me that was in Wit's shoes, you'd say, 'Fuck off, boys, and let me be. This is my call.' And you'd be right, far's the unwritten code's concerned. But I don't think Wit's gonna deep-six anybody. I think he's gonna skedaddle, just like he said in the church, and October's crazy if she follows him, but she might. Ye never know about a woman like that. Old Doc Porterfield's a'messin' with fire. Well, it's late, and I'm damn sure tired. Thanks for ye help, boys. I'm gonna put the juice to this old truck and take Wit Odin home and throw him in his bed, and then I'm gonna do the same with myself. Adios, boys. Oh, ah Billy . . . you staying with ye Grandpa?"

"Yessir."

"You'll see to things, won't ye?" Hart said to Doody, and Doody nodded that he would.

The men got in their cars and trucks and pulled away, their lights bumping ahead of them down the dirt road back into town. No one needed headlamps. The night was lit and glowing under the ripe harvest moon.

The only thing Doody said came after we got Grandpa upstairs and into his bed at the town house. Downstairs in the office, I'd stripped to my cotton shorts and was pulling a quilt over me and Grandpa's cold leather couch when Doody, passing out the back door to walk to his Kushtown, paused, looked back and said quietly, "Billy Porterfield. You remember this night. I reckon Wit Odin's right. It may be the twilight of the gods. And that don't bode well for damn fools like men."

When Wit Odin didn't show up for his classes the next morning, Mr. Terry took it upon himself to teach his students and Wit's at the same time, crowding us all together. Doody and I went out to Sessrymmer to check on Wit and he was gone, nowhere to be found. As far as we could tell, he had taken nothing but himself and the clothes on his back. The thousands of books, art, antiques and instruments—the sum of his personal and cultural mythology—he had left behind with the woman who had betrayed him.

After a few days, October returned to Sessrymmer and did not show herself for months. Grandpa hid in the town house, growing old as Methuselah in a matter of days.

AMAZING GRACE

From the Salt of the Earth Church, the Board of Deacons moved quietly to remove Grandpa from their ranks and replace him with Granny, the first woman elder ever, and Brother Reid had to go along with it. But Alice Austin refused the appointment, saying it was no elevation for her to rise upon the fall of her husband. She said if they did not reinstate Henry like the forgiving Christians they were supposed to be—after, of course, a proper penitence on his part—she would move her letter to another church. This stunned me. I never knew she had it in her. It made me feel guilty for all my prejudices against her. When the elders backed down, I marveled that she had transcended herself. Of course, that was premature on my part.

The deacons did not need to cast out October. She stopped coming to church on her own, and they got another pianist. Brother Reid and Mrs. Reid, mistaking the extent of Granny's grace, sought her help in welcoming October back into the fold. She said no, that the Jezebel would drive her and her husband crazy, and that was that. I was greatly relieved to see our old Granny flare up. Now, you see, I could go back to hating her and loving October freely.

For his part, Grandpa was contrite in his return to the fore of the congregation. His conduct was so deferential and mild that I feared for his vitality and wondered if Wit's revelations had, indeed, ruined him, sapped him of his manhood. I brought it up to Mother, and she withered me with her response.

"You think he's decaying?" she said.

"Well, he's not the same. He reminds me of a steer instead of the little bull he was. I think Granny's leading him around with a ring in his nose."

"Humph," she said. "It's about time. They are married, you know. Why can't you give him some credit and assume that he's maturing instead of being broken down into dry rot. Life is a lesson, Billy Mack, even for adults and elders. Grandpa doesn't have to stop growing just to suit you."

I felt flattened. I tried another tack. "I don't understand you, Mother. I thought you liked October more than Granny. In fact, from what you've said about Alice, I thought you despised her."

"Right on all counts. But that has nothing to do with this. In this mess, Granny's right and October's wrong. You feel Granny fell back down when she didn't extend to October the same forgiveness that she gave her husband, don't you?"

"Yes ma'am. Don't you?"

"In a high-minded way, yes. But not in a worldly way. Granny can't afford to let October back in again, or Grandpa's a goner and Granny's a loser. And she's right. Isn't that strange, Alice Austin and Wit Odin agreeing on something? October is that goddess everyone around town's talking about. What's her name, Friday—?"

"Freya. Do you think she's evil?"

"October? Oh, come on, Billy, of course. We're all some of both, even you, my little devil of an angel."

"But what about love?"

"You mean between Grandpa and October?"

"Uh huh."

"I'd guess, and this is only a guess, that there's more lust than love to it." She started laughing and said, half to herself, "Imagine, at his age. Just like Papa Harrell."

"I don't know lust," I said.

"I know," she said, leaning over and kissing me on the cheek, "but you will. Right now, you're not perfectly innocent, but you are, still, at least for a little longer, my curly haired angel."

A few minutes later, when Mother went out to hang wash on the line, Daddy drew me aside and said, "Hey, short pecker. I heard what ye mother told you a while ago about Grandpa. But don't you believe it. He's not done for, not by a long shot. He's still got some piss and vinegar. You just wait. Give 'em a little time. Takes longer at his age. Now don't let on that I've said anything to you. If you do, I'll pee on your boot."

Now I was really confused. Daddy had always been sweet on his sour old mother and at odds with his father. But now he seemed to be taking Grandpa's side. Grownups! How could you figure them?

It was the winter before we Little Egyptians gave up on Wit Odin and decided that he would not come back.

I was beginning to see, as Daddy had suggested, how some people, even old coots like Grandpa, could suffer the most calamitous setbacks and still get up and go on, maybe limping a bit and favoring one leg or another—whatever—but not surrendering their sass or dare to be nervy fools all over again. And if this was going to be true about Grandpa, what about Wit Odin? I wasn't sure which to count out.

6

★ ★ ★

Sunday Dickens

LITTLE EGYPT
Winter 1935 and Spring 1936

FREEWILL, GRANNY AND THE DEVIL IN ME

ONE SUNDAY AFTER CHURCH, GRANNY SAT ROCKING IN THE parlor of the big house. She was dipping snuff and catching a wink or two while Mother washed the dishes from lunch. Alice kept a pinch between her cheek and gum, and it took her a week to swallow and spit her way through a couple of bottles of three-button snuff, the strong stuff. Stirring in her rocker, she'd handed me the coins I would use on Monday to fetch her some new makings from Cude's when she looked up to see Daddy walking into the parlor with a cigarette in his mouth. She called him over, reached up and pulled the smoking Camel from his lips and threw it into her dirty spittoon. "Smoking's a sin," she announced. "I won't have a son of mine flaunting it in my presence."

This was hardly news. We all knew her litany of sins. That was why Grandpa kept his cigars in the town house and why Daddy kept his cigarettes to the fields and the little house. Daddy had just forgotten to snuff his out and stick the butt in a pocket. He accepted her condemnation, offered a fumbling apology and got the hell out.

When we were alone again I said, "Granny, if God has already charted the course of our lives, why should we bother choosing between right and wrong?"

"Because He wants to test our mettle," she said.

"You mean it's like an obstacle course soldiers go through?"

"Why, I swan, Billy, that's exactly it. Yes, that's a very good way to put it."

"He must be mean."

"Who, Billy?"

"God."

She looked at me with astonishment. "God save you, boy. Why do you say such a thing?"

"'Cause it's like a torture chamber. He already knows what He's gonna do with you—let you go or singe you into eternity. But He puts you through it anyway, just to see you squirm and crawl."

Granny slapped me so hard I dropped the coins for her snuff.

This was not about the dawning of doubt in a simple boy of the country after years of blessed faith. The fact that we subscribed to the twin doctrines of predestination and freewill was, to say the least, confusing, but that's another story. What this was about was Granny and me and the little war we waged between us.

She was, in many ways, an admirable woman. She had been bountiful in child rearing, had kept a large and boisterous farm family clothed and fed while her peacock of a husband paraded about like a lord. And if all her children did not tread the straight and narrow, it wasn't because Granny hadn't tried. At this point in the story I needn't remind you she was quick to point out the failings of others, and this is where we came to a parting of the ways. I may have been a kid, but I saw she was a hypocrite. She convinced me of that from the beginning, and neither of us wavered in our regard for one another. We saw the other as the devil. I thought she was a worse one than me because she passed herself off as Mrs. Rigidly-Upright, which she was, but in the meanest little ways.

I let her stinging slap stop smarting before I asked for another. When I was ready I said, "Granny, what's the difference in your dipping and sniffing snuff and Daddy smoking cigarettes?"

"It isn't the same thing," she said, surprised that I was challenging her. After all, she was God's older sister.

"No difference?" I insisted. "It's all tobacco, whether you're smoking, dipping or sniffing."

I turned the other cheek as she fired away a second slap, and although it brought tears to my eyes I managed to say, "Thanks. You make me feel like Jesus."

The worst thing you could do to Granny, other than wink at her, was to upstage her on the Christian virtues. And already, within the space of a minute, she had allowed me to play Christ to her casting of stones. It was one of my memorable triumphs over her, and I was not through. Alice hated any show of affection. What she demanded was fear, respect and obedience. So my coup de grace was to fall upon her sour bosom, hugging and kissing the mortified woman and showering her with moist declarations of my undying love.

"The dickens is in you!" she cried, and managed to free herself and stagger from the room. She knew better than to seek Mother's sympathy, so she retreated to the only place she felt safe from me. Without grabbing a coat, she ran out the back and shut herself in the outhouse.

Now that was dumb as a chicken. All I had to do to achieve total mastery over the old hen was to slip up to the outhouse and lower the outside latch over the door.

She banged and called out for a shivering hour or so before someone heard and came to let her out. Alice was a severe and imposing woman, and this reduced her considerably.

Of course, I did not get away with it. She had what she thought was the last laugh, watching her son and my father thrash me with a leather strop. He adored her, so my rump was bleeding when he got through with me.

But not even Daddy's whippings stopped me. Like a witch I ground a dried tarantula into powder and mixed it into her snuff. As curiosities, Grandpa kept at his medical office in the town house various specimens from patients, and I managed to borrow a set of wooden dentures that Grandpa had plucked from the mouth of an expired chain-gang convict. One night while she slept, I removed her regular false teeth from the jar of soda and water beside her bed, and replaced them with the dead convict's teeth. The blinky-eyed old woman wore them for a day or two before realizing, in the grinding gluttony of a box supper feast at a church social, that she was chewing with someone else's teeth.

Grandpa looked at them and said, "Good Lord, Alice, what are you doing with these in your mouth? These are those nasty old things I pulled from the mouth of a dead murderer. I had them in my office. How'd you get ahold of them?"

She came right for me. Even Grandpa was mad. He slapped me around a good bit in front of everyone at the social, and Granny swore more vengeance upon me once my father got home from a drilling rig. And, of course, he did come home and gave me a beating that took the hide off.

Rue and Shame

I thought my campaign against Granny was worth the slaps and floggings until the icy morning we got up to go to church and found Granny dead, sitting cold (if somewhat fresher) as "The True John Wilkes Booth" on the throne of the outhouse. I hasten to say the door to the toilet was not bolted from the outside, and that Grandpa ruled she'd died of a heart attack brought on by constriction of the bowels. A proclivity for cheese inclined Alice to constipation, but my conscience kept reminding me that the poor woman's closure could have been aggravated, if not by tarantula dust, then by the fear that once she committed herself to the outhouse, she might never get out again.

I was shaken by the reaction of my father. I had never seen him cry. He went out in the backyard among the chickens, got down on his knees in the dominicker dung and beat the frozen earth with his fists. Mother went out and held him until he calmed. At the funeral he bent over Granny's coffin, lifted the veil from her rock face and kissed her on the mouth. I wept rue and I wept shame.

Death Mask

It was strange, Grandpa calling a halt to the burial just as the pallbearers were lowering her into the grave. "Stop!" he gasped. I heard him, but the words were muffled in his emotion and the sons who bore her did not hear, or if they did they ignored him, perhaps thinking he was out of his mind with grief, unable to accept her departure, her return to the earth. The ropes slipped through their hard hands. The coffin descended.

Grandpa stepped from our sniveling huddle to the edge of the hole, raised his black-suited arms and cried, "Damn it, Doody, hold the rope! I forgot something."

Doleful Doody. He turned, his black face spouting white frost, and gaped up into Grandpa's eyes. Then he looked at Hamilton Hart, the blacksmith, and nodded knowingly.

"What have you forgotten, Doc?" rumbled Hart. He was down on one ponderous knee for the launching, and he squinted up through the brush of his brows at the scarecrow figure of my grandfather. Grandpa trembled, and came down. He wiped a cuff across his white goatee and bent, unsteadily, to lay a hand on Hart's arm. "I don't have a photograph of Alice," he said pathetically. "How am I going to remember her without a picture?"

Daddy moved to Grandpa's side, his arm around the old man, gently pacifying. "Papa, let's step back now and go on with the buryin'. Why, we got pictures of Mama. There's bound to be some."

"Where?" Grandpa asked, looking at Daddy.

"We'll get some, Papa, now let's just—"

"But where? She never had one made. By Jess, I remember that. We talked about it not long ago."

Daddy looked to Mother for help. "Jennie," he said, "don't we have pictures at the house?"

Mother shook her head. No.

My father looked to his brothers. They were no help.

"Doc," the blacksmith Hart said softly, reasonably, "if you don't have a picture of Alice, it's too late now to get one." He paused. "A man doesn't forget what his wife looked like. Alice'll be in your memory as if she were beside you." Hart waited again, then said with finality, "Boys, let's ease her down."

"Amen," said Brother Reid.

But Grandpa would not have it. He stopped trembling. He rose up, as the elder, as the husband of the dead woman, and stopped the burial. He asked that we believe in his reason. He said in ancient times masks were made of the dead to perpetuate their memory, and he said he intended to get a photographer in Ardmore to open the coffin and make a likeness of Alice's face. Meantime, the body would be kept in a cold locker.

And that is what happened, more or less. The photographs made of her in the coffin were those of a dead woman. No amount of retouching and fakery could open the eyes or soften the cold set of death about the mouth. The photographer was paid and the pictures were taken to a Mexican artist in Dallas whose masterwork was a mural for a Brownsville cafe. He painted from the photographs and then, to Grandpa's distress, insisted, in an unfortunate choice of words, that he would do better painting from life, and that Granny sit for him.

"I'm afraid we'd have to break her in two to achieve that," Grandpa shot back. Or I could have slapped her sharply the way she did me. Sorry. Couldn't resist.

Finally we allowed the artist two long peeks—he called them studies, Grandpa said they grew into careers—of the very cold corpse. Alice had to have been his most patient subject. The painter was a fat fellow who took pride in his work. But he was tedious and slow to a fault. It dragged on much longer than even Grandpa had expected. Winter lost its grip. March blew by and cleared the landscape for the new. Grandpa himself, who had seldom ventured from the big house since Alice's death, suddenly stopped moping, perked himself up with some libation and set about to inter the body. By this time we had no heart for tears or ritual. But a Christian and a wife and a mom was being buried and Grandpa, though weary as the rest of us with the spectacle of Granny's coffin being toted about and opened and closed like a trunk in a carnival, saw to it that she was buried with dignity. We gathered one noon in the cemetery before Brother Reid and deposited her with dispatch while singing that relentless refrain, "Asleep in Jesus."

Daddy wanted to return to the rigs in Texas, but hung around to see that Grandpa was steady. After the burial, Grandpa went to town and got a haircut. A good sign. When the painting of Alice was delivered, Grandpa looked at it, shook his head and shrugged his shoulders, and hung it in the darkest hall of the big house. Granny was history.

Like hell she was.

She surfaced in all her sons as they aged. If you put a mop on Daddy's head, he was Alice all over again. I even feel her in me when I'm at my worst as God's older brother.

RAFF ARDMORE'S WHATCHAMACALLIT

Summer 1936

Raff Ardmore was said to be half Mexican and half Negro. No one could remember Raff as a boy, so it was assumed he had attained an age between, say, Doody and Lonnie Mareain. He was a skinny, smoky little man with yellow slits for eyes and a grin Satan could not match for wickedness. Never saw him without his derby hat. Most of the Negro and Mexican men worked for the white man as cowboys and farmhands. Raff worked for no man.

He lived in a tiny, tin-topped house on the bank of the Little Nile, alongside the dusty red road that followed the meandering line of the brook toward Sessrymmer, now glacial and remote as an iceberg with October's seclusion. Most times of the day you would find him hidden on the town square, slouched like an old tomcat under a wagon, in an alley—one afternoon I saw him yawning and licking himself on top of the shed behind Hamilton Hart's blacksmith shop—just taking it easy in the sun or shade. He never allowed himself to fall fully to sleep, somehow managed a watchful dozing with one eye slit open like a lewd dog. A stranger passing through Little Egypt in the daytime—say a drummer with a sharp eye—would have guessed Raff was lazy. And he would have been convinced of it if he had seen the peach tree Raff grew next to his bedroom window down on the creek. In season this tree grew peaches so tempting and conveniently at hand that all Raff had to do for breakfast was raise out of bed, reach through the window and grab one.

But Raff wasn't lazy; he was storing his energy to prowl at night. This was one of the things that made him sinister. You would be coming home late, say from a visit to a neighbor's that had lasted into the evening, maybe rounding the bend of some obscure dirt road miles from anywhere and dark as hell, and Raff, his yellow eyes glowing and his mouth set in that queer grin, would loom up in the headlights. He would slide back into the darkness as you bumped past, and even your daddy would say with a shiver, "What in the world do you think he's doing way out here at this hour? And afoot! He has to be able to run like a cat."

Bobby and I would scramble toward the rear window of the car and press our noses against the glass.

Naturally there were stories about such a character. Most had him in the role of satyr for black bacchanals that went into the witching hours in the woods along the Nile. You'd hear of Raff and naked women flitting about through the fern and rollicking in a pool below the bridge that ran to the church. We imagined he was a chicken thief, a witch doctor and a murderer who never slept and smoked all the yellow-john he wanted. But the most persistent story was that Raff had a tail.

Most had it long and whipish, cougarlike. I preferred Doody's version. The second summer of our carving in the tombs, he said Raff was an Egyptian god, part beast, part man, and likened him to the black jackal Anubis, who, when he wasn't looking after the mummies in the underworld, slinked about on earth, hiding his dog's head and his tail, which was no longer than his prodigious phallus. Whatever, Raff was supposed to keep his tail hidden by running it down his right trouser leg.

That winter I determined to settle the matter of Raff's tail. I would have a look. I knew that Raff rested from his black magic orgies on Sunday nights, that on these evenings he dropped into bed like any other normal person, and I reasoned that if I stationed myself in the peach tree at his bedroom window, I doubtless could watch him undress.

I enlisted the aid of Bobby—not because he could be of any earthly value to me in the mission, but because I was afraid to embark upon it alone. I had enticed him to accompany me on such forays into the dark as carrying the supper's trash to the burning barrel behind the barn, and I had found his stupid fearlessness comforting. Besides, he would do anything I'd tell him. Well, most of the time. No, I can't even get away with that. It's a stretcher. We already know Bobby did damned little I told him. I was so scared of doing what I had to do that I would have taken Joyce if she'd been big enough. Brother was at hand.

But as the time approached to peek into Raff's window, I began to feel that Bobby and I needed the presence and poise of an older boy, so we asked Terrapin Cude to join us. Terrapin was a natural choice, I reasoned, because if we accidentally aroused Raff and he started out after us, the slowest would so engage Raff that the other two could get away. Terrapin came by his name honestly. I figured I could outrun him with Bobby on my back.

At the appointed time, we started out. In a cluster as close as atoms, we walked across the pasture and down into Raff's cornfield, bearing toward the river and Raff's house. It was a still, clear evening and the dry shucks from summer's harvest cracked and popped in the field as we walked between the rows. We had to stop twice, to let Terrapin catch up and to let Bobby tie his shoelaces. My brother was a lot of trouble and usually I was impatient with him, but that night I helped him tie his shoe without complaint. I looked at his fat little face in the moonlight. The dust from the field had turned to mud on his sweaty cheeks and his tow-white hair was down in his eyes. But I thought he was a brave little guy and I thumped him affectionately on the noggin. I began to feel guilty about bringing him along. Suppose something terrible happened?

But we were at the end of the dry corn and there was Raff's shack beyond the fence and down in the trees beside the river. The flickering light from his lantern lit up the bedroom window with a yellowish cast. The yard smelled of burnt offerings, the mnemonic air evil with the whisper of hideous incantations. We crawled under the barbed wire fence and crept toward the house, alert for signs of Raff's dog.

The plan was for Terrapin, being the better shot, to stand back with my air rifle and cover us while Bobby supported me as I shinnied up the peach tree near the window. From the veil of naked branches I would peer into the bedroom. Everything went accordingly. The dog was away or asleep. The window was high, but by tiptoeing I could see inside.

I could not bring myself to do it. I chickened out. I closed my eyes. I just knew that if I opened them I would see something that would haunt me for the rest of my life. I quivered silently, almost suffocating in my sweat. It was a cool night and we all were sweating. I wanted to drop and run, but the urge to know about Raff was still strong.

"Hurry up," Terrapin whispered from behind us.

Bobby was looking up into my face, waiting, a hushing finger on his fat lips.

"Bobby," I lied into his ear, "I can't get up high enough to see in. I'll lift you up and you can look in. Okay?"

"Okay." His round eyes narrowed manfully, his lower lip jutted out with resolve and I heard him say "Upsey daisey" as I hauled him up and let myself down.

At that moment the silence was shattered by an outcry, a crazy kind of sing-song more shrill, and a thousand times more unwelcome, than a Tasmanian devil's whisper in your ear when you think you're blissfully alone and free of any prying eye. I dropped Bobby and danced a jig in every direction at once. It lasted only seconds, my little dance, but it must have been a splendid bit of choreography, depicting, as you see from the program notes, a boy in hair-raising midfright. I managed to steer myself toward Terrapin, an armed ally, while in the confusion reminding myself that I had indeed seen Bobby after his descent, that he had come up off the ground, fat legs pumping in magnificently stunted strokes, and that he was at my heel grunting and picking them up and throwing them down like a very agitated and in-a-hurry piglet.

But Terrapin was nowhere in sight. As I heard the thunder and crack of his progress through the corn brake I realized that he was not slow of foot after all but well ahead of us. He was the author, the creator of the outcry and that it had sprung out of him not in fear but in meanness, I had no doubt. What he had crowed at the top of his lungs was this:

> *Eeny meany*
> *Miney male*
> *Catch a Raff by the tail*
> *If he hollers*
> *Make him pay*
> *Fifty dollars*
> *Every day.*

I realized all this in flight, and I did not stop until that barbed wire fence rose up and smote me. We resumed our run, which slowed to a lope and then to a walk as weariness, and not Raff or his dog, overtook us. All we knew of Terrapin was his dust. He had not only been mean but thoughtless. He'd left my air rifle at the scene. I resolved never to speak to Terrapin again. Some people, I huffed to Bobby, could not be trusted in tight situations.

That night I dreamt I was swimming in the Little Nile and found myself floating out to sea, which was farfetched in terms of geography as the closest sea was the Gulf of Mexico, almost two hundred miles away. But in my dreamscape it made sense. I came upon veiled mermaids, who sang songs of unearthly beauty and beckoned me to swim with them into the deep. On some distant shore, I could hear Grandpa and Daddy shouting silently at me not to go with the sirens. I told Mother the dream. She said nothing, but I could see she was troubled.

HEARTS

Spring 1936

That spring, with Wit gone—not to speak of Granny—October grew back like a frostbitten rose. She came out of Sessrymmer. In the mild sunlight her ripe petals blushed a deeper, darker crimson, almost purple, and we saw beneath the bloom of her old vivacity that the shadow was the red of rue. It did not embitter her. If anything, she was sweeter, quieter, not so bold and thorny. Even those who had been critical warmed to her again, and she and Grandpa, in passing, could even stop and chat with one another without setting whispering mouths in motion.

But she was still Freya, and she could no more resist the king of dwarfs than Dain could stay away from her. She and Grandpa began appearing in public together. We did not know how to react. So we said nothing and tried to mind our business, leaving a slight but civil chill. In time we saw them so much together they became a habit, a part of the scene, a warm and mature couple with just enough flair—theatrical good looks and clothes—and just enough dash— the pepper of sin, the salt of suffering—and just enough grace of redemption that we opened our hearts to them, and at last celebrated their love.

The disappearance and death of their mates had freed them to follow their hearts, and it was a wonderful thing to watch. I never saw Grandpa happier. His bristles had dropped away. He had no need to connive and fight to get what he wanted. All he wanted now was October, and she was at his side, her hand in his at last, and no public shame to it. It was, of course, too soon to talk of marriage, and so they simply enjoyed themselves. At the planting dance, October wore, for the first time in years, fireflies in her hair. In my mind's eye, the picture I most cherish of her and Grandpa was framed at that dance, when, long after the other couples had retired, they remained embraced in a slow dance, his white head nestled upon the half-moon of her proud and partly exposed bosom, circling and circling under the arbor while the yawning fiddler, leaning against the bale of hay on which I drowsed, dared not stop his sweet nocturne until Grandpa called it a night.

7

★ ★ ★

Oil Fever

SUCKROCK SWANSON AND HIS SCIENTIFIC BOX

☆ I WAS IN THE BARN HAMMERING TOGETHER A SELF-FEEDER FOR the new sow when Daddy came in and said, "Hey, boy, you want to see a doodlebug? Come on."

To me a doodlebug was one of those seed-sized predatory larva lions that burrow in the sand and prey upon ants. A doodlebug to my friend Terrapin was one of those seed-sized larvae he called ant cows, because he said big red ants liked to capture them, haul them beneath the ground and nourish and milk them like Holsteins and Jerseys. Bobby and I collected doodlebugs by the jarful, stirring them from their pits with a stem of grass and the incantation: *Doodlebug, doodlebug, house on fire! Come and get your bread and water!* It was the kind of childish and idle pastime my father was loath to comprehend, especially when he thought we should be doing our chores. So I was puzzled by his sudden interest in doodlebugs.

"Doodlebugs?" I asked, thinking I had heard wrong.

"Yeah, boy, put 'che hammer down and let's go."

"You mean those little bugs me and Bobby—"

"Naw, shit, son, I'm talkin' about them oil diviners. One's in October's pasture. Let's take the Ford."

Daddy was not the only one who had noticed the stranger. The three black widowers who lived behind October had congregated at the gate that led into the pasture, and the mailman, Jim Walls, was there too, his truck engine idling. Parked on the side of the road was a long, black, heavy-wheeled Packard Eight, which obviously belonged to the stranger in the pasture. My father eyed it appreciatively. Walls touched his hat brim and said, "Hidy, Tice," and gave me a nod.

"What 'che got here, Jim?" Daddy said, smiling like a man who knows the answer to his question.

"Damned if I know, Tice. Some kind of surveyor, looks like to me."

"You know what he's lookin' for, don't 'che?" Daddy said.

Walls and the Negroes took their eyes off the stranger, who was beyond hearing distance fiddling with what looked like a black, boxy camera on a tripod, and turned to my father.

"Oil," Daddy said.

The old Negro men murmured.

"Well, I gotta get a good look at this if that's what he's doin'," Walls said, climbing up on the gate and straddling the top board. The widowers, their legs thin and veined as thermometers, climbed up beside him and sat there like crows on a fence. Daddy squatted and looked through the barbed wire, chewing a stem of johnson grass. His blue eyes were squinted but keen, and he had a grin on his lean face, as if he knew something we didn't. The stranger was a distant figure in white, maybe three hundred yards out and gradually making his way northward, away from us. He would stick the legs of the black box into the ground about every twenty-five yards, peer down into the top of the box and then consult what appeared to be a large map.

"Looks like to me he's takin' pictures," Walls said.

"Naw," Daddy said. "That idn't no camera, and that old boy idn't no doodlebug, Billy Mack. He's the real thang: a geologist."

"Daddy, what did you say a doodlebug was?"

"Man who says he can find water or oil with a divinin' rod, you know, a witchin' stick."

"Can he?"

"Oh, I reckon some do. But they no match for that old boy out there. They ain't no hocus-pocus to him. He's scientific. See how he uses that box."

"Mistah Tice, what is that box, anyhow?" Widower Gate asked.

"It measures thangs under the ground, magnetic forces and such that give geologists some notion as to whether there's oil down there or not."

"A man wouldn't want to lose that box, now would he?" Widower Gate said.

Daddy heh-hehed. "Oh, that old boy'd tear up the countryside lookin' for it, I guarantee. I'd hate to be the man that stole it."

The men rumbled with easy laughter.

"Yessiree," Daddy said, "that is one valuable box, and don't 'che know he paid a wad for it, same as he did his automobile."

Already, the stranger was becoming someone special, someone to look up to. There was his car to consider, and it was a considerable car, more than any of us could afford. And then there was his box, no less magical in its science. Once accepting my father's evaluation of the box, and it did not occur to any of us to question his opinion of it, as his knowledge of machines was well known, we were free, indeed eager, to enjoy the stranger's good fortune. We did not know him, did not know his name or where he came from or what he looked like up close, but that did not matter. He was a man who had two things of rare value, and it could be that he was bringing us something of value as well. And now my father was deciding for us that the stranger was also a man who could keep what he had, that he would be a hard man to cross. Widower Page could steal Widower Gate's chickens and get away with it, but he wasn't about to steal the stranger's box. We did not feel toward the stranger the green envy that women have for one another that makes them enemies. None of us felt threatened by him. My grandfather would feel differently, and with justification, and that would cause misery for a good many people. But right then at the beginning, out there in the field, we were one with the self-assured stranger with the box. It wasn't because he himself was admirable—he would prove to be rather chilling, for all his manners—but because he represented the new world: the silver of excitement and the mercury of change. Even when October rode out of her stables and headed for him on her stallion we were privately rooting for him. She wore pants and straddled the stud like a man.

"Uh oh," Daddy said. "Here comes the red-headed woman."

"Reckon he has permission to be out there?" Walls wondered.

"I don't know," Daddy replied. "He could or he couldn't. I thank we're fixin' to find out."

The stranger must have seen her coming on the big stud, but he went on with his business with the box, did not acknowledge her until she and the stallion were right over him, and then he did the damndest thing, something we had never seen a man do. He curtsied. He extended his right foot and bent at the waist and waved his arms like wands. It was an exquisite bow, straight from a seventeenth-century farce by Molière. But out there on the Oklahoma prairie it was entirely out of place. We did not know what to make of it. It left us looking at one another. The glances we exchanged would not have been any different if we had come upon two men kissing. My father, who had built up the stranger in our minds, blinked, and then turned to Walls with an embarrassed grin. "He's kinda silly, idn't he?" he said weakly.

October was talking to the stranger, but we couldn't hear. Finally, she got off the horse. The stranger led her to the box and motioned for her to look at what he had seen. They talked some more, she holding the reins to her mount. It was then we realized how tall the stranger was. October was a big woman with a full figure, but beside him she looked as little as Grandpa.

Directly, October swung back into the saddle. The stallion spun like a statue come to life, and they loped back toward the house. The stranger closed the legs of the box, slung it onto his shoulder and walked briskly toward us. He was thin as Doody. He wore a light linen suit and lavender Leatherette shoes. He was an older man, but his face was pink and fresh as a baby's, as if newly made. He smelled of perfume.

"Gentlemen," he said as we fell back, and with his free arm he steadied himself on the swing post and stepped over the creaking gate, hardly breaking stride. A lace handkerchief fell from his pocket. I retrieved it, noted its monogram and handed it to him. "Thank you," he said, and shook my hand politely. He was in the Packard and gone in an instant. We watched him take the turn to October's house, spin up dust for a quarter of a mile, slide to a stop in her yard, just like he owned the place, and disappear through the front door.

Daddy whistled. "Now what 'che make of that?" he said, more to himself than anybody else. "Billy," he said, "what did the initials on his hanky say?"

"The fancy cursive was too hard to read," I lied.

I lifted my tingling right hand and stared at it. It was wet with frost, as if I had exchanged five with a snowman. I put it quickly into my pocket.

A Fake Strad or a Gusher?

At supper that night, Daddy was fit to be tied. All he could do was talk about the geologist. Had he found anything on October's land? Formations. Structures, that's what they called them. The fancy old boy must've found somethin' or October wouldn't have asked him to her house. If there was oil on her land, then there could be oil on ours. 'Course, id be silly to get all excited at this point. Makin' an oil well was an iffy business. And how did we know that geologist was legit? He might be up to no good.

"I stars, Tice," Mother said. "You're getting all worked up before you know a thing about it. Look at your peas. You haven't eaten a one."

"Shit, woman. It's somethin' to be excited about—"

"I wish you wouldn't use language like that around the boys."

"Awww, a little shit never hurt two towheads." He reached over the table and playfully thumped our heads with his horny thumb. Bobby beamed.

"Daddy, you're sure feeling your oats." Mother went on, "You don't really think there's gonna be an oil boom—"

"Naw, you're right. I don't know enough to thank that. But I tell ye, woman, it makes my hemorrhoids hum like yo-yos to thank about the farmers that got rich from oilwells."

"Why, who? Nobody around here!"

"Naw, not in Little Egypt, but all around us. You reckon the Ringlings ain't rich just west of us? Closer to home is Healdton, only one of the biggest producing fields in oil history. Healdton's what put Oklahoma on the map, Jennie. And here's Wilson, its oily ass practically sittin' on our necks. If Wilson's run out of oil, do you thank L. B. Mason would still be offering free coffee at his cafe? Shoot, woman. If oil's in the next town, it could be next door or under this house. It was under the Bolstons' barn this side of Ardmore. Look'it the Bolstons! Now they sittin' purty!"

"Why, I wouldn't call them rich."

"Well, Mama, they right well off. Hank put both of his boys through college and that girl, didn't she take some typin' course?"

"Yes, but—"

"But what? That takes money, woman, lots of it. More'n we got for these two peckerwoods."

"Well, if Hank Bolston's got money, he doesn't act like it. Still living in that old house, Sally flopping around in feed sacks—"

"People that has it don't need to show it off. That's my point, woman. Shit fire, you beat all I ever saw! Are you tryin' to tell me that a man with two oilwells pumpin' day and night—quick as you breathe—ain't got money?"

Mother got up abruptly and went to the stove. Her back to Daddy, she said, in a hurt voice, "Tice Porterfield, I don't know what's the matter with you. You've got more than most men in the county, but it doesn't seem to satisfy you. You go around wishing for what someone else's got."

"Is it wrong to want better for ye kids?"

"No, but you talk as if we can't do a thing for Billy Mack and Bobby Lee."

"I didn't say no such of a thang."

"You said we couldn't send them to college."

"Well, as thangs stand now, we can't."

"Tice, you know good and well that even if we couldn't, Grandpa would. Even dead, he'd see to it that—"

"That's right, but whose boys are they, his or mine? Lordy, I tell ye, for one time I'd like to be able to do somethin' for them myself, and to hell with Papa. I get so tired of Grandpa this and Grandpa that—"

"Why, Tice, what a prideful thing to say! Your daddy's been wonderful to us. If it wasn't for him we might not have got married, the way your mother felt and everything. And look how hard he's worked to leave something worthwhile for you."

"Woman, what are ye talkin' about? He ain't done a lick of work on this farm since I can remember, and I'm a grown man with kids of my own. Doody and me did it, and then me and the Reds and the kids."

"I'm not just talking about the farm. Sure, you've worked it, but you're going to get it too and you know it, Tice, and that's no little thing. There's all the rest—"

"All the rest? What rest?"

"The saloon, the big house, the rent shacks in Froggy Bottom, all his money. He isn't going to leave any of it to your long-gone brothers."

"Jennie, a man could go to the poorhouse for all the money made in Hecker's. You forget it's dry. Nuthin's sold in there but a game of dominoes and a little soda pop, and that'll brang ye one thin dime an hour, and Hugh gets half of that. You talk like the old man rollin' in money, and that's the impression he likes to make, but he ain't. What's he got? You thank he makes money doctorin'? Hooey! They's always more people owin' him than they's people payin' him. He's got mostly people that mean to pay and never will, just like Buck and Carrie have at the store, and ye know how they complain. As for the big house, you forget it's twenty-five years old and ain't had a new nail or board or bucket of paint on it since it was built. Now, as to the farm—"

"Tice, I don't think we ought to talk this way in front of the boys—"

"Lemme finish, woman. You started it and I'm gonna end it. This has been in my craw a long time. This farm ain't no bonanza as it is. It's little as most farms go. I do the work and I get half, so it's no better'n sharecroppin'—"

"But Daddy, someday you'll get all that's made on it!"

"When, when I'm too old to work it?"

"Tice Porterfield! You sound as if you can't wait for your own father to die!"

"No. I wish him many more years, but I'm just lookin' the facts in the face, Jennie. I ain't gettin' any younger, and as long as the old man is alive he's gonna run thangs the way he wants. Why do you thank my brothers lit out? I'll always play second fiddle, and the way we die off, I figger I ain't got that much time."

"Oh, Tice."

"Well, that's the way I feel. Can't help it."

"What would you do, Tice, if you just hauled off like your brothers and hit the road for good? What would you do if you just did it?"

"I'd not go to the rigs. I'd get some kind of mechanical work. Lordy, Jennie, I tell you, mechanics make big hourly money. I'd love to hire on as a transmission man in one of them big auto repair shops like they have in Dallas and San Antonio."

"That would mean staying in Texas for good," Mother said soberly. "And that would kill Grandpa. You're the only one he has left, and he'd never forgive you. And from what we've seen of Texas, I don't think I'd like it either. I'm happy here and so are the boys."

I watched Daddy's face fall. He was quiet for a spell. Finally, he sighed deeply. "Awww, I guess it's just all talk. I don't guess I'll ever get up head enough steam to do much of anything."

He sat there dumbly, stirring the cold peas with his fork. Mother went to him and put her arms around him. When he didn't respond, she went to the sink. She was clearing away the supper dishes when October appeared at the door.

"Jennie, is Henry here?"

"Why October! Come in. No. Grandpa's gone to Ardmore. But come in and have some pie. We just got up from the table."

"No, no pie, thanks. I was hoping to catch Henry. I need to talk to him. What's he doing in Ardmore at this hour?"

"Oh, there's some violinist giving a concert in the high school gym, and Grandpa took his fiddle over to let the man have a look at it."

"That Henry! I thought I had talked him out of that idea. His is only a copy, an imitation. There must be hundreds, maybe thousands, like it."

"You know how Grandpa is when he gets a notion in his head."

"Humm. I wish he were here. Jennie, talk about something of value. Which would you rather have, a fake Stradivarius or a real oil-well?"

Daddy raised his head from the supper table. "You don't mean to say it's true then?"

October looked puzzled. "What's true?"

"About the geologist and ever'thang."

"God, how word gets around. How did you know?"

"We saw the man with the black box," I said. "Daddy figured it all out."

Daddy was grinning.

"That was very observant of Tice," October said, smiling back.

"The man is a geologist. Swanson is his name, said he was with the Royal Crown Drilling Company out of Oklahoma City. I was a little peeved to find him out in my pasture without permission, but after he told me what he found I almost hugged his neck."

Daddy was all ears. "Wha'd he find?"

"A lot of magnetic rocks."

Daddy whistled.

It didn't mean anything to us, so he explained. "When you have rocks like that near the surface, it usually means a dome is under them, and when you have a dome like that, there's a chance in five, say, that you have an oil bed."

"Why, Tice," October exclaimed, "that's exactly how Mr. Swanson put it!"

Mother looked at Daddy with new respect.

"And look," October said, pulling out of her riding pants a wad of one hundred dollar bills. "He gave me this earnest money. Said he wanted a few more days of testing before he'd commit to a lease. God, Tice, I'm excited!"

"Woman, you oughta be," Daddy said. He jumped up and jigged, hooped and hollered.

"Now don't say anything to Henry," October said. "I want to surprise him with it tomorrow."

"Oh, he'll be surprised awright," Daddy said with a chuckle. "He may not get over it."

When October left, Daddy rubbed his hands together and slapped Mother on the behind.

"Tice!" she scolded, "almost made me drop a dish."

"Whu'd I tell ye, Jennie. Whu'd I tell ye? Old Tice was right. Wudn't he? Lord, if they ever was a time to pray, it's now. I mean now!"

"Pray for oil, Daddy?" I said.

"Yes! Oil, son. Dirty, stinkin', filthy rich oil! Gonna stop prayin' for rain and start prayin' for oil. Oil for October and oil for you and me, oil for ever'body! Balls of fire, let it gush to high heaven and we'll catch it by the tubfull. If it don't fill ever furrow on this sorry-assed farm, then I'm gonna know why, 'cause that's exactly what I'll be prayin' for!"

An icy reserve came over Mother. I could see forebodings clouding her brow. I beamed in on her, and what she was saying was that we all were headed for hell.

But I was excited for Daddy. He'd gotten so dour lately it was good to see him a little drunk on something, even if it was a sticky, smelly thing like oil. I went to bed and prayed for gushers.

THE MYTH OF SUCKROCK

Now it was said in Hecker's, when my grandfather still had the sentiment running with him, that Suckrock Swanson was made a fool the first hour he spent in Little Egypt. They told the story that Suckrock came mincing into town wearing a white suit and spats, carrying a fancy-edged oil lease in his breast pocket a'peeping from behind a lace hanky, and that he was asking directions to Widower Page's, one of several old Negroes who lived on the Ney place.

"Widower Page?" Miz Cude at the store was supposed to have said. "Why just take this road that runs past the store. Follow it until you cross the Little Nile, and then take the first dirt road to your right. That'll take you right on up to Sessrymmer, the Ney place, but you don't want to go all the way to the house, although it's something to see, all old and castlelike. Just as you get even with the house, you see a dirt road to your left. Take it. Widower Page is in a shack back at the edge of the pasture."

They said Suckrock followed those directions and came to a shack and knocked on the door. When an old Negro appeared he asked, "Widower Page?" and the old Negro said no. He was Widower Smith. Frankie Smith. Widower Page didn't live there. Well, where was Widower Page? Hummm. Widower Page? Hummm. Pro'bly down the road. And the men in the saloon said Suckrock went on down that road and came to a shack and knocked on the door. When an old Negro appeared Suckrock said "Widower Page?" And the old Negro said no. He was Widower Gate. Brandenburg Gate. Now, Widower Page, he might be down the road. And they said Suckrock went farther on down that road and came to a shack and knocked on the door. When an old Negro appeared, he screamed in a shrill voice, "God damn you, you'd better be Widower Page or I'll see you hung!" And the old Negro said yeah suh, he was, but that he was sorry for it if Mistah John Law was gwine to take him to jail for stealing Widower Gate's chickens, at which point Suckrock was supposed to have thrown up his hands and said that either they were all crazy or he was, that he was only a geologist, and that all he wanted was to make some tests in the pasture out back.

Apocryphal, no doubt. If Suckrock was really who I thought he was, he would never have talked down to a black person. He talked up to them. But the story shows how, at the beginning, Little Egyptians in cahoots with Grandpa took Suckrock to be a figure of fun. Oh, they came around to his side, almost everyone did, eventually, out of greed. But for a time there, before they knew he could put his money and his men where his delicate but daring mouth was, Suckrock was fair game. Widowers Smith, Gate and Page were, indeed, neighbors, and Page was a notorious chicken thief, ranked right up there with Raff Ardmore, and perhaps Smith and Gate were as evasive in their directions to a white stranger as caricature implies, but Page was no fool. He would not have taken Suckrock Swanson, of all people, for the sheriff, most certainly not an Oklahoma sheriff. For all his height, Suckrock Swanson was as delicately put together as some twilight man from the future. His head was large and beautifully sculptured, the brow protrudent and veined as marble, his eyes as large and liquid as we imagine an alien changeling's to be. And he was a fop. It is true he carried his lease papers in his breast pocket and proffered them up like bouquets, whereas the ordinary landman of the time carried that lease in his butt pocket where he could reach back and whip it out like a pistol to mow down some land-rich, dirt-poor farmer. But these were only matters of style, and although they reflected on Suckrock's personality, they did not detract from his substance, his prowess as an oilman. Beneath the finery of his dress and manner (he never would have allowed a "God damn you" to escape his lips, as they had him saying to Widower Page) lurked a shrewd and adroit operator. If Suckrock had a bead on the Ney section behind Widower Page, he knew exactly where it was and how to get there and felt no obligation to announce his intentions to some old black squatter, unless, of course he meant for the word to spread, for the Trojan horse of oil fever to weaken whatever inner resistance there was in antediluvians like my grandfather. But Suckrock may not have been who I suspected he was. He could have been who he seemed to be to almost everyone else. In that case, I could see him hitting town and going directly to the Ney place to get his readings, and if they were not what the map told him they might be, he was going to get out with no landowners begging him to test every foot of ground they had.

As Mother sensed would happen, all hell broke loose. Suckrock Swanson didn't leave as abruptly as he came. That afternoon, he rented one of the rooms above the saloon.

On her part, October changed her mind and decided not to consult with Grandpa about Suckrock's proposition. We all kept our mouths shut about oil, even Daddy, for we knew the old man was dead set against the changes a boom would set off in the community. Oklahoma had known oil speculators and exploiters since the Nellie Johnstone No. 1 well of 1897, and the evidence was all about us of the price homefolks paid for, as Grandpa put it, "leasing our arcadian prairie to petrophobia and its attendant evils." So it was button-your-lip and wait-and-see time for Daddy and October.

Their alliance of discretion was helped by a mild heart attack Grandpa suffered. It so frightened him that he retreated to his upstairs bedroom at the big farmhouse, where he remained so uncharacteristically prudent in his recovery that he received no guests except the family, October and Doody, and did not come down for weeks.

October came in the evenings to fawn over him for a couple of hours, leading the rest of us in a conspiracy of silence about the tornado of oil speculation that struck Little Egypt with the appearance of Suckrock Swanson. For the longest, Grandpa didn't even know about Suckrock. He did not know Hecker had rented him a room. Indeed, he would never see his adversary. And, like the rest of us, he would not know, until after the fact, of the ultimate prize that Suckrock would pluck from him before stealing away into the oblivion of other dimensions.

By the time Grandpa made his way back into the world of men and his throne at Hecker's, it was too late to stop the maelstrom that engulfed all. The nature of men is such that he, not even a healthy and vigilant Henry, could have prevented it.

He was right. It proved to be demonic. More lost than gained. And when the vampires and new rich left, having sucked the fount dry, so followed the exuberant young, leaving the unambitious and aged to dream in haunted doorways before joining the ghosts of the weedy necropolis that Little Egypt became.

Meanwhile the incubi poured on more betrayal and surprise.

The first came at the end of summer, when, with Grandpa acting fitter and starting to get about, my father got up the nerve to face down the old man on leasing the farm to oil interests. Around us derricks were sprouting thicker than trees, and Daddy came bearing a written proposition from Suckrock Swanson. He placed it beside Grandpa's morning coffee, and took the chair across the table. When Grandpa came down and started to sip and read, he sputtered and spewed forth a fine mist of java.

"By Jess!" he roared, pounding the table with his freckled fist, "I'll have no more of this perfidy from you or anyone else about this petroleum business. So stop pestering me about it, Tice. They can fence our boundaries with greasy pipe and ruin the stock tanks, and every damn fool of a neighbor can get rich as Rockefeller, but I'll not lease a foot of my grain and grasses and creek to any sorry speculator—"

"But Papa . . . " Daddy began, and the old man threw a livid finger into his face and told him to follow it to hell.

"Okay, old man," Daddy said, repelled but still venomous, "it's your call. I think you're dead wrong, October thinks you're wrong—"

"What's she got to do with this?"

"She's doin' it!"

"Doing what?"

"Lettin' Swanson and Royal Crown drill. They're plugging in two wells right now."

"You mean—?"

"I'm sorry to be the one to let the cat out of the bag, Papa, but with you up and on the mend, you would've found out anyway. October wanted to tell you, but she was afraid for your heart."

"I can't believe this. What the hell is going on around here?"

"What's going on is life and reality, Papa. Wit and October lived on the skinny for years, and what with Wit and his income gone, she's hard pressed to make ends meet."

"Boy, don't tell me my business. And it is my business because I've been helping her get by. I can do a hell of a lot more for her than Wit ever did."

"Yeah," Daddy said, "but you can't make her rich like Suckrock Swanson can."

"Who in the hell is this Suckrock Swanson?" Grandpa roared. He stood up and started for his hat pegged on the kitchen wall, but fell into Daddy's arms in a purple-faced faint. It was another heart spell. Back upstairs he went, looking like death but still proud and now very aloof.

Mother was so mad at Daddy she did not speak to him for days. Grandpa would not see October, and Mother said that that was just as well. He needed sedation and rest, not excitement, and excitement was October's middle name.

The second and third visitation of the incubi waited until after the following winter—a hard freezer which had upon us the merciful effect of a stupefying hibernation—before trying us most terrible.

8

★ ★ ★

Carnival Malarkey

LITTLE EGYPT
Spring 1938

THE WINTER OF '37 I CAN'T REMEMBER MUCH OF NOW—RUNNY morning noses, pork sausage and biscuits for breakfast, hastily packed sack lunches of sausage and biscuits; the countryside a frosty affront on the filly to school, the cool precision of Mr. Terry's teaching in the face of so many fools crammed before him in an overheated room; the fantasies on the way home; the gore and ritual of Daddy killing a screaming hog to butcher to eat and his bending down to wash red sins away in the white snow; the coughs and colds and liniment-filled nights; a recovered Grandpa up to his pestle in prescriptions. The winter I can't remember much of, so apocalyptic was the new year's spring. March's last wind swept through Little Egypt with a tumbleweed broom and lost itself in the moaning chaparral. It was late in the spring, after the rains when the Christweeds were sweet with their bloody blooms, before we learned what October had done. We were still stunned with that when we learned that Lonnie Mareain had died back in the winter without a peep to any of us from Doody. The reason Doody remained silent became evident to all, and was such a ghastly indictment of him that everyone in my already mad family was made madder by it. If Doody stood at the center of this curse, I, his altar boy, felt a part of the damnation. Of these bedevilments I must speak carefully and as rationally as I am able, for they shake me even at this remove. In this telling I stick to the order in which they came. And so we begin with October.

FROM THE MOUTH OF A BRASS GARGOYLE

When Grandpa was able to get up and about and see for himself the extent to which Little Egyptians had welcomed the oil companies—he said the village looked like a little Tulsa with the derricks going up—he showed his pragmatic side and stopped playing the stubborn puritan. He forgave Daddy for causing his second heart attack. He even said Daddy and his brothers should go ahead and line up a lease to drill on the farm, but not to execute it until after his death released the place to them. He forgave October her speculation. He returned to his medical practice and his office, but, curiously, he never again set foot in Hecker's. This was, to the family, the most telling of his spring of surrenders. It meant he had resigned the senate which he owned, but now in name and profits only. Others held forth there, the new blood and rowdies drinking their black-market whiskey from sacked bottles. Among them, of course, was the strange and austere Suckrock Swanson, who drank but mead and said little. He had no need to speak, for the tongues about wagged him into mythic proportions. And Grandpa, perhaps testing his own stout heart and finding it wanting, choose not to risk a confrontation—for that is what it would have been—with the fabulous stranger with the fabulous name. Grandpa saw his patients in the office and in the countryside, sat quietly in church and resumed his relationship with October—but in a way that remarkably altered its intensity. He saw her only on Tuesday nights at the farmhouse, in a benign family setting that began with dinner and ended with her reading him to sleep on the divan in the parlor. They were still in love, but in the tenderer expression of aging friends.

That first Tuesday when October didn't show up for her evening with Grandpa at the farmhouse, I offered to ride my filly over to Sessrymmer and check on her. But Grandpa, who had bathed and dressed and was awaiting her in the parlor, said no, that we shouldn't press, that surely there was a reasonable explanation for her absence. He and the scent of lilac water followed me into the kitchen, where the dinner Mother had prepared them was turning to toast in the oven. "Jennie," he said, scratching his head, "it seems to me now that October may have told me she wouldn't be here tonight. Do you recollect that?"

"Well, no," Mother said, "or I wouldn't have made dinner for both of you. But then I haven't seen her since she was here last Tuesday. She could have said something to you, and it slipped your mind. Half the things I tell Tice he forgets. Did you see her over the weekend?"

"No," he said. "I had sick calls Saturday, and, of course, then I had church Sunday. And we never see each other on Monday. It seems to me now that she said that tonight she had to go somewhere, Ardmore maybe, and try to sell those two old grand pianos to . . . ah . . . yes, that music teacher, that deaf German—"

"Madame Sweelinck?" I said.

"Yes, by Jess, that's it. How could I forget that woman's name."

"So you think that's what she told you?" Mother said, turning down the gas and opening the oven.

"I'm afraid so, Jennie. I'm sorry you went to all this trouble. The roast and everything smells so savory. It flat slipped my mind. We've made such a habit of these evenings, I just didn't think."

"Shush," Mother said, hugging him. "Now Grandpa, sit down here in the kitchen and eat some of this roast. We'd join you, but we've all eaten. Billy, get him some bread out of the cupboard."

"Humm, good," he said. "Did you have this?"

"No, we had pork chops. I made the roast special for you and October. Guess what I put in it, besides onions?"

"Wine?"

"Some of your brandy. Elegant lovers like you two shouldn't have to settle for watery gravy. I hope it didn't turn too dry."

He winked at her and said it was worth the wait, even if he did have to dine alone. Boy, was October missing a treat. She'd probably come home with a sore throat, having to shout at Madame Sweelinck's hearing horn. Well, tomorrow night would be her turn as host. It was time she opened up Sessrymmer to some fresh air and sunlight and have him over for a change. He'd see to that in the morning.

And he did, taking me with him in the carriage behind the bays. Approaching the grounds of Sessrymmer from the road, we saw a great column of smoke, its color rich as dark wine, rising above the house, hidden by trees. Grandpa cried and whipped the bays to hurry. We thought the place was a'fire. But as we drew closer we saw that the smoke came from a great bonfire behind the house. Grandpa laughed in relief. "She must be burning my love letters," he quipped.

As we pulled up in front of the gothic monstrosity, I sensed, behind the smell of burning wood and something more acrid, so much the shroud of Wit Odin about the house that I glanced at Grandpa, fearing he too had felt the phantom. But Grandpa was jaunty. "Billy," he said, "hop out and bang the knocker. And when she comes to the door, tell 'er she's got some explaining to do, standing me up like that and burning my letters."

I started to bang the knocker, but Grandpa signaled me to wait. He pulled from beneath the seat a jug of hum, from which he swigged most prodigiously. He slapped the cork back in the jug, hiccuped and said, "It ill becomes the sober and meek-hearted man to knock at the door of the muses, for he will serve no one in his inquiry. Now, bang the knocker, Billy my son."

I banged the knocker.

She did not come.

I banged the knocker.

She did not come.

Grandpa banged the knocker.

She did not come.

Grandpa banged the knocker.

She did not come.

Grandpa banged the knocker.

She did not come.

It was then that we noticed above our heads an envelope addressed to him in her hand, and Grandpa reached up with trembling hand and took it down from the mouth of a brass gargoyle. He tore it open and consumed it. The blood of the gored bull burst from his heart and bled into his eyes, and he fell to his knees, steadying himself with an arm against the cold stone of Sessrymmer.

"Grandpa?"

"She's left, my son. She's gone. Forever."

He handed me the letter, which shook with his hand.

Henry, I cannot stay. I must follow him. It is my destiny, greater
than my wish or will. Forgive me, my love. There is no time here.
I pray we love again.

October Millstrom

"Grandpa, are you okay?"

"I'll be fine," he said in a gargling rattle, shifting to a sitting
position on the steps. He was breathing heavily. He took out his
handkerchief and wiped his eyes until the cloth was red and his
vision clear. Then he spat blood and whiskey into the handkerchief
and looked for a place to dispose of it.

"Here," he said in a cleaner voice, "help steady me. I want to see
what's burning in back. I can throw this bloody rag in the fire."

As we made our way around the house, he stopped and took the
letter from me and read it again. "Who do you think she meant by
him?" he said. "It could be only Wit, right?"

"I expect so," I said.

"Then he was a prophet, wasn't he?"

"Yessir. I guess it looks that way. Grandpa, I'm real sorry."

"Bless you, boy. I guess I deserved it. Come on, let's see what
they burned."

Grandpa said it was the biggest bonfire since Bull Head Well
No. 3 burned itself out at Healdton. Frankie Smith stood before the
fire, a hoe and some wet toesacks in hand.

"Widower Smith," Grandpa said, "what are you burning?"

"I'm not bu'nin nothin', Doctah Po'te'field. I'm justa watchin' it
fo Miss October."

"What's October burning?"

Widower Smith turned to us and said it was the craziest thing he
had ever seen, that for four days Miss October and Suckrock Swanson had directed a crew of roustabouts to attack the house and clean
out every stick of furniture, on down to statues and iron men, wall
pictures and bare carpets, and stack it all like kindling in the back
and put gasoline and a match to it. They paid off the men, told
Smith to guard the pyre from spreading, and the two of them—
Swanson and Miss October—had jumped in his long black Packard
and driven away. And it looked to the widower like they were gone
for good, 'cause they sure didn't look back.

"So it wasn't Wit, but that Swanson fella," Grandpa said to me.

I didn't say anything back. The less I said, the better. I could see Grandpa was going to be all right. His flat voice seemed to have hit bottom, and I imagined that his wet, ruptured heart had burned to ash before the blaze and that he couldn't be hurt anymore, at least not by her.

I could only look at the fire and see going up in smoke a treasure of civilization—all those books and instruments, all that learning and art. The sum of it would have made a wonderful museum and library for Little Egypt, if there was going to be a town after all this was said and done.

"Widower Smith," I said, "did you see them put a long, old spear into the fire, or did they take it with them?"

His eyes lit up. "They sho' did," he said. "Mistah Swanson said that was one thing he had to have."

Grandpa threw the red hanky into the fire, and we went to the town house, where he fell to putting his books in order, a task he usually put off until he was up against the wall.

More Calamity

Lonnie Mareain died that December, and Doody had gone about burying his mother with unusual quiet, even for him. He had her in the rock, embalmed, wrapped like a mummy and entombed by the Jesus Brothers out of San Antonio, and, as I have indicated, months passed before anyone in town realized she was dead. My first reaction was one of hurt, not at her passing but at my being left out of her putting away. It was true I had seen little of Doody since school had started, but hadn't I spent the summers carving prayers for Mrs. Mareain's vault, keeping my mouth shut about it all through the semesters when I could have enriched the experience in confessions with Mother and Wit Odin, and perhaps even Grandpa? I fumed but a little before I cooled down to a chill that kept me mute. The playground gossip had Doody and the Mexican morticians in the county jail, charged with everything imaginable. I couldn't wait for the bell to ring, and when it did I mounted my filly and lit out—not for the farm but for Grandpa's town house on the square.

After October's exit, Grandpa had, with the help of whiskey and sedatives, taken to napping in the afternoon before supper, and on this day I burst through the door of his study expecting to find him stretched out on the leather couch. He was at his desk, and it was as though he were expecting me. I started to speak, but he waved me to silence and finished addressing a letter. His pink, freckled hand made the ink sail in a cavalier cursive that masked these sudden sorrows that had befallen us. He stamped the envelope and turned to me. I opened my mouth to ask the questions that had been building in me, but Grandpa was already speaking, telling me what I wanted to know without my having to ask. He went directly to the point.

Yes. Doody was in jail.

Why had Doody been arrested? Because he and the undertakers had buried Mrs. Mareain without a death certificate. No doctor had been called in to confirm her death was of natural causes. Now Doody and the Jesus Brothers were facing a coroner's inquest. The old woman's body was being disinterred for an autopsy.

"What are they looking for?" I asked calmly as I could.

"For evidence of murder."

Grandpa had said it softly but succinctly. Drawing on a cigar, he blew smoke rings from his pink, puckered mouth and looked at me steadily. I felt queer, and sat on a wooden chest that contained his patient logs.

"Grandpa, you don't think that Doody—"

"You know him as well as I," he cut in, lifting a devilish eyebrow, "maybe better."

I could not hold back my tears.

"Hush now," he said, coming to me and running a shaking hand through my hair. "You'll have me crying too. And I've had enough of that lately. I'm sorry I spoke so sharply. Now dry up and listen to me. It's important."

He poked his face into mine and I saw myself as I now am, and our old eyes were earnest as they gazed into my youthful tears.

"This may be a lot of fuss over nothing. The autopsy will be reported in a few days, and it'll probably show Mrs. Mareain died of old age. Hell, she was ancient, several years beyond a hundred. In that case Doody will have been guilty of an oversight, and we can all go back to work and play and love's disappointments."

I screwed up a smile, more out of hope than relief, and Grandpa tried to match my attempt at optimism. But we fell serious again. I couldn't help it after all I knew of Doody from the previous summers. That old mystic easily could have done his mother in, thinking he was doing her a favor. It was fantastic, but possible. Grandpa was thinking the same thing, because he said, "Now, on the other hand, we've got to be prepared. . . ." He paused to catch my eye. "Suppose," he said, squinting at me, bending down, bringing scents of old serge and cigar, "suppose the autopsy shows traces of poison in the body, something like that. What then are we to think?"

"The worst," I said.

"Exactly," he said, nodding his white head.

We stood up, looking at the floor.

"I've written to my attorney in Ardmore," Grandpa finally said, clearing his throat.

"Good," I croaked.

"There is one thing, well, two really—"

"Yessir?"

"You must promise, Billy Mack, that you will not tell a soul about you and Doody's subterranean sorties of the summers, and you will not—"

"You knew?"

"About that monkey business in the cave? Of course I knew. By Jess, I should have put a stop to it, because it damn sure bothered me. But I was up to my neck in enough hell already."

"It was innocent," I protested. "I can't believe that all along Doody was planning to kill her if she didn't hurry up and die."

"You were innocent," Grandpa said, "but was Doody? That's the question, and you know damn well that under the circumstances the question is not all that outlandish."

I began to whistle under my breath, a habit of fear that still betrays me.

"That's the reason, son, that you've got to keep your mouth shut. I admit it's unlikely, but you could be implicated if anyone within ear of the courthouse knows you were down there in that insane sepulcher, designing her tomb! Goddamnit, I ought to tear your head off! And that crazy old fool of a nigger. I should've sent him off to his pyramid a long time ago."

Grandpa wheezed and trembled like a winded horse.

"Stop that infernal whistling!" he roared, and slapped me across the head with the hand that held the cigar. I tasted tears and ash.

"And don't," he gasped, "and don't you even think of trying to see Doody until this mess is cleared up. Do you hear me?"

"Yessir," I cried.

But I could not go home.

After we calmed down, Grandpa send word by one of the men at the saloon that I was spending the night with him. He had been treating me somewhat as an equal, and I supposed he felt he should make up to me for his sudden violence. But it was more than that, it turned out. We would never again be as close as we were that long and strange night. While I bathed, he had steaks brought over from his private slaughterhouse. He cooked them himself, striding about the kitchen in a scarlet evening robe. He allowed me a sip of wine. We sat up till dawn, he drinking and talking and I listening with a question now and then, and it was as if I were a boy in another time and place, years back, and Doody was still my friend, though not the same man at all as I now knew him. You see what Grandpa was telling me, for the first time, was that he too had been a boy with Doody, back before they came West into Texas and Oklahoma, all the way back to the time in Georgia. I knew of their long friendship, but I had not known the particulars of any of it. And yet, as I say, I felt it was my story as much as Grandpa's, since I was a sprig from his trunk, and in so many ways more his son than my father. That is what he said, and this is what he said:

CARNIVAL

Now, first off, you should know that Doody Mareain's claim to some ancient and high-falutin' African heritage is pure carnival malarkey, dreamed up by a sideshow barker Doody and I used to travel with out of Savannah. Now don't raise your eyebrows. I'm giving you the straight of it as I remember, and by Jess, I remember it well because I was at an impressionable age—just about your age, well, two years older—when I first ran into these fellows. It was along about 1885, thereabouts. I was already on my own, fiddling and stepping-and-fetching for room and board wherever they'd take me in. Well, anyway, I was holed up in some ramshackly place that didn't have much to offer in the way of an audience. I think it was Watkinsville or Winder. Whatever, the townspeople had not taken to my fiddling and I was feeling the need for some pocket money when this drummer on the boarding house porch says, Hell, Henry, why don't you strike for Athens tonight? They's some doings there that might interest you.

Like what?

A carnival for one thing. I saw it day before yesterday over in Comer, and it generated a right smart little turnout. They got this giant nigger buck of a prizefighter who whupped ever' white man the crowd threw at him. I understand they're layin' for him in Athens with some ringers that won't say quit.

Well now, they didn't seem at all bad, so I rode over to Athens and took in the sights for a while, and then got a ticket for the fight.

You paid a silver dollar to the barker and crowded around a ring set up in a tent. The barker was a young black man, and he had a pitch that turned the head of everyone within earshot. It was a taunting kind of thing no white man could hear and ignore. What the barker was saying was that he had a nigger in the ring inside that tent who could bring the best white man to his knees. What he implied was that the black man—not just his fighter but any Ethiopian—was, when it was all said and done, superior to your white man. I mean he drew a crowd quick, one of those well-let's-just-see-about-that mobs of men who were willing to lay cash on the line that their own kind was not to be humiliated by the likes of some nigger, no matter how strapping. But the barker you had to admire. He was a little fella with sass and a sense of himself that would take no intimidation. He looked you right in the eye and smiled with such contempt that you wondered, in the deepest part of you, if maybe he wasn't right.

THE GREAT HAMMERCULES

When the barker enticed the men he could into the tent—the women would have none of it—he entered the ring and became announcer and master of ceremonies. He was a magician at that too. I'll never forget his introduction, because I was to hear it hundreds of times over the next several years.

Ladies and gentlemen, he began, and then corrected himself in such a clever way that it made us feel that to be men and to be watching what we were about to see was somehow select and special in an elemental and undeniable way. There we were, whiskey-drinking, cigar-smoking, spraddle-legged males, jingling the money in our pants, pawing the sawdust with our boots, a fraternity of roughs who liked a good, bruising fight, while the little ladies, bless them with their faint hearts fluttering in dainty breasts, had to remain outside. I even felt a masculine pride building as the announcer introduced his fighter.

Gentlemen, he said, the management of the Patrick J. Owens Traveling Roadshow and Circus is proud to present to you its giant of the African earth, Hammercules! But before I bring him out, to meet any and all challengers in the manly art of fisticuffs, I must warn you that this man is one of the mightiest to ever walk the earth. Since joining our company the Great Hammercules has faced in the ring more than fifteen hundred challengers, on the average of three opponents a week over the past ten years, and he has yet to bow to any man. Only four have had the distinction of knocking Hammercules down, and they paid dearly for that all too brief moment of glory. His skill and strength is such that only the hungriest prizefighters will step into the ring with him. We have had, for the past few years, a most remunerative standing challenge to the bare-knuckle champion of the world, John L. Sullivan. But he, perhaps wisely, has refused to meet Hammercules. Gentlemen, a hand of applause please, for our African Apollo, that hammering Hamite, that walloping Watutsi from Ruanda on the River of the Nile, the Great Hammercules!

Well now, out he came from a canvas dressing room, and I tell you when the men saw him they fell back and only a few of us could muster up a clap over the oohs and aahs. Doody was something to see in those days. He was past forty then, and where now you see bones you still saw muscle. Not just seven feet tall but broad as Brautigam. Biggest man any of us had ever seen, and black as ebony.

I thought to myself, well no wonder the little nigger's so sure of himself. He can hide behind the giant seven days a week and not be found.

I happened on the drummer from the boardinghouse in the crowd. He turned to me and says, Hey kid, ain't he a specimen? Wait'll you see him fight. He's as mean as he looks.

THE HORNER TWINS CHALLENGE HAMMERCULES

I laughed, and allowed that the white boys who had been conscripted to take him on might well be wishing for an out. But I misjudged the grit of the Athenian men. Two stepped forward from the murmur of the crowd and talked at ringside with the announcer, who was soaking Doody's fists in a bucket of brine. The men around began digging into their pockets and placing bets with one another. I studied the two white boys. They were big men, but just boys, really, neither much over twenty. Outsized country lads with blunt, come-on-and-hit-me-it-don't-hurt-but-I'm-sure-as-hell-gonna-hurt-you faces. Then it was that I realized they were brothers.

I heard one of the townsmen say, well, if Tommy or Tooter can't whip him, no one around here can, because they've whipped everything that walks in ten counties or more. I mean you can't get much tougher'n the Horner boys.

The brothers drew straws to see which would take on Doody first, and Tooter stepped into the ring and removed his shirt. He was a pink-nippled Celt, one of us, Billy, and his hide was as white as Doody's was black. And yet I could see he was a bleeder, that his blood lay just under the skin. Otherwise he was an impressive strongman, his girth thick and muscular, although not as tightly defined as Doody's. The announcer gave him a dandy introduction and then started taking bets against the house. Within minutes he had almost fifty takers, and the match began.

The first thing you felt watching them circle and swap blows was a disappointment in Doody. There was a brittleness and a caution in him. Oh, he was strong, mighty strong, but you could tell that years of fighting three nights a week in every other decent-sized burg had sapped him. He was closer to fifty than Tooter was twenty, and he was having to coast to live up to the claims of the announcer. And that's what he did with Tooter Horner. He paced himself and fought defensive. Well, hell, you couldn't blame him. After Tooter there'd be his brother, fresh and avenging, to contend with. Well, as I say, those boys were young enough to be his sons, and they gave the old pro some bare-fisted commotion before it was over. They came on fast and furious, and the only reason Doody whipped them was because he was cagier and more experienced. He didn't bull them over, he just outboxed them, cutting them up so badly that they were drenched in their own blood. His fists were like surgical instruments. And the Horner boys were man enough to admit they'd been bested. All in all it was a good show, and it didn't bother me at all to learn that the drummer from the boardinghouse was on the payroll. His job was to pull in customers, and I was glad he had enticed me, because I made up mind right then and there to join the troupe and take his job.

The Great Rexrotti vs. Sutton Griggs

I went into the dressing room and right up to the barker-announcer, whose name was Sutton Griggs. Listen, Griggs, I began, I'd like to hire on—

Call me Mister, you little cracker, he snapped.

Doesn't bother me at all, Mister Griggs, I returned, looking him in the eye. I was a street kid who survived by wit and wile, and always tried to come on strong.

Hey, Griggs said, what do we have here? A nigger-lovin' white boy. Looky here, Doody!

Doody looked down on me, and I trembled in new respect for the Horner brothers. He was more than damned awesome up close. I grinned weakly, but he didn't respond. He just stared at me like a stone god.

Why should we hire an impudent little ass like you? Griggs said.

Your tent was half full tonight, I said, and in Athens! You need a new drummer. You could use a cut man, I went on, and you as the boss, a swell-vested entrepreneur and all, why you ought'n be groveling in the crowd collecting money. I could do that for you—

Entrepreneur? Boy, where you get such fancy words?

Same place you get 'em.

Griggs was grinning. I doubt that, he said. The only Ph.D. you got is in sass.

I figured I was in.

What do you know about cuts?

Pine tree rosin will stop bleeding quicker'n steptic, and I gotta sackful. Wax my bowstring with it.

Your what?

My bowstring. I'm a fiddler. Got a great idea for an act. Dress me up in tails, like a longhair, and bill me as the Great Rexrotti. I come out all dignified and pompous and start grandly into Beethoven's Concerto for Violin, which naturally the crackers hate. But then, just about the time they're starting to cover their ears, I swing into a good old reel, "Turkey in the Straw," somethin' like that. They'd love it.

Uhn huh. I'm sure. We'll have to think on that. About three seconds worth. Kid, you get sassy around here and I'll tell everybody you're not only a nigger-lover, but a queer as well. What's your name? The Great Rexrotti won't do.

Henry Porterfield. But call me Doc. Most everybody does.

*I can see why. You got the snake oil. Alrighty, Little Doc. Let me
hear you fiddle.*

I didn't got much more than a bar into Beethoven when he stopped me.

*Enough! Enough. God save our ears. Here's the deal, Little Doc.
You go ahead of the troupe and beat the drum for us in the towns. And on
fight nights you tend the cuts and be our second fiddle and watch your
manners and we'll get along fine. I have but two commandments to hand
down to you. The first is that in public you are to always and unfailingly
address Doody and me as Mr. Hammercules and Mr. Griggs. Now,
Doody's white man's name is Mareain, but in public it's Mr. Hammercules or, if you feel up to it, the Great Hammercules. Got it?*

Yessir.

*And the second thing is that you are not to make a sound on your
puling fiddle as long as you are with us. I will break it across your bony little butt and send you packing if I catch it out of its case.*

What's the pay?

*Two percent of every night's take, and you can eat with us if you sit
at the foot of the table and lick the leftovers.*

Two percent! That's nigger wages. I gotta have at least five.

*On a top night, which are few and far between, we'll take in about
one-hundred and forty dollars. If I paid you five percent you'd be getting
seven dollars and fifty cents, and you know damned well even on a good
night no white boy is worth that. If you don't draw better than that drummer
you're replacing, you're going to have to get by on an average of a dollar fifty
to a dollar seventy-five a night, and sleep in the stable with the horses.*

*That was at least seven smackers a week, not bad, so I stopped hag-
gling.*

THE TROUPE—QUEEN MAKEDA—HER HOLD OVER THE MEN

*It was the beginning of a ten-year engagement with Griggs and the
Great Hammercules. We made quite a team, and when Doody's mother
joined us she brought an added touch of class. Regal she was. Griggs didn't
trust me, so he had Lonnie Mareain go down among the crowd and collect
the bets, and this always caused a stir. She was so tall and beautiful and
well-set-up, looked exactly the way Griggs wanted her to look when he
dreamed up all that stuff and such about her and Doody being aristocrats
of Africa. I've got to hand it to Griggs. He could enhance Heaven with his*

introductions. And Lonnie was heavenly. She would descend among the men as Queen Makeda, and even in her coming down we had to look up and marvel at what Africa had wrought. You could believe she was Queen Makeda, and that Makeda had been the Sheba who journeyed to Jerusalem to seek Solomon's wisdom and returned with his seed, to give birth to Menelik, who became a great warrior and turned the ancient pastures of Abyssinia into the Kingdom of Ethiopia, all a thousand years and more before the coming of Christ. Oh, Lonnie Mareain was as much a showman as Griggs. After her fingers were fat with greenbacks, she would hold them up like fans and turn toward Doody and Griggs in the ring and say, in a rich, exultant way, a strange and beautiful chant that went:

Through wisdom I have dived down into the great sea, and have seized
in the place of her depths a pearl whereby I am rich . . .

and here she would wave the money and the men would whoop and holler and cheer her on. She would acknowledge the rowdies with a smile and a nod, and continue in her contralto:

I went down like the great iron anchor,
whereby men anchor ships for the night on the high seas,
and I received a lamp which lighteth me,
and I came up by the ropes of the boat of understanding.

And up she would go into the ring, to walk around it once waving the money. And Lordy, the men loved it. Then she would kiss Hammercules, shake the challenger's hand and disappear into the dressing room, where, I knew, she would become all business and turn to counting the take.

THE STRETCHERS GRIGGS PUT INTO HAMMERCULES'S HEAD

Hell, the truth of them, as far as I was able to tell, was that all three had come from Waco, Texas. Now that they had their genesis in Africa there could be no doubt, of course, but my point is that they made their African geneaology a damnsight more magnificent and continuous than it probably was. I know for sure that Doody had been a cowpoke like his daddy until Griggs latched onto him and his mother. The word I got from other carnies was that they had been run out of Waco by the Klan because of Griggs's radical politics. It was said he organized the niggers and tried to create a separate black state. Brilliant, he was, but crazy. Dangerous. Doody's the way he is now, and in the trouble he's in, because of Griggs. I tell you it was a sin the stretchers that Griggs put into Doody's head.

Apparently at least a shadow of that was true, because years later, after the act broke up, Griggs wrote a novel about an attempt to set up a black utopia in Waco. He sent it to Doody and I read it. Imperium in Emperio it was called, and it was a good read, I had to admit, a lot more moderate in its tone and sympathies toward whites than I would have expected from Griggs. He wrote several books, and Doody let me read them all. The Hindered Hand comes to mind. He and Doody kept in touch.

And Doody came to believe them. The poor fool was convinced he was Ethiopian with a little Arab thrown in, that his ancestors had come down from the Kingdom of Nubia and the courts of the black pharaohs of Kush to settle in East Africa along the Lake Kivu. And he was full of Griggs's notions about the superiority of the Watutsi, and all that nonsense about how they had conquered the peasant Bahutus who lived on the plains and the pygmy Batwa who lived in the forests. The logical step, naturally, was to extend their supremacy over even white people. And that's how Griggs primed Doody for the boxing matches. He had Doody believing that most white men were worth killing, and in the beginning, I understand, when Doody was in his thirties, they said it was like feeding the scent to a great dark serpent, and for a while there, before he settled on Hammercules, Griggs toyed with calling Doody Typhon, which I understand is the ancient Egyptian serpent-satan. If anything, Griggs was Doody's Typhon. He made each bout a symbol of the nigger's struggle against the white man, their own personal crusade, and so goaded Doody that sometimes they'd have to stop the fight to keep Doody from pure and simple murder.

But that had changed by the time I came along.

HAMMERCULES AND HENRY BECOME FRIENDS—THEIR DREAM

When I got to know him, Doody was pretty much run down and tired of doing battle with every white-trash lunkhead. Behind all he was a gentle man, and he didn't hate the way Griggs did. I'm still not sure why Griggs took me on. My grit and gab, I guess, and then he liked lording it over a white kid. It was always jab and parry between us.

With Doody it was different. We became friends, and during those *years I reached my pride while Doody, as an athlete, went over the hill and into rheumatic late middle-age. I spent many a morning after a fight the night before working the aches and pains out of his body. Hell, I went to medical school on him. Some days he just couldn't get up, and we found it harder and harder to get him warm and loose for a match. Niggers aren't supposed to bleed, but Doody did, and I put a forest of rosin in his old sore hide. I got big arms from rubbing him down. He used to lie there and get whiffed on the alcohol I was soaking him in and talk about what he was going to do when he retired from the ring.*

He was going to get him a farm down in South Texas, get him a fat Mexican wife, and do nothing but pleasure in the woman and eat the corn and milk the cows he raised. The white bread and red beer life, he called it. Damn it, boy, because of your age I feel a little constrained, like I'm telling you something I ought'n, but, by Jess, if you can sit there and sip my best Beaujolais like it was soda pop I guess I can give you the straight of it about Doody and me and our adventures. You've been around barnyards and a certain hunting cabin long enough not to blink, eh? That's what I thought. Well, let's enjoy it, at least the telling of it. That's about all an old man and a boy can do, hey! Well, now, where was I? Oh, yes, Doody was daydreaming. He said he hoped to make love as many times as he had fought, which made sense to me at the time. It seemed the proper balance for any red-blooded man, and goodness knows Doody needed a little realignment, as we say in chiropractic. The poor devil. Between living with his mother and fighting for Griggs, he didn't have much time for the ladies. Why he even said Griggs put saltpeter in the meals they fed us to keep Doody celibate and strong for the ring. Now I never believed that, or maybe I was just immune, if you know what I mean. But Doody was convinced of it, and once in a while he would skip eating all but the poke salad so he could slip out with me on an off night and make the whore houses.

Oh, the women loved him. They would wait in line to service him. He enjoyed himself. We were a pair, I tell you. Take our little side trip to San Antonio, the summer of '93 or '94, I believe it was. It was an initiation I'll never forget.

For the first time I laid eyes on Mexican women. Doody had assured me we would find a special and refreshing welcome, and the man did not lie. The river that takes its time through the heart of the city was brimming with life. It was Saturday. The market on Military Plaza was packed with traders, and along the river bank all manner of humanity was in proces-

sion. Reminded me of the parade of people I used to see on the Mississippi as a kid. Merchants and minstrels, adventurers of every sex and scheme, skin and tongue. Why, we saw Canary Island girls speaking Spanish with Texas Indian boys, barbed wire drummers from Chicago buying whiskey for maverick cattlemen. There were more Catholic fathers than the pope ought to allow, and even more soldiers. In almost any other public square, Doody would have stood out like quills on a porcupine. But we passed almost unnoticed, so varied were the freaks and strangers. It was probably as much from our sense of being sprung as it was the spirits we were drinking, but we were ready for anything.

Well, we were coming around the riverbend when I see a sight that stops me dead in my tracks. There, ahead of us, just as unconcerned as ladies at their toilette, are some women and girls, laughing and chattering and playing in the water, and son they don't have a stitch on to hide their luxurious buoyancy. A barefoot brother in a woolen gown coming down the other bank of the river sees them and averts his eyes, but such probity never enters our mind. A woman at her bath is a pleasure to behold, and the sight so rare, that we both draw closer for a better look. They are such sensual creatures the way they lave themselves in the warm water, so sleek and plump in the right places, and so direct in their black-eyed gaze. I'll never forget it.

Doody said he could stand it no longer. I followed him along an acequia between Old Mission Road and the Market Gardens. We came upon the twin towers of Mission Concepcion, which was pretty much in ruins. I couldn't figure what Doody was up to until we entered the walls hiding a great domed hall. A German madame opened the massive door, and we walked into a den of iniquity so seductive that we did not leave for two days.

It was while we were on our way back to Texarkana that we agreed to throw in together on that Texas farm. I think the promise of it helped sustain Doody through his servitude to Griggs.

THE HORNER BOYS AGAIN—THE TIDE TURNS—RETREAT TO OKLAHOMA

It was a shame, really, the way Griggs pushed Doody. I don't know who I hated the most: Griggs or the Horner boys, the way they dogged him. You see those brothers wouldn't give up after that first fight in Athens. No matter where we were playing, they'd show up at least once a month to *challenge. Doody must have fought those rednecks fifty times. First one and then the other. Well, after ten years of Tommy and Tooter and all the opponents in between, it just wore him down. And all the while Tommy and Tooter were learning, and the tide began to turn. The matches got closer and closer, until finally, one hot July night in Senatobia, Mississippi, just below Memphis, Tommy Horner let rip a damn stunner. He caught Doody on the right side of the head with a left hook. Blood gushed out of his ear and sprayed us at ringside. Doody went down like a rubber tree. He bounced up five times before Tommy put him down for good.*

Doody wasn't out. He was just whipped, a worse humiliation. I can see it now. Griggs was standing over him, screaming and cursing for him to get up and fight. I have never seen a man so worked up. His eyes were popping out of his head and his voice was as high and shrill as a crazy woman's. When he finally realized that Doody wouldn't get up, that Hammercules was done for—after twenty years and twenty thousand rounds— Griggs ran from the tent and lost himself in the midway crowd.

We never saw him again because as soon as Doody came around and Lonnie and I got him into the tent and showered and dressed, we packed our horses and struck for Memphis. We put up at a nigger hotel on Crump Boulevard. It wasn't too many weeks before I came into the property here in Oklahoma, and Doody and Mrs. Mareain followed me out here. The year was 1896.

GRANDPA AND DOODY GROW APART

Now a lot has passed between Doody and me since we first came out here. Forty-one years, for one thing. In that time we changed, and I guess you'd have to say we grew apart. I didn't realize it until sometime afterwards, but that beating Doody took from Tommy Horner really changed him. Took the wind out of him in a way that's hard to explain. He went right on working as hard at farming as he had at prizefighting, and for a while he made a hand. But there was a removal about him that hadn't been there before. He got so damned metaphysical, so superior to the things of this world that I had to let him do his thing and put your daddy on the farm.

You see the problem between Doody and me was that I was just coming into my maturity, and, hell, I'll admit it, my ambition. I came to want to walk in the world of men, to cut a swath through more than carnivals and cornfields. And Doody, who had mowed through men like a reaper, was no longer interested in them as opponents, except maybe as corpses. No, that's unfair. Let's say spirits. He got contrary and grim to be around, almost insolent in his derision of my storing up of worldly goods.

I remember one year I was all excited about the corn crop and he put me down for it. Told me off, said I had not dealt squarely with him in the partnership, and accused me of keeping him in a bondage that was only a little more pleasant than his years with Griggs. By Jess, that stung me, because there was some truth in it. I had taken over, but it was due as much to Doody's indifference as it was my bossiness.

You noticed Doody never took a wife like he said he would. Instead he got skinnier and skinnier and downright ascetic. That day we had the knockdown-dragout, I said, all right, let's go halves, you take yours and I'll take mine and we'll each work our own fields. But he would have none of it. No, he said, he didn't need it. All he wanted was a house and a small garden and his mule to ride around and think on. Socrates on an ass, that's how he saw himself. And, of course, his attitude toward me suggested that I had somehow missed the true meaning of life, the pursuit of wisdom. Well, I told the old fool off. For all his philosophizing, he cut a ludicrous figure. Fanatic old coot. Hovering about graveyards, whispering with children. Where had his manhood gone? I was sick of his superiority and his pretension to some pharoahic past, and sorry that I had let him influence me in naming the town and creek and every damn thing around here Egyptian the way we did.

I told him once he had about as much Watutsi in him as I did. I guess I was stretching it a bit, but I said it was my opinion he wasn't tall out of some noble lineage, but out of affliction. I said I had suspected for years that he and his mother were cursed with that bone disease that plagued Lincoln and made him such an elongated freak. The Marfan Syndrome is what we call it. Shows up about every fourth generation in certain families. This is where your giants come from you see in carnivals and sideshows. Lincoln inherited it from his great-great-grandfather, Mordecai Lincoln II, and I'm sure if you could go back a few generations you'd find it in Doody's line. What usually rides this syndrome is aortic insufficiency. The arteries that send blood to the heart can't keep up with the stretching of the bones, and they tend to go haywire, causing a leaky heart. And the surest sign of heart leakage is a shaking and trembling of the legs, which I'm sure you've noticed in Doody. He even had it when he was boxing, *though at the time I laid it to nerves. The only thing that doesn't fit to make Doody a black Lincoln is his great age. Marfan men usually don't live long. Take Abe. He would have been dead anyway, within six months, if Booth hadn't shot him in Ford's Theater.*

But hold on here, Billy, and mark my words. The impasse Doody and I have come to is equaled only by the carnival malarkey of our lives. We both have made a mess of things. And now, the only thing left to us— growing old and mellow together—has been taken away by his ridiculous attempts to get his mother into heaven.

THE VERDICT

Grandpa had talked through the night with great animation. But now, as the morning sun lit the room, his voice was thin and his face was haggard. And, for the first time, I realized he was failing.

"I'm going to bed," he said, rising from his deep leather chair. "You can do the same or you can go to school, I don't care."

"Well," I hesitated. "I guess I'd better go on."

He smiled. "One more thing and we'll not talk of this further."

"Yessir."

"Suppose this business of Lonnie Mareain's death does come down to a jury, and you and I are on it. How would we find Doody? That's really what we're asking, isn't it, because we know him best of all?"

"Yessir, that's about it."

Grandpa straightened up and took from his lips a cigar that had been cold and hanging at half ash. He made his fingers a crossbow, the cigar an arrow and shot it into a spittoon. As it struck the spittle he said, "Guilty. I have to say guilty."

The same verdict was in my heart.

"But without malice," Grandpa whispered, "with love afore-thought."

9

★ ★ ★

On to the Other Side

GOOD NEWS AND BAD

☆ GRANDPA'S THEATRICS THAT LONG NIGHT HAD LEFT ME WITH the distinct impression that Doody was headed for prison and the electric chair.

But already, my grandfather was executing a bold plan that would have freed Doody of suspicion of murder. Within a few weeks, Mother confided to me that Grandpa had made a deal with cronies at the courthouse to have himself appointed coroner in the case, and that he was prepared to swear in his autopsy report that there was no trace of poison in Mrs. Mareain, that medically she had died of natural causes. He was about to finish his report, and was so confident of its acceptance that he had convinced the sheriff to return Lonnie Mareain's mummy to the tomb and patch it back up properly. The latter had been done, but Doody would not be told and released until the judge had made it all official. My guess is that Grandpa never so much as touched the linen wrap of Lonnie's body, not only out of deference to her and Doody and their Egyptianism, but out of affection and respect for their long and bizarre friendship. The violation of her tomb by the sheriff had been offense enough.

It was the last thing my grandfather could do for his old companion, but Doody would never know it. An awful and absolutely unexpected development set in motion a train of events that would never allow Doody to realize that he and Henry Porterfield had begun to see things in the same, haunted light, so much so that Grandpa was willing to stake everything on saving him. As Mother put it, what did they have to lose? Everything was behind them.

All was in front of me. That is what Daddy began drilling into my head. For the first time, he pushed Grandpa and Doody aside and came to run point for me. Grandpa had forbidden me to see Doody, but now in his dream-walking he would not have enforced it if my father had not struck steel in the patriarchal backbone. The succession was complete. Daddy drew a hard line between Doody and me and warned us not to cross it.

WHISTLING DIXIE

I obeyed my father. It was easy to do, or so I told myself. I was weary of the dark, the invisible, the down, deep and under, the wretched dead. I thought I could return to daylight and join the living without a backward look. That June I ate and drank bright, cold, cheerful things: popsicles and watermelon, red soda pop and iced lemonade. I took up with Bobby and Terrapin again, threw myself into kid play. Went to the Saturday matinees in Punk and watched the stupid serial cowboys and Indians. After Doody, Mother and Grandpa, Snow White and the Seven Dwarfs was a tale for the nursery, but I kept my complaint to myself for Joyce's sake. Bobby and I stayed up late, our heads in the bedroom window, singing silly songs like "Flat Foot Floogee with the Floy, Floy."

MUMMY-WRAP DREAMS OF PROPHECY

And just when I felt I was home free, that my Pepsodent smile was real, something dreadfully familiar tugged at me in dreams, drew me down again into hot sheets, which held me like mummy wrap. And I knew as I fought for air that I had been whistling Dixie, that my single day will had no power over the twins of my night will. The gnomes of sleep and death whispered to me in the sultry nights, pulling me under, and I would fight them screaming. Weary Bobby, bags already under his little brother eyes, would wash my face with a cold rag until Mother came in her gown. She would have to reach deep to bring me to the surface, and for a time the best she could do was pull me halfway out of sleep's grasp. The souls did not want to let me go. When they held me with their swarm of shadows and ebony images, devouring me with an unearthly moan of all the dead that had ever lived, I could not crawl out of their black hole. But when they tried to speak intelligibly, in a day world way as if to reason me into submission, I had a chance because they fell into Mother's ken. It had begun to dawn on me how hidden she was, how much she too lived in twilight, on the edge between both worlds, and I learned she was more at home on the far side than I. She came and went through the shadows the way Daddy walked among hornets and never got stung. In tiny voices dry as mummy breath the demons would tell me I belonged to them, the hiders, that it was useless to struggle because they were stronger than anything visible. "*Under*stand," they whispered one night, emphasizing the "under," "*under*stand that We the Hidden are the true things." Even in my froth a semantic logic made me think they were right.

"Mother, oh Jesus, Momma-Mommy-Mother-Ma, my mommy mummy, mummy, mummy ..."

"Stop that, Billy Mack. Look into my eyes. Look! Focus."

"Yes, ma'am, I see you, Mother. You're a long way off, but I see your eyes."

"Good. Don't take your eyes off mine. That's right. Now keep your eyes to my eyes. Don't look back! Keep coming."

"But Mother, are they right? They sound right."

"What are they saying?"

"I'm not sure I overstand."

"Overstand? You mean understand."

"Don't say that! That's their word. We say overstand, don't we?"

"No, Billy, you know we don't. We say understand, too."

"Then they are right."

"No, they're half right, is all."

"Mother, why are your eyes smiling?"

"Because you are free of them now, aren't you?"

"Nearly, Mother. I feel one still holding onto my foot."

"Kick it off."

"Ouch!"

"Free?"

"Oh, Lord yes. God. Little shaky. Mother, don't leave until I'm all the way home. Can I have a drink? But send Bobby after it. You stay here. Lots of ice. I didn't wake Daddy, did I?"

The dream that blew our fuses came in the wake of what had been a listless, uneventful Fourth of July. We in Little Egypt had gone to bed ambivalent about the holiday. There had been no public occasion, no patriotic speeches, only the scattered pop of a few firecrackers toward evening. Even the president seemed pooped. His fireside chat on radio the month before had set the tone, mustering, in Daddy's words, a great big fizzle. If Roosevelt couldn't arouse us, not even the Thomas boys had a chance. They seemed to have recognized it, for we slipped into sleep both relieved and disappointed the day had passed without affront from them, not even a mild prank.

But my own bedevilers were not to be denied. The fantasy they hatched was so full of ill omen for Doody Mareain that it sent me naked into the wee hours, sleepwalking toward Kushtown to warn Doody of the peril ahead. Bobby remained in his half of our bed, locked in his own soul. But Mother sensed something was amiss and sent a barefoot father after me. Daddy was surprisingly gentle, and by the time he got me turned around and headed home, the dew washing our feet, I was awake and clear-headed. But the dream was still fresh in my consciousness. By now it was almost daylight, so Mother made breakfast, and over hot grits and coffee I related the vision while Daddy wolfed down biscuits and Mother made sense of it.

A mule with no name but with a star-spangled chain around its neck was trying to walk up a rainbow. But someone out of the picture was holding the glorious chain taut, and the mule kept slipping and sliding, eventually ending up in a heap at the base of the rainbow. When I ran to help the mule, it turned into a cadaver, a mummified old woman.

"Boy," Daddy said. "The thangs you dream up."

Mother's dark eyes narrowed. "Billy's right," she said, "it's bad news for Doody."

"How do ye figure that?"

A cloud came over her face.

"Well, woman," Daddy said, "are ye going to tell us what it is?"

"No," she said. "I don't want to help give it power by foretelling. Maybe it won't happen."

"Son," Daddy said. "I don't want to see you out of this house today. You understand?"

"Yessir."

Back in my room, Mother whispered, "Listen to Daddy. That dream was a warning to you as well as Doody."

"What did it have to do with me?"

"Well, first it is yours because you dreamed it. And its lesson is that God walks the rainbows of this world, not mortals like us. We are damned to fall if we get too uppity, and that's what Doody has done, and dragged you and his mother with him."

"Lonnie was in the dream?"

"Of course. She and Mule."

"Creepy."

"That may not be the half of it," Mother said. "Morning may tell the rest."

The Heroic Rescue of Lonnie Mareain

Almost as Mother spoke, Walter Brautigam was up in the sepia dawn, opening his feed store on the town square. He came into the store from the rear, turning on lights that scattered the rats and roaches, and made his way to the front and opened that door. As he looked out, he saw the breadman leaving loaves in the bread box in front of Cude's grocery. He waved at the breadman and started to step back into the feed store when he noticed something odd hanging from the flagpole in the park. It was something large, long and white, but without the furl and buoyancy of a flag. Uh aw, he thought, the Thomas boys have been up to their old tricks. What is it this time?

Brautigam walked toward the flagpole, and as he got closer he grew grim, and then white-faced. And he cried out. It was a mummy. It was the body of Lonnie Mareain, hanging grotesquely upright in her mummy's shroud, the snaps of the chain locked into the layered gauze at her right shoulder and right hip. What was more hideous was that the wraps had been taken from her face. This wizened old queen, black as a prune, gazed down on Brautigam with lidded eyes, her snaggled mouth awry in a final sigh, her tongue locked in the immutable memoriam of formaldehyde. A dust devil stirred up and slapped the chain against the flagpole. *Clink, Clink.* Mrs. Mareain turned slightly and swung. Brautigam thought of his pickled wife, Renata, and turned and fled.

In the feed store, he composed himself and called my grandfather on the new rural telephone system. Then he called the sheriff in the county seat, thought better of it and hung up before anyone answered. When he went out again to make sure he wasn't hallucinating, the mummy of Mrs. Mareain was gone.

Walter Brautigam began to look around and touch and feel things to make sure he was on the right planet. The sun was clearly on the eastern horizon. The ground was beneath his feet. With relief he spotted the breadman hurrying toward him. "Did you see what I saw?" Walter said.

"I damned sure did," the breadman said. "I saw you watching it, and then I saw it for myself. But just for an instant. Before I could get close, this creature bounded out from nowhere, climbed up that flagpole like a monkey, and brought the mummy down."

"Where did it go?"

"Thataway," the breadman said, pointing toward Froggy Bottom. "It put the mummy on its shoulder and ran like a wild thing."

"Creature you say?"

"Yeah, like a black man with a long tail. So help me, God. And wearing a derby hat. The most ungodly thing I ever saw, 'cept for the mummy on the flagpole. I didn't touch either one of them, didn't come within fifty feet, but I feel like I need to wash my hands."

"There's a faucet in the back of the store," Brautigam said. "Come on, I'll stake you to a cup of coffee. You need it as bad as I do."

ON TO THE OTHER SIDE

Of course, everyone knew—or figured they knew after hearing the story—who had taken Mrs. Mareain's body from Doody's patched-up tomb. There was no use in confronting the Thomas boys about it. The more you came down on them, the worse they got with their hijinks. And everyone knew who had sprung Doody from the county jail, just as we knew who had taken Lonnie Mareain from the flagpole. There was no need to talk to Raff Ardmore about either. He had done the proper thing with the body. He had returned it to Doody.

Or so everyone thought.

No one really knew, not even Grandpa. But it stood to reason, since Doody Mareain was never seen again, not by anyone we ever met, not even to this day. If Doody hadn't gotten his mother back from Raff, he would not have left. And not even Raff, if he had something sick in mind, could have stood up to Doody, mad as he was. Raff's motives were heroic. And he must have gone with Doody, because we never saw him again either.

That was the way most Little Egyptians put it to rest, and went on with their lives.

Some of us had a harder time forgetting. Grandpa and I dreamed of trailing Doody and hunting him down, just to make sure he was all right. But Mother picked this up and nipped it in the bud.

"Billy Mack," she said, "let Doody go, let him go on to the other side. You stay here. It's more dangerous than even your dreams. You've just gotten your feet wet. Don't get in over your head."

"Okay, Mother," I said, "but aren't you glad Raff got Lonnie down, and that Doody got away, and don't you think that Osiris would understand it as an ultimate compliment to him, and forgive them?"

"Probably. Wouldn't you if you were him."

I hugged her, and ventured one last question, "And won't you always wonder where they are entombed?"

She looked at me and winked. And then hushed me with a red-nailed forefinger to her lips.

Grandpa, missing strychnine from his medical satchel, supposed that Doody had done away with himself in some even more secret place than the rock proved to be. Suicide? I didn't buy that. Doody could not afford to die at that moment, without all the proper prayers and appurtenances, since it would leave him, if not his mother, in Nether Land for eternity.

No. I saw him suddenly taking very good care of himself and his mother's mummy, wherever he was, preparing another tomb and other petitions to Osiris. I prayed he would pull it off. Certainly he had a prodigious longevity on his side and a fierce passion for deliverance.

GRAVE ROBBERS

With the oil rush on in Little Egypt and environs, Doody's rock turned out to be a valuable piece of property, containing more treasure than the pyramids of four pharoahs. The rock sat on an anticline of oil and gas sands. When the geologists and lease hounds from an oil company discovered this, they had little trouble in the courts snatching the plot from an absent Doody. But before the claim was decided in their favor, other spoilers even more mendacious could not wait. They threw up a rig beside the rock, on land they legitimately acquired in a hurry, and drilled at an angle. They hit the sand and brought in a gusher that is still producing, if at a trickle.

I wanted to spit on the exploiters of the Mareain tomb, but Grandpa, mellowing, said it was saner, at least easier, to think of them as aping archaeologists, and archaeologists were no more than miners of antiquity, grave robbers really. As Daddy repeated over and over in his geological, but surprisingly theological, way, "There's nothin' older'n oil or a better distillation of the dead." Doody's and Mrs. Mareain's tomb was already one anyway, had been for billions of years.

It is a shame that men of Grandpa's and Doody's predilections get shuffled into the wrong age. It is such a waste of time and energy and inheritance. Sends anachronistic tendencies tailing off into the generations like time bombs. I'm one of the wounded, a victim of Grandpa's genetic shrapnel, of Doody's Egyptian spirit.

10

★ ★ ★

Diddy Waw Diddy

the road
    the heart
        the problem
            for life

—TRANSLATION FROM "PALABRAS MALO,"
A LITHOGRAPH BY TERRY ALLEN,
LUBBOCK, TEXAS

A TEXAS MONTAGE
1939 Onward

FANTASTIC

☆ I HEAR THE ENGINE OF THE TERRAPLANE AND THE WHINE OF ITS transmission: pistons pumping, chains driving and gears shifting with the intimacy of my mother's heartbeat. I smell the faded felt of the seats. The rural telephone poles and their crossbars flash past like crucifixes. We get so far out from nowhere we leave the wire behind, and there is nothing but the ribbon of the road amid all that strange space. We have the illusion of something known slipping away beneath our wheels, while before us, like a mirage, something unknown but compelling beckons on the horizon, which seems to run away from us no matter how we try to close the distance.

Like Ulysses, we wandered, out of the forests of East Texas through a country more vast and various than the Greek isles, and, in its mummified Amerind memories, perhaps older.

Robinson Jeffers once wrote that Plato smilingly carved dreams, bright cells of incorruptible wax, to hive the Greek honey. And Jeffers lamented that his own time had acids for honey, and for fine dreams the immense vulgarities of misapplied science and decaying Christianity. Doubtless this is true, if only a part of me agrees. But

there are other truths of our time as well, the sum of many perceptions that echo in each of us.

So as a sprout of a new man, a father innocent not only of Jeffers's romantic cynicisms but of Plato and his dreams, I could only go
forth fresh-eyed at the world before which we passed.

It was enough for me that the land was one of prodigious
extremes, that the shade of woods would be followed by mountain
glory, the desolation of desert, the stretch of prairie and the tug-and-
pull of coastal tide. It was enough that there was a three-legged calf
at Daisetta, that for fifty years Plennie Wingo of Abilene walked
backwards everywhere he went, that we camped at Buck Naked in
Parker County beside a Navajo couple from Chicken Bite, Arizona,
who called themselves Mr. and Mrs. Mike Cowboy. We crossed Can't
'Cha Get Over Creek and rode the Wobblety, Bobblety, Turnover
and Stop Railroad on its last gasp from Weldon to Livingston. The
WBT&S had started off the Waco, Beaumont, Trinity and Sabine,
but had so many wrecks it went into the receivership of a rollicking
ridicule that held it in the affection of provincial hyperbole long past
its demise. Not to be outdone in a testament to the whimsy of rail
and route-calling was the Gospel Railroad in Williamson County
and its switching stations: Matthew, Mark, Luke and John.

Why reach below the surface when the appearance itself was so
fantastic? If anything, we were inclined to climb the highest peaks—
Guadalupe and El Capitan—for a panoramic view of creation, and
even that enthralling ascent was not enough. Once among the nests
of the golden eagles, I yearned to follow them in flight across the
great Chihuahuan desert and the rivers of the Pecos and Rio Grande.
And there was a way of flying, I found, even as we rolled across the
terra firma in our Bark of Ra.

For after wonder and marvels came stretches of flat nothingness
that went beyond monotony into what Daddy, borrowing from his
father's medical dictionary, called damned near catatonia. So when
the distances got unrelieved by any wrinkle of interest he would say,
"Uh ah, let's snap out of it. We've long passed Monotony and Catatonia's just ahead. If someone doesn't wake up and talk to me we're
all gonna end up in the ditch."

Mother and I appeared to be snoozing, but we were off somewhere in our heads. Maybe all of us were. I occupied myself by turn-

ing inward and living in my reveries. This freed me from the hot
confines (there was no air-conditioning) of the sluggish car, which in
its crawl across the desert was an inchworm working its way across
the face of God. I found I could detach myself, and this emboldened
me to consider soaring through the roof of the Terraplane, not as
Icky might have, but as I did when I followed his flights with my
fancy. I tried it. And I levitated. I passed through the top of the car,
working my wings until I attained a great height. I played at being a
god, at least an anthropomorphic eaglet, looking down and musing
on the black speck of the car moving across the sand. I pretended to
be indifferent to it.

Even in the glare of day the car was insignificant, a dusty rattle
making its tedious way, of no account in the blaze of sky and the
sweep of plain. The land was a paradox, sunlit but brooding, open
but impassive, above all impersonal, and I pretended it took no note
of me grandstanding in its air or trapped in the mechanical contraption on the road. The car and its occupants were nothing at all. Our
hearts pumped but could not be heard. The engine was inaudible
below the silence that pervaded the country.

The game bored me. So I tried to defy time as well as matter
and gravity, and flew into the curved future. I was not sure it was the
one I actually would come to experience, but it was somewhere that
had for me a sense of déjà vu, as if I were damned to repeat things I
had forgotten. Had I mistaken past for future? Or was this both,
existing simultaneously with the present? What I saw was highly disturbing.

From out of the ether between Ozona and Sonora, circa 1939, I
had projected myself out of the moving Hudson to a cemetery in
Oklahoma, six hundred miles north, and, I now realize, thirty-nine
years hence, where the five of us minus one were sprinkling dirt and
petals upon a coffin just lowered into a grave. The missing among
the mourners was Mother. And from the static I was picking up from
the Hudson, she was onto my grim forecast.

It was the closest she ever came to damning me. And not doing
it, I mean.

All I had intended was to limn off Mother's lightshow, make my
own little magic lantern images the way I knew she did in her head. I
knew because sometimes I picked up her signals. Mental casts they

were, I suppose you could say, summoned from the psyche, flashed backward or forward into time, depending on whether you wired into memory or potential cause-and-effect ahead. I would never do it as well as she, but it seemed plausible that such connections were possible, since I was making them and still spotting freckles and loving peanut butter and jam. I was hardly an innocent of metaphysics. The old Salt of the Earth Church of the Absolute Predestinarian Faith and Order, and its grim reminder of the ordeal of salvation for the elect, had had its sway with me. And Doody Mareain had taught me the catechism of the Egyptian Book of the Dead, which was as dreadful and glorious as the primitive Christian gospel. All this, freighted by genetic and psychic predispositions, encouraged me to go with Mother on her trips, just as I was bound to Daddy and his peripatetic Terraplane.

The way I lived with the portent of Mother's death, however distant, was to accept that we were not necessarily limited to the time, circumstance and shape of this particular outing we call life. I'd spent enough time in the projection loft of Aunt Marguerite and Uncle Howard's movie house in Marshall, Arkansas, to know that cinematic images could be edited in any sequence the goofy god in the stifling booth wanted, that in the blink of an eye Greta Garbo's Camille could end up in the arms of Mickey Rooney's Andy Hardy instead of Robert Taylor's Armand Duval.

God knows who Mother would end up in the arms of after Daddy and us kids got through with her. It wouldn't take much of an improvement to be a better deal than what she had gotten from us.

I could think this and still love Daddy.

If I saw Mother and myself as changelings, it was a conceit. I had only to look about to see we were not alone. Counting my father, who was not so common as he supposed, none of us fit one another—not even the Pete and Repete often mistaken for twins, thanks to our matching cotton heads, so bleached in the sun that not even winter and wool darkened our noggins or erased the stain from our hides. Albino brains and wetback bodies, our uncles teased. About the best they could say for us was that we were Appalachian dunces at the foot of the class, full of hookworns, hominy grits and flapdoodle. All of it was true: the ignorance, the parasites and boils, the leached corn, the folkways and warps of perception. But this was hardly the whole of us. Bobby, behind the spectacle of his thin neck and jug ears, was quiet, sensitive and full of fellowfeeling—when he wasn't batting me in the head with a board.

NECKS

They became as important to me as faces. Children who grow up in cars will understand this, particularly in reference to their elders, who are usually up front with their faces trained on the road. It was the same perspective for me riding behind Grandpa on his hinny, though not behind Doody on his mule because Doody was so tall, sitting or standing, that I seldom got a good gander at his neck. Short of that, "By his cervix ye shall know thy father" is still a pretty good maxim. It seems after we left Little Egypt I spent most of my boyhood in the rear seat of Ra, staring at the back of Daddy's neck as we droned across time and Texas. I remember little of Mother's or Joyce's. Their hair was in the way. But I remember the guys'. There was not a pale male neck in that car, not in that country. We had played and labored long in the Southwestern sun. It made its mark on us. The variety of wrinkles and hues wrought on our vulnerable scruffs was a mask that, like a blush, seldom hid a thing. Grandpa's neck was in the grave rather than our long, black, bone wagon, but I remember it with affection. It was freckled but could burn irate red. For all his lividity, there was something in his neck, a delicacy, that told you he was more than a hot-headed country man. There was a mystery about Grandpa, as there was about Doody, and only a hint of it was in his neck. Naked Bobby's baked skin could be brown everywhere but on the back of his neck, where he wore a tender, pink expression. We fought like Cain and Abel, but all he had to do to disarm me was turn and expose his neck. It was dear.

Bobby would write later:

...BROTHERS (1930's)
The whine
  of the Terraplane Hudson
Combined with
  the whir of the road

Set in a rhythm of a one-night stand
Staid . . . and played as a kinder-ode.

To preserve a certain sanity,
* and slay each countless mile*
Games were played a'plenty
* with only a nod an' a smile.*
Our world was an anthem,
* sung in an empty hall . . .*
A writ with our own secrets
* wrought since birthing's caul.*

As vagabonds we "snaked" the land
* in quest of the mother-lode . . .*
Two small boys in the back of a car,
* perfecting a close-knit code.*

(. . . and though I walked through the
valley of the shadow of danger, I
feared no evil . . . because Billy was
always there to protect me.)

But my father's neck was the most contrary ever set on a man. On each end of said neck was a mule head and heart to match. His brothers used to tell that, horsing around on the farm, they'd get Tice down in the dirt and take turns—all eight of them—squeezing his neck in an armlock until his face was beet red and the cows had come home, and still he wouldn't say uncle. He'd get up hee-hawing. They swore he could have gotten away with murder, as Oklahoma was still executing men by hanging.

In the Octobers of our odyssey, my father's neck was a cured and furrowed red, the color and conformation that of the Santa Gertrudis bulls bred by the King Ranch. I'm changing beasts in the middle of my metaphor because we've left the mules in Oklahoma, if not Daddy's stubborn streak, and we're pulling into Mexican Texas and toro country, for which the King Ranch is legend.

By August, Daddy's neck was courting violet, not another woman, but a wanton pigment only two scarlet badges from black, which

meant Daddy could have passed as one of those little fighting bulls in
the rings at Juarez and Matamoras. Tice's heart and strength were
deceiving, whether Tobin Drexler realized it or not. Daddy's small
skeleton was bison racy, hocks and fetlocks slender and stomach and
rump so zip you wondered how he bore the bulk of his neck, shoulders
and chest. Even there he was not coarse, but compact and efficient—
en canal, the Spanish call it, meaning the net weight is better than
sixty percent bone, muscle and molecular dazzle. Tice the taurus, a
brindle with wee wild western eyes that caught every movement in the
arena, carrying a sniffer of a nose that jerked his head in every direction; the anima armed and revealed, a longhorned Logos of substantial
sensation. Lit by exuberance or affection, he had a dance or a snort
with a story that pranced right through you with delightful effect. No
wonder Mother, on the cusp between teen and twenty, had shown him
her red flag. But she found, I think to her everlasting regret, that this
minotaur, nine years her senior, was not to be flirted with. He could
hook you on the way back from laughter. Or drag you to hell and gone.
Or down to the town square to watch the freak show.

BANANA SATURDAYS

Fruit requires a cookie and milk, Aunt Ella used to say. And so
Oreos and sweet milk went with bananas on the seventh day of the
week when we rested from the road.

It was our Saturday habit to park on a town square, strange or
familiar, and watch the people come and go. In those days you could
count on every county seat having the same attractions, with little
variation. Every pharmacy had a soda parlor, next to which was the
theater. From town to town, the names of the movie houses—the
Majestic, the Palace, the Rialto—were repeated as often as the
scratchy and brittle films the projectionists rolled over and over
again through their cranky reels.

Daddy would park the Terraplane in front of the Rialto and
Mother and Joyce would wait in the car while we menfolk—Daddy,
my brother and me—would walk over to the grocery and buy a stalk
of bananas, a huge sack of Oreos and several quarts of bottled milk
with cream on top. We would sit for hours in the car, eating bananas
and Oreos and passing the milk—shaking the bottle to spread the

cream—utterly entranced by the human spectacle before us. We would cluck among ourselves about this person and that who passed before our gaze. It was our mission to observe, from the hideaway of the hooded Hudson, the flaws, virtues and general demeanor of every local we laid our eyes upon.

The Hudson had deep, cavernous seats and high windows. Mother could barely see out from her place up front beside Daddy. She arched her head high, her nose in the air like the huntress Diana sniffing the wind, and leveled her gaze down the bridge of her nose, just above the window line, aiming her arrows at those who caught her interest.

"My, my," she would purr softly, narrowing her wide eyes, "look at that man, Daddy. He's walking around town with the fly of his overalls unbuttoned. Isn't that the Mr. Gillespie who's on the school board? Reckon we ought to tell him?"

We would snort with laughter.

A key to a personality was the Oreo Cookie Test. "Daddy," Mother would say, "how do you think Mr. Gillespie eats his Oreo?"

"Well," he would snicker, "I wouldn't say. What would you say, Billy Mack?"

"No question," I would pipe up, "he eats them whole, in one bite, without a thought to what he's doing."

"I think you're right," Mother would say. "A man who doesn't take time to button his pants wouldn't separate the cookies and taste the filling by itself."

With or without Oreos, Mother drew dead-on conclusions about people from little evidence. Sometimes she took your breath away, and sent your new friends packing, with the accuracy of her observations.

Cutting as Mother could be with her eyes and tongue, she never laid a hand on us accept in affection. Daddy would beat the stuffing out of us boys. Her power was such that she never needed physical force. Her worst weapon was silence. When she laid it on one of us, the house or car turned into a tomb, and we felt for the victim— even when it was Daddy—and begged her to relent. It was utter damnation, those piercing black eyes and that locked jaw. A beating by Daddy was preferable to her mute malevolence.

She rarely damned us without cause. This was one of the reasons why her withdrawal into silence was so doubly terrible for a clinging child, or even a now wild, now milk-sopped and subdued husband. She was the red-hearted, warm-blooded goddess of our lives. Her fierce love and Gordian-knotted will kept us intact and centered in a centripetal world that pulled us in all directions.

Outside the house, before the world, we reversed the Comus mask. If it was sad we made it gay. We became an amused Greek chorus, united and commenting on the figures who paraded past. We would sit in that long, hearse of a sedan on that square and a hundred others in our gypsy life, and for all the Saturdays of our days became customers at a zoo, marveling and being entertained by the captives before us. The difference was that we ate the bananas. When at last we drove away, we left a rectangle of peels on the street that must have puzzled those who came upon them.

DIDDYLAND

At first, the people in a particular place lay light on me as we left them. But it got hard to say goodbye, and harder still to say hello with any conviction, knowing it would turn into adios before the last salutatory syllables were out. But we got used to it. We all take the best parts of our lives with us as we move, and that is what I have done with my journey as a son. Life on the farm in Little Egypt was slow and bound up in family, village and the pantheistic repetitions of rural life. And we had flirted with that in Gladewater. But now our pace quickened, shifting from a traditional and almost seamless narrative flow into the picaresque short-takes of life on the road. It is as well a metaphor of American life and its mule-to-motor launch which has brought us, lickety-split, to fast foods, fifteen-minute fame and thirty-second sound bites.

As I look back, I realize the road brought many more people into our lives than had we remained on the farm. Far-flung places called, enriching us with new friends and enemies. Some became so close, so knotted into the unraveling string of our lives that we hugged and hated them like family, and in the Southern way took on a host of aunts and uncles and cousins dear and dreadful as blood kin. From then on our parents did not always keep us. We passed from hand to hand, spending all too short weekends and all too long summers with the various branches of our extending family, a network that reached as far as the highways and byways would take us, and some places where they wouldn't. So there were pauses, more commas than periods in the sentence of our fate. The journey superseded everything.

And yet, our departures were not as neat, the severings not so complete as our dust and distance might have indicated. Life was a taffy pull that sometimes tugged us back with rubbery snaps of sentiment or reckoning. Posses following in our wake would have found themselves stuck with confusion in a crisscrossing welter of filigree and strand—materially and psychically—that stretched from one end of Texas to the other.

And not a one of them broken. Here, I hold the line. My job is to witness not only the journey but the destination. I am my mother's son as well as my father's. Daddy's reality was that what you see is what there is, and to go out and get it honestly but with great vigor, even if it's the pleasure of digging the best ditch in the world. He took rapture in working and figuring out the evident creation, which for him included the notion that man and his machines were an improvement over nature. This was heresy to Mother. Her reality was that what you see is not there of its own accord, but is a mask put there by an unseen hand; only fools and the dubious elect dare reach behind the mask. If Daddy had recognized the mask as false, he would have torn it off the face of whatever-it-was hiding there. But thank whatever-it-was, Daddy took it for what it appeared to be, and remained an innocent in Mother's world. Just as she was in his.

It was almost a blessing that on those endless odysseys, the destinations often proved to be mirages—dreamy half-stops half-remembered—for we never got to where we were going and have yet to complete the journey. We may have gotten to the rig or the patch where Daddy was to work, but even the work was transitory, a means to an end which came and went as chimera. If the work seemed real—it was clangingly loud in its effort and brutally demanding of a roughneck's body—it was only because a screaming drilling rig in the desert made a more immediate assault on the senses than the nagging dream that drove us across the Southwest.

The end we sought was more insistent than the Protestant work ethic that towed us from job to job. It was just harder to define. Each of us made stabs at it. Mother decided that Daddy's get-up-and-go was meant to drive her crazy. She fully expected that the heavenly journey was an endless circling about on the dusty roads of Limbo, the Porterfield-Joads on their way to God knows what and where. I think it is telling that in their dotage my parents lived on wheels. The trailerhouse on the hill in Seguin which became their last earthly abode was in no sense anchored. It was as buoyant to the winds of change as Homer's Ionian homeport, Ithaca, washed away by tidal waves. The tide of history waits for no man, my father used to say. We would whisper behind his back that Tice Covey Porterfield hardly waited for woman or child.

Now I put away his knighthood and saw him and his roughnecks as new cowboys as cussed and independent as the old saddlelads, slowed but not stopped by the baggage of wife and kids, drifting from ranch to ranch, stopping wherever there was work and a bunkhouse. Only the horses Daddy rode were the Hudson, the pickups and the drilling rigs. His ranch was the oil patch, the bunk a lease shack. Real cowboys sang of a'leavin' Cheyenne and a'makin' Montana their new home. And Daddy did the same, only in his refrain, the point of departure and the point of arrival were one and the same.

In thousands of stops and starts at roadhouses and gas stations, we heard the same exchange over and over between our father and the proprietor.

"Where you folks from?"

"Diddy Waw Diddy."

"Never heard of it. Must be a far piece."

"Well, it's not a town and it's not a city. It's just a place in the road called Diddy Waw Diddy."

"That's a fine lookin' lot of towheads you got there. Are they worth a hoot?"

"Haw! That's about all they're worth, a hoot. Yep, they're regular ring-tailed tooters from Diddy Waw Diddy."

At first it was funny, listening to Daddy's bull. But then we began to call him on it.

"Daddy, we've never lived in a place called Diddy Waw Diddy. Does it really exist?"

"Why, shore, boys. It's just up ahead."

The place up ahead would be Aransas Pass, Clarkwood, Driscoll, Los Ovejas, whatever. We never got to Diddy Waw Diddy. It became our dream place, the verdant rock, which, once gained, would anchor and harbor us from the road for the rest of our days. In our use of its magical pull, Diddy Waw Diddy could be high as heaven or low as the next sorely needed job. "I hear they're a-hirin' and a-payin' well up in Diddy Waw," our father would say, and we'd strike for a place that sounded as strange. Corpus Christi.

"Where you folks headed?"

"Body of Christ."

"What?

"We're from Diddy Waw Diddy, but we're headed to Body of Chris—"

"Tice Porterfield! Now that's enough. Let's go before that poor man hauls off and hits you with a monkey wrench. For all you know, he could be a Catholic who might take offense—"

"Why shoot, woman. What'che talkin' about? See the name over the door?"

We all looked. It was O'Connor, one of the oldest Irish Catholic families in Texas.

We howled from the back seat. Daddy grinned, rolled his eyes at Mother, and put the juice to the Hudson. We left Mr. O'Connor in the driveway, scratching his head.

This trip, we never got any closer to Corpus Christi than we did Diddy Waw Diddy. It too seemed just beyond our reach. Now, Daddy had seen the city. Bobby and I figured he'd seen everything worth seeing upon the earth. The way he held Corpus Christi out to us as something fabulous, something we all would appreciate, even travel-weary Mother and toddler Joyce, made us hunger for it even more than Diddy. Daddy made Corpus real in a concrete way that he'd never done with Diddy.

In fact, concrete was the only reason Corpus Christi hadn't been blown away by hurricanes. Daddy could quote the exact tonnage of cement that had gone into its seawall, which, below the bluffs on which Corpus had been built, faced with stair-stepped serenity the blue, white-capped gulf that was both a boon to the city and a caution. But the tropical storms could heave up upon the seawall the fabled: messages in bottles from the Robinson Crusoes of the islands off the South American coast; Aztec jewels and gold plundered in Mexico by the conquistadores, but given up to the tides as storm-tossed ships bearing the treasures to Spain sank off the coast. The strangest sights of all were the creatures of the deep that washed up, some astonishingly like beasts in fairy tales: water-gods, whirlpool whales, seahorses, sword-fish, sea-dragons, sirens, manatees that remind you of sea-satyrs . . .

"Sirens, Daddy?"

"Yep," he said, "mermaids."

"For real?"

"You'd better believe it."

"Dead or alive?"

"One come ashore alive."

"Is she still breathing?"

"Yep."

And thus we learned of the Mermaid of Zennor.

Someday, he promised, we boys would see this fish-woman when we were on the cusp of manhood and could accompany him there. For the city embodied more than the Body of Christ. It was a profane port of call to sailors from the Gulf of Mexico, the dive of buccaneers and the grave of Spanish galleons, and, in a privileged water palace upon its North Beach, there lived this special friend of my father, a flesh and blood, lunged and scaled mermaid who sang like a Lorelei to certain gentlemen who were allowed to pay her court. Our father's meaning was clear. Bobby and I knew he was our ticket to manhood and the mermaid. We knew as well he was a hard man, that mustering past him was hell. But we did not question the initiation—it had already begun—or the worth of the passage.

The girl of the sea was something else to remember. I got my stubby pencil and pad and put her down on my list, after the reminders to pray for safe flights for Icky, and to conjure up the most horrible death imaginable for Tobin Drexler back in Gladewater. "Grow up to see the Mermaid of Zennor," I wrote, and looked over at Bobby. Funny how brothers are. I was relieved to see he did not appear to be as interested in the mermaid as I was. At least, he hadn't put it in his book, the little copycat.

But that was a long ways off, our first sap and the unveiling of the naked mermaid, and we had to content ourselves with retellings and grins about Mr. O'Connor's confusion at Daddy's translation of the seaport's Latin name. But it was more than a joke, this play with words and their meanings against the backdrop of life and dreams. I was just a kid, but I had already learned that names were not personal property, but filial, communal, historical, and more. Doody Mareain had been right. A name was not something to toss about lightly.

NAMES

It is telling I remember the grades she gave me but not her name. The marks were very good, all A's, an auspicious start in Texas that would not fulfill its promise as the schools changed as often as the seasons as we and the miles and years marched on. She was my first memorable classroom teacher and she made an impression on me that is not diminished by my loss of her name. Now that I think about it, we—she, my brother and I—had a problem with names from the very beginning.

She must have been late into middle age, a heavy, round-faced woman with a definite schoolmarm air about her: the scent of chalk rather than talcum wafted from her bosom, and she spoke and wrote with a precision that reminded my father of a Rolls-Royce engine. This was reinforced by her forthright character, which expressed itself not only in her strong opinions but in her bearing and British accent. Bully girl she was. Hail Britannia and all of that. At least I remember enough of the spirit of her name to recall that it fit her heritage. Her last name should have been London or England or English. Whatever, having a strong sense of place and history, she took pride in her people.

But she was not so much an Anglophile that she could not appreciate the history and culture of other peoples. Fate had brought her to reign like Elizabeth I over a country school deep in the sand and oaks of the Texas coast. Aransas Pass was a hybrid settlement half salt and half manure, a harbor as well as a trading center for South Texas ranchers. We were there because an oil boom was on, living on the Dunn lease where my father was switching for P. W. Slimp. We were back in the trees on the Live Oak Peninsula, a few miles from Redfish Bay and the Gulf of Mexico. Gulls kept getting into Mother's garden. History kept getting in the way of Miss London/England's understanding of our names.

On the first day of class, that fall, Miss London/England had each student call out his full name for the record book. When she came to my brother, she stopped and corrected him.

"Bobby Lee Porterfield," he had called out.

"That may be your nickname," she had said, smiling indulgently. "But for the formal record, I'm putting it down as Robert E. Lee Porterfield."

"No, ma'am. That's not my name. It's Bobby Lee, not Robert E. Lee."

"Don't correct me, young man. Surely you are mistaken. Don't you know who Robert E. Lee was?"

"No, ma'am."

"He was the great Confederate general, a fine American hero. Many Southern families have named their sons after him. No doubt that is what your parents intended. You will go down in my book as Robert E. Lee Porterfield, and you should be proud of it."

I fared no better.

"Billy Mack Porterfield," I declared.

"Let's stop this nonsense," Miss London/England snapped. "What is your proper name?"

"Billy Mack."

"God save me," she sighed, staring a hole in me. "I will not, for the life of me, call you such a thing. Billy is the diminutive for William. Surely your name is William Mack Porterfield, which has a rather high ring to it. Doubtless you, too, are named after some historical figure, perhaps in your own family tree. The children may call you what they like on the playground, but in class you are William, you understand?"

"Yes, ma'am."

We couldn't wait to get home to Mother and tattle on Miss London/England. Mother hated people she thought were stuck up, and sure enough, she was stung by our teacher's supercilious treatment of the names she and Daddy had pinned on us. She wrote a curt little note correcting Miss London/England.

Miss London/England wouldn't believe it. She thought we had forged Mother's note. She sent word for Mother to come see her and clear up the matter of our names once and for all. Bobby and I waited with our ears to the door while they talked.

We could hear Mother saying in her soft twang, "It may sound backward to you, Miss London/England, but the fact of the matter is we named Billy Mack after his grandfathers, Billy Harrell and Henry Mack Porterfield. There's no William anywhere in it. We named Bobby Lee that way because it seemed to go with Billy Mack, since they're almost twins. We never even thought of Robert E. Lee when we did it."

What could the teacher do in the face of such Southern sloth and slang? We were a slouching people and Miss London/England had to accept it, grating as it was to her sense of erect posture, which applied to nomenclature as well as manners.

She wrote us down in the record as Bobby Lee and Billy Mack.

But she never called us that. It would have been too much. We were always Robert and William on her regal tongue. It was a subtle elevation that worked. She made us feel as if we were, indeed, worthy of such formality, and we came to love her for it. Out of the hearing of our parents, we passed ourselves off as Robert and William.

Thus it did not altogether nonplus me when, forty-three years later at my son's high school graduation, I heard his name called out with not only eleven letters added to it, but a hyphen as well. I thought I was mishearing, but there it was, written in bright green on the program. We had named him Winton Covey Porterfield. Without a word to us, he had added considerable panache by renaming himself Winton Christopher-Covey Porterfield. We've come a long way in two generations. Miss London/England would be pleased. And she would delight in my parents' ignorance, which surfaced a year or so ago when genealogical records revealed that Grandpa Porterfield was not Henry Mack but Henry McMahon, and, just as Miss London/England had suspected all along, maternal Grandpa Billy Harrell was, indeed, a William.

BOTH SPLENDID AND SILLY

Frances Gumm was seventeen and older than me, but she looked a kid. She lived larger than life on the movie screen. I lived very small, indeed, in the sand and ticks of old Aransas.

Still, I'd had my eye on her since the Andy Hardy movies. One Saturday afternoon we loaded up in the Terraplane and drove to the picture show in Rockport to see a double-header. Shirley Temple starred in the first feature. She was ten at the time, and the screen's number-one box office attraction, even ahead of Joe Yule and Spencer Tracy. But that night, I sure enough fell in love with Frances Gumm.

In that enchanting movie she was Dorothy Gale, the little Kansas farm girl who in her dreams was blown away by a cyclone to the Land of Oz. The friends Dorothy and her cairn terrier Toto made en route to Oz I would embrace for life. Ray Bolger was the Scarecrow who wanted brains. Jack Haley was the Tin Woodman who wanted a heart. And, of course, Irving Lahrheim was the Cowardly Lion who wanted co . . . co . . . courage. Margaret Hamilton was the Wicked Witch and Mary William Ethelbert Appleton Burke the Good Witch.

And who can forget Francis Wupperman as the Wizard of Oz himself? "How can I help being a humbug when people make me do things they know can't be done?" he lamented.

And when Dorothy unmasked him, scolding him as a bad man, Oz protested, "I'm not a bad man, just a bad wizard!"

He proved to be a marvelous wizard, in spite of his human frailties, indeed because of them. And when he gave Ray Bolger brains and Jack Haley heart and Irving Lahrheim courage, we were all the stronger, for these were the very things we would need in the war that was growing in Europe and about to shake the world.

Francisco Franco had won in Spain. Germany had invaded Poland and Italy had taken Albania. Even we kids sensed that the Wicked Witch was a pushover compared to Adolph Hitler and Benito Mussolini. That year American school children voted the devil as their third most-hated bogeyman. Two fascists were ranked ahead of him—the Fuhrer was first, il Duce second. Franklin Delano Roosevelt had been president so long we tended to confuse him with George Washington, ranking him slightly behind God in the most-loved category. God must have smiled and forgiven us, and Roosevelt as well, because He was merciful and saw us through to victory.

In the meantime we were both splendid and silly.

On the way home from the movie that autumn night, I giddily confessed I was in love with Frances Gumm. Daddy teased me, reminding that Frances was too old for me, that they had flattened her bosom to play the part of Dorothy Gale from Kansas. Besides, he said, Joe Yule was waiting for her in the wings. The year before, Frances and Joe had been thick in the movie, *Love Finds Andy Hardy,* which I had yet to see.

(Later I would see Gumm and Yule together in several films, but by that time Parthena Pappuga had come into my life and I was no longer jealous of attentions paid to Frances Gumm, though my admiration for her talent continued to grow. I even gained a grudging admiration for that little twerp Joe Yule. Never expected in my maturity I would look like him instead of Frank James Cooper. I should note that Parthena Pappuga was doubtless the Eudoxan theory of proportion Edna St. Vincent Millay had in mind when she said that Euclid alone had looked on beauty bare. At thirteen, Parthena was 35-20-34—sorry, but that's the way we measured girls in the dark ages—and already a beauty contest winner on the beaches of the Body of Christ, which were being overrun by Euclidian sailor boys from the new naval bases. Splendid Parthena let silly me carry her sun tan lotion—"Keep it out of the sand"—that she allowed the older guys to rub on her geometry while I flunked elementary addition and subtraction.)

If in '39 Angelo Sicilano was the Charles Atlas of pulchritude, Joseph Louis Barrow was the heavyweight champion boxer of the world. John Donald Budge was the top tennis pro, Thomas Dudley Harmon the collegiate football star. They were all splendid, even Henry Louis Gehrig in his decline. Old John Pierpoint Morgan II was selfish and spoiled. While sailing to Scotland to shoot grouse, he had whined, "If they start the war, certainly my shooting will be interrupted, because everybody would rush off to do what they'd have to do and I wouldn't have anybody with me."

Edward Kennedy was a rich little menace who would cheat on exams when he got to the university. After the new Roman pope, Eugenio Pacelli, gave private audience to Mr. and Mrs. Joseph P. Kennedy and eight of their nine children, said Ted, then seven: "I wasn't frightened. He patted my head and told me I was a smart little fellow." Teddy would lose his oldest brother in the war. The rest of us around the world would lose a generation of young lions hardly cowardly.

It seems so long ago. Everyone I've mentioned is dead but for Ted Kennedy and his sisters, and Harmon, Budge, Joe Yule and Shirley Temple Black. Lou Gehrig went in 1941, J. P. Morgan II two years later. Joe Louis Barrow hung 'em up in 1967. So did Spencer Tracy. FDR didn't last out the war, and neither did Hitler and Mussolini. Franco hung on until 1975. Pope Pius XII died in 1958.

When Oz gave the Tin Man a heart, he warned that hearts were a fine and kind thing, but that they tended to break. Well, sure enough, the Tin Man's heart stopped running. But his was a good and strong heart for a long time. Before he died in 1979, Jack Haley had outlived every major player in the Land of Oz except for the Wicked Witch and Scarecrow. Margaret Hamilton died in 1985, Ray Bolger in 1987. Before that, Oz (Francis Wupperman) died in 1949; the Cowardly Lion (Irving Lahrheim) in 1967; Dorothy Gale (Frances Gumm) in 1969; the Good Witch (Mary William Ethelbert Appleton Burke) in 1970. I don't know when Toto died, but he was really a she named Terry.

I thought it strange that on the day the Tin Man departed out in California, I went to a play opening in Dallas and, backstage, met Liza Minnelli, daughter of Dorothy, and John Lahr, son of the Cowardly Lion.

11

★ ★ ★

Uncle John, FDR and the War

UNCLE JOHN AND THE STRADIVARIUS

☆ THAT SPRING, APRIL 1940, WE MOVED TWELVE MILES ACROSS Corpus Christi Bay to the Texas Conservative Oil Company lease between Robstown and Driscoll. Daddy's job was to check the flow of oil and gas wells and to maintain storage tanks and their fire walls. We put up in a tiny house that stood on piers, the better to see over the corn stalks which hid us from U.S. 77, a two-laner that ran alongside the Missouri Pacific Railroad tracks plying the coast of the Mexican Gulf. We watched the race of men and their elegant, Pullman car ladies go by. Of course, the one fellow Daddy chose to befriend turned out to be as bad as he was good, and certainly as foolish as wise.

It was a spirit of dubious enterprise that brought Uncle John Pierson into our lives that April. You see, he didn't belong to us by blood or marriage, but by misfortune, which masked itself as its opposite.

Daddy brought him home from the pool hall in Robstown, all aglow with liquor and the likelihood that, at last, after all the years of living from payday to payday, we were about to come into a fortune. Daddy went directly to his closet and brought out a special inheritance—Grandpa's violin—the red little jewel he had gotten from his father. Out of all the boys, Daddy had gotten it because he was the only one willing to fiddle with it. Now it lay in its case, gathering neglect. One day I had come home from school convinced that Grandpa's fiddle was worth more than sentiment. I had been reading in an encyclopedia about the great Italian violin maker, Antonius Stradivarius. Wasn't that the name carved into the pegboard of Grandpa's? I copied the Stradivarius mark and brought it home to Daddy, who got out Grandpa's and compared its label. They were the same! On the neck, imprinted in the wood, was "Concert Violin," and below that the name "Stradivarius." Inside the label read "Antonius Stradivarius Cremonensis," and below that "Faciebat Anno 1734," and below that "A5" circled and a fancy cross circled. A true Stradivarius would be worth thousands. Was it possible?

"I don't know," Daddy had said. "All I know is that Dad always said this fiddle was older'n he was."

"Yeah," Mother said, "and October and Wit Odin said it was a cheap copy, worth no more than a thousand other fake Strads."

"I still think we ought to check her out," I said, forgetting that Madame Sweelinck had dismissed it as worthless.

But Daddy squelched me quickly. "Don't be crazy, boy! We can't claim nuthin' Eye-talian right now with old Mussolini about to join up with Hitler and Hirohito."

Still, none of us could resist, from time to time, bragging about our masterpiece. Apparently John Pierson had gotten the full treatment from Daddy at the pool hall. Now, looking back on it, remembering the expression in John's coyote face when he took up the fiddle to inspect, perhaps it had been the other way around. For John Pierson was as wily as he was eloquent. We had a Stradivarius. No doubt about it. He looked at it lovingly, as though it were alive, a fine, long-lost friend of the highest art and he the connoisseur. He ran his long fingers along its lines, held it up to the light and plucked its strings. He sniffed the varnish and tapped the wood, noting the detail and delicacy of design. He said it was small, a woman's concert violin, and he explained to us why it was not an Amati or a Guarnerius or a Guadagnini or a Bergonzi. Beyond a doubt, a Strad! There were only 540 of them in the world. No telling what we could get if we handled its sale shrewdly. And, of course, John was the man for the job, our agent, as it were.

He tightened the strings, put the fiddle to his chin and drew the bow across the gut. Ah! The big warm tones. Unique to the master. He was almost tempted, he whispered, to play his own concerto upon it.

"Play," he was urged. "Play a little of your own music."

"No," he sighed, "it has been so many years I forget Pierson. Beethoven I know better."

He swung into what we recognized as the D Major Concerto, because that was what Grandpa had tried to scratch, but John stopped abruptly because Daddy was on his feet hushing him.

"Don't play no German music!" Daddy shouted. "Good God, John, we're just about at war with them!"

"I am very rusty," John said impatiently, "so it's just as well. I abuse both the music of the German and the instrument of the Italian."

After that performance, John Pierson was the star boarder at our house. He stayed and stayed, fattening his gorgeous thin self up on Mother's cooking and drinking Daddy's medicinal whiskey for his cough. We all competed for him. Daddy wanted John to join him out on the oil lease; John, of course, diplomatically declined. He did show up at summer Bible camp one afternoon, to my delight, when we were jock deep in P.E., and stunned us all by clearing the high jump at six feet. If we had the father and son banquet then, I would have preferred Pierson to Pa, but that tricky temptation never presented itself. I did get John to Boy Scouts one afternoon, but most of the time he remained at home with Mother, helping with the meals and housework and fixing things around the place Daddy hadn't gotten to. He trimmed the suckers from the budding fruit trees and repaired the washing machine wringer, all the while keeping Mother company.

He gossiped with her in a way Daddy never did, complimented her every other minute, did her hair, of all things, and crowned the week by accompanying Mother and me to Church, where he somehow convinced the pastor, Brother Potash, to take a breather while he, John Pierson, a pool-playing, profane drifter with the tongue of an angel—Lucifer, not Gabriel—delivered one of the damndest sermons we had ever heard. It was in the form of a eulogy to his dead mother. He took the story of Sodom and Lot's wife and, like an alchemist, transformed sodium chloride into a metaphor for Christian virtue.

His mother, he said, was the salt of the earth. That was the highest accolade he could think of to bestow on a mortal Christian. Mrs.

This is a sketch by my brother, Bobby, of Grandpa Porterfield as he looked in the summer of 1935, when Doody Mareain and I were hiding in the cavern of the tomb carving prayers to Osiris for Lonnie Mareain.

Grandpa
circa 1935
BLP

This is brother Bobby's profile of Doody Mareain as he must have looked just after he quit the boxing ring and came to Carter County, Oklahoma, with Grandpa.

Doody Mareain
circa 1900
BLP

In this sketch, Bobby ages Doody. He was about eighty-seven in 1935.

Doody Mazeau
circa 1935
BXP

Daddy Harrell and Mama Harrell, Mother's parents, on the stoop of their porch in Carter County, Oklahoma, in 1927–28, when my father-to-be was after first one of their daughters and then another.

My mother-to-be, Janavee Elizabeth Harrell, sits on a tricycle in front of a wagon pushed by Ola Mae Austin, just before Ola Mae married Carl Porterfield and "Jennie" married his younger brother Tice.

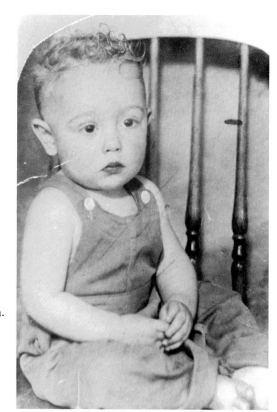

The author, about sixteen months old, in Graham, Oklahoma.

This fading photo of Daddy, the first figure at left with his knee on a bench, and his drilling crew was shot below the floor of the Barr No. 1, one of the hundreds of gusher oil wells that were tapped in Oklahoma City during the boom, which started in 1928 and did not let up until the mid-1940s. On the State Capitol lawn alone, there were twenty-four wells pumping day and night. Daddy said the Barr No. 1 produced six thousand barrels of oil every twenty-four hours. To Daddy's left are bareheaded Lee Swindler, derrickman, and then the floor hands: Daddy's younger brother, Earl Lee Porterfield, L. G. Riggs and K. L. (Keig) Kendall.

This sketch by Bobby pictures Wit Odin as he appeared the night in 1935 when he stood at the pulpit and brought damnation down on Grandpa and October Ney Mills. I would have drawn Wit a little longer faced and looser skinned, more like a polar bear, but Bobby said I had had my way with him in the text— now it was his turn.

Wit Odin circa 1935 BLP

This is how Bobby saw Wit Odin as the young Norse god shortly after Odin and his brothers killed the giant Ymir and made the earth from his body, the sea from his blood and the heavens from his skull.

Wit Odin ...as a young god BLP

October Ney Mills, as sketched by Bobby. She stands before the Mills home, Sessrymmer, somewhat out-scaled in the artist's imagination. She often wore fur when leaves were on the trees, perhaps to keep her warm from the frigid Odin.

October Ney
BLD   circa 1930

Mother, "The Empress of Roughnecks," on the porch of our first house, the forty-dollar one, in Gladewater, Texas, circa 1938–39. At back was the water well Tatum and Larreaux dug.

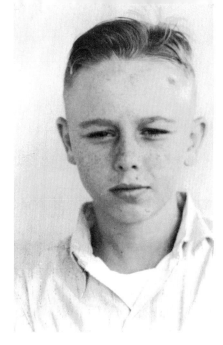

This picture was taken of me after we said goodbye forever to Grandpa and Doody and hit 'em once again for Texas in the Terraplane Hudson I called the Bark of Ra.

Billy, Bobby and Joyce in a musical mood after having Christmas with Uncle Earl and Aunt Arbie at Corpus Christi, Texas, shortly before World War II. My somber face was because I was miffed. We had wished for guitars and a real piano instead of ukuleles and a toy. Aunt Arbie blamed it on Santa, but she didn't fool me.

On the hill in Seguin, Texas, the summer of 1984. Mother has been dead for five years. Pictured, left to right: brother Bobby Lee Porterfield; our old man, Tice Covey Porterfield, is holding my youngest daughter, Oren, and, on the end, a jaunty me who, without Ma's prescience, can't see the shadows around the corner.

Pierson may not have been a saint, but who among us was? We were all frail, yea, below Jesus. But by God, his mother was salty!

"Now if the salt has lost its saving power," he shouted, "it is good for nothing but to be cast out, trodden under the feet of men! But my mother was good, Christian salt, and she did not lose her saving power.

"Every child of God is a lump of salt. Every time you pray, you salt somebody. Every song you sing, you salt someone. Every home you visit, you salt a sick one. Mrs. Pierson went all over her country sprinkling salt.

"Now, natural salt kills insects and snakes. Epsom Salt kills infection. Spiritual salt, friends, spiritual salt kills sin! That is the message my mother is sending us from High Heaven. Get out and sprinkle a little salt on someone. Get out and sprinkle a little salt on someone."

John made it a sing-song. Sprinkle a little salt on someone. Brother Potash sang it. We all sang it. The church house shook under our stamping feet, and in our salty hearts and above our hymning heads halos shone.

Monday, Mother went down to the bank in Robstown and, somehow, borrowed one-hundred dollars and gave the wad to John. That was a considerable sum in those days.

Daddy's enthusiasm for John began to pale, and he said as much in a subdued, troubled way. Mother got his message, but, again, she dealt with it in her independent way. A morning or so later, she packed her husband off to work, and, allowing Bobby and me to skip Bible school, she let Joyce and us join her as she drove (yes, John had taught her how to drive!) him into Robstown and dropped him off on the busiest highway headed north, suitcase in one hand and a lunch sack and fiddle case in the other. John would thumb his way to Chicago, where a Greek he knew would find a big-time buyer to relieve us of the Stradivarius. "You can count on it," were his last words to Mother. He kissed her on the cheek, tossled our towheads and took off walking up the road like he owned it.

CHILI TODAY, HOT TAMALE

June had hardly made a freckle on us when Daddy came home from the tanks to say, "Boys, we're takin' off any day now. Ye mother's gonna have her hands full, so I want you peckerwoods to stay around the house and help her pack."

"Aw, Daddy, it seems like we just got here. We were looking forward to the summer—"

"Shit, son, we been here long enough for any but the lazy. They's better money on a rig about to spud in down in Diddy Waw Diddy. I'll be head driller and we'll get a practically new lease house."

"Daddy, where's it at, really?"

"Well, ye right. It damned sure ain't Diddy. In fact, it'll be just the opposite, more like hell. Hot. Down in Zapata County."

"Where's that?"

"Mexican border."

I screwed up my face and looked at Bobby. He had just picked up the mail out on the highway, and he held a postcard in his paw. "Whad'ya say, Brother?"

"Same old story," Bobby said glumly. "Chili today, hot tamale. Here today, gone tomorrow."

"Is that another one of your poems?"

"Just a saying," he said.

"What'che got there, Rapid Robert?" Daddy said, eyeing the postcard.

"It's from Uncle John."

"Well, well, hand'er here and let's take 'er inside and see what John's Greek is gonna offer us for the fiddle."

Mother was at the kitchen sink peeling potatoes.

"Jennie," Daddy said, flipping the card to her. "This is from John. You oughta read it."

"Why me?" she said, throwing her head back and giving Daddy a sideways glance.

"Hell, he's your honey, not mine."

"Daddy, now you hush, saying such a thing in front of Billy Mack and Bobby Lee. No, here, you read it yourself. I couldn't care less about John and that stupid fiddle of Grandpa's."

Daddy looked at us and winked. "I reckon she cared a hunnert dollars worth. Boys, wonder if we can leave town without paying that bank note?"

"Daddy!" Mother said, her face a blister now, "I did that for us, not John Pierson!"

"Well, let's see how he's farin' with our money and our fiddle."

Uncle John hadn't made it to Chicago. The postcard was from Earline's Truck Stop in Evening Shade, Arkansas. That's on Highway 167 between Bald Knob and Thayer. The reason I know is because that night Daddy traced it on the map, his big finger angry and shaking like a guy wire in the wind. He wanted John Pierson's neck, and he wanted his fiddle back.

Mother never said a word, but I noticed she began putting extra sweets in Daddy's lunch sack, and she took to rubbing his back at night. And every Sunday afternoon from three to five, she reinstituted their "Grownup Recess," the time for us kids to bug out and not bother them so they could retreat to their bedroom behind a closed door and not worry about us barging in every other minute to ask for something. And she never made a peep of a complaint about having to make still another move.

THE WATER CLOSET AND WAR ABROAD

LOS OVEJAS
July 1940

It was July 29, a great day on Los Ovejas Creek in the county of Zapata on the Mexican border. Daddy and some roughnecks off the drilling rig crew had just put in our first indoor toilet and pronounced it ready to flush.

Every five minutes, we kids kept running to the beautiful white porcelain commode to try it, even though there was not a tinkle left in our scrawny bodies. Daddy threw up his hands and declared it off limits, at least until after supper. "You're gonna fill up the septic tank with nothing but water the very first day!" he roared, lecturing us about not wasting water in such a dry country. It was droughty, had been for years, and Daddy was surprised we could tap water for the commode. We'd been drinking bottled water from Mirando City. There may not have been much water beneath all the cactus and mesquite, but there was oil. Daddy was a driller on one of the rigs.

He said we'd need the oil for the war effort. Everybody thought President Roosevelt would declare war against Hitler, even though the presidential election was four months away. Daddy said FDR would win a third term because we shouldn't change horses in the middle of the stream. It was scary, listening to the war news on the radio. Mussolini was aiming to goose-step with Hitler, France had fallen, the RAF and the Luftwaffe were fighting over English skies. The grownups talked so much of war it gave us kids nightmares. The world seemed to be coming to an end. Tom Mix had just died and Kate Smith kept singing "God Bless America" as if we were in for something terrible. The new bath and commode room was a relief.

We wondered when Daddy whipped us if he'd take us out to the old bathhouse beside the rig boilers, as he usually did, or if he'd shift to the new bathroom. Bobby was for indoors. He thought our cries would bring Mother to the rescue. Hard to say. If Mother interfered, Daddy would sure beat her, too. He had such a temper sometimes we wished he would get drafted and aim it at Hitler instead of us. But at least he tried to be funny about the commode as well as nagging. He came in with a sign he and the roughnecks made to put on the wall over the contraption. It said: *The Country Commode and Septic Tank creed: When yellow let it mellow. When brown flush it down.* Mother said the sign was tacky and wouldn't let them put it up. The outhouse was never this much bother, though the bathroom seemed cleaner and a lot more convenient. We kids hated the spiders and wasps in the privy, and at night we dreaded using it because of the snakes.

Now it was night, and Mr. Munoz, the fat little widower with the pencil moustache who ran the store at Escoba, had come to sup with us (he always brought wonderful hot tamales) and to listen to the news on our radio. His had been broken since June. It stopped right in the middle of a bulletin announcing that Italy had joined Germany against the Allies.

Now on our radio we were hearing FDR speak from the basement of the White House Radio Room, and, big surprise, he said he would accept a nomination for a third term.

The news that night was less interesting than what Mr. Munoz had to say at the table. He had said some college students up East had done a study of the speeches of Hitler, Mussolini and President Roosevelt, and that it showed that Hitler said "I" every 53 words; Mussolini every 83 and FDR every 100. Daddy reared back and said it sure showed the difference between conceited dictators who appoint themselves and duly elected presidents chosen by the people. Mr. Munoz pointed out that Hitler was elected, but Daddy never heard him.

It was getting late. Daddy and Mr. Munoz were out on the screened porch about to wind up their talk. Bobby had been eaves-dropping from the window in our bedroom, and he, always the calcu-lator, said Daddy had said "I" more times than Bob Feller threw strikes.

"How many times is that?"

"Daddy said 'I' every 79 words (worse than Mussolini) to Mr. Munoz's 'I' every 120 words," Bobby said.

It might have meant a whipping if we told it at breakfast the next morning, but we decided it would be worth it. Mother would enjoy it. We would be leaving soon, as we always did, and we would miss Mr. Munoz.

We'd gotten several cheery notes from Evening Shade, Arkansas, which suggested Uncle John had fallen in love with Ear-line. Daddy was not amused, although he was encouraged that John kept writing, since it indicated that maybe he hadn't pulled a fast one on us and intended to do right by us and Grandpa's fiddle. If he hadn't hocked it.

Then another card came not from Evening Shade but from La Grange, Texas, where it seemed Uncle John had gone into business. No mention of Earline. Uncle John said he'd opened himself Cap-tain John's Cowboy and Indian Village on Highway 71 between La Grange and Smithville. He said it was a kind of miniature frontier town tourist attraction. Daddy wondered where in the hell he got the money to put up a sideshow right in the heart of Texas.

Speaking of the heart, the reason we were leaving Los Ovejas was because Daddy'd gotten a high-paying offer from a driller up in the hill country of Mason County, which Daddy claimed was the eyeball bull's-eye heart of Texas. So he wanted to go up there and show us that and cash in on that good money. And he said at the same time, we could kill a third bird with one stone. That bird being Uncle John. "We just might pay him a visit," Daddy said.

I had a hunch Mother was putting a mild Mickey Finn in Daddy's coffee to calm him down. I knew they did that to the chow at Texas A&M to keep the Aggies in line. I wondered if what

Mother was slipping Daddy was salt peter. I thought that's what they called it.

No Takers

SMITHVILLE
August 1940

Mother and I thought Uncle John's Cowboy Village tourist attraction was kind of cute. Well, knock off the last two words. Hardly any tourists were attracted. Several cars slowed in passing, but John had no takers. Of course, it was a Sunday on the hottest day in August. The only people on the stifling grounds—not a breath of breeze—were the cigar store Indians John had grouped around some tin tepees, which were hot as skillets. John himself sat whittling in the shade of a Roy Bean–like shack, wearing a moth-eaten cavalry uniform left over from Custer's Last Stand. He kept a wary eye out for my father, who so far had been noncommittal and so mild it made us all nervous. Behind John, inside the shack, department store dummies, dressed as cowboys and Lillie Langtrys, stood in mute attention before an array of whatnots John had for sale—the kind of junk we gave Native Americans in exchange for the New World.

Daddy showed a singular, if silent, interest in the merchandise, which gave us relief until it dawned on us that what he was looking for was his fiddle, or else a noose by which to hang Uncle John.

But Daddy didn't bring it up. We thought it was because, surveying the tourist attraction, he had come to feel as sorry for Uncle John as Mother and me. John was charging a dime to see the whole village, a stiff fee considering the offerings. At that rate and Sunday's pace, he was bound for the poorhouse.

We sat out front sipping lemonade and listening to the bugs frying. We counted thousands and smelled a million. The sun was melting the asphalt in the road, and grasshoppers would stick in it and scald. John had a radio in the window, and even that which came from it was depressing.

FDR had returned from a secret shipboard meeting in the North Atlantic with Winston Churchill, and the networks were full of war talk. No way we could stay out of it, Daddy guessed. Hell, the German Swastika flew over the Balkans, the Netherlands, most of Scandinavia, and now Belgium and France had fallen, and Britain seemed to be tottering on the edge of defeat. Hitler was not having to go it alone. In June, Mussolini and the Italians had stepped up as the second leg of the Axis, and Hirohito and Japan seemed sure to follow in Indochina, the Pacific and East Indies.

Mother shuddered and turned the dial to some music:

> Now the Rawlson is a Swedish town,
> The Rillerah is a stream,
> The brawla is the boy and girl,
> The Hut-Sut is their dream.
>
> Hut-Sut Rawlson on the Rillerah . . .

"I'll swan," Mother sang through her nose. "I can't for the life of me figure out what that means."

"Some war code," John said.

Daddy removed his straw and scratched his head.

"I'll tell you this," Uncle John said emphatically, a new resolution stirring him. "I'm tired of watching grasshoppers die out here on this sorry excuse for a highway."

"There ain't much traffic," Daddy agreed.

"And what there is isn't giving me the time of the day," Uncle John went on. He shook his head and grinned. "It's all going to Miss Jessie's down there past the railroad trestle."

"You talkin' about the Chicken Ranch?" Daddy whispered, suddenly alive, eyeing Mother to see if she was onto them, which she wasn't. She was picking grassburrs out of Joyce's sneakers.

"I couldn've sworn I saw the governor out there the other day," John said.

"You mean Coke or Pappy?"

"Naw, not Coke. Pappy. Least it looked like him."

It didn't surprise me at all that the governor, or rather the new U.S. senator from Texas, would be hanging around a chicken farm. It made sense from what I knew of him on his radio music show. Why, Wilbert Lee O'Daniel, or Pappy Lee as we called him, was the kind of country boy who was more at home among hayseeds than he was the high muckety-mucks that hung around the statehouse up the road in

Austin. I could just see Pappy and his Light Crust Doughboys out at the La Grange Chicken Ranch, stroking their fiddles and selling Hill-billy Four to beat the band, singing: "Chicken in the breadpan scratching up the dough, Mama in the kitchen saying, 'No child, no.'"

It would not be until I was in high school, and roughnecking summers, that I learned, in a baptism of lurid and comical desire I shared with Larry L. King and several generations of Texas kickers, that the Chicken Ranch was the best little whorehouse in Texas.

Meanwhile, Daddy said to John, "Now what were you doin' at Miss Jessie's?"

"Ah, heh, heh. I was trying to forget the tidy little fortune I put into this ghost town."

"Was it your money or mine?" Daddy said flatly.

"Neither," said John. "It was a banker's."

Daddy's head shot up with his voice. "But my old dead daddy's fiddle as collateral. Right?"

"Now Porter—"

"Tice?" Mother said, stirring from Joyce and looking at him uneasily. "I think it's time to go."

All Daddy could get away with was to crush John's hand when he extended it in a farewell shake. Uncle John took it without a sound, although beads of sweat popped out on his handsome face. But his counterattack was sly. He kissed Mother goodbye on the lips, which sent the blood to Daddy's hard face.

On the way to our new home that night we crossed the Col-orado River so many times I thought we were circling back on our-selves. Daddy grew glum in the gloom. Now and then I would hear him stomp the floorboard of the Terraplane and swear. He had let Uncle John off the hook on the whereabouts of Grandpa's fiddle, and now it was haunting him. Someday, he swore to me on down the road as we stepped from the car to take a leak, he would settle with John Pierson, one way or the other. I looked at Pa's pecker and won-dered if my "Vienna sausage," as Mother called it, would ever get as frankfurter big as his.

The driller at Mason had gotten impatient and hired another hand, so Daddy felt lucky to land another switching job back down in Mex-ican border country. But it wouldn't start up for a month, so Daddy decided it was time for us to relax at Uncle Earl's hunting cabin down in Goliad County.

DEVIL WAS IN DADDY

EL PERDIDO CREEK
September 1940

We were going through hell on Little Perdition Creek, but I was still making mental notes to put in my journal.

Right then, we—Mother and us kids—were hiding under bunk beds on the back screened porch of Earl and Arbie's hunting camphouse out in the mesquite of Goliad County. Daddy was on a drunken rampage. He was stumbling from room to room and closet to closet looking for rifles and shotguns, swearing he'd kill us when he found us. But first he had to find the guns, and Mother had them with us under the bunk beds. It was a good thing she thought of that, or we'd have been goners for sure, because Pa was crazy on hum and whatever else ate at him. Ma had shells in both chambers of the shotgun, and she said she'd blow his head off before she'd let him beat us all again. I felt it was my responsibility to hold the shotgun, since I was already taller than Mother, but she said she didn't want me taking the blame if we had to shoot Daddy. Our hearts were pumping so hard we were afraid he could hear them. Listen? Oh, shit. He was in a closet where Ma thought she overlooked one of the rifles. Joyce started to cry, and we were trying to hush her. Jesus H. Christ, little sister. What if Daddy found the rifle? Don't panic. He'd have to find shells and load it, and the way he was lurching from wall to wall, we didn't think he was steady enough to get a shell in the chamber. Lord, he was tearing the closet apart. Sounded like an animal. Devil was in him. I hated him. If Ma wouldn't pull the trigger on him, I would. No Daddy had a right to act like that. *What was wrong with our father?* I goddamned him and goddamned God and Jesus too. *We hadn't asked for this!* I tried to calm down and think. Lordy, Lordy, even if everything turned out okay by morning, I'd never forgive him, and neither would Mother. Strange how it had begun on such a good note.

Uncle Earl and Aunt Arbie had come in from Corpus for the night before's big dance at Schroeder Dance Hall. It was a dance floor out in the country northeast of Perdido, about a twenty-minute drive, and we met Earl and Arbie there and had a terrific time. Ernest Tubb, the Texas Troubadour, was appearing for a one-night stand and we danced our feet off. Ernest took a break after singing his hit, "Walking the Floor Over You," and Daddy got up on the bandstand, borrowed a fiddle and led us all in a hoedown. Reminded me of Grandpa. I was right proud of him. But after that the night went to pieces.

Daddy got loaded and started smart-mouthing Uncle Earl. It's not as if he had all that much to drink. Pa was like an Indian. He could sniff a cork and go nuts. He made such a scene Byron Hoff asked him to leave. We were all red-faced with embarrassment. Mr. Hoff owned the dance hall. He was a nice man, and Schroeder's was as sweet and homey a place to dance as there was in Texas, perfect for families. Except for ours, I guessed. Our name would be mud, you could bet your boots on that. I goddamned Daddy again. Uncle Earl hadn't wanted us to ride alone with Pa back to the cabin. He and Arbie wanted to take us on to Corpus for the night, but Mother had said no, and they had dropped us off before Daddy got to the cabin. We had time to get the weapons and hide under the bunk beds when he drove up. Our hearts sank. We were praying he wouldn't be able to navigate the narrow Coleto Creek bridge and crash and kill himself. No such luck.

No good could possibly come of it. It had been half an hour since things had gotten quiet, and we decided to crawl out and see where he was. Mother thought he'd passed out in the front yard. We had heard him leave the house and clamor onto the porch, heard him puking and gagging. If he had managed to get in the Terraplane and drive off, we hadn't heard it.

It was almost daylight, and it looked like our nightmare was about to end. Yep, Mother found him snoring in the yard. He'd be cowed when he woke up, and would try to get on Mother's good side. But we'd made a pact. Not a one of us would smile or speak to him for thirty days, no matter what he threatened. Of course, we didn't dare show up at Schroeder's again.

STRENGTH IN NUMBERS

NORIAS
October 1940

I wrote in my journal that there was strength in numbers if everyone held, and what we held was our mouths shut, snapped tighter than a turtle on a trotline. Now we knew how to handle the mean old buzzard that was our husband and father. And he was broken, at least for now, which found us down on the switching lease we were promised up in Mason. There was not a soberer or more contrite soul within a hundred miles than T. C. Porterfield, who turned himself inside out to be nice to us. So Mother gave the signal to let up on him and try to be a family again.

RADIO VERSUS REALITY

NORIAS
July 1941

Radio was it.

Almost all I knew of the world beyond the Texas oil fields came to me through our old Zenith console. Saturdays were for the picture show, if we were within fifty miles of one. Sundays were for church, fried chicken and the "funnies," the Sunday comics. But every day of the week was for radio.

Daddy got up at the crack of dawn to the weather report, had breakfast listening to the news, which, with World War II looming, was as global as it was local. During the day, Mother did her chores while listening to the soaps, especially "Ma Perkins" and "Stella Dallas," and during the summer mornings my brother and I lived every exciting episode of "The Lone Ranger."

I first heard a symphony orchestra play when we tuned in to Arturo Toscanini conducting the NBC Symphony, and I came to know a president from his fireside chats. Franklin Delano Roosevelt made almost three-hundred radio talks, and I guess I heard most of them. There was as much comfort in his voice, through the Depression and into the war years, as there was later to be in the voice of Edward R. Morrow and, still later, Walter Cronkite.

Daddy had turned forty that spring and would have been grouchy about it if we hadn't continued to hold him to his best behavior. I'm sure part of his sobriety lay in a sense of lost youth, and part the fear that he was not too old to be drafted if we got into the war abroad.

Politics were no better at home. That trashy hillbilly singer, Pappy Lee O'Daniel, had just whipped a young New Deal Congressman, Lyndon Johnson, for the Senate, and in addition to all that, Daddy was drilling a dry hole on the Armstrong Ranch down in Kenedy County.

The only bright spot that summer was Joe DiMaggio of the New York Yankees. About the middle of May, Joltin' Joe began a batting streak that lasted into July. It caught the fancy of the whole country, and diverted us, for a while, from the specter of war. Down in Norias, Texas, near the Mexican border, we were just as enthralled as any fan from Gotham City. Of course, we couldn't see the Yankee Clipper—the nearest major league club was in St. Louis, eight hundred miles away—and there was no television. We hung by the radio, and Daddy was the most faithful of all. He never missed a Yankee game, even when they played during work hours. He kept a radio on the rig and swore by Joe DiMaggio, tolerating no slurs against this son of American Italy.

On July 1, 1941—I think it was a Sunday because Mother was out in the yard ringing fryers' necks for supper—Daddy went off his rocker. He jumped out of his radio chair and ran outside, whooping and hollering and clearing barbed wire fences like a high hurdler.

"What's got into that old fool?" Mother asked me, a chicken head in each of her fat little hands.

"DiMaggio just homered against the Red Sox," I said. "That breaks the record. Old Wee Willie Keeler's record. You know, of hitting safely in forty-four consecutive games! Well, Old Joe just did it, Mother, he just did it, and that's what's got hold of Daddy."

When Daddy settled down, he made a major, prewar decision. For once in our lives, before the Nazis and gas rationing got us and the rest of the country down, the Porterfields were going to see a major league baseball game. "And what I want to do," Daddy said, "is to get up there and see DiMaggio before his hitting streak runs out."

We were still driving the old Hudson Terraplane, which these days Daddy seldom pushed past forty miles per hour, which meant we had to make tracks. Daddy called in another toolpusher to strawboss the drilling, and on Sunday, July 13, we loaded up the Hudson and struck for Cleveland, Ohio, fifteen-hundred miles away, where, in four days, DiMaggio and the Yankees would be playing.

The day we left we got off to a late start because Daddy had to listen to the game on the house radio, since we had no set for the car. Joe kept his string alive in a doubleheader against the Chicago White Sox. It was dark before we drove off.

Since we didn't have a radio, and couldn't afford a battery-powered portable, we used gas station attendants along the way to keep us posted on Joe's progress. DiMaggio's heroics, heightened by broadcasting, exploded across the land like Fourth of July pinwheels. Along our route the excitement was that of a national grandstand. One was not a stranger with the magic question—"How's Joe doing?"—on his lips. It was the only time in our family history that Daddy was willing to make Mother's pit stops every hour. We ate cheese and crackers and Cokes and spent the nights in tourist cabins that advertised a radio and a gun of bug spray in every room.

On Monday, as we bore down on the Louisiana-Arkansas border, the Yankees lost to the White Sox, but DiMaggio beat out a bounder to third and kept his string going at fifty-four.

Tuesday, between Memphis and Louisville, we heard Joe had doubled and singled against Chicago.

On Wednesday, stalled in Columbus with a boiling radiator, we listened to a service station radio as Joe kept on with a double and two singles against Cleveland. That made it fifty-six.

We roared into Cleveland the next day, in plenty of time. It was a night game, and I had never seen so many people in my life. There were sixty-seven thousand—at that time a major league record—and Mother said most of them were standing in line ahead of us. She and Joyce got tired of waiting and chickened out. They begged off and went to a movie. (It was Greer Garson and Walter Pidgeon in *Blossoms in the Dust*.) Daddy was profoundly disgusted with the women in our family.

We men made it in. It didn't matter that the diamond and the players seemed as small as fleas in a circus. We had finally made it to the majors.

All night long, the great DiMaggio never got one out of the infield. On Joe's last swing, when he hit into a double play, Daddy turned to me with a sour look and said, "Them Eyetalians will do it ever' time. Fold in the stretch!"

Things weren't as good in real life as they seemed on the radio. We headed home to Texas to winter and a war that would drag us in for the duration, a long and exhausting death knell that in four years would take FDR and make way for Harry Truman's inauguration, which people in sixteen cities saw on television. Already things were changing.

By the year I graduated from high school, my father and seven-million Americans had TV sets. On the tube we even got to see an old Joe DiMaggio play a time or two. But he was never as good on television as he had been on radio.

But this was all still ahead of us, so much that I must not hurry over it.

VEAL, THEN SPAM

PETRONILA
December 1941

The sun that rose over America that clear Sunday morning gave no hint of the malevolence that would follow from the East.

It brought to our barn a new-born calf, so pretty and red Daddy dubbed it Maureen O'Hara, after the fiery-haired actress we had just seen in the movie, *How Green Was My Valley*.

"She's a prize-winner," he said.

"We won't eat her, will we?" I asked.

"Naw. We'll keep her for a brood cow and a milker. Id'nt she a sight!"

Dawn broke benignly upon the farm we were share cropping, bathing the dewy winter stubble of cotton and sorghum in a glistening imitation of the Christmas lights to come. Back in the house, Daddy gulped coffee black as the gumbo on his boots, went to frying bacon and eggs while Mother got herself and us kids ready for church. We had Maureen O'Hara's first birthday. Now we were ready for the Lord and his birthday. Daddy went out to start the car, but it wouldn't. "Even if I fix the Hudson," he said, "I can't get you to church on time, so let's forget it." We certainly were not ready for the nightmare history was bringing.

Even had our radio been working, we would not have heard that, at that moment, Japanese war planes were attacking Pearl Harbor, the U.S. naval base in the Hawaiian islands. In Washington, not even President Roosevelt and his high command would know of the sneak attack until 2 P.M. In those days, news came after an event.

The Old World had been at war for years. As early as the fall of '36, Japan had moved into the Axis fold with Germany and Italy. And the bad guys were winning. That December of '41, the Germans occupied the Balkans, the Netherlands, most of Scandinavia and France, and now they were blitzkrieging the British. The Japanese were in the Pacific and most of China and Indochina, and were aiming at the Philippines and the East Indies.

We were up on our strategic geography, especially boys who read the war comics and moved toy soldiers not only in imitation, but in anticipation, of the real thing. The president himself was fit to be tied, had just fired off a letter to Emperor Hirohito, demanding to know Japan's intentions in Indochina. His mind wasn't on Hawaii. We had long since broken the Japanese's secret code, and FDR used that to advantage. But he did not know Dutch intelligence had warned us Pearl Harbor might well be the target. Somehow it never penetrated the fog of bureaucracy.

Down on the Texas coast, a few miles inland of Corpus Christi, we Porterfields sat with hundreds of Clara Driscoll oil and gas wells at our front door, and just as many King Ranch/Kleberg wells at our back. And there we whiled away an innocent Sunday, moving from calf-birthing to chicken-eating and *Caller-Times* comic-reading.

It was not until Monday, when met by neighbors and headlines, that we realized our isolation had been breached, that we were at war along with the rest of the world.

We gathered one another around, out of not-knowing and out of fear. Some daddies did not go to work. A lot of kids were kept home from school. We exchanged rumors. Both American coasts were under alert for signs of enemy planes, ships and submarines. The mayor of San Francisco reported sighting Japanese fighter planes in the Bay area. The governor of California called out the National Guard. Smack-dab in the middle of an oilfield the way we were, and only eighteen miles from the Mexican gulf and the U.S. Naval Air Station at Corpus, Mother made no objections when Daddy got out his rifles and shotguns and began oiling and loading them. Mother began putting provisions in the cellar. Bobby and I, feeling manful, took turns keeping watch on the skies from the highest perch of the windmill. Daddy hurried and fixed the Terraplane and the radio.

The most respectful, attentive and throat-swallowing thing we did was gather that noon around radios to hear the president speak before a joint session of Congress. FDR had been the father so long he was like a god.

"Yesterday," the president's patrician voice began, "December 7, 1941—a date that will live in infamy . . . "

Overnight, it seemed, we mobilized, and as Daddy put it, our lives went off ever' which way. Out at Voca below the San Saba, Wild John Davis, the eighty-year-old "Law West of Lost Creek," resigned as justice of the peace and lit out for Frisco to help Californians protect their coast.

"We could've used him here," Uncle Earl, Daddy's brother in the Body of Christ, opined, observing that lightning can strike in the same place.

"What does that mean?" Daddy asked.

"During the Civil War," Earl replied, raising a meaningful eyebrow, "Corpus was bombed twice by Yankee gunboats. Now that we've got the Naval Air Station and all this oil around us, I figure Corpus has to be a prime target. The Japanese ain't dumb."

"We ain't lost a war yet," Daddy said, "and we been havin' them since 1775."

Earl shot back: "And Japan hasn't lost one since 1598."

From then on, when Daddy was away, he insisted Mother keep Grandpa's old double-barreled shotgun at the ready. There were rumors of enemy submarines surfacing just off Corpus in the Gulf of Mexico, and reports of farmers and ranchers seeing men drop by parachute into the thickets along the coast. We canceled outings at the beaches.

At the historic Kleberg mansion on Broadway, the fanciest street in Corpus, Congressman Richard Kleberg packed his bags for Washington. The day before the attack on Pearl Harbor, he had seen his newly married daughter off to New Orleans. Now, he stood in his bedroom, talking to *Caller* reporter Tom Mulvaney.

Rats, the houseboy, came in with another suit for the congressman's bag. "Do you want your golf clubs?"

"To hell with the golf clubs," the congressman said. "We're not going to take this war business lightly."

Mother didn't.

One night when Daddy was away, and we kids asleep, Mother saw the shadow of a man crouch-stepping his way toward our back door. She picked up the shotgun and blew away with both barrels a marauding Japanese soldier.

The blasts woke me, and Mother, covering me with both barrels reloaded, made me go outside in the dark and make sure "the Jap" was dead.

He damned sure was. An awful bloody mess.

Except that he wasn't a he, or even a soldier or a Japanese. It turned out to be Maureen O'Hara, the new calf. Before he left, Daddy had put her inside the yard fence to graze and didn't think to tell Mother.

That's why we ate veal and then some for our first Christmas dinner of the war. After that it was Spam.

12

★ ★ ★

Bad Karma and Good,
Circles and Squares

Washington—In new images from the Hubble Space Telescope, astronomers have for the first time distinguished the
shapes of galaxies as they existed in the universe at least 4
billion years ago, before they were violently rearranged by
collisions and other forces.

Where before they were blurred images and scientific
speculation, the Hubble has revealed pinwheels galore,
elipses, rat-tails, spheres and the slicing and dicing of one
whirling galaxy by another. It also shows that spiral galaxies like Earth's Milky Way were several times more abundant than they are now.

—KATHY SAWYER,
WASHINGTON POST NEWS SERVICE,
DECEMBER 2, 1992

TEXAS AND OKLAHOMA
1942

A 15 TEX 851

★ THE GREEKS WOULD NOT LET US ALONE. THEY KEPT HAUNTING
us with the efficacy of their tragedies.

My cousin Icky Adams did not plummet to his death after we
left him in the fall of '39 with Oklahoma Settlement's great aeronaut, Sam Longmeyer. But while we were at Clarkwood Aunt Ella
wrote that Icky had fallen and would never fly again.

Here we were just hearing from her in the spring of the follow-

ing year after his fall, this after Icky had undergone a long convales-
cence and was able to walk out of the hospital in Houston. She said
she hadn't wanted to write us until they knew one way or the other
about Icky, because he had lingered at death's door before recovering.
"I didn't want to leave you hanging," she wrote, "but now am
relieved to say that the worst is over, and that Icky has rejoined us at
the farm. We would love for Billy Mack to come see him, if only for a
few days before the summer chores set in with a vengeance. Billy, if
you are able to come, you must prepare yourself for the change that
has come over Icky. He is not the same as he was, and never will be.
He rarely says a word. When he does speak, it is only to say 'A 15
Tex 851,' which was a mystery to Eck and me and the doctors until
Eck realized it was the license number of that old Model T Ford we
had before Icky was born. It's been laid up in a back stall of the barn
gathering dust and dirt daubers all these years. Eck went to see if it
still had its license plate, and it didn't. How and why Ecky fastened
onto that old missing license number as something to remember
remains a puzzlement to all. And to tell the truth, Janavee, it breaks
our hearts to think that out of all the things we shared with our only
boy, this is all he can remember—something so trivial that Eck and I
had forgotten it. Well, the Lord has His ways.

"We do hope Billy can come. He might joggle Icky's memory,
though that's not the reason we invite him and don't want him to
come feeling a burden has been placed on him. It's just that he and
Icky were so close it would do us a world of good to see them play
again. You ought to be able to put Billy on the bus out of Corpus to
Houston, where we can pick him up. Let us know. Love, Eck and Ella."

"This is all damned inconvenient!"

That's what Daddy said when Mother read us the letter from
Aunt Ella. Already, we were about to make another move, and
Daddy was counting on me to be, as he put it, his cabooseman. By
now, we were hauling so many trailers in a train behind the Hudson
that in heavy traffic and the tight squeeze of close turns and backing,
he needed someone to ride the tailer and signal him clear. I was first
in line for this manful and even dangerous work, for which Daddy
had been priming me, despite Mother's misgivings. But, shoot, if I
had to go hold Icky's hand, then Rapid Robert would have to take
my place.

That was the way Daddy had put it, and Mother came down on him like Tobin Drexler, only she did it with her tongue. This time, he deserved all he got. Still, as the bus pulled away from the depot at Corpus, Bobby waved at me with a smirk on his face. I could not but dread what awaited me at Uncle Eck's and Aunt Ella's.

He stood with them at the bus station in Houston. At first, I didn't recognize him. It had been a little over a year since I had seen Icky, and almost that long since his fall, but you could hardly say his setback had stunted his growth. Icky of the airy bird bones had grown gluttonous and fat. His wild-blue-yonder eyes were clouded and crossed now. So it was, in a sense, a blessing that they were reduced to two tiny, confused raisins peering out from a bloated, pumpkin of a face. A shiver ran through me. He had just as well be dead, I thought. What a come-down for Sam's eaglet. They had him in overalls, which he had despised.

I swallowed hard and reached up to embrace him, for he was huge. He grunted like a porker, but did not return the hug.

"Icky," Aunt Ella said, "don't you remember Billy? He's your cousin and favorite friend. He was here last fall with Aunt Janavee and Billy's brother Bobby. He's come all this way just to see you. Can't you say something to him?"

I looked into his face, raised my hand in an awkward sign of "Hi." Nothing. Nothing came from him except drool running down the corner of his mouth. I looked up at Uncle Eck, and he grimaced. Everything that had been knocked out of Icky was in his eyes.

"Take his hand," Aunt Ella instructed me. And when I did, Icky went along with me, a Saint Bernard to my whippet, his huge, clammy paw dwarfing mine. I was reminded of the spectacle Wit Odin and I must have made holding hands on the train from Dallas to Ardmore, except that Wit's hands were smaller than mine. Icky took short, choppy steps, each stride stunted by a massive confusion of motor skills.

I stayed for three weeks, and the time was not as hellish as I had expected. I accepted right away that this Icky was not my friend of old, that in fact he had undergone a sudden and jarring reincarnation into a Mongolian idiot, that this poor creature had been sent us in his place. Bad karma, but as Aunt Ella said, the Lord had His way. I wondered about that. Icky saw his flying as a great reaching out of himself, a bird on the wing in the universe, noble and free as thought itself. I saw it that way, too. Still do, or I wouldn't be flying on my own with this fable. Aunt Ella's remark reminded me, as if I needed it, of the dark side of fate, and I questioned if Sam's and Icky's thrusts into the air were what they supposed, or something aggressive, even predatory. Was Icky—this beautiful feathered arrow of the Amerind—actually the white man coming to contaminate and annihilate? Another lichen or fungus spreading its musk and lust from sea to shore to space? If he was, he was Grandpa, Daddy, Sam Longmeyer and my Great-Uncle Ben, whom you will meet shortly. But then I realized he was also Doody, Mother and me. We too were on our journeys.

Of course, there was no answer. It was too complicated, and too simple. All I had to do was live with the result: my two Ickies. I guessed the two Ickies had the same soul, if different bodies, and I tried to keep my heart open to the one before me. He needed all the kindness of which I was capable. I also squinted my potato-bead eyes, furrowed the brow of my turnip face and did some detective work.

In his maiden flight for Sam Longmeyer, Icky had lofted himself upon leather wings from the great skyscraping windmill beside Uncle Eck's barn. It seemed reasonable to suppose that the last thing Icky might have seen other than the oncoming ground could have jammed in his memory upon impact, that what he repeated over and over must have been apparent to him from the air. So I went up into the towering windmill and looked about, taking note of everything that could have caught his eye. Since I knew what I was looking for—A 15 Tex 851—it leaped out at me almost immediately from the tin roof of the barn below me to the left. Years before, Uncle Eck or one of his hired hands had removed the license plate from the wornout Ford and had tacked it onto the roof to cover a leaky hole. Icky read the license as he fell past the roof, its obsolescent code apparently the only cognitive data that wasn't knocked from his head.

"Icky, what's your real name?"

"A 15 Tex 851."

"Icky, do you like ice cream?"

"A 15 Tex 851."

"Icky, how about a radish?"

Silence.

He had back problems, which he bore up stoically. The chiropractor we took him to said Icky was confounded because his bones and brains had been rattled—a brilliant diagnosis—and thought to straighten out his head as well as his spine. So he beat and massaged Icky three times a week at a buck a treatment. Uncle Eck's pocketbook, already depleted by the hospital bills, could not stand a lot of that.

Desperate, Aunt Ella took him to a priest at Nacogdoches. He said Icky had had his soul knocked out of him, as much by disappointment as the fall. I thought the priest had something, and so did Aunt Ella. But Uncle Eck, ever the son of the Protestant Reformation—in spite of his pagan past—wasn't taking any advice from no Catholic.

Icky never went back to school after the fifth grade. Day and night, he sat on the front porch in the rocking chair, rolling back and forth, stuffing himself on peanut butter and saltine crackers, which Aunt Ella bought by the case. Eventually, she got him a cot for the porch, and he slept all but the coldest nights out there. He bothered no one, but he was a bother to have to look after. He got so heavy the only thing they could clothe him in was overalls. He understood us, because he would do what we told him. But he never laughed. And he only cried when Aunt Ella would wring the chickens' necks before frying them for supper. He refused to eat the earthbound fowl.

INTO THE CARTESIAN BLUE

In no way did Uncle Eck and Aunt Ella blame Sam Longmeyer for Icky's fall and its consequence. It was Sam's loss too, and he suffered; though it has to be said with no dimming of the passion that had so maimed his fledglings. But there were some in the family who thereafter avoided Sam. It was easily done, and without offense to Sam, since the ones who felt funny about him were in Rexroat, almost five-hundred miles to the north. The only slight Sam may have felt would have been from Great-Uncle Ben Scott, who, for reasons that will become apparent, went out of his way to make friends with Sam down in Texas, only to withdraw after Icky's fall.

Save for the totally unexpected secret letter I got from Wit Odin, who would say only that he was somewhere in the universe and for me not to betray him, Uncle Ben was the only one who said anything outright critical of Sam. Wit was compelled to write to explain in a very lofty way why physics would never have allowed Icky to fly in the manner Sam had launched him. In Rexroat, Oklahoma, Ben would say the same thing to my father, who had gone up there to pick up trailer wheels Granddaddy Harrell had made for us. Typically, Ben made his charge against Sam sound like an observation that was both empirical and analogical, the detached conspectus of a fellow trailblazer in that high but hazy realm that groped between instinct, art and science. And Ben was right. He too was a quester, a barrier-breaker pushing himself to do, essentially, the same thing Sam was about. Both were long, lean Apollos trying to break the bonds of the material earth and send themselves out into the immaterial, up to heaven's door. And, I realize now, like Wit Odin, Ben saw the flaw in Sam's science.

"Longmeyer knows well the gravity of Newton's Laws," Ben said to my father, no slouch at engineering, "and he's up on aerodynamics. But he's obviously in the dark about thermodynamics, and that's his limitation, the one that led to Icky's downfall."

"Refresh my memory," Daddy said.

"Let me put it this way," Ben said. "Sam knows that the heavier you are, and the faster you fall, the harder you hit. And he may even know that only God creates energy, that man can cup but a bit of it for his own power . . . "

Daddy raised an eyebrow. "Yep, I'm right with ye, Ben. But what's the but?"

"The but is that Sam hasn't realized how much of God's energy is wasted in the universe, much less in a cup wafted up by Sam's attempt at wings. He and Icky could wave their arms to beat the band, and even outwit the odds for a while, but the heat of their exertion exhausts them, and entropy sets in. If they could cool themselves down to zero they could hold the energy. But God has said that's a no-no, absolutely impossible. But even if they could freeze, they can't and still keep flapping. So, you see, in a sense we're all in the same fix."

"Falling down, running down, kaput!" Daddy said.

"Exactly!" Ben said triumphantly, as if he were excused from it.

You would never have heard Uncle Ben having such a conversation with Mother's father, Daddy Harrell. The latter gave me, among other things, my barrel body and Bacchus nature. He was, as I told at the beginning, a blacksmith, and one of the reasons he stayed busy at the forge when he wasn't carousing was because his competitor, Uncle Ben, refused to make anything circular.

Ben, as angular as Daddy Harrell was round, would fashion you something straight. And if it had to go sideways and then up and down, he would angle it in a way to do Hipparchus proud. The closest thing he came to a circle was a square.

Although, like all my fathers—and this includes Doody—Ben had no formal schooling, he had a sense for logic and a gift for abstraction. I found him a wonder at trigonometry. As a schoolboy, I had not even a tangential interest in the hypotenuse, much less the hypoteinein, and when I was in Oklahoma I went to Ben with my homework, watching with amazement as he set me straight on sines and cosines. He could look at a trapezoidal roofline and figure in a jiffy the angles of incidence and repose. He was great at making Christian crosses, lightning rods, pitchforks and pyramids.

But when it came to the spherical, Ben would send you to Bill Harrell. And that explained why, in an age that had tilted, in its bias and manufacture, from the flat to the round, that Daddy Harrell was up to his drawing compass and protractor making hoops and wheels and rims with zodiacal zeal. Ben was in no way resentful. Let Bill spin himself to an early grave trying to keep up with the unending demand for the cyclical. Rhomboidal Ben was happiest at the forge of his own invention. And more and more he made things no one wanted.

In his shop yard and about his house Ben began planting his creations, which got taller and taller. Ben took angle iron to new heights of intrinsic abstraction, welding thin slices of metal into such high reaches of the unrecognizable and absurd that villagers in Rexroat strained their necks and gawked in stupefaction. When storms made of the waving towers monstrous wind chimes, people began complaining of earache and asked that he take them down. Ben refused, saying he owned the space above his property line as well as within and below it. "Yes, but do you own the soundwaves that come from your towers and accost our ears?" a wag cried.

Ben's wife, Maude, who loved him almost in spite of herself, was tested to the limit by Ben's intransigence. She tried earnest plea and wile to get him to listen to the neighbors' complaints. Maude was my maternal great-aunt, Daddy Harrell's sister, and she looked like my grandfather in drag. No Nefertiti, Maude. She had none of Ben's sleek, Apollonian lines. Maude was the Venus of Willendorff, the fat nature goddess of thirty-two thousand years ago. If opposites are required of marriage and art, she was perfect for Ben. Her matter and his spirit had mated to make, up to this point, a harmonious whole.

The only thing missing was children, and none of us were sure why this was so until later. They welcomed nephew and niece as their own. My mother observed that the want of their own children had created an empty space in Maude and Ben, and that was why they kept filling up her house and his shop with things. Ben wasn't the only creator.

Maude spun and sewed everything she and Ben wore, except shoes. And when she wasn't baking bread and curdling cheese she was sculpting and firing clay pots and weaving baskets for kitchen and garden. Like her brother, and quite unlike her husband, everything she made was for a use. A form's function was her answer to the riddle of life. The locus of her imagination was close and sensate. All she needed to run her house and garden were ears, nose, mouth and hands. Ben could have his soaring eye and vertical mind. She was curved horizontally, like the earth, parallel to soil and nature, and she humped and bumped busily about like a hedgesow, this round drum of a woman, listening to the rain on the roof, sniffing her pork pie and Ben's haggis, tasting the new corn, singing old Irish airs and kneading everything within reach into the vessel and fuel of life. She smelled of flour, flowers and garlic, and to hear her earthy tread and fertile voice was a great reassurance, especially after a gaseous day at the forge with Vulcan himself, the incendiary, sooty Ben.

For him, the village crank, space around a form was reality. I didn't understand this as a boy, and thought him daft on this invisible point. Now I see his eye was Western, if Eastern in its quest for the immaterial. The unseen was greater than the seen, the form itself only a shadow of something far more substantial. This is why he tried to reduce his pig iron shafts to insubstantial needles, flat ones, and sent them out of sight, into the Cartesian blue. He was God-crazed, and the wands were his temple.

At least they were the keys. Early on, Doody Mareain noticed they resembled the Egyptian neter, symbolic turnlatch to the temenos, the sacred precincts. Ben could not have known this, except in his unconscious.

It was after a tornado broke the iron towers like shards, sending great, whistling, rusty knives slicing through Rexroat, that Ben repented of his "affront to God" and went about collecting what was left of the totems, as Daddy Harrell called them. Totems to hoity-toity. Fortunately, no one was killed or hurt except some livestock, for which Ben made restitution. When he got back home, he found Maude had left him. She had had enough.

He wooed her back, but when she discovered he had not learned his lesson, that he was secretly experimenting, at a reduced scale, with blowing glass towers (which he kept angular by molds), she left again.

This cured him.

Ben remained so contrite that Maude returned to bear him a child, a daughter. Ben wanted to call her Hypoteninousa, a term he had gotten from one of my math books. It is the Greek feminine for the thin side of a right-ankled (sic) triangle. But Maude put her thick, round foot down. Cora, they named the daughter, and she grew up to be skinny Ben all over again, but weighted with Maude's common sense. She was a whiz at trig.

Let Us Speak No More of Space, Infinity, Nothingness or Miz Tarbutton's Brassiere Straps

CLARKWOOD

Up on the wooden platform of the windmill, Bobby and I sat in a sweat, for it was high noon under a burning July sun of an arid year. The wind was still and we did not have to duck the mill blades. Just as well, for we were intent. We licked forefingers and stuck them into the spout of a Morton Salt box, withdrawing the briny fingers to put them into our mouths. Better'n salt blocks and tablets, we said.

But our taste for the saline was not the ultimate thrill that came from the pasteboard container. Something far more mysterious and hypnotic lurked there, a genie of illusion and paradox pretending to be a girl the age of our Joyce. On the label she was pictured in the rain carrying an open umbrella in one hand and a cylinder of Morton Salt in the other. The spout of the box was open and the salt was pouring out. The trademark said, "When it rains, it pours."

What fascinated was that the pound of salt she carried bore the same emblem as the package she was pictured on. There she was, repeated again, although considerably reduced. And of course it fol-lowed that the tiny, second girl held an even smaller pack of salt which featured an even tinier third girl, and that this mite-sized girl held a smaller yet fourth girl, and so on past the point of seeing. You get the idea. I did not know the term ad infinitum, and the eternal I left to heaven. So I thought we had made an amazing discovery. Bobby and I stared at the girl on the Morton Salt box until we were goofy trying to figure out if she and her smaller sisters—or were they daughters?—ever ended even when they went out of sight.

He tired of it, but it was not easy for me to put aside the notion that something could repeat itself endlessly, or be replicated perpetu-ally, however reduced, by someone else. The artist had chosen to sus-tain an image of a girl holding a salt box. I put myself in place of the girl, and in my mind kept reducing the images of myself past the point where the limitations of the human eye and physics had stopped the artist and his pen. I found I could indeed do this best from the vantage of the windmill platform. But I needed to be by myself. So, one morning, I banned Bobby from the windmill. He went and crawled under the house and sulked, swearing he'd get me back.

Alone up there for hours, I stared through a cloudless sky with all the concentration and focus I could muster, projecting my serial and shrinking selves, piggy-backing on them into space. I sensed, in a vague way, that I was swimming against the stream, growing smaller in macrospace and not microspace. But starting out as big as I was, compared, say, to a germ in a slide under a microscope, I felt more comfortable growing smaller in an expanding world than in the other. I reasoned that except for my illusion of comfort, the larger space made no difference. In my innocent knowing it struck me that there had to be as much room in a drop of water as there was in the universe. I trembled in joy and dread at the thought that my blood was a sea, my body a continent, and that I was a host to swarms of life so small that I was unaware of them, an indifferent god. If it was so in me, it could be so in the god that held us in a time and place teeming with anonymity. At one end or another of a cosmos wee or grand lay the beginning or the end. If, indeed, there was a beginning and an end? What was before the beginning and what was after the end? The most frightful possibility was nothing, which I could not wrap my sappy brain around.

As nervous as I was in my projections, I was strangely compelled. I saw vast reaches of cold light and hot dark, heard what I took to be music of the spheres, and passed through galaxies galore with pyrotechnic displays of geometry and geomancy so brilliant that Uncle Ben and Daddy Harrell would have been struck dumb. But it was Icky I took with me, the one before the fall, and he was enchanted. I got so dizzy and discombobulated that I fell behind Icky, returned to my body in the windmill, swooned and almost fell from my perch. Icky, never wavering, went on out of sight. I would never see him again, I told myself with an immeasurable regret, not this Icky. But he might have reached back to me in dreams, for I vaguely remember someone in those sultry Clarkwood nights whispering from afar, suggesting that this reality to which I had returned was a pale shadow to what he had found. Of course, it could have been Doody as well as Icky, or even Wit Odin.

Mother knew by the look in my eye that I was up to something in the windmill, for I could not but return there, and she made me wear a baseball cap to protect my noggin from the sun. I took the sun shades she gave me to rest my eyes. She too, for all her energy, was given to sitting, her dark eyes stuck in a stare more inward than mine, agape at God knows what. If Bobby could sulk under the cool of the house and draw naked women—I was relieved to discover he was not a diarist after all—then there was no harm—cross my fingers in King's X—in my daydreaming in the windmill, long as I didn't fall or get sunstroke. Or not come back like Icky.

And so I resumed my incredible shrinking odyssey. One day I became so infinitely small, and reached a place of such quiet and purity, it frightened me. Was I approaching the border where Icky was lost? Was it the realm where matter surrenders to the mystery of the invisible, the undetectable, the nothing? Was this the end of the

Universe? Suddenly it was absolutely horrible in its absolute nothingness, and I turned away and came screaming back through my chain of expanding selves. I managed to scoot down from the ladder and start for the house, white as a ghost.

I came to that night in my bed, in a sweat and babbling nonsense. Joyce was bent over me, holding an ice bag to my throbbing head. I could hear Mother and Daddy talking at the supper table. Joyce wiped my face with a damp rag. She whispered that Mother and Daddy were so mad at mean ole brother that they had sent him to her room without supper. The story was that when I started for the house from the windmill, Bobby, waiting in ambush, had stepped from behind a corner of the house to powder me with a two-by-four. Daddy reasoned my gibberish was the result of water on the brain.

I was rational the next morning. But Daddy missed work to take me to a Doctor Woolvin in Corpus. The black-bearded doctor examined me. He swung his gold watch before my eyes. He asked Daddy to leave the room. He sat and talked to me, drew out of me my obsession with the girls on the Morton Salt boxes and my attempts to solve the riddle. At last, he winked at me, called Daddy back into the examining room and said that what had hit me in the head was not so much Bobby's board—which admittedly had raised a right smart lump and some disorientation—but the idea of infinity.

"What?" Daddy said. He thought the doctor had said the idea of divinity, and he was about to get pissed. After all my promises not to pine over lunatic mystics like Doody Mareain and Wit Odin, here I was, backsliding.

Daddy looked at me as if I had betrayed him, and said, "Son, I just don't understand."

Doc Woolvin, still on his track and thinking he was going to have to explain infinity to my father, sighed and said it was beyond most men's understanding, that it was a harmless notion of Euclid's that Einstein had shot down, and that I would get over it as soon as I was old enough to have pimples and notice real girls instead of those on Morton Salt.

"Girls? Is that your prescription?" Daddy said.

"You bet. But in his own time. I wouldn't rush him."

On the way home in the Terraplane, Daddy was silent as a clam. I didn't dare speak. At last he said, "Son, I thank we've found the perfect doctor for you in that fella. He's either a very smart man or a damned fool, I don't know which."

"Yessir," I said, looking at the infinite road ahead and wondering if we'd ever get off it. I wanted him to turn the car toward North Beach and take me, right then and there, to see the Mermaid of Zennor.

I asked him if he would, and he said, no, that Woolvin's medicine would have to wait, that when my time came, he'd let me know. Until then, I was not to bug him about her.

In lieu of the mermaid, Infinity continued to pull at me. I managed to keep quiet about it until one night when, sitting around a radio so full of static that we'd turned it off, Daddy began challenging Bobby to solve some long tables of addition and subtraction. Daddy was good at figures. Even summer evenings he liked to drill us on arithmetic. He called zero aught and sometimes naught, which struck us as cute but awfully old-timey.

"Daddy," I said, "I know your aught and naught stand for zero, and zero stands for nothing, but what is nothing?"

"Nothin's nothin'," he said. "It's somethin' that don't exist."

"How can it be something if it doesn't exist?"

He cackled. "Boy, if you don't take the cake for askin' questions that'ud cross an angel's eyes. Jennie, did you hear what Billy asked?"

"I thought it was a good question," she said.

"Naw," he shot back, "it's a trick question. He's tryin' to trip me up. But I'm no angel and I can answer it. Son, by my callin' nothin' somethin', I'm just tryin' to get a handle on it, same as you are, same as the first fella that called it zero. Ye gotta call it somethin', even if ye can't see it, touch it or feel it."

Pa, as Bobby and I in our first pimply strut were beginning to call him—of course not to his face—could be a cagey old dude.

"Space, Daddy. It is something or is it nothing?"

"Well, shit, Billy Mack. I reckon it's somethin' if it's got us and our world, and worlds upon worlds a'spinnin' around in it. Air and electricity and all such as that. Energy. I hear tell of protons and neutrons and elements like that in it too, but I'm not an educated man. Why don't 'che write Uncle Ben and ask him, heh? If he don't know ever' thang, he'll make up an answer anyhow."

I wrote Uncle Ben and awaited his answer.

Only the torpid and slack-jawed could doze under the illusion that there was nothing to do in that tropical heat wave.

Daddy was doin' tha mucho, as he put it, pulling double duty. He was drilling the graveyard shift on a well in the Ramada oil field. Sunup, he would leave that job and drive five miles north to another lease where he worked into the afternoon as a pumper—a caretaker and fixer-upper—on a bunch of old pumpjacks—praying mantis pumps, we called them—so cranky they needed all the grease he could give them. After a night of drilling and a day dealing with oil-suckers and blood-sucking fleas and ticks—which thrived in the coastal sands—Daddy came home looking like a vampire had drained him dry.

We'd rented an old Mexican farmhouse on Oso Creek between Violet and Clarkwood, southwest of the Body of Christ and its beautiful bay, ever so close to North Beach and the naked and still-beckoning Mermaid of Zennor. Bobby and I fancied swiping the Terraplane and driving into Corpus for a peep at her. But Daddy took the car to work six days a week, so we were stuck out there in the flats. We were too chicken to have done it, anyway.

The house was like an oven, and the little floor fans Mother set out circulated hot air, their drone adding to the torpor that lay like a suffocating quilt on the gasping countryside. The much-touted bay breeze was petrochemical and possum-sull still. All around us out on the flats, mirages danced in the distance, and people, when we saw them, moved like they were tramping through molasses.

There was a store down on the Violet crossroads, run by a Miz Tarbutton, where we went to buy block ice to set before the fans. Tarbutton moved so slowly in ringing up the price of anything, but most particularly ice (it seemed to freeze her into inanition), that the block would melt to a cube before we left the sweltering store. But, by God, Pa complained, she wadn't about to melt the price. A bovine intelligence dulled by a cloudless drought was only part of her problem, Pa observed. One dirty strap or the other of her brassiere was always falling off a shoulder and working its way down so you could see it hanging out of the tacky open-sleeved blouses she favored, and Tarbutton couldn't ring up one red cent on the register without grabbing at a bra strap. Daddy swore that once, when she lifted an arm to turn up the ceiling fan, he saw a mouse peep from the yucky bush of her armpit. He figured Tarbutton'ud be rich as Clara Driscoll, the doyenne of high society along the bay, if ye'd give 'er a nickel for every tug and pull she gave her filthy old bra. On an ice run, the thing to do was to tell Tarbutton on coming in that you were going to get a block of ice, and wait and make sure she was ringing it up before you even started toward the cooler. This way, she'd set to ringing it up before you went and got the ice. And if you didn't show your hand and took your time, and didn't open the freezer until the register rang out the totaled price, which was always the same and always a mystery to Tarbutton until the register told her, July might pass into August but you were still out of there in a wink with some ice left, so it could all melt in the hot car on the way home.

Mother and Daddy seemed inoculated against the drag of heat. When she wasn't in one of her trances, Ma matched Pa's zealous drive. She had such a passion for spit and polish and the rightness of work that we called her Mrs. Perpetual Motion. When she was not at the stove stirring up something, she was on her knees scrubbing the linoleum, or out back at the roller washing machine and clothesline or bent over the ironing board pressing khakis and jeans with a heavy steam iron. She even ironed the bed sheets and Daddy's boxer shorts. The only time I saw her relax was Sundays, when she let Daddy cook so she could clip commonplace verse from the Corpus Christi *Caller-Times* and paste them in her book of memories. She smelled of soap and starch and scorched cotton, and there was bluing on her shapely fingertips to go with the red of her nails. She liked for us to say we could eat off her floors they were so clean, or that Daddy wore the only starched and ironed underwear in the oil patch.

To keep us from wasting away with metaphysical ennui—Bobby sulling under the house and me mulling up in the windmill, Mother began dividing the kid day into various activities and expectations in an attempt to relieve the Mongolian monotony. The idea was for us—Joyce was picking them up and laying them down by now—to get outdoors in some safe rumpus spot and play hard until noon, when Mother would call us for iced tea and sandwiches. Lunch, which we called dinner—what you call dinner was supper for us— was followed by an attempt at naps in "the ice box," a small, dark room that Mother covered with pallets and cooled by putting several of Tarbutton's cubes of ice in a washpan, positioning it on the floor in front of an oscillating fan aimed at us.

Fresh from our naps, Mother would send us out again, but not to the same place we had spent the morning. The afternoon play places had to be different environments. You see what she was doing here. She was challenging us to keep changing place and perspective—as if we'd not had enough of moving—and therefore play itself.

The pickings around the dunes and flats of bitterweed and railroad vine would have seemed spare to kids used to parks and playgrounds, but we made ourselves Bedouins in a New World desert, and, riding stick Arabian ponies, fought enough stick fights to win enough oases to satisfy us. These open and strenuous sandlot battles were best fought in the relative cool of morning; the quiet and imaginative games sent us in the glare of afternoons to the shade of cool, wet places, of which there was a scarcity.

Finding these special places, and keeping them a secret from Mother, became a game. If she found us, she would flush us out and make us help with the chores.

We couldn't hide in the cornfield. The earth was so hot, the stalks so dry and yellow and razorlike, the husks so full of spiders and bugs and the rows crawling with rattlesnakes, that it was alien territory.

We couldn't hide in the scabby wood that led to the oil-slicked creek. It was the pits—steamy, rutty ravine land, scarred by oil field bulldozers and erosion, polluted by crude, soured by stagnant swamp, crawling with cotton-mouth moccasin, alligator and gar that fed on one another to stay alive in the hydrocarbon soup. Even the vines and vegetation fought for life, entwining and squeezing one another in a mad, upward spiraling for air and sunlight. Lungs and gills and pores struggled to breathe in the humidity.

But we were safe and cool under the wooden water tower beside the windmill. Daddy had wrapped the substructure in canvas, had plugged a couple of holes in the bottom of the tank so that water would drip down on the crocks of milk, butter and cheese that Mother kept there. Bossy the cow was now a part of our family caravan, along with Boss, the German shepherd dog; Mack Mary, the white rat; and the heavy, hand-me-down dictionaries to which Bobby had become addicted. Beneath the water tower, Bobby and I would lift the linen off the jars, dip dirty fingers into the sweet cream, and skim it up and suck it into our parched mouths as we threw fancy words at each other in a definition bee while Joyce held her ears. Whenever Mother caught us stealing cream, she would get a switch and reach for us. We would run out and go around and around the water tower, naked little savages, giggling and shrieking at the sight she made. Her breasts jiggled when she ran, and Mother couldn't for the life of her catch us. She would see how absurd it was too, and start to laugh. The windmill turned and squeaked in the hot wind, the pump sang, the water trough filled, and she would join us as we raced the cows to drink and skinny dip. For all the switches Mother brandished, she never laid a one on us. Daddy would take the hide off, but Mother did not, could not even cuff when she cornered us.

Banned from the milk house, we were buoyant in the boughs of the chinaberry tree. It grew in a clearing at the edge of the slimy creek, green in all that wilt, and from its crown of camouflage we would throw berries at the great, horned spiders that had fenced the wood with their webs.

Throw pebbles at anything, and it will retreat or attack. We did not take into account our own aggression against the natural world of the creek bottom. It seemed to us berry throwers that everything out there was mean and hostile and laying in wait, that all manner of things—mineral, vegetable, animal and man—either pricked, pounced or was poisonous. Even the lizards wore cactus spikes. Daddy said the only soft white things in that country were heads of warm cantina beer and sweet cream, featherbed down and the underbellies of horny toads and women. During the day reptilian creatures and their females lay on rocks at the edge of their holes, sleeping with slit eyes, the better to see you coming. At night they came alive and crawled and thrashed about, hunting, killing, crunching and swallowing, moaning and groaning, crying out mating calls as I lay on my bed with my head in the window. Listening to that swarming din, I felt a tide of shivers ebb and flow the length of my spine. My only comfort was the deep rumble of Daddy's snoring.

> But the nights off the bay turned cool at last.
> And there were tins of iced tea at noon.

And the mail came in the afternoon.
And Daddy came home after that.

The mail truck was too far away for us to hear. But we knew. A little alarm went off in us. We gathered on the porch ahead of Mother. She came out in her bonnet, and, at our urging, removed her shoes. The challenge, the delicious pain of going for the mail, was to scamper through the blistering sand of the driveway all the way to the mailbox and back. The box wasn't at the end of the yard. It was out on the county road, maybe a mile going and a mile coming, and the only relief to bare feet was an occasional patch of shade from the thin mesquite and *huisache*.

That poor woman. The soles of our feet were callused, hers as soft and tender as the underbellies Daddy dreamed of, but she walked on fire with us. If you had to stand still, you stood on one foot and then the other. How sweet the reward of a bit of shade. We walked through heaven and hell to get the mail.

When there was nothing in the box, the road back home was a long one. But that was seldom the case. If there wasn't a letter, there was always something, a circular, a catalogue. The junkiest missive was reason to rejoice. It meant that as far out in the sand as we were, as hot and miserable as the live-long summer was, that someone, somewhere, was thoughtful enough to send us something, even if it was an advertisement or a bill. We would hotfoot it home, but not to read it. That was the old man's perogative, his and only his, even if it was a letter to Mother from one of her sisters.

Mother would take the mail—no matter how significant or insignificant it might be to our lives, no matter if it was thought to be Uncle Ben's answer to my space-on-the-brain dilemma—and leave it on the smoking tray Daddy kept beside his easy chair. When he came stomping in from the lease, deep-voiced and heavy-booted, smelling of oil, mud, sweat and tobacco, and now and then of whiskey, before he took off his tin hat, he would stride up to Mother, who by this time was back at the stove, pinch her on the butt and say, "Jennie, any mail today?"

"What came is where it always is."

The ritual began. He would settle in his chair and light his pipe and open the mail while we kids unlaced and removed his boots.

Then we would settle around and he would read the mail, first to himself and then aloud.

"Hummm. The Sir Walter Raleigh Smoking Tobacco Club wants me to join up for an initiation fee of a dollar fifty. For that I get a free tin of tobacco and a certificate of membership suitable for framing. And let's see. A good deal on future premiums."

"Why, how nice, Tice," Mother said. "That's awful thoughty of them. You getting a nineteen-cent can of tobacco and a certificate a soul would die for, and all of it only a dollar fifty! Why don't you go ahead and do it? It would look nice hanging on the wall over your chair."

"Well," he said with a big wink, "I'll have to thank about it."

"Now, come on, Daddy, quit putting it off. Billy's about to pee in his pants to hear what Uncle Ben says about space. You know which envelope it is. It's the one I put on the top, the one you shuffled to the bottom."

"Son," Daddy said, flipping the letter to me, "you're gettin' big enough to read your own mail. Take it to ye bed and digest it, and then tell us about it after I've had my bath."

"Do I get to read mine, too?" Bobby said.

"You didn't get any."

"I mean when I get some."

"Nope, not yet."

"Well, what about me, Daddy?" said a little girl voice. It wasn't Joyce.

It was Mother, fire in her black eyes. Her voice dropped back to a menacing alto as she told him, "Tice Porterfield, the day a son out-ranks me in this house is the day I leave. I've put up with your Big Daddy bull for as long as it was sweet and fun and family-like, but what you just did is an insult to me and my womanhood."

"Why, good God woman. You sound like October Ney. I was just giving the boy some credit he's earned, now that he's about to come of age."

"How large of you, Tice. Billy Mack, you run on and read your letter. And if any letters come for you tomorrow, you take them and read them too. From now on, no one, not Bobby or even Joyce, has to wait till Daddy gets home to open the mail. And that includes me, even if I get dozens a day from boyfriends in all the towns we've been through, and Tobin Drexler to boot. And no one, not even Daddy, has the right to go through another's mail without permission. Am I understood?"

We drew our heads down into our necks and remained silent, even Daddy, who whistled before he lowered his periscope. I went to my bed. Mother returned to the kitchen, where she threw pots and pans and slammed drawers.

Daddy got up and went to the bathroom, where, for the first time in years, he filled his own tub, removed his own armor and soaped himself with the harsh grit of Lava, mild to the scalding Mother had given him. That night, not so slick as a whistle, his belly sour from a slack-jawed supper, he did not sit by the radio and fall asleep smelling of aftershave, a shot of whiskey, Sir Walter Raleigh pipe tobacco and fatherhood. He smelled of smugness and stupidity and called-to-account (a new fragrance in our house), and of painfully mute regret, like a man who'd bitten off his tongue and soured the sugar that would ease him. He went out on the porch in his khakis and undershirt, and sat smoking Camels until the house was dark and silent with sad sleep.

We spoke no more of space, infinity and nothingness. There was too much of it between us.

But before I went to sleep, I imagined the conversation Daddy and I would have had if things had gone according to routine.

"Was Ben any help to ye on the space business?"

"A little. He said space doesn't go on forever, that it curves back on itself."

"That make sense to ye?"

"Oh, I don't know. It makes me feel better knowing that things, even space, have endings. Well, it's probably hard to separate the beginning from the ending in a parabola that comes back on itself, but Uncle Ben was definite about space not being infinite. So it has to have a boundary, and I guess I'm relieved. It was hurting my brain trying to imagine something going on and on without end.

"The only thing that bothers me now is nothingness. If the universe stops and there is nothing else out there beyond it, then what is nothing? Is nothing infinite? Or is it finite, too? I can't conceive nothing. In my mind, it keeps turning into pure space, which is something."

"Shit, son, that's where we came in. Let's get off it. Even I've got the sense to know no mortal can answer questions like that. So it's silly to keep at it."

"Daddy, you keep on looking for Diddy."

"Yeah, and I'm a damned fool. I hoped you and Bobby'd turn out to have more sense."

Doc Woolvin in Corpus was right though. I did grow and graduate to more serious pursuits of time and space and physical matter. I was trying to fathom in my dreams the profound curves of the Mermaid of Zennor's heavenly body.

Awake, I feared she was a mystery that might elude me, since Daddy was talking of still another move, not toward the Body of Christ and the curioshop siren of my pubescent imagination, but away, southwest, deeper into the bloody, brooding thorns of Mexican Texas. I wondered if I might run across Rosita Colorado. I remembered with a pang our goodbye, and found her easier to embody in my dreams than a mermaid I had not seen.

Bobby must have read my mind because he said he was sorry for having hit me with the board, and to make up allowed me to gaze upon his sketches of naked women. As an artist, I saw he was ahead of himself, certainly beyond me in his intuitive grasp of the Copernican delights of feminine curvature. I promised to try to get the old man to include him in my introduction to the mermaid. In return, he dedicated a poem to me he had written under the house, his face buried in one of his dictionaries, after I had barred him from the windmill. He called it "Of Our Disaccord":

> You are free
>   to try your wings
>   and do the things
>   I can't enjoin.
>
> We had our time . . .
>   and for a while
>   magic seemed the answer.
>
> Now winds of change have blown,
>   and the requiem behests

the cadence of the tolling . . .
while somewhere in the darkness
somber tears flood tiny wrinkles
meant for smiling.

The Tree, the Singing Fence and Chubb Talbot

DUVAL COUNTY
August 1942

There is, one knows not what sweet mystery about this
sea, whose gentle, awful stirrings seem to speak of some
hidden soul beneath . . .

—ISHMAEL, IN
HERMAN MELVILLE'S
MOBY-DICK

The Tree.

Joyce.

Her green eyes lit up the sweat on her pug nose as she stared at
it. The two of us were lost hiking on the naked and exhausting
prairie, somewhere out of sight of our new home, a lease house on
Macho Creek in the Conoco Driscoll Oil Field of Duval County, fifty
burnt miles from Zapata and the Mexican border. We were close to
despair when we saw the tree loom on the horizon, its billowing olive
green canopy a heady challenge to the bleached emptiness of the
adobe land and the bald dome of blue sky.

In our grateful minds the tree offered a redeeming reference and
lookout tower amid the vast and featureless savanna that confused
us. It promised the only relief on the horizon. There was the sun, but
it was directly overhead and stupefying in its mirages. The circling
buzzards were a source of unease. They followed as if expecting us to
wilt and collapse any moment into carrion. We saw not a pumpjack
or a gas flare, nor any evidence that anyone on two feet or four tires
had been out there. But now there was the tree.

I hugged Joyce and we jumped up and down, almost crying in
our hope of deliverance. "If we can climb high enough in it," I
hooted, "maybe we can see our house, or something that'll set us
straight." I didn't have to tell her to scoot for the tree. She hadn't

tagged after Bobby and me all over creation for nothing. Joyce was a tomboy, as game as they came and a kick to run away with and do things we weren't supposed to do. Which was why we were out there so far from the house. We raced to the tree.

It was huge, a spreading live oak, wide as it was high, broad and thick in its truck, expansive in its branches.

Instead of shooting up into the sky, its burly limbs, the girth of elephant trunks, reached out parallel to the ground and stretched out longer than a train of giraffes' necks before rising to the sun, creating a pavilion beneath which a herd of cows could walk horn-high and shelter themselves.

Between us and the tree was a shiny, five-strand wire fence, the first sign of man! The fence was so distant and airy it was almost an abstraction until we came upon its taut lines and sharp barbs, which sang like fiddle strings when we plucked them. We slipped under the barbs of the singing fence and made our way to the skirts of the tree, awed by its grandeur and cathedral calm.

Joyce started to step beneath the shade of its branches, but I held her at my side, cautioning that this tree was very alive, like any creature, and while it appeared to be majestically alone, and benign, it was probably home to a host of eyes and ears and mouths that would like nothing better than to pounce upon us. "It's like one of those New York City skyscrapers we see in the movies," I whispered. "We gotta make sure the tenants are friendly. You look up through the stories on the right, clear to the top, now, and I'll do the same here on the left."

"What're we looking for, brother?"

"Oh, I'd say anything bigger than a finger. If it's a lizard, I wouldn't bother about it. But anything bigger or longer we need to talk about before climbing up there with it."

"I already see the biggest spider I've ever seen in a web," she said with a shudder.

"I expect she has company, Joyce," I said, "but we'll have to put up with spiders if we hope to get to the top. Come on, now. I'm right beside you. Let's step under it real quiet-like and start looking. If you see anything, nudge me and point it out. But don't cry out or act afraid, okay?"

"Alrighty, brother," Joyce said softly, bugging out her eyes and

lifting her head back as far as she could. I reckoned she was as nervous as I was, but I couldn't think of anyone I'd rather have as a sidekick in situations like this. A wee bellibone was Joyce, but all spunk.

I guess my imagination and the hot sun and my cotton mouth
got the best of me. The tree was of such great and shaggy age that the
scales of its bark seemed to rise against us like thick armor plates, the
crevices between the plates so wide and deep we could lose a finger
in them. I first pictured the Spanish moss hanging from the tree as its
beard. But as I became more attuned to the tree and could separate
its body from that of its parasites, druidic stirrings heaped and
steeped in me. Blood rushed to my face as I began to see things I
hadn't seen in many lifetimes. Like a pagan Celt glopped on mistle-
toe mead, I took the moss to be the beards of malicious little wood
demons nipped and tucked away in hiding, but for the betrayal of
their chinny-chin-chins. Their whiskers moved to leprechaunlike
whispers as Joyce and I scanned the tree, but just as quickly their
hoary host silenced them, for now I heard the humming and breathing of the tree itself, expanding and contracting its coat of mail like a
great organ. I grabbed Joyce by the hand and pulled her behind me as
I made for the fence.

We were almost upon it when we heard a loud snap and a long
twang, followed by a furious whirling. The top wire of the fence had
broken under tension, and both ends were twirling and whorling
back upon themselves, throwing staples from the posts and gaining
momentum, each forming a great flailing tumbleweed of barbed wire
that in raveling back upon itself was creating a bristling cyclone to
confront whatever lay in its path. The end nearest us missed us by a
few yards, and Joyce and I stood in stupefaction, watching it tumble
and scream away into the distance, scattering birds and Mexican
hawks along it and the buzzards above, until what was left of the
standing fence relaxed and sagged, releasing the torque that had
driven the wild wire. It must have been a large ball by the time it
stopped, house-high, but it was so far from us it seemed no larger
than a prickly sweetgum ball. The same thing had happened in the
other direction—toward what I now know was the northeast—
except that the horizon was closer because of an almost impercepti-
ble fall in the floor of the prairie, and its ball of wire had dipped
down and gone out of sight. Now all was quiet on both ends. Joyce

and I remained still, afraid to move. Not even the fowl returned to the fence, although the buzzards glided back, their coiling cycle above us matching the malevolence of the wire.

Now, in silence's stead came the most welcome sound we had heard all morning. It was that of a man cursing. And it came from below the horizon on our left. Directly a broad-brimmed hat appeared on the rim, followed by the round figure of a bow-legged cowboy on foot, who brandished a fence-mending iron in his hand while shouting down invectives upon the fence, and all creation, including the almighty.

When he saw us, he came running, crying, "Are you babies all right?" I stiffened a bit at "babies," but replied, "Yessir. It missed us, just barely."

"I knew I was tasking it when I took that last bite with me come-along," he said, squinting down at us, his two red eyes beady orbs between red mutton chops that ran down to his chin. "If the bloody thing 'ad 'eld, it would have been the tightest fence in Christendom, ye can bet ye booties on that, me lad. I like me strings tight as rigging. Say, wat, laddie? What're you and the lassie doin' way out 'ere?"

"We're kind of lost."

"How come?"

"Our folks just moved into the lease house on the Conoco Driscoll, you know, on Macho Creek?"

"Aye, I know the place."

"Our father's the new switcher. T. C. Porterfield's his name."

"Well, I'm sure I'll be pleased to meet 'im, and ye shrimp as well, but not out 'ere, Laddie. Ye and ye sis are adrift in dangerous waters when ye out come this far."

"Where might this be, sir?"

"Off limits, 'at's what. Talbot is the name," the strange-talking cowboy said, extending to each of us a rough, waddy hand nicked with wounds and covered in red fur. "But call me Chubb. I'm fore-man for Miss Clara's Realitos Ranch, and this here fence I'm string-ing is the line between the ranch and the field she's leased to Conoco. You babies stay on ye own side of me fence. On this side is bad business. Now, I know ye lost, but mark this, boy, on the port side ye can only come to grief. So stand by for it, and live to a ripe old age, the both of ye."

"Bad business, sir? Grief, sir?"

"Aye. There are whales hereabouts! If ye see a white one, split your lungs for him! A white whale—did ye mark that, laddie? Look ye—there's something special in the wind."

I did feel a chilling waft of something in all that heat. I looked up at Chubb Talbot. I looked down at Joyce, who wrinkled up the sweat on her button nose and stared trustingly at me with her green eyes, squeezing my hand in hers.

Whales in the Coahuiltecan desert? This sailor who talks like Popeye is no saner than I, I who have seen a tree breathing bearded elves and a fence do the St. Vitus. Pray that our Chubby-Chubb-Chubbo is a guy in a white hat, even if it is black and his hands are bloody and his jeans sour. Oh, Lord, keep us in wonder, wandering and wondering for Diddy in this thirsty Eden.

"Sure," I managed to say to Master Chubb. "We don't want trouble. We just want to get home."

"That's me hearties," said he. "Ye tads come swim with me to the ranch house. Me lady'll give ye lunch and drink, and then I'll take ye home to . . . wat's 'is name?"

"T. C. Porterfield."

"Aye, Master Porterfield, it 'tis and t'will be forever more and amen, eh, me laddie? I 'eard yer earnest prayer, don'tcha see."

A mile down the rise, we climbed into the filthy seat of his battered red pickup and bumped across the flats.

FAY TALBOT AND THE WORD

If Chubb Talbot was a mouthy red mullet out of water, his wife, Frances, was a little house mouse who served us iced mint tea and dainty but delicious cold cucumber sandwiches garnished with dill. Perhaps I should call her a ship mouse, because Chubb (she confessed it was his doing, but that she hadn't minded) had done what he could with nets and ropes and great rusty anchors from Port Isabel to make the ranch house look like a boat, in specific what I came to understand was a nineteenth-century New Bedford whaler with the name *The Pequod* nailed over the front door. None of this meant anything to me except for the realization, informed by Frances, that Chubb was homesick. Before his reincarnation as a ranch foreman, he had started out as a merchant seaman from New Bedford, one whose people had been whalers and lamplighters of the world before whales had disappeared almost as fast as bison.

The family testament to this storied past was Melville's *Moby-Dick*, which I saw for the first time when Frances fetched it up to explain her husband's insistence on seeing the arid prairie as a sea, and its cattle as whale. Chubb himself was a busy foreman with his few wetbacks, hundreds of cows and thousands of acres, and was not party to these family soundings conducted by his wife, who grew in my estimation as our friendship deepened into the summer. I came to see her not as a mouse but as deep and sensitive an Ishmael as Chubb was a rollicking Stubb. She was as drunk on the word and as God-crazed as I found Melville and Emily Dickinson to be, only the first of five writers she would introduce me to before our voyage was over.

I had never heard of a public library until I met Frances. We moved so much across the outback of Texas we were lucky to find running water and electricity. Cultural amenities were not a consideration. Even years later, when I finished high school, there were no public libraries in one-hundred and fifty of the two-hundred and fifty-four Texas counties, and we lived in all the stingy ones. Practically none of the people we knew had books, this side of a Bible with gray whiskers on it. Now that Sessrymner was a gutted memory, a drought withered my reading, save for Bobby's dictionaries, which I read to keep up with him. Even there, neither of us learned to read diacritical markings, and slaughtered with our redneck tongues the uncommon words whose meanings we gleaned. Like our Celt fathers, we drank the heat of words like Vulcan sucked fiery metal, and bent them in the anvils of our mouths to our own purpose, mixing them with the almost-lost words of an oral tradition that ran on kindred tongues for hundreds of years throughout the British Isles. But as to reading material, by 1942 in the desert of Texas it was an event to get a Sunday paper and a Sears, Roebuck catalogue. So it was Frances who took me to my first public library in Hebbronville, an old cattle-shipping point suddenly rich with oil, twenty miles to the south. A few wealthy Catholic families, inspired by the literacy of their priests at the Franciscan College, had started the free library, and Protestant Frances was not only a patron but on-call as a substitute clerk at the check-out desk. A daughter of West Texas, Frances had become literate simply by reading great books, and that summer she launched me into European writers in translation whose names neither of us could pronounce. We got all excited about Goosestav Flauw . . . bert and Joe Hand Goe . . . the. We read *Madame Bovary* and *Faust* and discussed them. We also began reading that French Jew, Marcel Prow . . . st. His *Remembrance of Things Past* took us into the fall to read, and after Christmas I still wasn't finished when Daddy said we had to move on. So I never got to sum up Mr. Prow . . . st with Frances Talbot. She was the first to encourage me to keep writing in the journal I had begun, and she was my first guide to literature. I thought Daddy's natural sense of mathematics, and his innate mechanical ability, held him in good stead on his oil rigs, and that was beautiful. But after Frances Talbot the most beautiful things to me were stories, and, of course, the words that make them.

My father and his brothers were wonderful storytellers. They had the tricks and nuances down. They knew how to pause, how to lead the listener off in one direction and then jerk him back with a twist. They were great in describing characters, good with dialogue, and, of course, being rugged men, their stories were full of fun, action and adventure. Not much psychology. But they never put any of it down on paper. Bobby and I were the first in the family to scribble. To this day, when I hesitate to think how to pronounce French and German writers' names, I recall the resonantly nasal Ms. Talbot.

But it was her husband's historian, Melville, who transported us back a hundred years to Bedford and the Whaleman's Chapel of Father Mapple, where upon a wall Chubb's kinsmen, John Talbot, lost overboard near the Isle of Desolation, off Patagonia on November 1, 1836, was immortalized in the grandeur of Melvillean marble. Now this was a writer Chubb himself could smoke 'is pipe over, and it was through his and Melville's telling of Ahab's quest of Moby-Dick that I came to see the prairie and its beasts through rigadig Chubb's practiced cetology.

THE MYTH OF MOBY

Chubb Talbot was a landlocked sailor of fortune who found himself shipwrecked, but blessedly afloat, upon a wide-rolling prairie-sea of drought-drowned dreams and dreamlike reveries as the great shroud of the prairie rolled on as it rolled five-thousand years ago.

Like Job and Ishmael, Chubb was escaped to tell thee and me as we float for our day and night on a soft and dirgelike main.

But I got a little seasick on the metaphor.

One day, as I helped wise Chubb unravel the top strand of the fence and stretch it back in place, hammering it tight with staples, I asked him if there really was a Moby-Dick–like bull plying the port side of the fence, all full of bad business and grief, like he had said.

"Aye," he said, working the fence iron. "Our Moby-Dick is real enough, but seldom seen. He cruises the remotest latitudes of these waters—"

"Chubb," I said, "could you talk about him like the dry land bull he apparently is, you know, with legs instead of flippers—"

"Lord help such jollies!" he swore. "Crish, crash! here comes the jib-stay! Blang-whang! God! Duck lower, Chubb. No more talk of the white whale, says he. Oh, thou big white God aloft there somewhere on yon swells, have mercy on this small skeptical white boy by me side; preserve him from all men that have no bowels to feel fear!"

"Good gracious, Chubb. How you do go on."

"Just wait'll ye see 'im, laddie, and one day ye will. And then ye understand me flappin' lip, which is only mimic to me 'eart. It is not so much 'is uncommon bulk that separates Moby from the 'erd, or 'is peculiar snow-white wrinkled forehead, or 'is high, pyramidical white hump or even 'is ancient and godly eye, an orb as knowing as the first star of the firmament, an eye that takes in all in the sweep of 'is lordly 'ead."

"Then what is it, Chubb? If it isn't all these things you say about Moby, what is it?"

"'Is vivid aspect," says Chubb. "Whether seen gliding at high noon through a light blue sky, or looming in the moonlight, 'e has an inner sun or moon that makes 'is milkyway aura most eerily incandescent, as if 'e's super-charged by divine fire. But Melville escapes me, laddie, and without 'im I'm a'tongue-tied and all a'jabber."

"Is our Moby mean as Ahab's whale?" says I. "Does he have a deformed lower jaw? Is he indifferent to tarpoon? Is he heaped with unexampled, intelligent malignity, Chubb?"

"Aye, boy. Melville moves in thee, I see."

"Thanks to you and Frances. I've 'bout driven my family mad with the crew of the *Pequod*."

"Not fitter company," Chubb said seriously. And then in a wink he came back with, "not if ye be a fatalist."

"Mother is. Daddy isn't. Bobby's wary and Joyce is nervous, but game."

"And you?"

"I just get curiouser and curiouser, Chubb. And you're not answering my question."

"My answer is that this Moby's not mean, laddie. At least not unless 'e has to be. I reckon 'e's a good god in 'is home on the range."

"But I thought you said he was all bad business and grief."

"I expect 'e can be, laddie, and I wouldn't test him for the world. By that bad business I meant the other bulls and cows, especially the cow with calf, and in particular some of them big old black, brindled bulls with their harems. Ye know they're all Brahmas from India, and used to 'avin' their way, being sacred and all, even if we eat them over here."

"Yes, Chubb. I've seen 'em for years now, not out here yet but I know them. But no, Chubb. I remember you said something was in the wind, and to look for the white whale and split my lungs in warning, something like that."

"I meant that too. It's been my experience, and I been out on this ranch for years, though not as long as Moby, that 'e only appears when there's trouble a'brewin'. 'E seems to sense it, and suddenly 'e's 'ere."

"And what happens?"

"It stops. The trouble. Whatever it is, it subsides. The storm slackens. The wind rests. The ragin' waves of the deep stop their foamin' assault and settle down, and all is as quiet and still as death, except the creaking of the ship."

"Really, Chubb?"

"From what I've seen."

"The other bulls don't fight Moby?"

"All but one. All give him sway but one. One stands up to 'em."

"Have you seen them fight?"

"I've seen the others fight one another over rights to a herd, but I've never seen Moby fight the one."

"The one. This one. What's he like? Do you think he ever wins over Moby?"

"Not least so far."

"And yet he keeps coming back?"

"'E always comes back."

"Now, Chubb, it seems like to me Moby's strong, but not mean, or he wouldn't let this other one keep coming back."

"Oh, 'e never comes back. We find 'im dead or mortally wounded and have to shoot 'im. No. Moby doesn't mess around. That's for damned sure. Ask the Mexicans, they'll tell ye."

"Chubb, you're talking me cross-eyed. You're not making any sense."

"'Ow's that, laddie?"

"You say the one always challenges Moby. And I say Moby must not be all that mean to let him keep coming back. And you say no, that Moby never lets him come back because he either kills him or hurts him so bad he has to be shot. But here comes the one again. You can't have it both ways, Chubb. It's got to be one way or the other. That or you're pulling my leg."

"Laddie, me boy. The one that fights Moby is not always the same one. In every pasture there's always a king of the 'ill, one bull that stands out over the rest. He usually has the most cows and calves, and the lesser bulls take the hindmost. In that very same pasture there's always a young bull that's a comer, one so newly muscled and willful that he challenges the champion for the big 'erd. In our pastures here on the Realitos, there's always one that thinks 'e has the mustard to take Moby. So far, not one 'as done it, because we keep leavin' them to the buzzards. There's a boneyard of them from 'ere to the border. But 'e keeps comin' back, this one of the moment, laddie. And Moby keeps puttin' 'im down."

"Oh."

"There's more gab in this than work, boy. Have ye any other questions before we get back to the fence?"

"How many cows does Moby have?"

"None."

"Chubb Talbot!"

"I never said Moby has cows."

"You did!"

"I said in every pasture there's a king of the 'ill that 'as the most cows and calves, but I didn't mean Moby. 'Ere on the Realitos, Moby's above all that now. He used to 'ave a stampede of cows and calves and young bulls with 'im all the time, but now he's the old man of the mountain, the old god, and he stays aloof from the blood and rut, except as a referee, ye might say."

"And he remains strong enough to do that?"

"Apparently."

"How long will he last?"

"Well, not forever, laddie. Nothin' last forever, not even a monarch of the prairie, not even a god."

"Sad."

"Avast with ye, lad. 'T'isn't sad. It just is. Whatever's father is always killed. Whatever's killed is always father."

"I don't understand what that means."

He ruffled my head roughly with a rough old hand. "Ye will, laddie. When ye feel the young bull in ye, ye'll start to understand, and there'll come a time when the saddest thing you can think of is not bein' able to put old Moby down. And if ever ye manage to do it, you won't have time to shed a tear for the old god, because you'll be up to your 'aunches and 'orns siring and fighting off pretenders to your estate.

"Mark ye this, scamp. Reign long as Moby, ye time on the hill'll be brief as a joust with a bawd, compared to the eternity you'll spend in the boneyard, in gentle and affectionate recall with all the fathers before ye.

"Now what say let's get this fence fixed."

I looked at his hand that had touched my head. Chubb was an old bull himself, much older than Frances, as nicked and scarred and seemingly impregnable as the myth of Moby. I was glad I would not have to fight him. He was a load. But then I thought of my father and shuddered. That prospect was a load and a half.

The Tree and the Minotaur

That summer the tree still beckoned, and Chubb Talbot's admonitions could not keep us away. Joyce and I continued to slip away, slide under the fence and brave the branches of the oak, which became as safe to us as Mother's arms.

Sometimes, the cows were a problem, especially when a herd wanted to use the tree at the same time we did. When the cows were without calves, they were docile enough, and I could shoo them away. But this was when whatever bull was in charge was away grazing. When a bull was under the tree, forget it. The tree was the only relief on the horizon and therefore coveted not only by us and the cows, but by all creatures, arboreal or not. But when the cattle came, most everything skedaddled but the flies and tick birds.

Once, I got cocky when a big brindled bull saw us in the tree and came for it. I left Joyce in the branches, jumped down and kicked dirt at him, hoping to discourage him. But he moved up even more deliberately when I challenged. He wasn't so much angry as ominous. He planted a great, Big Foot Wallace eye on me. Big Foot had been one of the legendary goliaths of frontier Texas, known for his bovine strength and the unerring menace of his eye, and I could see Big Foot coming to get me, as he had Indian children, in the sham of a minotaur. Amassing his muscles, awesomely collecting himself, Big Foot shook his hump and moved faster toward me, breathing as if in hell-bent karma. I turned and ran for the fence, sliding under.

"Well, thanks a lot, brother," Joyce called from the treetop. "Now what am I gonna do?"

"Just sit tight," I said, safe behind the barbed wire. "He'll go away in a minute. His cows are drifting out."

Satisfied he had rid me from his stomping ground, Big Foot did turn away with a lazy waddle. But it was hours before Joyce could get down.

"What kind of bull did you say Big Foot was?" she asked on the way home.

"A Brahman. You saw the hump on his shoulders. That's the meanest kind. He would've killed me if I had been a man."

"Don't tell Mother."

"No . . . and Daddy neither, not if we want to keep coming to the tree."

I stopped and tugged at Joyce.

"Do you still want to come to the tree, even with the bull and everything?"

"Long as he's out of sight, Billy. Long as you promise to stay between him and me."

"Joyce," I said, "you don't worry your head about it. I'll take care of you. If that old bull comes around and catches us on the ground, I'll see to it he chases me and not you. I'll do like the clowns do in the rodeo. I'll distract him."

That night, lying in her bed, the thought of it chilled her. Maybe next time the bull wouldn't be so lazy in chasing her brother away. We were just two kids. The bull weighed a ton or more, and he had horns. Was the tree worth it? Was it worth our lives?

Joyce had a nightmare, woke everybody in the house. Mother took her into the bathroom and washed her face with cold water, all the while Joyce babbling about the bull bearing down.

"What is she talking about?" Mother kept asking.

Awake and standing by in my shorts, I kept biting my lip and rolling my eyes and saying, "I don't know, Mother, I don't know. Joyce's just having a bad dream, that's all."

Finally we got her awake and calm, and Mother put her back to bed and went back to sleep herself. I waited until things were quiet. I slipped up to Joyce's bed and pinched her.

"You almost blew it," I whispered fiercely. "You almost blew it."

"I'm sorry. I didn't know what I was doing."

"I'm not going to take you to the tree again if you can't handle it."

"I can handle it, Billy. I promise I can."

"God, girls! Yawl are more bother than you're worth."

The tree pulled at us, drew us back. It was too magical to resist. It stood out there on the prairie beckoning, its power stronger and stranger than the threat of a minotaur. We wished we could fly to it like the birds that nested in its boughs. But I had not learned to fly except in my head. So we continued to crawl through the barbed wire fence and walk toward it, eyes peeled for Big Foot. We swallowed bloody throbs, spat sticky cotton at snakes as the sun bore down on our bleached heads and buzzards circled. And the tree danced like St. Vitus in the crazy haze of refracted light. And arrow-tongued horny toads scurried at our burning feet. And, watching for the minotaur, we attenuated our eyes so far out of our heads that they drooped on thin stalks and made us dizzy as Dorothy in the poppies of Oz. We were frazzle-eyed wanderers in a fairy tale, breeching obstacles before reaching the enchanted place.

As we got closer on a good day, we would see that the cows were not under the tree.

"They're probably down at one of the windmills' tanks," I would say, and we'd run toward the bosom of the tree, nestling like chicks under the wings of a mother hen. In the sweet shade we were safe, and could turn our delirium down a degree past fear to pleasure.

For hours we would play in its branches, climbing and swaying and exploring, peeping into a cardinal's nest, pulling moss to fashion wigs and moustaches, matching ourselves in feats of climbing, chinning and swinging. One day, we climbed to the topmost branch that would hold us, and there in the crown we clung, and swore we could see the green rise and blue glint of the Mexican gulf in the distance to the east.

In the boughs we played so hard we did not realize it was growing dark. We did not know how late it was until we heard the cows lowing and gathering beneath us. The beasts had come to spend the night under the tree. We could smell their swarm, their hot breath and foul dung, and felt like the complaining tree bark the young bulls were scraping and sharpening their horns against was our hide.

"Billy," Joyce said, "what are we gonna do? You know Big Foot's down there with them."

"I know," I croaked.

"Well, what do we do?"

"Wait until morning, wait until they move. We have no choice."

"Mother and Daddy are going to die, just die."

"I know. They'll just have to, but we're not moving until it's safe."

"What if we fall asleep and fall out of the tree?"

"I'm too scared to do that."

Every time we dozed off, we came awake with a start. It seemed night would never end. At last, secure on the broad arms of branches, sleep insisted, and as we gave in to languor I felt my blood thicken and run in rhythm with the sap. I felt myself growing into the oak, like a graft, and felt my toes stretch and reach down with the tap roots into cool clay, and give suck to some deep quenching spring. In mossy dreams the night oak was a Tower of Babel, a broadcast booth from which the strangest gibberish came, noisemakers that buzzed and bandersnatched, churred, whirred, cooed, cawed, croaked, crunked, cricked and chirked, sawed, screeched, tuwhooed, whooped and whistled and strangled most mugiently and much more magnificently than Lewis Carroll. For all my initial caution, there were things in the tree I had never suspected, a host of jabberwocks and creepy crawlers that grow bold in the night and bump and thump and callooh, callay a body. Joyce came awake with a cry, and scrambled into my lap. "Brother, we've got to get out of here. Now I don't feel safe in the tree, not at night."

Fret thee not, little sister, for I think we are delivered.

I turned her toward the descent of the moon, which seemed to throb with greater luminiscence, and between us and its glow there appeared on the horizon the imperial white bull of Chubb Talbot's Melvillean tale. There was no mistaking His Royal Highness. Already, beneath us, Big Foot's sleeping cows, aroused by this great lord's appearance, were milling about and mooing.

"What is that?" Joyce said, her eyes round and moonstruck. In each of her pupils I could see the white humped bull, reduced like the Morton Salt box girls, and imagined his image being repeated, being burned like an icon into the eyes of the cows and calves and every creature within sight.

"It's Moby," said I, transfixed. Herman had been right, and so had Chubb. In his lofty, overscorning carriage, Moby looked down on us with the dignity of a thousand monarchs. Even in his flip-flop of Moby's motive power, I had to go with Chubb. In this Moby I saw no evil. Like Melville's White Steed of the Prairies, our Moby's whiteness was noble wampum, an unbreakable pledge of honor.

He lifted his great head to the heavens, and in a bellow round and deep as a Cathedral organ, he called the cows out from the tree, and they obeyed. All save Big Foot. He remained beneath us, black and bitter, moaning and wrestling with himself over what to do. At last, he went out from under us, but he did not put himself between his herd and Moby. He stationed himself between the herd and the tree. This was prudence on his part. I know he knew we were up in the tree, but that was not his attachment to it. It was a sturdy thing to put between him and Moby if Moby came down breathing hell.

"Come on," I said to Joyce, "let's get down now and go. We can walk to the fence. Don't run. Walk. Whatever happens, don't leave my side."

"What about Big Foot?"

"Joyce, his concern is Moby, not us. Now, come on!"

Every Apis eye followed us when we emerged from the skirt of the tree. I did not dare look at the animals, but turned away from them and, holding Joyce's hand, walked with tortured measure toward the fence. But I could feel in the boy bulls their charging instinct rising and jumping hot like boils beneath their sleek flesh. But they contained themselves under Moby's unyielding gaze.

Big Foot could not. He broke and moved toward us menacingly, followed by a few young braves from the herd. Joyce's grip tightened. She had not looked back, but she could hear them coming. The clump-clump of their hooves was increasing. I measured the distance to the fence. "Run, Joyce," I said, releasing her hand. "Run as hard as you can. I'll stay behind you."

I could hear them gaining.

I could hear them gaining.

Great god move the fence closer.

They are almost upon me!

"Go, Joyce. Go . . . !"

Blackout.

Silence.

Stirrings.

Moonlight.

Slow motion.

Joyce was sliding under the fence, ever so slowly, frame by frame inching past. She was turning now in her slide, and out of the moon dust she raised an arm, unclinched a forefinger, and pointed behind me. I was still running, as if on a treadmill, and, swiveling my head, I saw not Big Foot behind me but Moby. He was not running. He stood still, as if planted, perpendicular to my path, parallel to the fence, putting all his length and mass between me and Big Foot and the charging bulls. They almost crashed into him, but swerved away at the last moment, dissipating their force out of bounds. He spun around and was after them, lowering his horns and prodding them away into the void.

I was upon the fence by now, and felt myself being lifted down from the other side, and when I wiped away my disbelief I saw the face of Chubb Talbot, who, cradling me, passed me to the arms of my father, who bore my sister as well. Daddy buried his cactus face into our naked necks and wept, pricking and almost strangling us in his emotion. Even tough Chubb was bawling. He sounded like a bull, at least a minotaur.

Silent and red-eyed, we rode in the red pickup to Chubb's house, where Mother, paler than I would ever see her, even in the coffin, waited with Frances. Daddy got on the phone and called off the sheriff patrols and ranch posses and thanked everybody. Himself again, he said he ought to beat us, but figured we'd had enough for the night. At the lease house, Mother bathed and licked and cooed us to sleep. And when we awoke the next morning, we found her curled beside us. Daddy's bed was empty. He was already in his tin hat out on the lease, switching pipelines and tanks.

We never went to the tree again, but we'd conjure it in play and dreams, and remember, and it remained a golden olive green, and worth all the trouble.

As for Moby, we thanked him most profusely in our prayers. And we would see him again, but not for a long time. Meanwhile, what kept him in my mind, and even Joyce's, was not so much our own visions of him, which were awesome, but that of Daddy and Chubb. They said that when he came down off the horizon to intercept Big Foot and the young bulls, he did not seem to hoof it heavily across the prairie floor like the others, but glided silently across the expanse, coursing in the spangled moonlight like a hermit leviathan upon the great waters. None of us on the lee of the fence that lunar morning remembered him leaving. He vanished as he had appeared.

Bobby, who had been in Corpus with Uncle Earl and Aunt Arbie, upon his return wrote Joyce a poem of his impression of our adventure. In "Of an Old Moon," he ignored the tree and wrote of the moon:

> What grip hath thee on me . . .
> > old moon?
> That transfixed smile perplexes
> > my knowing.
> And my tendency to paw the ground
> > and snort in flanks
> > is an indication
> > of something!

The Lady or the Stallion?

Daddy loved the sweet, nutty smell of horses and mules, even their dung. He had grown up with the beasts, riding their backs, working them in the fields. Later, when the sap moved in him, he went courting in a one-horse surrey before he could get him a car. On Saturday afternoons on the prairie, he raced horses in the quarter mile at country fairs. He never felt surer of himself, not even at the wheel of a car or a rig, than when he was astride a big, spirited stud. He was in the saddle so much it became a part of him, like his hat and his boots, and eventually he got in the habit of using his saddle for a pillow, not only around the camp fire but in bed in the house. It took some doing for Mother to get used to that.

He had on the Conoco Driscoll a dream horse, a white-eyed, dappled gray stallion eighteen-hands high. War Cloud stood so proudly that Daddy could not reach up and touch the horn of Cloud's saddle. He mounted by jumping for the horn while spearing the toe of his left boot into the stirrup, like a boy would. Cloud was off and running before Daddy got his other foot over and his rump in the saddle. Every dawn, before he made his rounds checking the wells, he spent an hour in the stable, feeding War Cloud crimped oats, currying and brushing his coat. Evenings, he rode until sunset.

Daddy had outfitted War Cloud's stall with every amenity: a running water trough, salt block, tack box, blankets of various weights and pelts for changes in the weather. There was even a fan to keep the flies off, and, in a cabinet on the wall, every kind of salve and ointment and pill an ailing horse would need.

Mother said he'd furnished the stable for his stallion better than he had the company lease house for her and us kids.

"Shoot, woman," he said, "why do you haul off and say a thang like that?"

But he knew there was some truth in what she said. He was an old skinflint, just like his mother. About the only thing he splurged on was horseflesh, and that was just like Grandpa. But Grandpa could afford it. Daddy couldn't.

The oilfield, for all its saga and promise of riches, proved to be a better payday for the producers and landowners than it was for the roughnecks. Big surprise, right? The food chain is always rigged, no matter where or what the spiel. The money on a drilling crew seemed good, and it was while the rig was running. But it didn't stretch all that far when the well was finished and the producer had to shut down and move to another lease. A man on the drilling crew could be laid off for weeks before the rig was ready to spud in again, and it was hard to find work in between. Besides, you didn't want to blow your in with the toolpusher or driller, who was waiting to put you to work soon as he got the call.

That's why my father would stagger drilling work with roustabouting on a lease looking after wells and tank farms. The hourly wage was lower than on a rig, but the work was steady and the check came every week. And the living was nicer than it was follow-ing the rigs and taking what you could get in the way of housing. The lease houses weren't fancy, but they were off to themselves, a plus, and we made them home, however short our stay. If we had time in season, we'd grow vegetables, peppers and flowers. And drift though we did, we carried with us a menagerie of barnyard animals. But War Cloud was a luxury for Daddy.

Now Mother wanted to indulge herself as well. She prettied up the lease house, making oval throw rugs out of rags and hosiery for the living room and bedrooms. But she still wasn't satisfied. She wanted a new dining room suite. We ate at a table a neighbor had given us, and Mother hated it. It was rough and unpainted, and she kept it hidden under oilcloth. She had spotted a highly varnished oak table and six chairs at a furniture store in Benavides. She could see it in our dining room, covered with a lacy white tablecloth. The only catch was that the oak table and chairs cost a hundred dollars, and Daddy wouldn't go and look at that price. Had the woman lost her mind? He put his foot down and that was that.

It galled him to see her going around the place with a hurt look and a tremble in her voice. He remained aloof and on his horse, and all in all if it hadn't been for the tree and Moby and the Talbots it would have been a piss-poor summer.

That fall, Mother came down sick. She ran a fever and had chills, vomited all over the place. All along, we had sensed she was strangely fragile for all her power, and we lived in dread that the slightest ail-ment might crush her. Her dark nature was delicate and sensitive, and that took its psychic toll. And yet her will and drive was prodigious.

And so she pushed her tiny body beyond endurance, weakening her resistance against contagion until something flattened her. An old Mexican doctor came out from Benavides, bent over the bed, and concluded that Jennie, already rundown and anemic, had eaten something spoiled. "She has ptomaine poisoning," he said. "It'll be touch and go because her fever's so high and she's terribly dehydrated."

Mother lapsed into a coma, and we thought she was going to die. When she came out of it, briefly, as if to say goodbye, she cried and kissed us all and settled into a strange calm. The doc said there was nothing to do but wait and pray. Every morning he drove the fifteen miles from Benavides to check on her. Fay Talbot moved in with us to keep Mother full of aspirin and liquids. Every morning, she bathed Mother in bed and changed her gown and sheets. Daddy slept on the living room divan.

On the morning Mother was at her lowest ebb, Daddy went out to the stable where he thought we couldn't see him and bawled. He was a rough, profane man, but he found himself babbling to God, promising anything if Jennie got well. He got carried away, even promised to sell War Cloud and buy Mother that new dining room suite if God brought her around.

We were never sure if it was God, the old doctor's medicine, Fay Talbot's nursing or just her recuperative powers, but Mother recovered. The day before she was to get out of bed and try her legs, Daddy slipped out of the house, hooked up War Cloud's trailer to his truck and hauled the stallion to the stock auctioneer in Benavides. He sold his pride to the highest bidder for one hundred and fifty dollars.

Why he then went to the cantinas and got drunk has always been a matter of debate in the family. The reader's guess is as welcome as any. I lean to the side that has him drowning in self-pity for losing his head and making such a sacrificial promise to God. When it came down to death's door, he chose wife over horse. But now that death had been set back and the woman on the mend, a man as lazy to theology as my father was ready to second-guess himself, and to figure he might have gotten by without the loss of either.

After stupefying himself in the ointment of his shallow, now sentimental, now selfish soul, my father staggered to the furniture store and bought a dining room suite and a lacy white tablecloth.

When he got back to the lease house, he got us kids, laughing and whispering, to help him set it up in the dining room. That he was tooted made it all the more fun. We got Mother out of bed, helped her into her robe and slippers, and walked her into the dining room for the surprise.

Mother's heart rose. Daddy had done a wonderful thing.

Mother's heart fell. He was so drunk he'd bought the wrong suite. This furniture was painted blond. It was tacky, something white trash like that platinum Jean Harlow who broke Clark Gable's heart would buy.

"Well," he said, swaying beside her, "what do you think?"

She looked at her red-faced husband. She looked at her beady-eyed children.

"Why Daddy, my darlings," she said, leaning on tipsy Tice as tears came into her eyes, "it's perfectly beautiful. I love it. I thank you all, so much."

She confessed to us later that she hated it. Still, we used the blond table and chairs for years, moving them along with our other possessions wherever whim and work called us. Daddy said the chairs were a hell of a lot safer to sit in than War Cloud's saddle. Indeed, we used them for forty-seven years, until Mother really did die.

Now my sister has the suite for her dining room. It isn't just for sentiment's sake. She removed the blond finish and found the natural grain pleasing. I have to give it this. The suite's proved sturdier than War Cloud, and Mother.

THE FIRE OF DREAMS

It seems such a waste now, but in the oil boom days, when there was a glut of fuel, gas wells were considered something of a disappointment. The bonanza was in oil, so many a light-producing gas well was abandoned, left to spew its vapor into the wind. The stuff was volatile, of course, and foul, so it was piped up and out of the ground a dozen feet or so and lit so that, eventually, it would burn itself out. These oilfield flares, as we called them, dotted the Texas prairie like candles on a birthday cake.

Conservationists cringe at the memory. One flare could have heated the homes of a small town for twenty years. But this was in a green and bountiful time when prodigals were more easily forgiven.

To a child, the flares were wondrous wands that lit up the night and made the vast and mysterious prairie a warmer and more hospitable place. How epically aching was the sense of loneliness and desolation one felt at times on the Rio Grande Plain. We came in after the tent cities had folded, after the wells were drilled and the fields established. The farmer or rancher who had gotten rich off the royalties had long since moved into town, so we were left to shift for ourselves in his old home, or in a house the oil company had thrown up. The nearest neighbor would be miles away. We lived in many such a place, but the early winter at Conoco Driscoll proved to be our worst ever, as hard as any Daddy remembered from his Panhandle days. It was as cold by November as it had been hot in August.

The ice and howling wind kept us stoved up in the lease house. What roads there were in and out of the ranch were tundra and too treacherous to use unless you had a truck with tire chains, which Daddy did. Still, one ventured forth cautiously.

Icicles hung so heavy on the rural electrification lines that the lines sagged and broke, knocking out our power and party-line telephone. We lit candles for light and butane for cooking and heating, and we had the fireplace, which Daddy fueled with dried cow chips since there wasn't a tree within sight. But we were used to extremes of cold and heat, used to shifting for ourselves. It was invigorating, in a kind of Hole-in-the-Wall outlaw way, to be stuck in all that time and space in such an existential box. For it allowed interior freedoms and adventures as vast as dreams.

Bobby and I prayed Mother Nature would continue to keep us in quarantine so we would not have to return to school when the holidays were over. The school was as far away as the trees. A bus had to come for us at the crossroads miles from the house.

Meanwhile, we lost ourselves in the world of our imaginations. That's what staring at a fire in the hearth will do to you. Physically bound, unable to move much more than your mind, your head starts to do funny things. Now I understand what Frederick Remington meant when he carved into the mantel of his hearth: "We sat before earth's greatest philosopher—the fire." It was the hypnotic attraction of the flame that caused my father to puff on his pipe and muse. It was the fire that set me to dreaming. Like Chubb Talbot, I dreamt that our house was a ship, that the prairie was a sea and that the cattle and coyotes and snakes beyond our door were creatures of the sea: whale, dolphin, shark and eel. It is curious how the dream matched our actual circumstance.

We were not headed anywhere in our stilled ship, but were adrift, waiting not so much to be rescued as we were waiting for something, someone, to come along and relieve us from the tedium of ourselves. In my daydream spring had come and gone and we were dry-docked upon the prairie again, and it was nice to dream of warm days and warm companions.

In those summer dream days visitors came calling without invitation or notice, though never often enough to suit us. If they were tired of eating their own grub, they came at suppertime. If they came too late for the main course, they got milk and cookies or coffee and cake. Womenfolk tended to sit in the parlor, the men out on the gallery. The visiting went past dark, until kids were sleepy and ready for bed.

Goodbyes were drawn out. When callers finally tore themselves away, Daddy walked them out on the porch, down the front steps, out through the yard and the gate and up to their car, jawing all the way. They would get in, the man would turn the key in the ignition and start the engine. Daddy would stick his head in the driver's window, right in the fella's face, and keep on talking. The fella would let out the clutch and start moving slowly away, nodding and grinning but not saying another word in hopes that Tice Porterfield would shut up and let him leave. Daddy would move along with them, gradually pulling back from the window as the car picked up speed, but still yakking. He'd go all the way to the cattle guard, hang with them until they were going so fast he had to quit and let them go. Shoot. Do you think Tice Covey Porterfield turned around and headed for the house? No, friend, not yet. He would stand this side of the cattle guard and wave. We would stand on the porch and wave. We all would stand as we were and wave—Pa, Ma, Billy Mack and Bobby Lee, and little sister Joyce Dawn. It was flat and you could see forever in Mexican Texas. We would stand there and wave until they were a tiiiiiiiinnnnnnnnyyyyy speck on the horizon. Until they disappeared.

The plain dissolved into the sea again, the prairie house became a boat, the season turned back cold and we came upon a shipwrecked sea captain, a white-whiskered old salt in a dinghy, a kind of Santa

Claus who came aboard and railed us with good stories as we plied him with food and drink.

The salty Santa we really were waiting for was Daddy Harrell, Mother's father. One of the great freight hobos of his time, he was due in from wherever, and, his postcard said, he would make it by the first of December.

He hadn't, and Mother was fit to be tied. "There's something wrong," she told Daddy. "It's not like Papa to not show up this way."

"It's the ice," Daddy said. "If he caught the Texas Mexican Railroad through San Diego and Benavides, it's likely he elected to stay in Benavides until a thaw sets in. By the map he can reckon how far off the track we are, and only a fool would set out walking across the prairie in ice like this. There's frozen cow carcasses from here to the border."

"Papa's no fool, but then again, he is. You know how he gets up a head of steam. He swore he'd be here by the first. That was two weeks ago. I'm worried."

"Jennie, where do you think he is? For all we know, the railroad bulls could have caught him and put him in the brig."

"No, he's out here on the prairie. I can feel it in my bones."

When Mother said that, we listened.

We men—Daddy, Chubb Talbot, Bobby and me—made ourselves a search party. Chubb put ice shoes on his saddle horses, and, bundled up and fortified with whiskey-milk, we set out the next morning east across the flats toward the Texas Mexican tracks.

"If he's out there," Daddy had told Mother, "he'll be at one of the gas flares. The old man's got more sense than you give him credit for."

We rode toward the water depot between Concepcion Creek and Realitos, each rider branching out to cover as many flares as we could while keeping a line between the lease house and the railroad track.

Each flare was a hearth, a circle of warmth and shelter for every creature on the ranch. Implacable enemies called a truce to bask before the rings of radiant heat. And that is where we found Papa Harrell. He was curled up asleep in his bed roll beneath a flare, sharing the accommodations with cattle, coyotes, rabbits, prairie dogs and prairie hens and thousands of scorched bugs. At least the hibernators, the cold-blooded rattlesnakes and horned reptiles, were not out.

"Hell, boys," he said, "you needn't have come for me. I'm running late, but I would've made it in another day or so. I had it down to where I could make four or five flares a day before tuckering out. Ain't this cold a ring-tailed tooter?"

He was a marvel, and I loved to look into his handsome face. Compact and hard as an anvil, he had thick, iron-gray hair, a fine-boned nose and eyes so blue and naughty they promised fun. Women were drawn to him, and he was a scandal with his loves and wives. This same romping maleness he had passed onto his son, our Uncle Glen, but where Papa Harrell was strong, Glen was weak. The sisters said their brother's dipsomania was Daddy Harrell's fault. They reasoned he had been so easy on them that he had to be hard on Glen. I knew the tough side of Papa Harrell, just as I knew my father's, but I figured Glen's wasted life was his own fault.

I gave Daddy Harrell my seat in the saddle, and sat behind him on the horse, one arm around his waist and the other holding his tote bag, laden with gifts. We made for home, some eight miles west.

We were waylaid by a neighbor's misfortune. South of Concepcion Creek we saw a dark rope of smoke rising on the horizon farther south, and Chubb said the only thing out there that could make that much smoke was a house or barn burning. He said it had to be the line cabin or barn of Juan De Ariste, a caballero on the 666, the ranch on the border of Conoco Driscoll. "Come on," he said. "Let's ride hard. Juan's got a wife and new baby in that shack."

We and the heaving horses were spouting frost and dry-mouthed by the time we got to the De Ariste place. A huddle of people stood before the smoking ashes of a burned-out shack. Before them in woolen robe stood Father Flaherty, the Catholic priest at Realitos. He was swinging a pot of incense and chanting a prayer: *Non intres in judicium cum servo tuo, Domine, quia nullus apud te justificabitur homo, nisi per te omnium peccatorum ei tribuatur remissio. Non ergo eum, quaesumus, tua judicialis sententia premat, quem tibi vera supplicatio fidei christianane commendat: sed gratia tua illi succurrente, mereatur evadere judicium ultionis, qui dum viveret, insignitus est signaculo sanctae Trinitatis: Qui vivis et regnas in saecula saeculorum. A-men.*

We horsemen, sensing tragedy, held back but for Chubb, who

knew everyone. He got off his mount, removed his hat and walked up to a tall Anglo, the 666 foreman, Seth Joiner. They talked, and Chubb joined them. His Irish face drained of color, Chubb rejoined us with sad tidings. Juan De Ariste's young wife and infant son had perished in the fire. Juan, who had spent the night in Realitos buying supplies, had ridden up to find the consumed cabin in a last paroxysm of flame. He had rushed into the dying pyre, only to find the hideously baked bodies of his wife and child, now covered by tarpaulin and laid upon the bed of a truck. I stole a long look at Juan De Ariste. He was a mature man about the age of the foreman and priest, even in soot and sorrow a splendid figure in his wide sombrero and snug black charro pants, which he wore with a proud and slender-waisted carriage. There was in his bearing a quiet, aristocratic élan I had not seen in a Mexican before. He had his arm around a grieving boy, whose face I could not see. About De Ariste were handsome caballeros, standing stiff as sticks in their grief and in the cold, cutting wind as the priest blessed the ashes of the fire and the dead. When Father Flaherty was finished, the caballeros stirred as if choreographed in elegant movement, the spiked rowels of their spurs singing as they turned away from the smoking ruin and followed De Ariste to black-shawled women who fingered rosaries and silently chanted prayers. The caballeros hoisted their women upon the backs of horses and waited for the priest.

Pudgy Father Flaherty, who lifted a finger for them to wait with his horse, approached the tall foreman, who had beckoned him.

SETH JOINER: Father, Juan and his nephew can stay at the main house annex until spring, when they're supposed to go back to Mexico. My wife and kids are in San Antonio until May, so there's room. I won't mind long as they keep their peppers out of my chili.

FATHER FLAHERTY: That's good of you, Seth. But I'm sure they'll want to stay with their own people. The Herreras will take them in.

SETH: It's going to be tough. Juan and the boy lost everything except what's on their backs. I know for a fact that their money went up in smoke. It was several months of savings they had in a coffee can. I know Juan kept it there to send home to El Burro. I tried to get him to put it in the bank at Benavides or Hebbronville, but he wasn't having any of it. He said he felt better being able to look at it every night before turning in. I guess I ought'n to be talking about money when he's lost a wife and baby, but—

FATHER: The church . . . we will try to do what we can, but . . . well, you know we have a poor parish. But we will bury the wife and child and see that Juan and the boy eat. We can feed them, and I guess the whole retinue—

SETH: It isn't all your responsibility. Father, I can't speak for Mr. Wade and the Triple Six Syndicate, but as their foreman, as the man who hired these people, I feel the outfit ought to bend a little and chip in, too.

FATHER FLAHERTY: (He bit his chapped lips and looked up at the cowboy.) Now, Seth. You're confusing the hell out of me. Didn't you just fire Juan and his boys last Friday? I hear you threw a fit and gave them their walking papers, told them they had to be off the place when the cold snap broke.

SETH: (He looked down and nudged the earth with a boot toe. He stretched his neck and gawked at the sky. He slapped his dirty felt hat against his thigh.) I damned sure did. And I'd do it over again. I'd do it in spite of everything. Well, no, I guess I wouldn't. But how was I to know that . . . ?

They stood silent for a moment.

JUAN: (He left the other mourners and approached the priest, keeping his sombrero over his breast.) *Padre, ya es hora de irnos, con su permisso.*

FATHER FLAHERTY: *Siga usted, Juan. Hasta prontito.*

SETH: Juan. *Lo siento mucho.*

JUAN: *Gracias. Hasta luego.* (He turned to go, but paused, saying to Seth:) No hard feelin's, amigo. Adios.

SETH: (Nodding and kicking at the ground, gave Juan the Indian goodbye, a sweeping hand gesture, right palm flat and moving from the left shoulder to the right hip, that is the highest sign of respect between equals.) *Te deseo, de corazon, que venzas cada quebranto y goces cada ilusion. Vaya con Dios, amigo.* (I wish, from my heart, that you may overcome every difficulty, and enjoy every dream. Go with God, friend.)

SETH: (turning back to the priest) It is hard out here.

FATHER FLAHERTY: It is that. It is that. Well, I've got to get back to the rectory. You talk to Wade or whatever, see what you can do for Juan and his boys. I'll see they're out of your hair soon as the weather turns. (He looked at the ashes.) Lord, that old shack was dry. Went up like a matchbox. See you, Seth.

SETH: Thank you, Father.

FATHER FLAHERTY: Seth? One thing. Exactly why did you fire Juan and his boys? I thought they were good hands.

SETH: Father, they were the best.

FATHER FLAHERTY: What was it, then?

SETH: They wouldn't work machinery. They were purdee cowhands, the best at riding and roping and branding and all such as that. But when it came to driving tractors and bailers and fixing windmills and doing general mechanic work, why, they flat wouldn't do it.

FATHER FLAHERTY: The old story, huh?

SETH: (with a rueful laugh) Yep. You know, vaqueros used to do that all the time, making those old distinctions. Even the old gringo cowboys did it. But these fellows were the worst. They're throwbacks. Father, they wouldn't touch anything that had metal in it, except spurs and the rigging in halters and saddles and the spangles on their pants. They'd work with leather and hemp and animals, and that was it. Technology's all around them, but they were contemptuous of it. I told Juan I was surprised they'd come up out of Mexico in such a modern conveyance as a truck. I told 'em they should'a come on horseback, since they were so uppity about locomotion. They acted like knighthood was still in flower.

FATHER FLAHERTY: How'd they treat your horses?

SETH: Beautifully. Hell, they know the horse better'n we do. The cow was another animal entirely. They were, to my way of thinking, brutal toward the cow. In fact, they didn't like to be called cowboys or vaqueros. They say they are caballeros, strictly horsemen. I can't blame them. I'd rather be identified with a horse than a cow, especially considering what we do with cows.

FATHER FLAHERTY: Yes, and the sad thing is that out here, which is really their country and not ours, Juan and his pure vagabond riders are the cows. Like you say, they're headed for their last roundup. Not many left of them. You're right, Seth. They're throwbacks.

SETH: On an outfit like this, we can't afford specialists. That's it. Plain and simple. What kept my dander up was that Juan was so above it all. It wasn't what he said. It was how he carried himself. Made me feel like a common laborer, which, to tell the truth, is what I am.

FATHER FLAHERTY: It's hard out here.

The priest left with the Mexicans, and we headed our horses home, leaving Seth alone at the ash heap.

As full of stories and adventure as Daddy Harrell was, he couldn't make us forget Juan De Ariste's wife and baby. Not even his tote bag of gifts he had made for each of us at his anvil—rings and knives and exquisite tools—could lift us from our melancholy. One night before the fire, Mother burst out crying, saying we knew that poor girl. She went to her bedroom and sulled, refusing to explain what she meant.

Daddy Harrell meant to stay into Christmas, but the close house and our mubblefubbles were too much for him. That and the indoor toilet. All his life he had relieved himself outdoors. "Tice," he said, "I've always liked you as a son-in-law, for what it's worth, and I'll go on liking you. But I'll be damned if I'll spend another night under the roof of a man who shits and pisses in his own house. I'm out'a here tomorrow. Ridin' the freight to Little Rock."

We all stood on the iced porch the next morning and waved until he was a tiiiiiiiinnnnnnnnyyyyy speck on the eastern horizon. I could see him laying in wait for the Texas Mexican to come around the bend at the water tank north of Realitos. As the train slowed, he would hop, agile as a cat, aboard an empty box car for the long rattle north. I thought he was right about a lot of things. I never got to ride the rails as a bum, but when I get the chance I'll sure enough shit in the woods.

Daddy Harrell hadn't been gone a day or two before a subdued Chubb Talbot appeared at our door with a boy about Bobby's age. We recognized him as Pepito, son of Señor and Señora El Colorado Grande and little brother to Rosita, and welcomed him. "What are you doing way out here?" we cried.

The answer was a killer.

He was the "nephew" of Juan De Ariste Father Flaherty and

Seth Joiner had been talking about. He had followed Rosita to Eagle Pass, where she had, indeed, lived with an uncle while working in a five and dime. But she had met this older man, a caballero from El Burro across the border, and had married him and had borne a son some time before he and his saddlemates had gone to work on the 666. She had joined her husband at the ranch, and had sent for Pepito to come and live with them. And, well, Mother had been right.

It was the saddest, strangest, most cockeyed winter. And it wasn't over.

Behold, a Man Named John Came Out of the Campo

I was miserable and so hard to get along with that even Daddy was glad to see Uncle John Pierson burst upon the scene, bearing gifts and breathing whiskey. Alcohol was the antifreeze in his radiator, and he exuded excitement and a sense of the road that my father, Prometheus bound, must have envied.

The moment John strode into our hot little rooms, startling us with his icy stamp and frostbitten visage, burly as a bear in his great coat, I felt exhilaration.

"Tice," Uncle John said vigorously, shaking Daddy's hand and reaching to hug Mother. His voice was piston-powerful, like the engine of his roadster idling out front.

"Cut off ye engine and stay a while," Daddy said. At this, Mother sprang for the medicine cabinet in the bathroom and got the sour mash. Daddy never so much as gave her a look. He took a snort too. Just one, and by his graciousness Mother and I felt he was not going to haul off and demand to know where Grandpa's fiddle was.

After the niceties and family catching up, Uncle John seemed impatient, as if something pressing but sweet awaited him on down the road. Shortly, he asked when I was supposed to return to school. Mother said if the freeze didn't let up the holiday might last into the first bud of spring.

"Then pack some duds, Billy," Uncle John roared, "I'm taking you with me, boy. That is, if Tice and Jennie are agreed?"

"What for?" Daddy said.

"I've started me a new venture down in Brewster County," Uncle

John said. "Pierson Resorts is what I call it. I've bought me a moun-tain, just off State Highway 118 about halfway between Alpine and Nine Point Mesa. I'm selling the mountain off in lots, a little down and a little bit a month. Already got my signs and streamers up."

"Who in the hell would want to buy way out there?" Daddy said, leaving his mouth flapped open until he added, "The last time I was way out there, the road out of Alpine—and it's a rough mother—petered out before it got to the Mexican border. The only people who take it are ranchers or hunters."

"That's all about to change, Tice."

"Because of your mountain lots?" Daddy said, heh-hehing above his skepticism.

"No. Because the state and the federal government are fixing to turn the Big Bend Mountains on the Rio Grande into a national park. They've already started extending State 118 through Nine Point Mesa and the Christmas Mountains. By next year, it'll run par-allel with State 227 right on into the road between Study Butte and Boquillas on the river. Pierson Resorts will be set to take earliest advantage of the traffic that'll build up when the tourists and road-houses and merchants start swarming down."

"Whad'a'ye need Billy for?"

"Company, mainly. As you and Jennie know, Tice, I'm a man slightly ahead of my time, which means, being a sociable fellow, I get lonesome out there ahead of the herd. I've beat the band to Brewster, so I'd welcome Billy's company. Besides, he can help me stake out the lots. And he'll love the big country and the big views. It's some-thing else, I tell you."

"Why, Daddy," Mother said, "I think Billy'd have a wonderful time. As long as John will bring him back in time for school, when-ever it starts, I don't see any harm in it, do you?"

"Well, no, I guess, long as ye put it thataway. We'll have to give him some money—"

"No you won't," Uncle John said. "I'm going to pay the boy wet-back wages, so he'll have plenty of money for the things he'll need, which won't be much. I'm furnishing room and board in my trailer, and you both know I'll look after him real good, just like a daddy."

"Just don't lose 'em like ye did my dead daddy's fiddle," Daddy said.

John chose to ignore the remark.

"Billy Mack," Mother said quickly. "Run on to you and Bobby's room and start packing your things."

"Mother, I want to go," Bobby said.

"Nope," Daddy said. "Two peckerwoods is too much for any man without a woman. Ye don't have a woman now, do ye, John? Whatever happened to Earline down 'nere in Evenin' Shade?"

"She run off with a Mexican who painted Aztec virgins and bullfights on black velvet," John said with a grin.

"Broke your crocodile heart, didn't it?" Daddy shot back with a leer.

"Hell no," John said with a triumphant wink. "I paid him a hundred to take her away from me. She thought it was because he loved her."

"Now you men beat all," Mother said lightly, changing the subject to admiration of John's car, which was a sporty red MG convertible. "How'd you drive that light little thing through the ice?" she wondered.

"Custom-fitted chains," he said smoothly.

We shot forth in his roadster, tire chains biting the ice, bearing southwest toward Laredo and the border, where we would pick up the highway northwest along the Rio and follow it west four-hundred miles to Alpine and the Chihuahuan Desert beyond. Before we were over the first cattle guard out of the Conoco Driscoll, John was declaiming above the thrust of the engine and the hum of the ice chains about the great things we would do the rest of the winter. We would turn a mountaintop into a hideaway for the rich. We would open a racetrack on the Mexican side and make a million racing quarterhorses. It all sounded so grand and fancy-free compared to the dreary quarantine of ice that lay upon my family behind us. Uncle John looked so cavalier, even heroic at the shaking wheel of the roadster.

But John Pierson was a man whose guardian angels were as mercurial as he was. One minute he would be in high cotton, the next down and out in a ditch. In the flush of the moment, I had forgotten the latter, this comeuppance to which he was heir. Just before we crossed the county line, the gods looked down and, remembering John's inordinate hubris and crossed stars, conspired against him.

From out of a side road, hidden by mesquite, loomed the long, cat-tailed pursuit car of the high sheriff, known far and wide not by his birthright, but as Boo Boo. Boo Boo wailed and flashed us down, moved up into John's handsome, ice-sculpture face like a brutal heat wave. "You musta been making seventy, at least that," Boo Boo said. "It's a wonder you didn't throw your ice chains and kill a cow."

"That fast? Well, gosh, Sheriff. I don't think the little Blimey can do that. To tell the truth, I wasn't paying attention. Billy and I were flapping our jaws, and I guess we might have crept over the speed limit. Lonely highway, nothing to compare yourself against. Didn't mean to break the law. 'Preciate you stopping us, though. John Pierson's the name. I guess you know the Porterfields on the Conoco Driscoll. Billy here's my nephew, so to speak."

"Hidy, Billy. Tice and Jennie know where you are?"

"Yessir. You know school's let out for the weather, and I'm going down to Alpine with Uncle John."

Boo Boo turned cordial. But he wrote out a ticket charging John with speeding. I knew he would. Never did Boo Boo not write a ticket, regardless of the circumstance. Well, it was something to do, an event in the life of a lawman out there on the lone prairie. Chubb Talbot said Boo Boo would write his mother and Jesus Christ a citation if he caught them hurrying past the stations of the cross. And pious Boo Boo was a mother's boy—he had never married and lived with his widowed mom.

When he took the ticket, John should have let well enough alone. But he was kin to no such restraint. Boo Boo had no more than turned back toward his big, bad car, still switching its tail slowly in the wind, when John said something in Spanish which I won't repeat here.

It was a cheeky obscenity, one particularly aimed at the fat ass of authority embodied in Boo Boo. Dumb, I thought. Boo Boo could spit out Tex-Mex like a peon. And when he heard what John had said, his thick back snapped, his head shot up and he turned back toward us and planted his sorry-that-you-said-that-bub pig eyes upon my stupid-no-account-step-uncle-who-could-not-hold-a-candle-to-my-father.

John's hummy breath didn't help matters. So Boo Boo and the justice of the peace found it easy to sentence him to the pokey for two weeks or a fifty-dollar fine. It was John's call. I was relieved to see he had the money.

On the road again, I was more sober about what might lie ahead.

BEHOLD, A MAN NAMED JACK CAME OUT OF THE CAMPO

We were selling lots upon the mountain, my Uncle John and me. At least that was our intent. But no one had come to our desert. Happiness was not, as our streamers and pitiful little signs suggested, a retreat on Mount Morning Air.

We approached Christmas out on the ragged road in front of the mountain in a tiny trailer house that shook in the wind of all that desolation, every day Uncle John falling deeper into the Second Book of Samuel, and his second bottle of Jack Daniels, while I played solitaire—not with cards but with the primordial play of hawk and cloud and prairie dog, burrow, butte and arroyo.

Magnificent scenery. A good place to hide, but who would want to live there? History said no one, and prehistory seemed to suggest the same thing. The mountain had been there for millions of years, unperturbed but for the elements, pretty much left alone until Uncle John came along. Still, John was encouraged by the truck traffic along the road. Huge convoys bearing bulldozers and other earth-moving tractors bellowed past us toward the dead end of the road at Nine Point Mesa, some twelve miles south. They began clearing through the rugged mesa, exploding rock with dynamite, and John said they'd be through the Christmas Mountains by Christmas. "You just watch," he said, "the snowbirds will be right after them, hungry for a home in the sun."

Surely, he was joking. Christmas was a week away, and just from reading the map I could see it would take the road crews until Christmas after next to level and pave the nine miles to Big Bend. "Uncle John," I said, "I don't want to be a kill-joy, but it looks like to me we're way early on attracting snowbirds. Ought'n't we come back after a year or so? The park's not even developed yet."

"The early bird gets the worm, Billy. There must be a hundred men on these road crews, and that's not counting the dump truck drivers. They know what's coming down out here. They know they're paving a way to fun in the sun and profit. You just watch. They see our signs and streamers. One of these days one will stop and look at a lot, and he'll go home and tell his old lady, and they'll come out and buy one. The word'll get around. It may take a year to lay the road and everything, but we're getting a head start. As a matter of fact, I've decided to launch a gala Christmas opening of Mount Morning Air."

"You mean Christmas of '43?"

"I mean this Christmas!"

"Why, that's eight days from now."

"That's right," he said. "No time to waste. It's now or never, William."

He reminded me of an old prospector playing out his last grub stake, a little crazed by it all.

He sped into Alpine in his roadster to place an ad in the weekly *Avalanche* inviting everyone to our "Gala Christmas Opening!" He came back with balloons, cartons of cokes, a hock shop drum and trombone and a galley proof of the ad, which the *Avalanche* would print two days before Christmas. The ad said Pierson Resorts was offering a Christmas special on mountain lots for only $25 down and $5 a month, come one come all.

"What's the drum and horn for?"

"To greet every hundredth customer," he said. "Make a big ta-do over it. Every hundredth customer gets his picture in the paper and a ten-percent discount on a lot."

Every hundredth customer? Now I was still a kid, but there were times when I was astonished at Uncle John's lack of proportion and scale. I didn't mind correcting him if I saw him heading hell-bent for disappointment. Our mountain was small, and slicing the lots wafer-thin, we hadn't been able to get more than fifty lots out of it. But compared to the available population, Mount Morning Air was a Rushmore. I pointed out a story in the *Avalanche* only the week before that showed that in Brewster County's six-thousand-mile radius, there was one person for every 1.1 miles, which meant that in the twenty-two miles between us and Alpine we'd be hard pressed to come up with two-dozen residents. Hadn't we better go ahead and root and toot for every sucker that showed up, just to cover our bets?

Uncle John studied that over and said I was right. We'd give everybody the big treatment.

Well, we went ahead and blew up the balloons and hung them between the streamers, most of which had already flapped to death, and Uncle John painted larger signs and arrows to line both sides of the road. Every morning he stationed himself out front in a lawn chair, watching first one horizon of the road and then the other with a brass spyglass left over from Marco Polo's travels to China.

The road crews had quit for the holidays. Over the next six days, a couple of pickup trucks gave us a moment's panic. They turned out to be ranchers who saluted with a forefinger to the hat brim in passing. And that was it.

Maybe the paper forgot to run the ad, Uncle John reasoned. That night he drove to Alpine to check it out. The *Avalanche* was closed, but he found the paper in a sidewalk stand, and the ad was in it. Well, he said when he got back, we're just impatient. It takes time for new things to catch on. So let's just sit tight. And that's what he did, right on up to Christmas Eve, sitting out front of the trailer, spy glass between his legs, sipping hum and reading aloud the good book, which he did with an actor's eloquence. And yet, there was an innocence about him that was disingenuous and touching.

To keep my blood running, that raw afternoon I went up on the mountain to hunt arrowheads. On the northeast horizon behind us, I saw a speck of a man, and what appeared to be a dog following him, making their way toward us from the Del Norte Gap. I drew Uncle John up on the mountain. He trained the spyglass on the figures.

"Friend or foe?" I said.

"Now it came it pass," he said, "that after the death of Saul, when David was returned, now it came to pass that, behold, a man came out of the camp with his clothes rent, and earth upon his head—"

"Who is it?" I said.

Uncle John lowered the spyglass.

"What does it matter?" he shouted. "He's a sight for sore eyes. Could be our first client. March out the band!"

I beat the drum and he blew the horn, and we went to greet what turned out to be a very startled and exhausted tramp, in tow with a baby billy goat. The dust upon his brow had turned to frozen tundra, and he almost collapsed in our arms. We helped him to the trailer, laid him upon John's bunk and revived him with whiskey.

"You've come to buy a lot?" Uncle John began warmly, taking a shot himself. He removed the man's shoes and socks. He poured a touch of the bourbon into a palm and rubbed his hands briskly until they were warm, applying them to the stranger's frostbitten feet for a stimulating massage.

"Oh my god," the old fellow said through his beard. "I've died and gone to heaven. I thank you, sir. My dogs were killin' me until I lost the feeling in them."

"You want a lot, don't you?" Uncle John said.

"Oh, rub 'em to a fare-thee-well," the tramp said. "I could stand this all day."

"Well, yes," Uncle John said, "what pilgrim wouldn't. But what I meant was business. You've come for a little business, eh?"

"Business?"

"You've come to buy a lot."

"A what?"

"A lot, a retreat on Mount Morning Air. Make you a good price."

"No," the tramp sighed. "I have no money."

"Hell, why did you come to us?" Uncle John said.

The tramp looked at us strangely. "I haven't come to see you," he said. Suddenly he smiled and said, "I was just out for a walk, and overdid it."

Rather than cry, Uncle John crossed his eyes and guffawed. "Oh," he played at laughing, "that's priceless. Went out of your way a bit, did you? Lord, man, what's your story? We don't have much in the way of vittles, but you're welcome to sup with us. Tomorrow's Christmas!"

"I accept with pleasure, and I thank you," the tramp said, adding that his goat would thank us for a piece of stale bread and some water.

I fed the tethered goat and heated tins of soup while the tramp, loosened by hum, began his story.

Right off, he admitted he was an escapee from an asylum. The time and place of his incarceration he did not make clear. All he said was that he had been placed there because he had lost his memory, and therefore his own sense of himself. He had escaped so that he might find himself. He had looked everywhere upon the road of life that unraveled before him, and he had yet to find himself. In his travels, in his marathon walk to identity, he avoided public thoroughfares, staying to the woods and fields and outbacks. Now and then he was drawn to towns, but always on the sly, trying to be as invisible as he could be in his search for himself. He had looked in telephone books, death notices in the newspapers, deeds at courthouses, almanacs, dictionaries, *Who's Who* and guides to periodical literature in libraries, even buttonholing great characters in fiction—especially detectives like Holmes—to see if they had heard of him. He would have preferred to approach real detectives rather than imaginary ones for clues to himself, but he couldn't risk it, being a fugitive in the manner of a Professor Moriarty.

"And what name do you look for?" Uncle John said. "Do you have a sense of your own name?"

"I don't know why," the tramp said, "but I always inquire about Rexrote, as if that's my name. I figure it might be because it comes to me every time I inquire about myself."

"How do you spell it?" I said.

"I spell it R-e-x-r-o-te."

"No," I said. "That's different. I was going to say there's a little place in Oklahoma called Rexroat, but it's not the same spelling."

"I bet it's r-o-a-t," he said.

"Right."

"Then I must go there and inquire," he said earnestly, "because roat is the obscure spelling for rote. It was a Teutonic twist on the Celtic *chrotta*, a medieval fiddle. Gradually, roat and then rote came to mean to perform something by habit."

"So your name, if it is your name," Uncle John said, "might mean the king of fiddling."

"Or of rotting," the tramp said with a shrug. "There are several possible meanings. A rote is a measure of weight, a wheel of torture, a roaring of the sea, a phalanx of warriors. To rote is to rotate, to flutter. But I think at bottom it is to be rooted in practice and skill."

"And here you are," said I, "uprooted in a most befuddling way."

"Yes," he agreed, sighing.

"I can see you've done your homework," Uncle John said earnestly, injecting hope. "I mean to have studied all the possible meanings of perhaps your name."

"I have been rigorous in the pursuit of myself," the tramp said, with what I detected to be more than a hint of pride which could have been described as approaching the royal, although not inordinately so. John and I liked him. "This is why," he went on, "that I ask the boy to draw a map of how to get to Rexroat, Oklahoma, where I certainly intend to make inquiries as to the origin of the name."

I drew directions for him as he and Uncle John continued talking. I overheard the tramp remind John that to rex not only meant to play lord, master and king, but to play pranks, which is what the fates had done to him and his identity. And he said it had made him more than a little nervous to learn that rex could also be a mutant rabbit or mouse, or a peculiar kind of cat from Cornwall. "It could be," he said sadly, "I am the king of the alien and outcast."

"Maybe if you stayed still, and stopped drifting around, it all would come to you," Uncle John said. "It appears to me you get around a lot, and have become a Jack of all places, and that would make you all the more confused—"

"And time," the tramp said, "a Jack of all times. I have a sense I'm living simultaneous time spans, which is one of the reasons I'm supposed to be crazy."

"Jack, it's doubly confusing," Uncle John said.

"Oh, many more confusions than that," the tramp said, offering his glass for more hum.

Suddenly, the tramp jumped out of bed, spilling his whiskey, hushing Uncle John. He bent his shaggy head to the thin trailer door and whispered, "Is that a car coming?"

"Jack, this is a dead-end road," Uncle John whispered back, humoring the fellow. "We hardly have any traffic—"

"It is a car!" the tramp said fiercely. "Someone's coming. They could be coming for me. I've got to go."

"Surely, no one has followed you way out here," I said. "Wait, your map."

The man was panic-stricken. Like a shot he went out the back door of the trailer and started up the dusk-laden mountain, scrambling through sotol and yucca. For a moment, frozen in the light of the door, we lost sight of him. The approaching car, or truck, passed, leaving only a shudder in its wake before disappearing over the southern horizon.

"Jack!" Uncle John called. "It's all right. Come back, Mr. Rexrote, come back! The danger has passed."

We pressed up the mountain and saw his silhouette outlined against the sky as he neared the top, heading east.

"Come back for your goat!" Uncle John cried.

At first the tramp didn't reply, nor did he break stride by turning around. But just before he dipped out of sight, he raised his arms and screamed to the heavens, "Keep him. I stole him anyway."

We dubbed the goat Jack Rexrote. It was all I could do to keep Uncle John from eating him for Christmas dinner.

We supped soup and crackers and listened to the radio, which was mostly about the war even in its music, dramas and commercials. Ma Bell was saying, "Please don't call long distance this Christmas." Fat chance of that. John didn't have a phone, and neither did Ma and Pa up on the Conoco Driscoll.

"Stout-hearted, shot to hell, but heading home," came the Bendix Aviation motto. I thought how far I was from my family and almost cried. It was a strange time, when love and hate fought for possession of your heart. One general, I think it was McNair, was quoted as saying, "We must lust for battle; our object in life must be to kill. There need be no pangs of conscience, for our enemy has lighted the way to faster, surer, crueler killing."

And then your heart would melt at General Electric's Christmas message of '42: "Christmas is a light no war will dim. It glows in the heart of every man in the armed forces of the United States; it glows in the hearts of those who gather scrap, who use less sugar and coffee and tea and meat, who walk to save gasoline and tires, who keep on buying more war bonds."

And who could pass up putting a little down and a little a month on a retreat atop Mount Morning Air.

On the morning I was to catch a bus to Hebbronville, where Mother and Daddy would meet me, Uncle John got up complaining that something had died and gone to putrefaction under his bed. He found the tramp's socks and shoes between his bed and the wall. Kicked off the bed frozen, they had defrosted most pungently. Convinced that Jack would not return for them, John burned them in the trash barrel while we said a prayer for the wild bugger.

The chances of a man surviving barefoot in the brutal terrain of

Hell's Half-Acre during its mildest season was not something to count on, but to attempt it in subfreezing temperatures was a death sentence more unrelenting than in the blistering heat. I thought of that poor old man as I sat in the bus, watching through a hole I had rubbed in the frost of the window as snowy, silver range and basin rose and fell like miles and miles of the furniture of heaven and hell.

13

★ ★ ★

Body of Christ

CORPUS CHRISTI, TEXAS
1943–1945

THE FLESHY COMMUNION OF SPA AND TRADE

OUR MOVE DURING THE MIDDLE OF THE WAR YEARS TO CORPUS Christi on the coast was a turning point in our lives, and everyone in the Hudson Terraplane sensed it. "Don't look back," my father said as we delivered ourselves out of the almost boundless interior ranch country, which, even given the mirages before you and the eccentricity and color of desert Bedouins, could be beekingly sloomy in its isolation. Corpus Christi was not only the largest place we would call home, but a port of call, a siren that beckoned adventurers who, restless and nomadic, sought the fleshy communion of spa and trade. The congregating extremes of sand and water make for interesting companions. "Why is it," Daddy used to observe, "that water or desert draws crazy people?" We all took our cue from the grande dame, Clara Driscoll, who could have been, who was, in fact, a wonderfully barbaric and generous pirate queen on this coast of buccaneers. And beneath and above the lurid carnival of last gasp love the wide-shouldered girls gave sailor boy and fly boy before they sailed off to die, Body of Christ was beautiful and balmy. Already, the war effort had made it a boom town of military marshaling and the production and refining of petrochemicals, but it would be years before the natural beauty of the city and its bay suffered the attendant congestion and pollution.

Indeed, it was the war and its opportunity that attracted my father to Corpus. By working in a Shell Oil refinery whose products were deemed necessary for the war effort, Daddy not only drew good pay, but got a deferment from the draft as well. We rented a cedar shake house off Shell Lane, which was near the refinery on the arcadian out-skirts of the city. By now, the string of animals we took with us was reduced to Bossy the cow and Boss the dog—who carried MackMary the white rat on his back—and we had pasture and coastal wood to accommodate them. Bobby and I milked Bossy morning and night, Mother sold raw milk and butter to the neighbors, and Daddy, tin-hat-ted and lunch-pailed, rode a bicycle he powered with a lawn mower engine back and forth to the plant. We kept a victory garden, saved things like leftover toothpaste tubes for war scrap, hoarded rationing stamps and canned goods, and hung a star in our living room window to let everyone know that we had a soldier boy fighting abroad. It was Uncle Glen, who had to sober up when Uncle Sam said he was needed for the infantry. The death toll was appalling, and yet it was only cold figures in the paper and on the radio unless it included someone famous or from the family. The other cost of the war seems cheap now: $3.37 a day for every adult in America. But then a man like Daddy rarely made more than $19.37 a day, so that was a sixth of his gross, and twice that if you included the tax on Mother, who earned nothing on the home front of kitchen and kinder. Well, that wasn't so, come to think of it. There was her milk and cream money from Bossy. I remem-ber what a setback it was to Mother's budget when margarine came out, and neighbors stopped buying our butter because it wasn't as pretty and bright yellow as the processed vegetable oil. Mother recov-ered, somewhat, by yellowing her butter with food dye. It was the enforcement of pasteurization laws that finally robbed her of our cot-tage industry. Filtering raw milk through a linen or cotton cloth would no longer do. Homogenized milk has never tasted like milk fresh from the tit. The only way I can describe the latter is that it was warm, with a wild blue taste that is, of course, lost in the homogeneous.

Even without having lived there, we had visited Corpus often enough, thanks to Uncle Earl and Aunt Arbie, to know the neat things there were to do. You'll do some of them with us in this chap-ter, but first you must come face-to-face with Earl and Arbie, who up to now have flitted in and out the edges of my journey.

EARL

Today in Texas, men wear their hats into stores and cafes, almost anywhere they please. This would upset my Uncle Earl, a Sir Walter Raleigh of the West. One of my father's younger brothers, anvil-jawed Earl was, like all the boys but Daddy, a rugged six-footer and then some. He was a tool pusher, a boss like Tobin Drexler of several drilling rigs, which kept him tooling about Texas in a long, snarling Oldsmobile 88. Cavalier he was, something of a gallant. Earl had his code. The way a man wore his hat, or perhaps it's more accurate to say the times a man should not wear his hat, were for him grave matters of social decorum.

Earl took off his hat—usually a felt with a flat and fairly wide brim—in the presence of every female, flag and cadaver he met. He'd pull off the side of a mountain pass to let a funeral procession pass; sit there belly pressed against the steering wheel of the Olds, balanced on the edge of oblivion, his hat over his breast, not moving an eyelid in honor of the dead, until every last car with its lights on had made him eat dust. Once, riding in an elevator at Joske's Department Store in San Antonio, he glared down at me because I still wore my Fort Worth crush. When we went to inspect the new-fangled escalators at Foley's in Houston, Uncle Earl, with great protocol, removed his hat. We buried him holding it across his ample stomach, just as he had done in life. The funeral was appropriate, and Earl would have approved. The Masons conducted it, and every time they mentioned his name, which must have been a hundred times, they took off their hats and held them over their hearts. Code of the Old West. You can wear out some wool taking a hat on and off every five minutes. It's made me bald. Earl was spared the rigors, for he went to his grave with a thatch of leonine hair. Come to think of it, Earl was even spared some manners, if you can believe that.

There was a side to him as uncouth as the Thomas boys back in Little Egypt. He'd order the most expensive rare steaks on the menu, even if it was at some highfalutin' petroleum club, and after he had chewed bloody steer and swallowed all he could hold, he'd push the plate back and belch. Then he would fish from his pocket a spool of dental floss, snip off a piece, open his lion mouth, insert the floss between his fangs, and start sawing back and forth, flip-

ping, or—as we called it, "thipping"—fumy tidbits of flesh all over
everyone within three or four feet of him.

He was full of fun and innuendos scatological and sexual, all this
implied in a manner of speaking as well-bred and proper as his hat
doffing. The most pungent expression I heard him use was the
euphemism, "break wind," this after he had stuck his big forefinger in
my face and said, "Pull my finger." I did and he let loose a fart that
would have blown the cuffs off Charlie Chaplin, who had just been
arrested for leching a teenage starlet. Earl himself was not above a
fatherly admiration for the nymphette carhops in shorts on skates
who made curb service beer drinking so popular around the boomtowns and military bases. He liked to reach under the leather seat of
his Olds and bring out for the girls his latest book:

WHAT I KNOW ABOUT WOMEN

BY

EARL LEE PORTERFIELD

bragged the embossed gold title of the leather-bound volume.

"Why, hidy do, Mr. Earl Lee. I'm right proud to meet up with a
real arthur."

"Go ahead, sweetheart. Open it up and read a little of it."

"Well, I don't have time to read . . . I'm afraid my boss—"

"Just flip through the pages," Earl would coax.

And they would. And what they found were blank pages.

What Bobby and I found in Earl was a surrogate father who took
delight rather than disappointment in our sonhood. He was not as
hard and single-minded as Daddy, and certainly he was more generous with his time and money than the old man. Part of it was that he
and Arbie didn't have children, and adopted us, in a manner of
speaking. We loved being with them, for the most part. They treated
us special.

ARBIE

Arbie Plummer Porterfield was as outgoing as Mother could be
withdrawn. Old Man Potter said you either loved Arbie or you hated
her. Now Potter was an expert on the latter. He was known as the

neighborhood grump. Little pleased him. He was out of sorts with the war, the sentimental patriotism and sacrifice on the home front. He hated Roosevelt, Churchill and Hitler in the same breath. But the person he hated most was my aunt. I think it was because Arbie wore britches and could cuss a blue streak. She also blew her whistle at him a lot. It was because he wouldn't turn out his lights during blackouts. Arbie was our Civil Defense Block captain, our air raid warden.

One evening when Arbie was parading around in her tin hat and uniform, almost wishing an honest-to-goodness real air raid would come so she could blow and show her stuff, Mr. Potter said to me with disgust: "Look at your aunt! I'm a silly old fool, but I've learned a thing or two. I used to think the only thing that would save man from destroying himself was for woman to take over the world. I thought they were different, superior somehow. Now, knowing old Arbie there, I'm not so sure. I'm afraid they can make just about as big a mess of things as men do. Rats! It'll be more of the same. Now that they've started to dress and talk like us, what's to keep them from acting like us?"

In a sense, he was right. If ever there was a woman who wanted to be one of the boys, it was Arbie. I don't mean to say there was anything butch about her. She could turn Earl around with one of her dark, direct gazes. She was part Choctaw. Earl said he had to chase her down barefoot in the woods of Oklahoma to woo her. He was big and barrel-chested, and she was five feet four and fuming, a slip of a woman who was frustrated in the limited role convention allowed for her sex.

On my wall as I write, I look at a tin poster from the era of the war. It shows a pretty, lip-sticked woman in factory overalls with her sleeves rolled up, flexing a nicely defined biceps. "We Can Do It" she says boldly. It was Arbie and a million other gritty gals who stepped into jobs the fighting men left behind. And with that move into the masculine, orchestrated with the blessing of the male powers that be, they moved in lock-step precision behind Eleanor Roosevelt, who would extend not only women's working field but their playing field. But I bet you the farm they didn't pay them what they paid the men. Capitalists are never so greedy as during war. Sharing the responsibilities of men, the Arbies also shared in the freedoms men enjoyed. At least they tried to. In times of war, this was hardly innovation, but a global practice that went back to Hippolyte, Cleopatra and Joan of Arc. But notice what happened to our hard-charging amazonian trio after they had served their purpose. As Father Flaherty would remind, it's rough out here.

My aunt was willing to pay the price.

Arbie was the first woman in our family—except for the old maids—to say flat out that she did not want children. By the time she got around to realizing that she loved us, and therefore children, it was too late for her and Earl to have babies. So they had us over a lot instead. The difference between Arbie and Earl and Mother and Daddy was that when Arbie and Earl got tired of us they could send us home. Arbie didn't like to be too tied down to anything but her own passions. Mr. Potter only knew half of them. Arbie's heart's desires Mr. Potter missed because she was very private with them. They were, in this order: a bed of her own, secret dreams, diaphanous bras and slips and high-heeled springalaters, a bank account and car of her own, Lucky Strikes in a gold case, jazz dancing and gin in high-stemmed glasses and secret assignations in the afternoons, Bing Crosby in the movies and on records and Humphrey Bogart in her bed of dreams. The public Arbie was another sister entirely. This one was into uniforms and weapons of various kind, Civil Defense and fire fighting, beers and card play with the boys, fishing and hunting with the boys, honky-tonking with the boys, dancing to Bob Wills's fiddle and Bob Wills's person, her neurotic little rat terriers, Earl as long as he stayed in his own bed and being Auntie Mame to Billy Mack and Bobby Lee. Her bathroom was populated with naughty naked ceramic and glass incubi, poupee and manikin pissers from the curio shops of North Beach.

After October Ney, Arbie was the first woman I knew to drive a car, and change a flat tire. If these two had ever gotten together, it would have been Thelma and Louise over the cliff. Earl was a big hunter, but Arbie was the best shot, and she took better care of her gear. She could cast a rod and reel as accurately as Zeus hurled thunderbolts, and, of course, her heroine was the great Babe Didrickson. When the Babe married and changed her name to Zaharis, Arbie got a little antsy. She was afraid the Babe would bloom forth with Greek child instead of staying free and easy to chase a golf ball 36 holes a day. She saw Bobby and me as scouts, and signed us up. Then she took us to Sears and not only outfitted us in uniforms and insignias, but bought livery for herself and became a saluting den mother.

Arbie had a uniform for every occasion. That's why I suspected she helped start the war. Just before the Japs bombed Pearl Harbor rumors were rife that we were going to war, and I figure that every night Arbie went to bed praying for it to commence. The men got kind of down on her. Heck, here Daddy and Earl were fortyish and draftable—certainly they could have gotten into it if they had wanted—but they chose, as they put it, to stay home and produce fuel for our fighting boys. Arbie, on the other hand, was fit to be tied. At breakfast, she would tell us how in her dreams the night before she had led the invasion into North Africa, or had slipped back to Bataan as a commando to rescue General Wainwright. It was all we could do to keep her from joining the WAVES or the WACS. She settled for being a Civilian Defense worker, and made of it an exciting, soldierly career through the war. She patrolled our block in a resplendent red, white and blue uniform with sergeant stripes and a helmet, blowing the whistle on slackers like Mr. Potter. Every night she searched the skies with a telescope, looking for enemy planes. None came that we knew of. But we did have some natural disasters, a couple of hurricanes, a defense plant explosion or two that allowed Arbie to do more than walk up and down the block. She became a fire fighter and drove one of those big red throbbers to the rescue. When it was all over over there, when the boys came home and Arbie had to hang up her uniforms, she did so with sadness. But it became a source of pride, her part in the war effort, and Earl bragged on her a lot.

THE TOUR

We were so proud of the things to see on the coast that we made a map of "must-sees" we forced on company from out of town. Every time Aunt Marguerite and Uncle Herschel, one of Daddy's brothers even younger than Earl, came to visit from Cement, Oklahoma, we would take them on the tour. Mother was afraid, after their fourth visit in two years, that they might feel put upon if Daddy brought out the maps for still another go-around of the now all-too-familiar places. But Uncle Herschel looked cross-eyed at Marguerite and said,

"Let's go, girl. What's worth seeing once is worth seeing over and over again."

The seawall was an impressive skirt around the city's sea legs, and it was fun to swim from it or fish off the jetties. We did those things with Marguerite and Herschel. Daddy would beckon them to the top of the seawall and, with a sweep of his arm and a rise in his voice, he would tell Uncle Herschel just how many tons of cement had gone into the making of the wall. He thought this was of terrible interest to them because they were from Cement. So every time they came they got the lowdown on the seawall.

Then we would ride to the top of the Driscoll Building on the bluff and take in everything from the observation deck. You could see across the bay all the way to Portland. This was as artless a pastime as you can imagine. It was Daddy who managed to bring the risqué element to it. He could not resist chortling and telling the story about how Clara Driscoll came to raise the highest building in town. It was low gossip of a high woman, the Daughter of the American and Texas Revolutions who had saved the Alamo for really the first time in history, since Colonel Travis had let it fall to the Mexicans; and then the rest of us, with faltering memory, had let it fall to time and ruins. Mother hated Daddy's feigned familiarity with the dope behind Driscoll's tower, but he would insist on reciting it with relish, swearing it was true in every detail, when, of course, he had no way of knowing. It is sufficient to say that Driscoll had been on the bluff first with a building, only to see a rival move in next door with an even higher edifice. Swearing she would someday squat and whiz on the top of the intruder on the bluff, Driscoll reached for the sky and built her crowning landmark.

The third attraction was North Beach, the carnival strip where Bobby and I took music lessons. Once it had been an amusement park for moms and dads and the kiddies, but now, with the war on and the town full of salts and fly boys from the naval bases, the fun had taken a decidedly adult and seedy turn. There were peep shows and B-girl dives along the strip, conmen and crooked games on the midway. You could still roller skate, dunk the clown and ride the ferris wheel and the bumper cars, but you had to pick your way through what Mother called a lot of riffraff. She went to the midway reluctantly, never letting us kids out of her sight. If Daddy showed the slightest interest in some gamy tent show, she would wheel him around, fasten a child to each of his anchorlike hands, and march her brood out of the park and toward the parking lot and the Hudson, vowing never to return. The only way we could lure her back was to talk of cotton candy, or have Marguerite and Herschel with us.

There was one other attraction North Beach offered that women and children could only wonder and whisper about. At the far end of Ocean Drive, just beyond the carnival grounds, an old salt ran a curio shop. The front of the store was open to anyone wanting souvenirs and sea shells, and we would browse among the bric-a-brac. The back of the shop was off limits to all but men.

A giant Chinaman stood guard at the door. He was bald-headed and bare-chested and wore a curving sword in his sash. A fearsome, silent sentinel, ever watchful. Above his head, tacked to the lintel, was a great, carved figurehead of a mermaid, an ornament that had graced the prow of a clipper. Around her neck hung a hand-painted sign. "Come Look upon the Mermaid of Zennor," it read. "See this living siren of the deep in all her natural glory. She lies in a glass aquarium, open to your astounded eyes. Her breath swells her bosom. She smiles. She sings. She moves her tail. She enters your heart. No man who has looked upon the Mermaid of Zennor can ever forget her beauty. $1 for two minutes. $2 for five minutes."

Daddy never went into the mermaid room with the other men when he was with us. But he had not hidden the fact that he went there often with Earl, though never with Herschel, who was in many ways a warm-blooded delight, especially in his eye for his wife and his love of family. But Herschel carried in his veins just enough of old Alice Austin's anathematizing formaldehyde of temperance to be a drag. He would have been hotly offended at such an invitation. So we did not make the house of the mermaid a part of their agenda. Seeing the mermaid was something more ordinary men did that their wives, even Mother, accepted as long as the men didn't ram it down their throats. Still, the stories filtered down. Daddy, of course, had long teased us boys with just enough of the mermaid to make us mad for her unveiling. I knew, in 1943, that it was about that time for me. But not with our innocents from Cement.

More to their liking was catching the Aransas Pass ferry to see Popeye. You looked up into the wheelhouse to see him. He had been the ferry captain for years: always at the wheel in a white sailor suit and captain's cap, the right eye closed in a squint, the left one bugged out mischievously. His nose dripped down into his toothless, wonderfully mobile mouth, which for gaping children and photographers would seam tight on the stem of a corncob pipe. The spitting image of the cartoon character.

Monroe Tabor was his real name, and Uncle Earl claimed to be one of his friends, especially when Arbie wanted us to eat our spinach. "If you don't eat your spinach," he would say, "I'm going to take you down to Port Aransas and report you to Popeye. Now, I'm not saying what he'll do, but if I were you I wouldn't risk it."

We ate enough spinach to make Del Monte rich, and so apparently did every kid in the country. It was, of course, in imitation of Popeye, who got his strength from the icky green stuff in the tin. A song always went with each serving:

> I'm Popeye the Sailorman.
> I eat out of the spinach can.
> I like to go swimmin'
> With bow-legged women,
> I'm Popeye the Sailorman.

Our bow-legged woman was Arbie. It was her only physical flaw. I remember being embarrassed because in summer she wore shorts that showed off her legs, which were as skinny as they were bowed. Earl kept her at home when we took Herschel and Marguerite to see Popeye. This was because Arbie could not help but become Olive Oyl as soon as she boarded the ferry. Olive Oyl loved to wave and flirt at Popeye up in his perch. Olive Oyl loved to smoke Luckies and drink Southern Select beer at the Hangout Cafe. She shopped for curio mermaids, especially the ones with moving parts that did something suggestive. We were never happy as we were without Herschel and Marguerite on those wicked interludes on Mustang Island. Earl and Daddy easily disarmed themselves of their mother's piety, and with Arbie sassy and strutting out front even Mother let down her guard. They wore out the boards of every dance hall on the island, while we kids watched the purses and slept between the rank ash trays and sour beer bottles.

Back on the mainland, Earl didn't do so well. He drove himself in trying to become an independent oil trucker, had a nervous break- down before he was killed in a truck wreck at the age of fifty-five. Arbie was confined to a wheelchair the last fifteen years of her life. When she died in 1983 at the age of eighty, she left me a ceramic mermaid we bought at Port Aransas in the old days. I always had a crush on it. The maid lies bare-breasted on an ashtray. Her finned tail arches up and wiggles back and forth when you touch it with an ashy butt.

The other day, riding the ferry again after forty years, I waved to the captain, a big, beefy guy who reminded me of Bluto, Popeye's nemesis, and I wondered what had happened to Monroe Tabor. Arbie always said he ought to be in the movies. I remembered the day Earl came home smelling of high spirits and bursting with news from Port Aransas. Cap'n Tabor was going to Hollywood, he announced. Talent scouts had found him on the ferry, and it would be no time before the real Popeye would be as rich and famous as the one in the funny papers. But nothing ever came of it, and Monroe Tabor spent his days ferrying folks back and forth between the main- land and the island.

Our last stop at Aransas Pass before heading home was always the historic Tarpon Inn, where we stood, hats upon our hearts at Earl's command, Arbie saluting, and stared up at the second story room President Roosevelt was supposed to stay in during his fishing jaunts in the Gulf of Mexico. There was a "Roosevelt Sleeps Here" plaque in the lobby. The Tarpon's wooden stairs were so narrow Daddy supposed the only way they could have gotten the president to his room was to lift him from his wheelchair and carry him like a baby. The picture in my mind of such a powerful and jaunty man being helpless without his aides, wheelchair and crutches made a poignant impression upon me.

It occurred to me that in bed at night, the president was as defenseless as any little kid, certainly less mobile. And that made me identify with him in an altogether new way. I reasoned that the paralysis he had been damned with sort of put him on an equal foot- ing with the rest of us, that otherwise he might have turned out to be another rich, tennis-playing Hyde Park snob who went along with the Coolidges and the Hoovers. Now I knew that he knew what it meant to have to go without things that others had, and maybe that was one of the reasons he was bound and determined to make us a New Deal in America.

As I grew up and began to peep past the auras that public men hold up before us, I learned that Franklin Roosevelt's character and political ambitions were not always as noble and heroic as we wanted them to be. His weaknesses were not always as benign as his paralysis. But this new reckoning did not ruin Roosevelt for me any more than it was ruining my father, whom I was also seeing in revisionist terms. What it did was make me more tolerant of the sins of the fathers, and, yes, the mothers, especially those who meant well and managed a decent balance between dark and light.

At the same time, it taught me to keep my sniffer on the alert for what my fathers called the buckram and hufty-tufty, the hot air that bellows from the stiffly starched and pompous, who with their manicured hands held out for us to kiss, would in turn save our family farms and the whole country to boot.

Thus it followed fifty-seven years later that when we saw President Bush take a moment off from his foreign affairs to be seen buying socks in a shopping mall like any other threadbare and gimpy hardy of the '90s Depression, I was reminded of Daddy Harrell's grace before we devoured haggis at the old Thanksgivings. "As for those who love us," he intoned, "may God bless their hearts. And for those who do not love us, may God change their hearts. And if he cannot change their hearts, may he turn their ankles. So that we may know them by their limping."

I was not as honest with my father about Franklin Roosevelt as I am with you about George Bush. I never told Daddy I had learned that the crippled FDR never got off the presidential yacht when fishing in the gulf, that the story of his staying at the Tarpon Inn was malarkey put out for publicity. And it could have been a Secret Service dodge to protect the president.

THE GARTLANDS

Uncle Earl and Aunt Arbie chipped in to help pay for instruments and music lessons for Bobby and me. I took guitar and he took fiddle. Our teachers were Professor Gartland and his wife,

Goldilocks, who had been recommended by Uncle Eddie, a distant but dear relative who was a circus midget and who sometimes appeared at the North Beach carnival, near which the Gartlands kept a studio.

Their beach studio was large, its screenless windows open to the summer gulf breeze. But the trailerhouse they lived in was said to be the tiniest in the world, no doubt because they had bought it from Uncle Eddie, who was given to hyperbole in every extreme. Daddy reckoned we could hitch the trailer to the rear of his motor bike and pull it out of the sand with only a push from Bobby and me.

The professor was a tall, rangy dignity who in his years as a violinist had gained little but a big belly, a perpetually bruised forehead, a mane of yellowish-gray hair and a beautiful blonde wife twenty years his junior. "Duck," she would say as they entered the trailer. But the professor seldom listened. He looked to me like Earl twenty years older, a kind of down-at-winged-heel Earl who had taken Grandpa's Stradivarius seriously, and the music that went with it. He smelled of Glen's whiskey pores, and smoked cigarettes down to his nicotine fingers. But he was gentle and patient with us, so complimentary at even the least progress we made, and so candidly and calamitously himself in his own rising and falling, that Bobby and I both adored him and worried about him. He must have taught dozens of string players, from children to oldtimers, and I can't imagine him being any different with them.

Goldilocks taught accordion, woodwinds and other horns, and she split the students of percussion with the professor. Well, that is, if he did not have a headache.

They couldn't have made much from their pupils, living as they were on the seedy beach. You knew they had started out with something higher in mind. Don't we all? They taught every day but Sunday. On those lazy afternoons, after the sun had mellowed, they emerged from their cramped little gypsy wagon, scantily clad for the time, toting the umbrellas, towels and ice chests they required, and hot-footed it across the dunes to a secluded spot near the water, where they stretched out on recliners beneath their portable shade and consumed in heirloom glasses bottle after bottle of cheap California wine while listening to the rhythms of the surf and the cry of the gulls. We were often on the beach those summers, and always looked for them in the same place, always the same place, to say hello. But not to tarry. This was their day, and we let them be. We would go down a ways from them and set ourselves up, to sun and swim until dark.

At cockshut, at always the moment when daughter tide was beginning to feel the pull of grandmother moon and sighing a dusky farewell to grandfather sun dying red in the west, we would hear the faint strains of music coming from the Gartlands' canopies. It began always as the same, cranky, scratchy waltz for piano, which the professor, on his bare knees, wound from the spring motor, stylus and wax of an old phonograph. When he got the motor going good, the romantic beauty and stately turn that Artur Rubinstein brought to the Chopin dance would bring the professor to his feet, and he would take his lady and waltz across the sand. Back and forth he went to the phonograph, putting on a mazurka, then a polonaise and, finally, a sublime nocturne, which he and Goldilocks, mad in love with one another and transported by American chablis, the lap of Mexican tide and the music of the two Poles, danced so beautifully that we watched and wept in silence.

THE CORN COBBERS

Eventually, Bobby and I practiced enough on our instruments and singing to make the Gartlands' band, the Corpus Christi Corn Cobbers, composed of the best of their students. The oldest members, other than the Gartlands, were twenty-two-year-old, yellow-haired twin beauties who blew very loud saxophones and libido. Our appeal was novelty, so mixed in age, sex, musical range and ability were the Corn Cobbers. Goldilocks played horn and accordion, and the professor led the band and played first fiddle to Bobby's second. On the guitar I thumped my four chords and sang in my soprano the lead while Bobby fiddled and sang harmony. Body of Christ was jumping with night spots during those deadly years. Eat, drink and be merry, for tomorrow we die, seemed to be the given. And probably it didn't much matter how good the food and drink and music as long as the night ended on the highest note imaginable: a duet until morning with the catch of the night. We played at honky-tonks and for USO dances until the end of the war.

We had a set opener. The professor would appear on stage before the curtain, if there was one, elegant in black tie and tails, violin under his arm. He would announce that he was opening the show with Beethoven. He'd cradle the violin into his neck, bend his great head down, and launch into the noble and dramatic Kreutzer Sonata. The audience, being sailors and their girls, would murmur and fall into a stunned hush. This was not what they had expected from a band billed as the Corn Cobbers.

Just as we could hear their hearts fall, the professor would shift gear and slide in an adroit bar that got him out of Beethoven and into that rollicking reel, "Turkey in the Straw." By the time he finished the room was his, every yahooing sailor in his hand. The curtain or the lights would go up, and the band would break forth behind the professor with our theme song, "San Antonio Rose," which we had picked up from Bob Wills. Now, almost a half century later, it is hard to imagine that the Corn Cobbers were any good or that those twenty-year-old sailors were very selective. The professor obviously was trying to make the best of a bad, sad time when the last tune a couple of kids about to part for war wanted to hear was something serious and European. We played some pop, but it was a poor imitation of Glenn Miller and the Dorsey Brothers. The only thing left was Spike Lee and corny country. But he kept us booked.

THE LAST SPRING OF OUR INNOCENCE

One Sunday afternoon at the beach, the professor and Goldilocks hosted a swimming party and picnic for band members. Toward twilight, the professor put down his wine glass, got up from his recliner in the sand beside Goldilocks, and, reaching his full height, wobbled like a stiff crane toward their trailer to take a pee. This was a routine stagger he had managed to negotiate for years. When he did not come back, Goldilocks got concerned and went after him, Aunt Arbie and I trailing her in our swimsuits. We found him lying half-conscious in the sand beside the trailer stoop, a gash in his head and blood covering him like a caul. Goldilocks had not been there to tell him to duck, and he had hit his head on the lintel and slipped, falling backward onto a sidewalk border of stubby creosote posts, one of which received the back of his head with brutal resistance.

He was not the same fellow after that. Neither were we all.

Strong men and a single strong woman had ruled the imagination of our war years. Thumb through the *Time* covers of the years between 1939 and 1945. It is the faces of the emphatic who made "Man of the Year"—people like Barrymore and Ben-Gurion, Al Capone and Madame Chiang Kai-shek, Gary Cooper and Hearst and Tom Harmon, Kilroy and Kai-shek (the Madame), Mussolini and MacArthur and Madame Chiang Ka-shek. It was a muscular, put-up-your-dukes gallery, and what it says is that Henry Luce, the *Time* publisher, had a thing for Chiang's wife.

What it also says is that a ninety-seven-pound weakling didn't have a chance in those *Times*, even though men and women as a rule were smaller than they are today. The 1944 girl of stage, screen, radio, kitchen and kinder stood five feet, three and one-half inches tall. She was longer in the leg, thicker in the waist (26.4 inches), and had slightly heavier hips (37.4 inches) and legs than the 1890 girl of E. L. Doctorow's *Ragtime*. But thanks to a bigger bust (33.9 inches) and torso, her figure looked better proportioned than granny's when she was a girl. Obviously, a ninety-seven-pound weakling couldn't handle a woman like that on Muscle Beach, so Charles Atlas stepped into my life.

Atlas's secret was "dynamic tension," which he shared in seven languages with Bobby and me and 69,998 other punks around the world. Mahatma Gandhi almost became a devotee. Two years before, Atlas had expressed pity and concern for Gandhi's frail body, to which the holy man replied: "I've met some inventive Americans, but Atlas takes the prize. Mind you, I would be delighted to have him work on me, if I could find someone to pay his passage to India."

Bobby never understood why Gandhi didn't take the course by mail, because it sure was working for us. For thirty-five dollars' credit we received weekly instruction in how to match muscle against muscle in dynamic tension. It required no equipment, just a kind of narcissistic dedication to working against yourself while standing naked and sweating before the dressing table mirror in Mother and Daddy's bedroom. It was a toss-up between us about which was the most important to our futures, music or muscles. For three years the soldiers had had the limelight. Now, it seemed to us singers were coming on strong. Jimmie Davis, that hillbilly bard, had been elected governor of Louisiana, and up in Manhattan, that skinny little crooner Frank Sinatra had to be rescued by police from a mob of thirty thousand bobby-soxers.

Besides, the war was winding down. In the Pacific the U.S. fleet dealt crippling blows to the Japanese navy, while our soldiers and marines leapfrogged from one Japanese-held island to another. The Germans, who in the preceding years had overrun Poland, Denmark, Norway, France, the Low Countries, the Balkans, North Africa and much of Russia, were on the defensive. But the most crucial battle, the liberation of Europe, was yet to begin.

Here at home, we were in a political stew. FDR was in questionable health and losing his touch with Congress, and the big if was whether he would seek a fourth term. Young, slick Tom Dewey tried his best to retire the old New Dealer, but FDR, of course, went on to victory.

By the following spring, however, FDR was dead. Harry S Truman was our man in midstream. And he was a question mark. What was it that Dewey's running mate, what's-his-name John Bricker had said about Harry? "Harry who?"

It was the last spring of our innocence.

In '44 Elizabeth Taylor was twelve years old and in love with horses.

In '45 she was kissing Robert Taylor.

It would never be the same. We changed in 1945. My voice broke. I quit singing soprano in the band and at church and began to worry about girls and pimples. We lost old FDR, the passing of the father. Oh, we won the war. But at a great cost. We would never enjoy war again. It was the year of the Bomb. The year of DDT and penicillin. The year of the ballpoint pin, the year Harvard and IBM brought out the computer.

It was the year Pa counted the hairs on my lip and took me to see the Mermaid of Zennor.

That summer we were leaving Corpus to go deeper into the Tortilla Curtain again. He pulled me aside and told me to get ready, that it was time I saw her.

I broke into a sweat, for I smelled whiskey on his breath and hazing in my future. "Oh, God," I whispered. "I'm not sure I'm ready. Daddy, I want to, and I don't want to."

"Ye ready, son. You can't put it off. It's something every man has to go through, and you're a little man. So get ready."

Now what did that mean? Get ready? He'd said it twice. Was there something savage, even atavistic, I should be preparing myself for? Were they going to whack off more than my foreskin? My first thought, of course, was to ask Mother. But I knew that wouldn't wash now.

"I thought I had to be twenty-one," I said.

"Naw, stop stallin'."

"What do I wear?"

"Wear your Sunday suit and tie."

This relieved me somewhat, but not enough. "Do I have to?"

"Have to what?"

"Go."

"Yep, and hurry. Uncle Earl and Uncle Herschel are goin' with us."

"Uncle Herschel!"

"Joke, son. Earl'll be here in a minute."

"Wow! Okay, Pa." With Uncle Earl along, I might not be so nervous and might even live to tell about it.

"And Billy, shower and shave."

"Shave? I've never shaved in my life."

"Damn it, boy. I said shave! Use my razor."

"YESSIR!"

Thank God Bobby was with friends for the weekend.

The three of us, very male, handsomely attired and sweetly anointed with Brilliantine, wedged into the front seat of the Hudson and drove to the curio shop on the beach. Daddy splurged. He paid six dollars so the great Chinaman would stand aside and let us go in and stand over the huge aquarium and look at the mermaid for five minutes.

I can't say what I saw, because Daddy and Earl, with fraternal gravity, swore me to silence about the particulars of the peep show. All I dare say is that what the old salt had written on the sign above the Chinaman's head was true. It changed me. It turned me from a boy into a man.

After that five minutes—which seemed a few seconds of eternity—I followed Daddy and Earl out to the car, where Earl took a swig on a pint of hum and passed it to Daddy, who knocked my socks off by passing it to me and insisting I take a tipple. Ritual. Initiation. Didn't dare not. It burned.

"Well, come on, gentlemen," Daddy said. "One more time."

I thought he meant another round of whiskey. What he meant was another look-see. And so we went back in and this time, Earl, as my second father, insisted on paying for another five minutes.

I can't say exactly what I saw, because Daddy and Earl again forbade me to speak of it in particulars. All I dare say is that she reminded me of October Ney in Grandpa's cabin, except the mermaid was much younger, not much older than me. And, of course, October didn't have a spangled fan tail. I think I'm allowed to say this about October's tail.

Again, we returned to the Terraplane, where Earl again produced the bottle, from which we again drank in most munificent brotherhood.

"Once more, into the breach, boys!" Daddy sshang out, and again we fell out of the Bark of Ra and entered the sacred precincts, paying dearly to sshee for the sscharmed time the beauteous maid of mer and myth.

Again, in these particulars regarding the actual appearance and comeliness of the Mermaid of Zennor, the admonition of sshecrecy was laid upon the mantle of my new manhood, and I would never be so spurious as to sully that secret, which thrice at the behest of my fathers was stitched with honor upon the unyielding seam of my mouth.

But they, being men of mechanical and chemical professions, held me to the real and specific, the objective corporeal manifestation of the mermaid; *but not the analogical or even the mythical,* although I feel in dangerous waters with the metaphorical, which omits the self-conscious comparison "like" or "is" or "was" and flat out says whatever it thinks she was. I shudder to think of the karma I would earn for such a direct description of the unmentionable maid. It would have me saying, strictly for example, that she was a dish, a buoyant-breasted, tender little Lorelei of a lungfish, kin to the snapper and red in the pink of her spots and wink-a-peeps, the white of her flesh and the silver sheen of her scales. But, of course, I cannot do that under the oath, any more than I could speculate that it was salt water she floated in from our very bay. My father and uncle, forever my fraternal brothers, would have fancied no such thing. Having drilled through many a water sand in search of oil, they would have, in the event of curiosity, conducted experiments on the maid's mer, and from that empirical data and a good bit of sniffing, would have come to deduce certain conclusions about her water; that perhaps it was saline, alkaline, but fresh enough to support organisms and sustain such delightful life as was embodied before us. And certainly that would have been the way they would have done it had they not gotten drunk and gamy enough to actually remove the glass lid and reach for the slippery little siren and try to lick her to see how she tasted. Her flowing strawberry blonde hair kept getting in the way of their slurps, that and her flips and screaming and quick deliverance at the hands of the bone-crunching Oriental, who dumped them in the alley, instructing me he never wanted to see their kind again before he slammed the door and closed up shop for the day. I was going to say that simile is left to me, but by now it's just like so much water over the dame, and I will let the mermaid go, just as we did the war and the city of the Body of Christ.

On the way in the Terraplane to a new home in Refugio County, Bobby taught us the Diddy "anthem" he had written with Goldilocks Gartland, who turned out to be a rich source of American folklore, especially that of blacks, whose musical play and figures of speech appear in Bobby's version of Daddy's diddy:

> *It's not a town*
> *It's not a city*
> *Just a place in the road*
> *Called Diddy Waw Diddy.*
>
> *Doo-waw-diddy-diddy-doom-life*
> *Doo-waw-diddy-diddy-doom-life*
>
> *Where da roof is made of pancakes*
> *And da roast duck fly by with*
> *Foik and knife.*
>
> *Doo-waw-diddy-diddy-doom-life*
> *Doo-waw-diddy-diddy-doom-life.*

14

★ ★ ★

Towns, Gowns and Liripoops
at Half Mast

TEXAS
1945–1955 and glimpses up to the present

JUST ANOTHER SMALL TOWN

WE LIVED A GOOD TIME IN A TOWN WHERE THERE WERE BUT
two telephone operators. Alice Ulrich and Viva Butler knew
everyone's business and where to find you if you didn't answer the
ring. This was intrusive at times but it was also reassuring.

Every wide spot in the road had a postmaster or a postmistress,
and a football team and a water tower to paint the class colors on,
and yes, a family rich and a family poor, a loose woman and a town
drunk, and of course more gossips than Carter had little liver pills or
Dewey had votes. And I declare it was wonderful, even if rival Refugio beat our butts in everything but basketball. And no, we didn't
have a traffic light, at least none that I remember stopping at. And
yes, Elsie Fay French would flunk me for ending a sentence with a
preposition.

It was Woodsboro, this place, and it was wonderful because we
were young, and if it was not yet Diddy it was for a while our stomping ground. The earth seemed very solid and good, now that the war
was over, and we were not afraid to dance upon it.

There were no battle scars upon our land, and those that were
burned into the limbs and hearts of our war heroes returned from

abroad were muted in manful stoicism. Everyone who could walk or roll in a wheelchair was home, and we relived the war only in VFW posts and the movies. The Saturday I ran ninety-five yards for a touchdown against Goliad, Daddy painted the dingy dining room walls with Kem-Tone, the new miracle interior, and we all went down to the Rialto to see Norman Mailer's *The Naked and the Dead*.

I wanted to take Colleen Glenn but I didn't have the nerve to ask. Colleen was a cheerleader. She had shot past me in height, but the real reason I was shy was because she was so pretty. As I write I am looking at her picture in the high school annual. With her mane of dark, curly hair Colleen was a Black Irish beauty, but I don't think she ever realized it. Nellie Jo Bunch and Jeanne Crowell were just as comely, in their different ways, but they were aloof and dated older guys. Colleen was just Colleen. She did the things for the class everybody else forgot to do. And she was crazy about her mother and daddy. Every afternoon she went home to Clyde and Mabel, who lived a couple of miles southeast of town on the curve of the New Bayside Highway.

We were full of mischief, even before the onslaught of pimples and puberty would make us howl at the moon. We ignored the POSTED signs and hunted possum in Mr. McCumber's wood. We smoked cedar bark and grapevine, filched watermelons from Mr. McCumber's patch. And it was frightful fun turning over outhouses on Halloween, or slipping up to the Masonic Lodge on Thursday nights and stealing glimpses of our Freemasons as they acted out their secret rites.

I remember Travis Naylor and I, walking home from a DeMolay meeting one night, swearing, like Tom Sawyer and Huckleberry Finn, that we would never get silly over girls the way Hugh Othal West had. Later though, when the sap moved in us, we took the girls out to Eddie Yoland's, where we kissed in the mesquite and swam in the Aransas river.

It was good salting down hides in the back of Gilbert Boenig's butcher shop. It was good pulling corn in the hot sun for Hugh Thomas and the Rookes. And the crowner was being inducted into the volunteer fire department, where every Tuesday night we played dominoes and practiced fire drills and only once in a great while had to fight a fire.

It was just another small town, I guess, no better or worse than any other, a reflection of the times. The whites looked down on the browns and the blacks, the browns did the same to the blacks, and the blacks, well, they worked hard and played hard and endured it all and never heard nothin' 'bout no welfare. The Scotch and the Irish owned the great ranches, the Germans and Bohemians tilled the rich blackland farms and every manner of man drifted through the chaparral and the oil fields. But you could cross racial lines in your work and friendships, and I loved the town. It was ours, after all, and everybody had his place.

A. C. Koontz was our doctor, Arno Walzel the deputy sheriff, Harry Cummins the banker, and Gilbert Boenig the mayor. Bill Kennedy was the weekly newspaper editor. Elmo Franklin Norris and Alvis Gregorczyk were the barbers, Helen Riskin Hamilton ran the drugstore and picture show, and Gordie Warren kept the hotel. The Carpenters had a general store, the Tuttles the biggest grocery and the Goldens a cafe. Graves Toland was the undertaker. G. E. Cavender was president of the school board, H. L. DeViney the superintendent and Juan Yanez the janitor. And everybody said The Benefactors were the nicest of the richest.

Having the sense to be in awe of The Benefactors was about the extent of my politics. Now that the war and all the excitement was over, I didn't care that Harry Truman had surprised Tom Dewey and the *Chicago Tribune*. I guess I knew that HST was still president because we saw him every Saturday in the Movietone News, but politics without war was boring. Jean Rooke and Dorothy Norris were probably the only ones in our class who could say for sure that Buford Jester was governor and Lyndon Johnson the new U.S. Senator, but then they (Jean and Dorothy, not Buford and Lyndon) were our valedictorian and salutatorian.

What was important was that Aubrey Dean Horner and Keith Hoffman were taking us to another district championship in basketball, thanks to the genius of Coach Meyer. What was important was that Colleen Glenn had led the girls to victory in the Orange Grove Basketball Tournament. I had a date at Teen Town with Phyllis Minor, who looked like Hedy Lamarr, and Daddy was going to let me take his new car. We would dance to "Goodnight Irene," and later on Lover's Lane I would hum into Phyllis's ear, "I'd love to get you on a slow boat to China, all to myself alone . . . "

But the best time of all for me in Woodsboro were the summer evenings, when the screen doors had stopped slapping softly upon the heels of children, and each family had withdrawn to its supper table, forming under each roof an intimate circle of blood and destiny where the ritual of sustenance made confession so compelling. Often, jaundiced by my own clan's stuff and nonsense and even the food we ate, I would bolt down supper and excuse myself, to walk up and down the streets gazing into the soft-lit dining room windows of those I considered our most mysterious and compelling neighbors. Across the street, I would see through the gauze of white-laced curtain the tall figures of Mayor Boenig and his wife, Mary, seated and eating with their elegantly elongated daughters, one with long yellow hair and the other with long, silky brown tresses. What a tableau! Their postures, their silhouettes, the outlines of their very noses—which were long and fine until they got to the tips, which flared out a bit like pigs, but very fetching pigs who otherwise were graceful as greyhounds. I would leave the pavement and slip up into their yard, sometimes almost into the hedges and mimosa trees that framed the window, and crouch close enough to hear through the screen of the open window the clink of fork upon china, and sometimes even snatches of conversation. I wasn't interested so much in the particulars of their talk as I was the inflections, which came out of their long noses with a charm I could never emulate with my pug button snout. It sounds low of me, but peeping Billy was drawn from great house to great house to spy upon the glowing dining rooms. I wasn't interested in the seamy or confrontational, but rather the graces of my townsmen as they softened from the drive of the day and gave themselves to the sweet communion of twilight and nourishment. I wanted to be all of them, the Boenigs and the Boones, to smell and taste and drink the meat and wine and hear the rich nuance of sound and spirit each household made at evening table. I resented the fact I was one person, Billy Mack, a kid imprisoned in but one mind and body and a single lifetime, hitched like a trailer to the genes and means of a family who, for all its wandering, seemed to spin in evermore concentric circles. I wanted to go every place at once, North, South, East and West and all the points between. I wanted to be everyman married to everywoman, to eat at every table and, shedding those skins and this earth, know all of creation. I could feel and hear my blood coursing in my growing mind and body. I gauged it flowing redder, thicker and fuller, as if fueled and drawn beyond my body to contain, pulled by some universal plasma and pump shared by all: man, beast, bird, bug and reptile, flower and tree. I was so full of fellowfeeling and anyfeeling I thought I would burst, and several times my heart ran away with itself to the point where I fainted. I would awake, wan and perspiring beneath some unsuspecting window, only to drag myself home in the dark to die blissfully and torturously in the salt and shame of my bed.

It was not long before I decided the only way I could get away with my spying was to lift it out of the covert and nocturnal, and make it my stock in trade as a listener and a voyager who might write someday for the Fay Talbots of the world. It was a large dream for the phonemic little cripple that I was.

But half of it is projection. I seemed to sense this from the beginning. And like my alchemist Cousin Crystal Ball who turned plastic into marble, I squinted up my potato-bead eyes, furrowed the brow of my turnip face and tried to imagine myself a parasite, a smalltime vampire. The blood I required was that from the heart, the rich, red seat of the soul, the fount from which flow the deepest secrets and longings. I saw myself doing anything for a story, falling in with bad company, falling in love, even marrying more often than is recommended. And so I would slaver for such drinks from the breast of intimacy and the cup of confession.

FOUR O'CLOCKS FOR MISS FLORA

The old house stood tall and bleak against Copana Bay, its weathered boards white and bearded with salt and seaweed, its shutters tight as the seams in a coffin. But there was life inside, at least an apparition of it. Now and then over the ebb and flow of the dull days that drifted like a dream into years, a slender, ghostly hand would poke from an upstairs window and push open the mask of the shutter, and a slender, ghostly face would peer out for an instant, blinking in the light. If someone in the street happened to glance up and see the face, it withdrew behind a curtain. The hand would come out and pull in the shutter tightly.

It was the Bayside house of Flora McSunder, and everything about it said go away, visitors not welcome. The gate of the white picket fence was locked. And, behind the gate, within the yard, was another fence—a few strands of electrically charged wire wrapped like prickly chastity belts about the skirt of the house. Flora McSunder never left the sanctuary. She was never so much as seen on the porch. This had been so for years, some said generations.

It was observed by those who kept count of such things that once a month someone from outside was allowed inside the gate and inside the stock fence. It was Uncle Ben, the fat old butcher who ran the village grocery beside the shrimp stand this side of the causeway.

At a certain time that never wavered, Uncle Ben would drive up in his delivery truck, gather sacks of groceries upon the shelf of his stomach and, belly and great moustache drooping, stagger to the picket gate. He would pause, fish a certain rusty key from his watch pocket, unlock the gate and enter. The charge in the wire would subside upon Uncle Ben's approach. He would step through the slack line and proceed around the house to the back door, which he tapped lightly. The door would open enough for a pair of slender white arms to reach out and relieve the deliverer of the sacks. Money would be exchanged and Uncle Ben would leave, locking the gate behind him. The wire fence would hum and tighten with electricity, and the high house would shutter and slip back into the inscrutable.

Uncle Ben was a cordial sort, even garrulous at times. But about Flora McSunder he would snap peevishly at me before snapping shut like a clam: "She's a long and faithful customer, and, obviously, a lady who likes to keep to herself. What little confidences she shares with me I honor, and that's it, Billy my boy. Now, what kind of candy do you want?"

But there were questions other than mine. There was gossip. Flora McSunder was the most mysterious resident on the bay. It was said she was the last of a family of great beauties, that in her youth she had attended the finest schools up East, and that at her coming-out party, every rich and eligible bachelor in Texas had hung on her every word.

Something terrible had happened, however, some calamity had descended upon the family, breaking not only their fortune but their spirit. The specifics were unclear. The only fact that seemed to stand out without question was the utter ruination of it. The family home, worn and severe as it was there on the bitter bay, had a hint of lost elegance. Flora McSunder was, without doubt, a haunted soul, condemned to hide to the end of her days.

The settlement around Flora McSunder was almost as stark as her own circumstances. The people who felt sorry for her were not setting the world on fire, either. In a sense, I told myself and Fred Fricks, the classmate who had me over to his house at Bayside, Miss Flora was better off, since, if you believed the stories, she at least had memories of a gay and exciting life, perhaps even a risqué life. But for Miss Flora, the villagers had little but the bite of the briny wind, the lap of the salt water, the cry of the gulls and the weight of the torpor that engulfed their pathetic passing of time. They had that and Miss Flora, and if they made little of themselves, they made much of her. This shut-in, this old recluse of a woman became the stuff of life and dreams to them, their only creation and recreation.

I had heard the stories, the little masterpieces of malicious envy that, in a strange twist, made her exotic and perfectly fascinating. More than a few men, in their cups and out of their minds, had penetrated her fences to bang on her door at midnight. Arno Walzel had always appeared to send them home. Like Uncle Ben, the deputy sheriff seemed to sense when he was needed at Miss Flora's, for she had no telephone. Tall and silver, Lone Ranger handsome, Arno was as tight-lipped and holstered as the sidearm he wore on his high hip. In all the years he had never drawn the gun. I sure enough respected Arno and his authority, but I dreamed of Miss Flora when she was a girl my age.

Something about outcasts and solitaires tugged at me. It was as if a signal, some semaphore, passed between us. One spring evening, just before sunset, I found myself breaking away from Fred and being drawn to Miss Flora's. Along the way, I gathered from the sand dunes flowers—four o'clocks just opening—and clasped them into a bouquet. I crawled over the picket fence, slipped under the shock wire and, straightening my shirt and pawing at my cowlick, knocked at the front door.

The window in the door was shuttered, but at last I thought I saw a face staring out the cracks.

I conquered my thumping heart. "Miss Flora," I called softly,

"I'm Billy Porterfield from down at the Fricks' house, and I've brought you some nice blue four o'clocks."

I held up the blossoms to the cracks in the shutter and listened, and thought I heard her breathing. I got no further response. I heard nothing more than my own excited heart. But I knew she had heard. I hoped she had seen the four o'clocks.

I knew as well that Arno Walzel was watching me. He sat in his big cruiser at the corner beneath the bearded live oaks, taking it all in, the cattail of his omniscient antenna arched like an eyebrow. The fist that held the flowers was so tight and sweaty I had to pry and pray it open. I scraped the flowers free from my palm with the other hand. I left the wilted nosegay before her door, and turned and walked away.

As I passed Arno's patrol car, I looked at him and nodded. "Good evening, Arno," I said.

"Good evening, Billy," he said pleasantly.

And I went my way and he went his, and we never spoke of it again.

Banjo Boy

They were small, thin, wary-eyed towheads, almost albinos. Stayed close to themselves. Didn't welcome company. They lived in a one-room house at the edge of town. It was plain and unpainted, but neat and in good repair. The yard was the most raked and mani-cured bare dirt you could imagine. The daddy and mother wore black, rode about in a black Model T. But mostly they sat in their house on hard, straight-backed chairs and stared at nothing in partic-ular. They had little to say, not to one another and most certainly not to anyone else. There was a stingy, self-sufficiency to them. They kept a garden, milked a goat, fatted a hog and cooped chickens. They spoke with a dialect and cadence I fancied was Elizabethan by way of Appalachia, but at the beginning of our experience I was not sure from where they had come. Wherever, it was old and backward. Their boy was quiet, gentle and shy rather than hard and standoffish. He had the yellowest eyes and the whitest hair, even after he was close to being a man. That combination seems strange, but I saw a beauty in him, felt an unspoken knowing pass between us. I was in the thick of things in that town, and I decided to draw him out, encourage him to become a part of the rest of us. Since we lived near each other, we often met on the path to school, he walking and I riding my bicycle. I began by asking him to come with me on my bike after school to slop my hogs, which Gilbert Boenig allowed me to keep at his slaughter pens southeast of town. Boenig was kind and generous to me, and I in turn helped him at the store. I told Boy the hog-slopping would take some time and effort, that we'd pedal along the back alleys of the town square picking up buckets of leftovers from Golden's Cafe, Poor Mexican's Kitchen, Dodie's Blue Moon Barbecue and Boenig's Market. I towed the buckets on a cart tied to the jump seat of my bike. He could ride on the back and keep the cart upright. And then he could help me mix the slop with the corn for the sow and shoats. I would have him home in time for supper. He seemed excited, and said he would ask his parents and let me know the next day.

At school the following morning, he confessed, with eyes averted and his pale face a livid rash, that his parents had said no. I could tell he wanted to be my friend, so I went ahead and fostered him along in spare moments at school. He was fine until a third party broke into our deal. Then he became as autistic as a possum set upon by dogs. He'd retreat into a corner, where he'd sull in a hunched curl and appear comatose. This made him even more an object of curiosity and ridicule. The other kids began calling him "Sull" and "Rip Van Possum," sometimes to his face, which he took with an impassivity I knew was a mask. I continued to befriend him, pursuing him on his home ground. The first time I rode my bike to his house and knocked on the door, a curtain parted and two furtive eyes appeared in a window, frowned and disappeared as the curtain snapped back together. But no one came to the door. I knocked and knocked, having been a paperboy who knew that the more persistently you knocked, the quicker you got paid for all the papers you've thrown people who can well afford to pay but won't because you're just a kid and they think they can get away with it. I called out his name, Boy, until I was sure the three of them inside had not only heard me, but had been tested. And then I went away, not in defeat, but with a chilling realization. It was confirmed the next time I saw Boy at school. He was in agony. But he would not acknowledge me.

I waited until the Saturday I caught his mother feeding and watering their chickens. The wire coops were up on sawhorses next to a mesh fence that ran alongside a dirt lane, and she was partially obscured and so intent with her chore that she did not see me ride up.

"Boy here?" I said.

She jerked her head up, eyed me through slit eyes, and said in a flat way, "What do you want?"

"I thought we'd go riding."

"Boy had better stay at home today," she said. "He's feeling poorly and we'd better watch over him."

"I'm sorry to hear that," I said, trying to sound ingenuous.

As we talked, I caught sight of Boy's face in a back window of the house. He did not nod or wave or give any sign he had seen me. I thanked Mrs. Boy and left.

I got to know the routine at their house so I could catch his parents when they had to come out. Now, Boy himself emerged only for school, or to accompany his parents in the Model T when they went shopping on Saturday afternoons. I could not catch him on the path to school because now his parents delivered him and picked him up in the tin lizzie. My only choice was to confront his jailers.

"Boy here?" I would say to either parent or both, and the answer was always the same, except that the father would grin after his discouraging report. Mr. Boy was Boy in forty years, a Boy whose shy grin had turned into what I took to be a warning to keep my distance, although he never came right out and told me to leave and not come back. Mrs. Boy was bad enough, but it took all the grit I had to confront him. The only thing that kept me coming back was the face in the window.

One Saturday, when I was salting hides back of Boenig's Market, Boy's mother came walking down the alley. Emboldened, I stopped her and asked the question that had been gnawing at me. "Why don't yawl let Boy be a normal kid?"

And for the first time, she softened. She took my hand in her worn ones, rough as a man's, and said she appreciated my wanting to be Boy's friend. I felt she was confiding in me, taking me into the family confidence. She said Boy would never be able to get along without them, that they would always have to watch over him because of his condition. Under the circumstances, she went on delicately, they were naturally inclined to keep him on a tight string. It was a burden, she added, but what could they do? He was their boy.

I never got straight exactly what his condition was. I didn't feel right about trying to pin down his parents on it, and I got no satisfaction from anyone else. Boy wasn't a dunce at school, although he didn't have much confidence. Mrs. French said she supposed he was smarter than he, and everyone else, thought. Mr. Surd, the choir teacher, said as far as he could tell, Boy had perfect pitch, but was so shy in raising his voice hardly anyone could hear him. There didn't seem to be anything physically wrong with him. I decided the only thing odd about him was his mother and daddy, that for some well-meaning but twisted reason they needed to convince him, as well as themselves and everyone around, that their boy had a screw loose. Now it was to the point where they never let him out of their sight. I figured that was the end of it for Boy and me.

But the unexpected happened.

Boy's father appeared at our door and asked for my father. I was shaken. I thought he was going to tell Daddy I had been hounding him and his wife to play with Boy, and was becoming a nuisance. Instead, he asked my father if I could come to their house once a week to help Boy with his new banjo, teach him a few licks. I had been picking one for a good while, knew a few chords and some blarney plucks, so, of course, I said yes when Daddy turned to me, being as delighted as I was baffled by Boy's parents' change of tune.

Boy ended up teaching me. He had a natural gift for music I could not touch. Soon he was plucking his banjo with skill and invention. His instrument was the most perfectly honed and toned banjo I've ever held. It had been made by Mr. Boy from elk, a piece of almost everything of the animal—bone, horn, cured skin, tendons, even it's wild heart and lonesome call—going into the banjo but the fur, which was used to stuff Mrs. Boy's pillows. Daddy said the Southern Appalachian forests still hid elk, which I had never seen except in zoos.

Once he got the hang of it, I immediately understood what the banjo was to Boy, and I decided to suppose that Mr. and Mrs. Boy had put it into his hands for the very purpose of release. Boy began composing songs, which he sang and played on the banjo. From that stringed tamborine and from our chained troubadour came the cry of all the diminished beasts and wild boys that had ever roamed the haunts of pristine America and Europe. Boy's ballads, traditional or freshly written from the mists of memory, confirmed what his family mien suggested: that their roots and racial memory lay deep in Appalachia, back to an almost aboriginal time when that part of mountain America, its Indian tribes isolated by almost impenetrable forests, was sparsely settled by herdsmen and tenant hunters from the British Isles while the mass of the Westward Movement marched on to the Pacific coast. Eventually, of course, the white horde, now machine-powered and tracked, its stacks puffing coal smoke, would curl back and chug into the Blue Ridges and Smokies to find in the hollows long-lost cousins who seemed quaintly clannish and anachronistic, having kept the ways of the old folk across the waters.

To sit on a stool in Boy's house was to leave Texas and the 1940s and return to the Kentucky of Daniel Boone. The house and every stick of furniture in it had been made by Boy's father, who used more pegs and notches than nails. The mother had made the clothes and curtains, behind which they hid with the purity and caution of milk-white moon crabs and cancers cowering under the fourth sign of the Zodiac. To sit on a stool and hear Boy pluck and sing while his parents sat upright, rigid in every expression save their toes—which in their tapping of time shamed metronomes—was to hear the first Kentucky Combses and Ritchies bring ballads like "Greensleeves" and "Dear Companion" to the New World. The latter was a simple tune: Dm, Gm, F and Dm, which went: "I once did have a dear companion, Indeed I thought her love my own, Until some black-eyed boy betrayed me, And now she cares for me no more." Boy's tenor was as objective and serene as an angel. And in its quavers and shakes lyrically true to the poetry of the folk genre's spare mathematics.

For spirituals, Boy would put down his banjo and sing a capella with his parents. Their hymns, which I knew from my father's childhood, came from the severe strictures of Sacred Harp Singing, or Shaped-Note Singing, an English solfeggio that reduces the diatonic scale to four tones: fa-sol-la-mi, the syllables noted on the scale in the shapes of triangles, circles, squares and diamonds. The best Sacred Harp Singing requires a baritone leader balanced by the harmonies of tenor, alto, bass and soprano. Since Mr. Boy sang lead and

Mrs. Boy soprano, and I was no alto or bass, the effect was not as satisfying, though they made heartfelt effort of it. Even Boy's love ballads seemed God-haunted; his laments for maids lost to others were almost bloodless abstractions, pure as myths. But then so would be the memory of the last sappy forests and coal-robbed mountains, cut down, sawed up, blasted out and consumed by the ravenous white prodigals—Yankee and Southerner, Sartoris and Snopes, timber baron and lumberjack, mine magnet and miner—who had borne us to a nationhood that would, after a few generations, exhaust its own resources and look abroad for fuel.

Was all this cause and effect a hint of the psychic ennui Boy and his parents suffered? Their people and mine had come from the embattled borders of the British Isles, where out of necessity the Celts hunkered down, their trust even in one another reduced from tribe to clan to family. This is what you do when foreign enemies abound, and between yourselves have no gift for statecraft. You end up haggling over haggis and murdering one another over the meaning in the glint of God's eye. Now Boy and his parents had been forced out of their Gothic American hollows to settle on a bald, sunlit prairie that afforded no cover, no shade and shadow save that which they could throw up. But this speculation was beyond me then. I could only see that where Boy's kin were fey hiders immaculate as lilies, mine were restless boundary busters freckled as the bloody blooms of the Christweed. Maybe an infusion of our vigor might help them. And it did.

One glorious Saturday evening, my father put down his fiddle—the one he bought secondhand to replace Grandpa's—my mother laid aside her mandolin, and we went, as arranged, to the Boys' house to make of our voices the sounds of the Sacred Harp. In the single-room house, Mr. Boy, as leader, stood in the middle, encircled by four Cotton Mather chairs. Boy, as tenor, sat facing my mother, an alto, and Daddy, bass, faced Mrs. Boy, the soprano. I held the Smith & Little hymnal, and chose the songs and kept time with my left boot on the hard pine floor.

It was an exhausting, transcendent experience. We sang into the night in a primitive Celthood that carried us back to an ancestry beyond the clouds of Christian dreams. We cried and embraced, and parted as brothers and sisters, promising to get together again.

Mother noted that Mr. Boy's face was red as a beet. But it never came to be.

It had been too much for the Boys, the blood coursing that way through their tight hearts and rising to inflame their pinched faces. Clearly, they were meant to be reincarnated in a life other than this, and they were of no mind to make the mistake of supposing, in a flash of emotional brotherhood, this a heaven. Perhaps they were right. I, on the other hand, being caught up in the rapture of the slightest goose bump, bent on reflecting myself and my fellows in the splendor of life, made one last attempt to draw out Boy. I encouraged him to sing his ballads, not his hymns, before a school assembly. He shook his head no, saying he would never play before anyone but his folks and me. About the best we could do was my singing his songs at school, and giving him credit.

He was not in the audience. Just like that, his parents threw up a wall between us that was never breached. They took him out of school, saying he had worsened, and kept him shut-in for the rest of their time in that town, which wasn't long. One day we looked up and they were gone.

Years later, the word went 'round that Boy had died in an insane asylum, but the story was never verified. I don't know what kind of man he turned out to be. But as a youth he was sane as anyone I knew. A notion nudges: What if the asylum story was true? What if he wasn't crazy, never at any time, not even at the end? It is a horrifying thought, in the dark of my conviction that it was his parents who insisted he was daft and drove him into retreat. But then I reason this goes on all the time, lest those of us outside the walls of dementia betray ourselves, in fair comparison, and must trade places.

STUDY HALL AND THE BENEFACTOR GENERAL'S CLOCK

Before puberty's swarm, I had a straight-A mind. It abandoned me at the first outbreak of pimples, and did not return until my libido had worn thin, some forty years later.

By high school, study hall was the dungeon of my otherwise halcyon days, the place where we were expected to bury our faces in textbooks and get a head start on homework. There was no escaping it. Study hall was held in the library and lorded over by the librarian and sometimes even the principal, W. A. Reeves, who kept a hawk-ish eye out for slackers.

At the beginning of the period you reported to the monitor what lessons you needed to do, and then you sat and did them until the bell rang. You ask the monitor for help, but no one else. You were not to talk, not to move without permission. Oh, you could get up and walk over to the big dictionary—so worn by my brother—to look up a spelling. And you could be excused for nature's call. Only after you had finished your lessons were you allowed to check out a book and read it. Study Hall was a damnation, especially for a kid so daydreamy he would graduate nearer the foot than at the head of his class of twenty-four.

But then something happened in the world and America that filtered all the way down to rural Texas and our school house and made study hall interesting and something of a challenge, at least to my mind.

Some saw it as a crusade. I guess it was, because it turned President Truman away from his domestic New Deal imitation and put him on another track: foreign policy. The president began to fight communism abroad while a new senator from Wisconsin, Joseph R. McCarthy, went after what he said were communists in the wood-work here at home. What did this have to do with a study hall down in the scholastic sticks of Mexican Texas? A lot, thanks to a local minuteman who was none other than the lord of the grand family of Benefaction to whom we bowed.

The Benefactor and his family lived in a high house at the edge of town, employing hundreds of Mexicans on their farms and ranches. Like their peons, they were Catholic, but there the similar-ity ended. Red-haired, fair-complexioned, coolly gracious in their home, cars and manners, The Benefactors seemed as above the rest of us as they were the brutalities of heat and poverty. They bought only their labor and some of their groceries locally. Everything else they brought from the big cities of Corpus Christi and San Antonio. His charming wife and polite son might appear, but The Benefactor himself was seldom seen at public functions, or anything so common as a local fair or football game. After all, he was a busy man. He was so active in the State Guard and attendant militias that they made him a brigadier general. It was an honor for The Benefactor General to speak or even nod to you on the sidewalk. This aura even enveloped his son, though the intelligent boy did nothing to encourage it. It went with being one of The Benefactors, who had an aristocracy of kin throughout South Texas. In the time I spent in that country, I never heard anything but good said of The Benefactors. In their personal and business dealings, they seem to have been brisk but benign, one of the early Irish families to make it big and benevolent on the Texas prairie.

One day, The Benefactor General donated a clock to the school library and study hall. His generosity had been so large the clock seemed a small thing, until you saw it told more than time. Even I, the befogged one, realized what The Benefactor General wanted to do with the clock was not so much tell us time as tell us how to think.

Not only did it tick away time, it served as a kind of billboard of sayings we took to be patriotic and appropriate for school children, a cuckoo way to teach us civics. Every time the minute hand changed, a maxim would drop into view and remain still for sixty seconds before being flipped over to make way for another. The Benefactor General had obviously had the study hall clock made to order.

I read the dictums from the clock with a comprehension and apprehension rare for me in my pimply pubescence. Their fascination remained fresh because once a month The Benefactor General sent a functionary to replace the old axioms with new ones. The theme that remained constant was the patriotism and the reminder that this star-spangled banner of a clock was a gift of The Benefactor General.

At first the quotations were mainstream American homilies, utterances with which few would argue. The Benefactor General seemed particularly fond of Teddy Roosevelt. I remember one Teddy-ism to the effect that the first requisite of a good citizen is that he pull his own weight; another a bully-boy challenge for us to put away fifty-fifty Americanism and make room for one-hundred percent Americanism. Exactly what Americanism was, Teddy didn't say. So The Benefactor General had Woodrow Wilson come along right after Roosevelt and declare that Americanism consisted in believing in the principles of America! Not a lot of help either. He and Noah Webster had the same infuriating habit.

It must have occurred to The Benefactor General to be more

specific because after Wilson he removed some puff by Henry Wadsworth Longfellow and replaced it with James Gordon Bennett declaring that it was our manifest destiny to lead and rule all other nations. After that stirring call came George Washington with "Put none but Americans on guard tonight." And then Augustus Gardener with "Wake Up America!"

Wake up to what?

In due time The Benefactor General told us.

It was after a new assistant coach had been fired amid controversy that the clock took on a more militant cast in its messages. The coach had clued us in on personal hygiene and birth control, no-nos then. He told us that in another generation or so, blacks would be going to the same schools as whites, much as the Mexicans were starting to, and that we had better learn to accept it. He had placed himself before the firing squad. The coup de grace the coach administered to himself was a word to the wise for us white kid athletes. Because anatomical construction varied with race, the assistant coach insisted, the black was superior to the white in physical prowess. "They will dominate sports," he declared, backing his claim with drawings on the blackboard of the deficiencies of Caucasian legs and arms and muscles when compared with the Negroid.

We never saw him again.

The clock on the study hall wall had counted him out.

And now it crowed in defiance of the things he had said during his brief time with us.

The Benefactor General started off with Lincoln saying "Anything that argues me into his ideas of perfect social and political equality with the negro is but a specious and fantastic arrangement of words, by which a man can prove a horse-chestnut to be a chestnut horse." Then The Benefactor General followed with a black, Booker T. Washington, who allowed that "In all things that are purely social, we can be as separate as the fingers, yet one as the hand in all things essential to mutual progress."

The Benefactor General's clock became as rabid and shrill as the whole country and its paranoia. His hero was McCarthy, old Tail-Gunner Joe, and their targets were the fellow traveling, pinko, commie-loving subversives who were plotting to overthrow the country. How would we know them? Look to the clock. It spat out the suspect types: longhairs, do-gooders, highbrows, bleeding hearts, liberals of any stripe, even some Democrats. Eleanor Roosevelt was the most hated with her one-world dreams.

The only ones who could save us from the commiecrats were men like McCarthy, Douglas MacArthur and Edward Teller, and women like Myrtle Glasscock Hance, the San Antonio woman who was having the works of every black-listed, socialist writer in the public library stamped with a red badge of betrayal. "Better Dead Than Red," The Benefactor General declared from his clock, and offered us Fulton Lewis, Jr.'s definition of McCarthyism: "Americanism with its sleeves rolled up."

When Senator McCarthy came to Texas to speak at the San Jacinto Day festivities near Houston, one of his sponsors, one of the hosts who accompanied the senator on the platform, was none other than our Benefactor General, a patriot if there ever was one, the town leaders said, and rustled up a reception to greet him home.

The Secret Colleen Kept

The day I got Mr. Moore's grade in chemistry I slipped off and hid in McCumber's Wood and wept. The Russians had just developed the atom bomb and I wished they'd drop it on me. How could I face my classmates, the whole town? Everybody turned out for Baccalaureate and Commencement. I couldn't not graduate. Heck, there were only two dozen of us in the whole senior class. It would look funny. Besides, everyone had already written goodbyes in my yearbook, including Colleen Glenn. Good Colleen. I had given up having the nerve to court her. But I still liked to look at her and think that we were friends. "Dear Billy," she had scribbled, "Best of Luck in the future." I know. It wasn't the cutest thing she could have written. As a matter of fact it was pretty matter-of-fact, which was cool, considering the secret she was keeping for me.

Mr. Moore had given me the word on a Friday. The next morning Coach Meyer was at our door before I had time to rush off to Boenig's Market and sell three-button snuff to the farm women. "Let's go outside where we can talk alone," he said. We stood under the pomegranate tree and he said that the man he really felt sorry for was Mr. Moore because they were going to have to go against him and let me graduate, even though academically and technically Moore was right and had no choice but to flunk me. Coach looked away and sighed. He picked up a rock and threw it onto the top of the chicken coop. Doody doing that kind of thing flashed into my mind. "Billy," Coach said, "you ought to have your butt spanked for goofing off. But there's just no sense in hanging around high school for a fifth year. Now, let's go see Reeves and DeViney and Moore, and whatever passes between us you keep to yourself."

We met in Mr. DeViney's office. Mr. Moore looked like a man who had been beaten by an ignoramus, namely me. I still didn't know red litmus paper from blue. I could hold Coach Meyer's football plays in my head but I couldn't remember Mr. Moore's formulas or make any sense of his potions. He was a new teacher, fresh out of college, and rather high-minded in his expectations. If I was a failure, the rest of the class was a disappointment, and after that debacle he left us, certainly with disillusionment, but perhaps with relief. Now he handed me the course textbook and a copy of the final test I had just flunked and told me to go home and get every answer right, even if I had to look up the answers in the book.

The only classmate I told my secret was Colleen. I knew she would understand and keep her lip zipped. If word got around town I was graduating only because Mr. Moore had been talked into giving me the test again, along with the correct answers, there would have been hell to pay for the whole lot of us. The graduation the year before had been a debacle in some parents' minds, because of how Mr. DeViney had handled it in the grip of a poliomyelitis scare. The trustees had voted not to assemble for graduation because of a statewide medical ban on crowds. But seniors wanted something to remember their send-off, so they had gotten with the superintendent and cooked up a kind of comic opera commencement on the last day of school. They put on toe sacks and marched down the hall with their diplomas. It was an antic leavetaking, as silly and light as a liripoop—a cheerful note in an otherwise frightening spring—and everyone enjoyed it but some old grouches stiff as mortarboards. How the parties concerned handled my graduation was, looking back from the perspective of time, the wise and human thing to do. I would make similar compromises on occasion for students I taught at Southern Methodist University. We live in an imperfect world, and we have to make allowances, especially for the young. My graduation was traditional and grand, and as I came down the aisle in board and gown I caught Mr. Moore's eye. He smiled and forgave me. And we all went our separate ways.

Colleen Glenn was married briefly to Eddie Rowland, had a son by him. She took her boy, Dennis, and moved back home with her parents out on the Bayside highway. Almost with relief, she went back to the high school and worked as a secretary to Coach Meyer, who had become principal upon Mr. Reeves's elevation to superin- tendent. And there she stayed. Meyer retired, Colleen's mother died and her son grew up and married, but Colleen continued. She still had her father to look after and all those kids at school. In a sense, in the best sense, she never grew up. Her whole life was centered at the school she had entered as a six-year-old. She kept up with the alumni, could tell you who had graduated when and where they were and what they were doing. She never ran out of school days.

Until a Wednesday in November of 1979, when she was killed in a car wreck between Bonnie View and Bayside.

It was ironic that she was the first of us to go. For it was she who kept us in touch in spite of ourselves. It was she who maintained our identity as old mates. It was a faint tie, held together by the cobwebs of occasional memory, held together by her steady regard in the face of our growing removal. And because of Colleen I write this and remember it all, much more than I can tell. Like Alice Ulrich and Viva Butler, our two telephone operators of old, she cared enough to keep up with us, even by long distance. How small town. And how wonderful.

DAVIDS AGAINST GOLIATHS

I was a sophomore at Del Mar Junior College in Corpus Christi, and I was feeling rejected because I hadn't been able to make the football team. The coach, Ox Emerson, had not even let me try out. He'd taken one look at me and had laughed, "Charlie Dollar'd make two of you." Dollar was Del Mar's smallest back, the guy who had punched me out when I dribbled under his basket for a lay-up in the Basketball-Box-Off. Yeah, the year before it had been Ox's idea for the freshmen and sophomores to settle their differences by playing boxing basketball with one gloved hand and one free hand, and the only fouling rule was that you couldn't double dribble. Low scoring, as you might imagine. But a lot of roundhouse bruises, contusions and butterflies.

So here I was living in the music dorm trying to make the choir and the tennis team, for God's sake. Uncle Eddie had been appearing with some carnival at the State Fair in Dallas, and was just passing through Corpus via the Continental Trailways Bus system—his favorite mode of transportation. I met him at the depot because he only had a two-hour layover. He was on his way to Mexico for a honeymoon with new wife, Tina, who had brought along her senile father, Roy, both of whom had made the *Guinness Book of Records*: Roy for being the worst driver and Tina for being fat. Roy had made it by getting ten straight traffic tickets in twenty minutes in downtown McKinney, Texas, a tour de force that had caused the crackup of a dozen other cars. And all he was trying to do was drive to the post office to mail a letter. Tina sniffed and said Texas was getting to be a police state. She weighed four-hundred and two pounds. Eddie weighed seventy-two. And he was fat. The World's Smallest Perfect Man was in decline, but he was kind and sought to soothe me, as I would later my own kids when they were hurt from being so small. Well, I was short, but I wasn't a midget like Eddie.

Tina dragged her father off to the pinball machine so he could watch the pretty, blinking lights, and Uncle Eddie held forth as we had coffee in a booth at the depot. He was done up in a nice little black suit that had to be custom-made unless you took it off a large doll's back. He looked like a foreign dignitary from Munchkinville in the Land of Oz.

"Look," he said, "by not making the football team you've saved yourself from the gladiator ring. Don't get down in the pit with the brutes. Go up into the emperor's box with the brains."

Uncle Eddie paused, and with a smile looked across the room at Tina. She was about to destroy the pinball machine.

"I see what you mean," I said.

"Think of it this way," he said. "Size and primitiveness go hand in hand. Anthropology supports it and so does religion. The Bible says in Genesis 6:4 that 'there were giants in the earth in those days.' And Lord knows that antiquity is full of titans: Polyphemus, Goliath,

Gargantua, Rubezahl, Gog and Magog. Science concurs. Two of our earliest specimens of man, the giant from Java—Meganthropus—and the giant from Hong Kong—Gigantopithecus—were bigger than gorillas. In the human evolutionary line, the more primitive the forms, the more gigantic the dimensions. Early man was much bigger than modern man. And yet who would deny our superiority? Dear boy, remember the wisdom of Didacus Stella, who said that a dwarf standing on the shoulders of a giant may see farther than the giant himself."

Uncle Eddie went on to sustain his theory through the march of civilization. As human history evolved it was quite clear that the little man with brains had lorded it over the big man with brawn. Occasionally, of course, there were role reversals: the dwarf who played the house fool, the intelligent giant. But, Uncle Eddie insisted, most of the movers and shakers—Socrates, Hannibal, Caesar, Mohammed, Montezuma, Cortez, Voltaire, Rousseau, Napoleon, Franklin, Einstein—were physically frail types who had used their wits and courage to prevail. Davids against Goliaths.

Winston Churchill had been a marvelous example. Here was a small, sensitive boy, bullied and beaten at school, who grew up into what the poet Wilfrid Scawen Blunt described as a "square-headed fellow of no very striking appearance." Winston was short and fat. He had a chicken chest with no hair on it. His arms were thin and his hands were a woman's. He spoke with a lisp and a slight stutter.

"So you see," Uncle Eddie said in summing up, "we have in Churchill an endomorph with a pronounced proclivity for somatotonia."

"Which means?"

"That he had the body of a mouse and the temperament of a lion. It was this very conflict in his own nature that drove him to greatness."

Well, that was all I needed. On campus I went about as Sir Winston. I adopted his waddle walk. I bent my head and went about scowling with bulldog tenacity. I gave the V for victory and spoke with Churchillian cadence. I wouldn't have been so odd if I had been matriculating at Oxford. But here I was flunking at Del Mar Junior College. When Prof Kelly, old paramecium John, caught me cheating on a test in biology—I was trying to pass the answers to a football player pal—he demanded to know what I had to say for myself.

I declared: "I have nothing to offer but blood, toil, tears and sweat."

Dean St. Clair took it out in blood, after which there were considerable tears and sweat for fear I would be expelled.

Charlie Camp, a tall, easygoing classmate, wrote in my annual: "To a fine little shrimp, but try not to be so salty."

And Uncle Eddie, back from honeymoon with his hippo and none the worse for wear, wrote from a circus wagon in Florida:

"Being short and sassy isn't enough. You have to be smart too."

NOT AT ALL GUNG-HO

Grandpa looked at the youth who would be my father and wondered, in 1918, if the boy would have to go to war. It wouldn't be anything new. That old patriarch, as I have told, had a lot of sons, some of them already in uniform, one sent home from France in a coffin and buried in a fresh grave out on the hill. If they took anymore who would tend the farm? The Armistice was signed. Daddy didn't go.

Again it was age, this time a little too much of it, that helped him miss the next war, one that came around as sure as the hands on an atomic clock. It came, the final tick of a great, atavistic time bomb implanted to go off in man, and my father stayed home. Oh, I guess he could have gone if he had been, as one of his brothers put it, a forty-four-year-old hellbent for leather, but Pa took his deferment and worked in the defense plant.

I was of draftable age during the Korean conflict, and damned if I didn't get the impression the old man was disappointed because I didn't haul off and do my duty. We never openly discussed it, but I could feel his reserve. Maybe he felt he had missed out on something, the ultimate initiation and rite of manhood, and now deep inside he wanted it for me, or, for himself through me. It wasn't enough that we had hunted together.

It was a football injury and student deferments that got me off. But I don't want to leave the wrong impression. Again, like my sire in his prime, I was not all that gung-ho. But there was more to it than inheritance. At least that is what I told myself.

After a couple of years of college I had turned from sweet conformity to disdainful rebellion, suddenly saw myself as a pipe-smoking intellectual, a sensitive flower in a patch of weeds. I came home preaching atheism and pacifism. I was willing to kill God but not gooks, the old man complained in defense of himself, for I was shooting at him the bullets of a new self-righteousness. Religion was stupid, war was insanity and a war that was not worth the name, left dangling as an undeclared police action, was hardly worth dying for. I felt before the Selective Service called that I would refuse to serve on the grounds that I was a conscientious objector. But I was never pressed hard enough to face that choice. And so I never got to know what kind of a soldier I would have made. It bugs me a little not to know, the Mussolini part of me that says war is to man what maternity is to woman. I'll not even know if I would have been a weenie even as a conscientious objector.

Eventually, Mayo Baugh, a Refugio brother-in-law against whom I played high school football, would be killed fighting the communists in Korea. After the telegram came, Mayo appeared in a dream.

We sat somewhere in the rubble of a city after a terrible massacre. The smell of decaying flesh was sickening, and I kept asking him why men kill so wantonly and why their leaders lie about it. Mayo of course had died young, but in the dream he looked old. He repeated my question, then began to play with it bitterly:

"Which is worse, the blood-lust killing, the cold killing or the lies? The killing is worse, I would have to say, certainly worse than lying. But to choose between killers, if that's what you want to call us, well, that's hard to say. It's like choosing between fire and ice. The result's the same. Death is everywhere."

"But what of the lies?" I insisted.

"You talk of lies as if they were terrible things," he said. "In war they are necessary things. No one could fight without them. First, the old men in government have to arouse the people. It's hard to fight a war when the people are not with you. The soldiers have to come from the people. The people have to believe in the cause to sacrifice and send their sons to die. Of course, they really don't believe it, since they really don't understand, but they think they have to, they think they have to go along. And, going along, it makes sense to go ahead and really get heated up about it. It's the same for soldiers, only more so since they have more to lose. They either get gung-ho and carried away and kill, as you say, with blood lust, or they get cynical like me and kill coldly because it is either them or the enemy."

"Whatever happened to patriotism?" I asked.

"Oh, it's still around," he said. "You see it in the very old or the very young. I had it once. But less and less you see it in soldiers like me who were caught in that battlefield between the old world and the new. Old soldiers like MacArthur had it. They had a clear idea about things, and they weren't afraid to act on them. Now, things are more complicated."

Before he faded away, Mayo told me something I'll never forget. He said the most brutal people in times of conflict are those who themselves have been brutalized. "You would think it would be the opposite," he said. "You would think people who had been terribly mistreated would know the pain and humiliation of it so well that they would never turn around and exact it of others if they ever got the power. But just the opposite is true. There is no difference in the brutality of partisans. One day they take it, one day they give it. One day they are victims of a massacre at the hands of terrorists acting for the devil. The next day they are victors in a noble fight guided by the hand of God."

Icky: Flying Again

But tragedy could be turned 'round.

During college breaks, I would drive the tenth-hand Chevy I'd bought for forty-five dollars to Oklahoma Settlement and take my cousin Icky to the picture show in Conroe for the Saturday westerns. This spelled Uncle Eck or Aunt Ella from having to take him. He liked Tom Mix. Well, I say that but I can't be sure. At the picture show Icky never said boo one way or the other, just ate his popcorn. But Tom Mix made four-hundred movies, and Icky saw many of them. Mix was the solitary knight who rode into town innocently enough, only to find himself having to stand up for folks who were being pushed around. Like Icky, with his Greek name and tragic fate, the townspeople and the sojourner Mix were pulled between troubles of their own making and circumstances beyond their control.

One summer afternoon in 1952, Icky and I shifted gears and saw actor/tenor Mario Lanza's debut in *The Great Caruso*. By this time Icky weighed maybe three-hundred pounds from eating no telling how many bags of popcorn and crackers of peanut butter while watching maybe a hundred movies without saying a word. So there we sat again in the darkened theater. Lanza, as Caruso, was singing "Nessun Dorma," an aria from Puccini's *Turandot*, when Icky burst into tears. I thought he was unhappy and got up to take him out, but he resisted, saying "A 15 Tex 851," and remained seated, staring raptly at the screen, sniveling and dribbling on himself. I never saw him eat so much popcorn.

That movie played several days at Conroe, and someone in the family had to take Icky to every showing. After the can of film went on its way to other theaters in other towns, I went to a record store in Houston and tried to buy Icky a recording of Lanza singing "Nessun Dorma." It had been bought out, so I got an old RCA recording of Jussi Bjorling and Birgit Nilsson singing the whole opera in the Rome Opera House. Never had I heard such melodious sweep and heavenly harmonies. Back home, Aunt Ella looked at Icky's face as he listened to the record and said, "Why, land sakes! The voices fly with the music. That's why he likes it. It's like flying!"

Later, I learned that Puccini's heroes and heroines were always star-crossed, fated against the odds of an overwhelmingly hostile circumstance, either one of their own making or one outside bearing in on them. And yet in their doom they triumphed in their passion. It was the tragic sense of life, the only worthwhile sense of life, the only one that could make Platos and Popes and Poes and Prousts and Puccinis, and Tom Mixes, Sam Longmeyers and Martin Luther "Icky" Rexrotes.

Icky wore out the wax listening to *Turandot*.

And then one night, after we had turned in, to our astonishment he woke us singing. He was out in the dewy grass of the front yard, singing "Dorma." It was unbelievably beautiful. He sounded like Jussi Bjorling. His eyes were rolled back in his head. He had left this earth. He was flying again, this time in Italian.

"O night depart! O ye stars grow pale. Shall die! Die! Shall die!"

FAT DREAMS IN FAT POLKALAND

It was the year Stalin died, the year a hollow peace came to Korea, the year Ike took over from Harry.

That spring, I dropped out of college to make forty dollars a week at the *New Braunfels Zeitung,* and Hilda wanted to get married. I wanted to strike for the Big Apple and hound the *New York Times* until they hired me. The half of me that loved myself more than Hilda wanted to go it alone.

On Wednesdays, when the previous Sunday's *Times* came, I would have a bratwurst and sauerkraut lunch at Oscar's Beer Garten and pore over the paper, which I took to be holy writ from Mecca. I was Meyer Berger covering the Manhattan police beat, and I practiced writing nifty leads for banner (yes, even in ye olde *Times*) crime stories. I decided that if Tony Anastasia, head of the Mafia's Murder Inc., ever got it between the eyes—say, while having a shave in a barbershop—my lead would be:

"Death came to the executioner today."

Not bad, huh? Too bad Berger stole it from me, I suppose telepathically, the day Tony really did get it.

Or I would be Brooks Atkinson reporting from behind the Iron Curtain, or even Alden Whitman making art of obituaries.

And I would convince myself there was no way I could take Hilda with me. It was no place for a Brunhilde who wanted babies so much they were almost sprouting from her asexually. I needed to live out of a suitcase somewhere on the lower West Side. Greenwich Village would be perfect, I imagined. Truth was, I hadn't been within a thousand miles of Gotham City. But I intended to rectify that. Under my breath, I practiced my swan song to Hilda.

I even tried it out on my roomie, Bad Dad Goode, who listened with half an ear. Bad Dad's sole ambition the year of '53 was to see Brigitte Bardot in *And God Created Woman.* From his immaculate cot he would call, "Listen to this, Port," and read from a by-now-tattered *Time* magazine, "'There lies Brigitte stretched from end to end of the Cinemascope screen, bottoms up and bare as a censor's eyeball.' Wow, Port, we've got to see it." Problem was, no small town picture show would touch it, and Bad Dad and I had driven one hundred and fifty miles to Fort Worth, only to find it banned there too.

A wedding band was the only thing Hilda could see, and she could make marriage sound like paradise to the half of me that loved her, for she was a-blush and so decent it made the other half of me who liked myself better ashamed. But this thing with Hilda was not all good. Her father convinced me he was the Kaiser masquerading in America as a Republican farmer of considerable substance. His favorite word was *verboten*. I, who had little to recommend me, was close to earning that designation. The only thing that kept me half afloat in the Kaiser's eyes was that I wrote the English part, the hind part of the German *Zeitung*, the last of the double language newspapers in Texas. In fact, I was the only question mark in Hilda's world. Everything else she did according to Father. She read the Bible and the positivist Norman Vincent Peale, the two best-sellers of the time. She swore by Martin Luther and danced the fat polka in fat polka-land.

Her prowess at the polka hints at a more ecstatic side to Hilda that Father did not know. She was the ideal Rubens woman, so exuberantly healthy and pink of mind and body I could not stop pinching her. And she could not help laughing and liking it, and pinching back. If it were up to the Hildas of the world, every day would be birds and bees and the passion flowers of spring, and a fount of milk, butter and babies.

It was this delightful Hilda that drew me down into soft Sundays at Landa Park, where we lay on quilts and planned, from the real estate ads in the *Times* from the Sunday before, our assault on New York. It had started out my assault. Now it was ours. We looked at the great homes on the High Meadows of Greenwich, with the Manhattan skyline in relief through big front windows, but they were too high, sixty-five thousand to three-hundred twenty-five thousand. It was the same on the Hudson and at South Hampton. Park Avenue was out of sight. We looked with a gleam at the old turn-of-the-century limestone town houses out on the East 60s. They were tempting elegant wrecks. But something pulled us on through a month of Sunday *Times*. And this was how we found the farmhouse in Katonah. This was how it came to be ours. We dreamed it true in Landa Park.

The marriage would be at the Kaiser family farm outside New Braunfels. Reception at the Sunday House in town. The honeymoon at Martha's Vineyard outside Boston.

Then the dash to Katonah, where, with Father's wedding gift money, we would pay down on the stately white eminence overlooking the Bedford Trail. I would not be a newspaperman, after all, dashing off to God knows where, leaving Hilda to cope with the babies.

Instead, I would retire upstairs to the spacious third-story attic, where, beneath a fan facing the window that looked out on the trail, I would write for Eustace Tilley's *New Yorker* my regular "Letter from Bedford" column, in the manner of Mollie Panter-Downes from London and Janet Flanner from Paris.

It was a wonderful life to imagine from Landa Park, for often it took me to Manhattan and right on down to the Hotel Algonquin, 59 West 44th Street, where I drank Manhattans with William Shawn, E. B. and Katherine White and, of course, James Thurber. One raced back to Hilda and the kids and passion flowers. We called the house and six acres "Landa-on-the-Bedford."

But we could not leave Texas without Uncle Eddie's blessing. I wanted him to see me in my new role as the elf of Epicurus, complete with my outsized queen. He would be flattered by my imitation. I wrote to him in Florida a glowing description of my Bohemian milk maid and asked that he and Tina come to the nuptial so that Eddie could be my best man. We exchanged letters. We made arrangements. He and Tina would come. They would catch the Continental.

But it never came to pass. Just as "Landa-on-the-Bedford" turned out to be nothing more than "Bedford-on-the-Landa."

Before the summer was out, I found myself fired from the *Zeitung*, which did not sit at all well with me even though I was wanting to leave as soon as Hilda got things worked out with her father. My dismissal set even worse with the American Kaiser, and Hilda and I had to cool it for a while, especially since I had to skedaddle to find another job so that I could finish my education. I figured I needed all the smarts I could get just to make it on another *Zeitung*, much less the *Times* or the *New Yorker*.

This put everything on hold. And I never got any of it back, not even Hilda. Eventually, I managed to make myself a hack of sorts, but I never got to New York or the farmhouse on the Bedford Trail, which I've always thought of as belonging to my Brunhilde and me and the kids we never had.

The other Wednesday, when the previous Sunday's *Times* came to my rural box on Topafossil Mountain, a half hour's drive from New Braunfels, the picture of a house for sale in the luxury homes and estates section of the magazine caught my eye.

Once, in a halcyon dream time, it had been mine. It is a boxy but stately white old farmhouse on six acres along the Bedford riding trails, an hour out of New York City at Katonah, the manse Hilda and I bought sight unseen. It was where we went as newlyweds to take on Manhattan and the world, and raise passion flowers and ruddy Katzenjammer kids. Great heavens! That was forty years ago. We paid forty-four thousand for the place. Now its current owners want almost nine hundred thousand. We shoulda stayed.

LOVE, MOM

After my forty-five-dollar Chevy gave out, I was hoping Daddy would let me drive the old Hudson, which gathered dust in his garage. But he said that would have to wait until my senior year at San Marcos. So I did a lot of summer hitchhiking between the drilling rigs that paid my spring and fall tuition. One July scorcher on the road between Kingsville and Raymondville, this woman in an old Cadillac picked me up.

We drove a ways and she finally said, "Well, are you gonna tell me where you're headed and everything about yourself, or are we gonna sit here mile after mile and stare at bug juice on the windshield?"

I was still on that self-conscious line between being a boy and a man, and unless someone broke the ice I didn't have much to say. The woman had broken it to smithereens. I laughed and told her my name and where I was from and where I was going.

She nodded her head and said, "In other words, you don't have anything particular in mind. You're between rigs and hoping to find a crew that'll take you on. Right?"

"Yes, ma'am."

We got friendly, talked all the way to Brownsville. Finally Miss Leona said, "Gonna be hard finding work on the border. This drought's got everybody beggin' for a payday. You seem like a straight kid. Why don't you throw in with me and make some real money."

I looked at her good for the first time. She was still a looker for an old gal, a bit hard and brassy—her hair was too yellow to be believed—but her eyes were nice. Reminded me of Mother's oldest sister, the widow Marguerite, not the one married to Uncle Herschel. "Just what is it that you're up to?" I asked.

Miss Leona slapped my thigh with the back of her heavily-ringed hand. "No good!" she cackled.

I giggled my James Dean giggle, more from nervousness than amusement. "That still doesn't tell me much, Miss Leona."

"Hummm," she mulled. "I guess there's no reason to beat around the bush about it. I run an escort service, provide female companionship to traveling gentlemen."

She eyed me taking this in. She saw my ears turn red. I hated it my ears were such a dead giveaway.

"It ain't what you think, Billy."

"I'm not thinking nothing."

"Yes you are."

"Well, what is it that you have your girls do?"

"I don't have no girls. I'm the girl. I'm the prez-za-dent and sole employee of my company. I rent myself out to gents. But it's strictly on the up and up. I'm a party girl, that's all. If you're lookin' for chummy good times, I'm your gal. If you're a lonesome fella that needs a lady on his arm for a little roadhouse dancing, that's Miss Leona's ticket."

Oh sure. But I didn't say anything. Just let her talk.

"But that's as far as it goes. A nightcap, a peck on the cheek and adios at the hotel or motel room door. That's all most mature men are interested in anyway, and they'll pay for it. Billy, I bought this old Cadillac new. I still drive it because it still goes, but I could get me another one just like that. Come in with me, and you could have yourself one."

"I don't want a Cadillac. I want a college education."

"You could have that same as the Cadillac."

"I don't see how I would fit in."

"I need what I call a door boy."

"Yeah?"

"Yeah. Six times out of ten, I'll end up having a nightcap with a guy in his room, and seven times out of ten he'll try to put the move on me, even though that's not part of the agreement. Nine times out of ten I can handle the situation. I mean I can get my money and get out without any trouble. It's that tenth time I need help. A guy gets insistent once in a while. That's where the door boy comes in."

"Lady, all the money in the world wouldn't get me to do that.

No siree. I can't go back to school all black and blue. Whew! That's just askin' for trouble."

"No it ain't. All you have to do is knock on the door and say, 'Mother?' You know, 'Mother?' with a question mark behind it. Loud enough for us to hear you."

"Aww, come on."

"That's all. I swear. Just call for 'Mother?' In the meantime I'll be sayin', 'Oh, that's my son! Please sir, unhand me. What will my son think?' It works every time. Even the meanest guys get all flustered and give up. Usually they hide in the bathroom while I straighten myself up and leave."

I turned her down.

Off Miss Leona went to work the border hotels and bars.

Off I went to the oil-patch cafes, where I hoped to find a driller looking for hands. She was right. It was bad that year. There wasn't much action anywhere. I looked for days up and down the border. I couldn't even get a job in the citrus harvests. I got down to the last change in my pocket before I dug up the note with Miss Leona's hotel number and called her.

Things went along copacetic for us.

It was just as Miss Leona said it would be, except that I found myself knocking on room doors every date she dragged up. I had to hang out in hotel bars and lobbies, because once Miss Leona and a guy started up to a room, I had to watch the clock and count the minutes and, if necessary (which it always was), knock in time to save Miss Leona from the clutches, so to speak. The guys all ran true to form. I didn't have to face them.

Leona split 70-30 with me, which I thought was fair and square since all I had to do was rap on the door and say, "Mother?" I was thinking, Jeez, what a swell way to work your way through college. Beats roughnecking. I'll do this next summer, and the next 'til I get out.

But then one night in Eagle Pass this guy didn't go for it. He didn't figure I was Leona's son. He opened the door and pasted me a good one. Miss Leona got the same. He took our money and beat it.

When I came to, Miss Leona was abject with apology. She had an eye that would blacken before she got downstairs. But now she was bent over me, wiping blood from my nose with a wet face towel.

What little nose I had was flattened so far into my face it was con-cave. She said it looked like a red little mouse peeping out of a hole. My face was bruised and two teeth were loose. At least I wasn't spit-ting them out.

"Now I know how Daddy felt," I said. "Tobin Drexler can sure hit hard."

"How did you know that was Tobin Drexler?" Miss Leona said with astonishment.

"Family tradition," I said. "His fists seem to run right into our faces."

"Well, I swear," Miss Leona said. "He is mean. I don't know why I mess with him. This is the last date I'll give him."

One of her breasts was hanging right in my face. When she real-ized this, she pulled herself together, fetched it and said she would meet me downstairs in the bar soon as she took a shower and fixed herself up. But I told her I had just soured on the job, that it wasn't up my alley and that I had best be getting back to college. And that's what I did.

Back in San Marcos, I worked nights in a gas station and morn-ings in the chow line and slept in class.

One day a check for one-thousand and five-hundred dollars arrived in the mail. It was from Miss Leona, who was carrying on in El Paso. It was what she owed me for the summer. "My son," she wrote, "it's always 70-30 between us. Love, Mom."

COTTONBALLS

Crane County on the Texas Pecos used to have as many oil wells as it had people, and this was fine with my friend Salida Cordona, since her family owned many sections of prime petroleum sands. But not even the subterranean wealth of that hot, hardscrabble country made it enticing, and once Sallie—as the gringos called her—got out of high school her family never saw her except for holidays and funerals. And then only for funerals. And then there came the time when there was no one to see her when she went home for the final funeral, that of her father, the last of the line but for Sallie.

Knowing she would be alone, save for the chanting priest, the cloying undertaker and the circumspect family lawyer, Sallie persuaded me to drive her back for the burial of Señor Cordona. I sat beside her in Dr. Wright's poetry class. We often met over coffee at the student union to compare notes on lectures, and literature in general. It was the spring semester of our senior year at the college in San Marcos, more than three-hundred miles and a dozen counties southeast of Ozona, the seat of Crane County.

We set forth that March in my father's hand-me-down, the ancient Bark of Ra, long and black as a hearse, which Sallie thought was mordantly appropriate. She brought along the deviant death mask poems of Emily Dickinson, which she read aloud with Sadean delight as we moved across a landscape which Sallie never bothered looking at, but which she fancied was purgatory, if not hell, casting me as her Vergilian chauffeur and her father as a stiff in the back who was being borne to the afterlife. It was a long day's journey into night, and I was sated with death and decadence by the time we arrived at the desolate Ozona.

We took rooms for the night in a cheap motel. Sallie, glassy-eyed, weary of the demons she had wrought, fell into her bed and went fast asleep, which I considered a godsend. I found a cantina and drank beer and danced until closing time. I thought my Dionysian devils were healthier than Sallie's.

At the mortuary the next morning, Sallie put on her highly magnified anteojos and gazed at Señor Cordona's cosmetic face in the casket. "You know," she said, "I hardly recognize this man. He was my father but I never knew him. I am grateful for the money he left me, but I know there was no sentiment in the gift. It was just a proper passing on within the family. He knew less of me than I knew of him, if that's possible. My, look at him!"

"What's the problem?"

"I remember him well enough to know that he did not have fat cheeks. He had a lean face, a lordly look. They've stuffed something in his mouth to make him look substantial and in the peak of life."

To my alarm, Sallie bent over the body and tried to pry open the mouth with her fingers. "Good God!" she said. "His face is as hard as rock. I guess it's the embalming fluid. His jaws are locked. I was going to take whatever is in there out so he won't look so ridiculous. Let's get the mortician."

"What have you got my father's mouth stuffed with?" she

demanded of the undertaker. He was a big, blowsy man in a cheap wig.

"Why, cottonballs. He was so emaciated we felt he needed something to—"

"Take them out!" Sallie ordered. "Break his jaw if you have to, but take them out! They distort his appearance. He always looked spare and aristocratic, because he was that if nothing else. It is horrible that you would turn him into a chipmunk like yourself." She gave the mortician a severe going over. We got through the graveside services with dispatch. On the way to the airport at Lubbock, Sallie cried.

"What a strange thing for me to have done," she wailed. "It is probably the first time in my life, at least in my memory, that I actually touched my father, and I found him hard as rock, just as I suspected he always was. You know, because of my eyesight, I have this terribly touchy, feely thing with fingers and toes and extremities, and I've always gotten so much communication and pleasure from tactile sensations, furtive and self-gratifying as they are. I don't know which is the stronger in me, the sensory or the cerebral, but I never got either of them from my father or from anyone in the family."

"What were they like?" I asked.

"Strangers," she said, and clammed up. We drove the bleak distance in silence.

She was to have boarded a plane that night, but Sallie proposed that we get a tourist cabin and touch and feel in the dark until dawn, when she would slip from my sleeping grasp and catch a cab to the airport alone. We were not lovers but friends, and her suggestion, bold for that time, stunned me. I did not know what to say. I stared at a road sign that said

TAHOKA 17

WOODROW 41

LUBBOCK 52

feeling relief that I had an hour to decide how to handle the situation. But I did not keep her hanging. It struck me that under normal circumstances Sallie would never have thought of such a thing for us to do. Our excitement in each other came from sharing ideas and books, not backseat gropes, and we might have gone on that way until the semesters ran out and we went our own ways. I knew she had a hopeless crush on my friend Evans, who had not read a dozen books in his life. She knew of my pantings over this girl and that. We had been honest with one another, very comfortable and now, suddenly, we were about to change all that.

"Great idea," I said, trying to appear casual, "I could stand a little snuggle myself."

Back on campus, we tried to go back to where we had been before, but it was never the same, at least not for me. I had found something in Sallie I had never suspected was there, and it was difficult to see her strictly as a bookworm. I died watching Evans treat her as just another weak-eyed Lit major. I wanted to strangle him when Evans described her as a frump, though she did come at you small and owlish, as if she had just put a masterpiece down, a brown little wizard who saw the world secondhand through literature. She did not trust her own weak eyes, magnified as they were by lenses so thick they distorted her appearance. She tried to save face by wearing the glasses only to read, or to see things like corpses when it was necessary, and that was not often. This meant she went about almost blind, but blithely. She had a radar that let her move without care, and only rarely did she bump into a post. Save for Evans. She let him hurt her. I never understood why.

She toyed with being a writer since she was such a reader and had exceptional verbal skills, but rejected it on the grounds that (A) she would never be as good as the writers she loved to read and (B) realizing herself as a second-rate writer would only cut into her first-rate reading, which to her was life itself. She decided not to do anything but read until her eyes dropped out. Her trust and inheritance would keep her comfortably.

It is not surprising that Sallie's favorite writer was Jorge Luis Borges. She was so precocious she had read him as a child, and she told me she remembered the stories and novels and imaginative characters of Borges better than she did the members of her family.

"I could see my friends in the books," she said, "because I had to wear glasses to read. I never wore the glasses for anything else, and it all was a blur, you know, so-called reality. Besides, everyone in the family but me lived outwardly, as if our cattle and sheep and oil wells, as if the buttes and mesas and the hurtful light were more important than our own interiors."

Fourteen years later, Borges would tell Richard Burgin almost the same thing about his childhood in Argentina. The difference was that Borges was encouraged in his reading and writing, and remained bound to his great-aged mother and younger sister.

There was another difference. Borges traveled broadly, but some of his pleasantest memories were of the United States, particularly New England and Texas, even though he could not see the obvious. After college, Sallie traveled the world over and became alien to her own land, especially Texas. She settled in Switzerland, looking to home only for money.

How strange came the news in the summer of 1986 from Geneva. First, that blind, all-seeing Borges had died there, at last, at the age of eighty-six. Then Sallie's letter to me, mentioning Borges's death and how it had affected her, for they had become friends. But with it her announcement that she was coming home for a visit, and the plea. Oh, cottonballs! She hated to ask but she had no choice. Would I take three days and drive her once again to that dreadful place, Ozona, the land she had hoped never again to see. After sixty-one years, the oil fortune had almost dried up, and Sallie had to go out there and settle matters with lawyers.

I drove her across the stark and brooding distances, dreamscapes, and Sallie, masked behind smoky glass, saw and talked of nothing but her friendship with Borges and her love of European and South American letters.

The lawyers in Ozona told her she would have to get by on less than she was used to receiving. "Oh, cottonballs! It is what I expected," she said briskly, and as soon as her affairs were settled we did not tarry.

"Do you want to stop by your father's grave?" I asked.

"No," she said, "all that is past now."

On the way to Lubbock, I read her a sonnet Borges was said to have written while drinking in Dallas's Knox Street Pub in the fall of 1961. It appeared under the title "Texas" in his book *El Otro, El Mismo*, published in Spanish in 1964, and was subsequently included in all editions of Borges's complete works. If Sallie had seen the poem, she had forgotten it. I read it to her in the Spanish. Here, I translate for English readers the last seven lines:

> Here too, the mystical alphabet
> Of the stars, that still invokes the fated
> Names the incessant labyrinth
> Of the days does not forget: San Jacinto
> And the other Thermoplylae, the Alamo.
> Here, too, that unknown
> And troubled and brief thing called life.

"Ugh! Cottonballs!" Sallie said. "Awful sentiments about Texas. Are you sure that's Borges? Frankly, I can't see it myself, never have, this thing about Texas. The last two lines were good though."

As we passed through Lubbock, the dismal tourist court where we had spent the night twenty-nine summers before came into view, and I slowed mentally as we passed, lingered briefly.

Sensing something, Sallie raised her face above the plane of the car window and stared at the light which filtered through her shades. "I can't make out a thing in this glare," she said. "Where are we?"

"Lubbock," I said.

"Perfectly dreadful place, I seem to recall," she said, "one of those towns you had to go through but hated."

THE DEATH OF A PRAIRIE LEVIATHAN

Daddy and Uncle Earl used to run the rigs that brought oil to the fabulous King Ranch and saved it from going broke. And, like generations of South Texas schoolboys who fancied themselves as Future Farmers of America, I toured the ranch several times with classmates.

I remember seeing the great thoroughbred, Assault, shortly after he won the Triple Crown in 1946. And I remember with what awe I first beheld a Santa Gertrudis bull, the ranch's claim to breeding fame. The beast was dark red and as monumental and mythic as the ranch itself. Our ag teacher, who was almost as big and burnished as the animal he worshipped, had taught us the breed's genetic history, had hammered it home with such pride and passion, that we approached the stall as if we were privy to royal chambers. The best bovine bloodlines of Britain and India were emboldened before us in this epic of Shorthorn and Brahman, and the old ag instructor couldn't control himself. He wept, bawled like a lost calf returning to the herd. It embarrassed the other boys. But I cried a little myself, in a secret aside, not out of respect for the bull but because I felt sorry for the great, rough man beside me. He had turned to teaching after failing at raising cattle, and I guess the love and lore of it were branded into his hide. From the day he wept for the great red bull, we called him Saint Gertrudis.

As I left high school for college, one of my parting shots was aimed affectionately at old Saint Gertrudis. I got up the nerve to tell him that the big red bull at the King Ranch was no match in size and splendor to the white Brahman on the Conoco Driscoll. No way, he said, and challenged me to prove it by taking him down to see Moby-Dick. But I went off in another direction and forgot about it.

Five years later, the summer I finished enough electives at Southwest Texas State to make a fool of myself in the real world, Saint Gertrudis finally caught up with me one morning upon a visit to Woodsboro.

"Is your Moby-Dick still alive?" he asked.

"As far as I know. I can call Chubb Talbot and ask him."

"Make it so," he said. "If Moby's still a'foot, let's go see him. I'll do the driving. And if what you say about him turns out to be true, I'm good for a room for the night and two steak dinners."

Chubb said yes, laddie, and come on down, and we were there on the Conoco Driscoll two hours and a hundred miles later.

It had been thirteen years since I had seen the Talbots, and I was disappointed to find that Fay was touring England with some other librarians. "Me lady's on a Virginia Woolf kick," Chubb said, somewhat mystified at the turn his wife's reading had taken. "Fay got me to try *Mrs. Dalloway*, but I couldn't stay hitched. No damn plot. Anyway, she and 'er girlfriends are touring the homes of the Bloomsbury crowd, which was damned effete if ye ask me."

"How do you know if you haven't read them?" I said.

"I guess by osmosis," he chuckled, "since Fay's drownin' in ever' tear they shed. But anyways, she won't be home 'til the sail's out of summer. She'll be sorry to have missed ye, laddie. But maybe Pepito and Moby-Dick'll remember ye. How're Tice and Janavee and the other two tykes?"

"Pepito?" I said. "Rosita's brother?"

"I hired him after the fire. 'E's almost big as you, Billy, and 'e's made a hand. He loves windmills same as ye, and will make a good *paplotero*. He ain't bad as a *valladero* either."

"Good Lord, boys," Saint Gertrudis stamped and bellowed. "You can catch up later. Take me to see the white Brahman."

It was only when I watched them walking together toward the corrals to pick up Pepito and saddle horses that I realized how much red and grizzled Old Saint resembled red and grizzled Chubb, the foreman being smaller but no less bullish. They talked nothing but cow.

Old Saint was pushing us, so Pepito and I hardly had time to say hello before we were on the horses and off toward the pasture. We rode through a gap gate and were about a quarter-mile out when we saw the vultures. One by one, they flew in from the west at an altitude so high they appeared toy gliders, each arcing his way into the thickening circle below until they formed a black funnel a half-mile high.

"Something's rotten in the state of Denmark," Chubb said. "But I can't smell it. Can you?"

"No, we're upwind," Saint said. "But whatever's dead must be huge to attract that many buzzards."

My heart leapt.

"Maybe a cow and newborn calf," Chubb said. "Several have died giving birth. It's got me and the vet stumped."

Chubb rode back to the red pickup and fetched his shotgun and some shells. We walked the horses under the great oak tree, which had new green upon its ancient branches, and waited for Chubb. Then we loped across the prairie toward the black funnel of fowl.

The buzzards had not touched down, but hovered in a holding pattern, waiting for coyotes to eat their fill. The wild dogs were tearing at the haunches of a great carcass. At first we thought it was a giant stag until I saw the horns and the great hump. The coyotes were so rapt on flesh they did not lift their bloody snouts.

"Damn," Chubb said. "It's Moby-Dick."

I moaned. "Are you sure?"

"Aye, lad. Turn this way and ye can tell."

"Oh, it is, it is," I said. I bit my lip so hard it bled.

Saint Gertrudis put his big red paw on my shoulder. "I'm sorry, son."

"It was bound to happen," I managed. "He was so old."

"So *viejo* he couldn't fight off the coyotes," Pepito said, his voice a husky treble beneath the thin hairs sprouting at his lip. Suddenly, he spurred his gelding and charged screaming and cursing into the bloody coyotes, who were not that intimidated. Chubb called him back.

"Whoa ho, laddie! Avast, damn thee. Give the dogs their day. All God's critters have to eat. Moby isn't of a mind to care any more."

"They killed heem," Pepito insisted. "You heard them yapping in *la noche?*"

"Aye, but I don't think they killed 'em. 'E was too strong for that. We would'a heard 'em a'snortin' and a'bawlin' if they had attacked. 'E must've got sick and died. Sure, the coyote sensed it and moved in, but I doubt they dared touch 'em until 'e was good and dead. No, old Moby was always self-possessed. I'm sure that's the way 'e went down."

"Let's go," I said, reining my horse around. "I can't bear to watch them dismember him."

"Señor Chubb," Pepito said. "*Donde esta* Ahab? *Muerto tambien?*"

"*Al vuelo,*" Chubb said. "Ye know Ahab got smart and flew away. He'll have to find him another mount."

"What's Ahab?" I said.

"One of them tick birds, laddie, ye know the white egrets? This one found such plenty on Moby's back he staked out a territorial claim, 'e did. They'd become inseparable the last few years. We fancied Moby looked healthier and seemed more at ease of summers, since ever mite and tick that moved upon 'is 'ide was pecked and eaten by Ahab."

Chubb insisted Old Saint and I stay the night. After barbecued steaks, beans and cornbread, Pepito and I slipped away from the table and sat out under the mesquite trees. It was a clear, moonlit night, and we talked of Rosita as if she were alive and we were still on the farm in Oklahoma, working sunup to sundown in the fields, and it was as if it had been paradise. Maybe it was.

The voices of the men carried from the kitchen window.

"Moby was a land mass," Chubb was telling Saint. "At least an island unto himself, 'e was, the ultimate host. 'E carried upon 'is back a world as botanically rich and biologically varied as a tropical isle. I tell ye, mate, Darwin would have busted a gut to see 'em. Caked with earth, 'e was verdant with lichen and moss, bugs and mites. Swarms of flies and grasshoppers followed 'is every step and excretion, gnats and mosquitoes swarming about 'is cuddy mouth. 'E was a great beast, 'e was, such a store of prey and predator and goodies the likes of which I've never seen on four 'ooves."

"Was he bigger than a Santa Gertrudis?"

"Mon, no red bull'd touch him. It was a sight to see 'em heavin' and swayin' upon the prairie sea like some ark. Upon 'em the elements rained everything that could be conceived, extremes of heat and cold and dry and wet, and on 'e 'ad sailed, old as the Biblical deluge, mythical-like in the rise of 'is white ghostly hump and in the pendulous fall of 'is dewlap. I'm sure I'll never see 'is like again."

It was past noon of the next day before Saint and I got out of bed and started for his car to drive home. Chubb and Pepito had been at work for hours, but they hailed us down at a cattle guard and said they wanted to show us something. They swung us up behind them on their horses and cantered out to show what was left of Moby-Dick after one night akimbo on the prairie.

Nothing of the great bull's remains, save the massive bones, was wasted. In death he was as nourishing as in life. The coyotes left much to the buzzards, who had fed until dark, they in turn leaving gristle, tendon and joints, odds and ends which nocturnal scavengers found to their liking. Of course, the flies had been first upon him, leaving the coyotes to draw second blood. The last may have been the ants, the most efficient appetites on the prairie. They were still swarming over the pungent clump of bones and scraps of hide, these big red mound builders. The tracks they cut through the sparse bluestem and buffalo grass were several hundred yards long. One continuous stream of ants headed for the bones, another came back to the home mound, each ant in the return line holding aloft a sizable morsel, obviously pleased and excited about it.

"A saddletramp 'at sleeps too still upon this ground is a dead mon," said Chubb. "Pepito, ye remember that."

"Si, Señor Chubb. I do not theenk I will forget it."

It could not have been long before Moby was reduced to a Georgia O'Keeffe painting. Upon her return from England, Fay Talbot wrote me she had taken the skull and hung it on the barn wall. Now, she reported, the spot where Moby had fallen was a fertile thrust of grass, the greenest in the pasture.

"I'm not sure it is a higher thing I did," she wrote in closing, "my little gesture of displaying his skull. In our sentiment, and even in our aesthetics, we are but predators, parasites and symbionts, and that includes Moby himself. Chubb tells me he and Pepito were having beefsteak the night Moby-Dick lay down for the coyotes, and even the night after with you and your old teacher. Ah, but a couple of his cows are heavy with calf. Shortly, while the grass is still green, we may see a baby Moby-Dick."

A Dream House for Amy Pierson

Early in their late marriage, consummated the summer I left college, John Pierson promised his wife Amy that one day they would live in a grand house, one that would match her childhood home on the Mississippi. They then proceeded to live in a succession of shacks and trailer houses from one dead end of Texas to the other. By the end of the decade, they were back at Alpine in the old Holland House Hotel, where old men coughed themselves to death in rented rooms.

If one disappointment after another only seemed to buoy Uncle John, they took their toll on Amy, who was of a delicate disposition anyway. At last, even the ever-optimistic John could see that Amy was on her last legs, that with all her ailments and ill humors she would not survive another West of the Pecos winter.

"Aim," he said to her upon the last November of the 1950s, "after Thanksgiving, I'm sending you to Clara's for the rest of the winter. You stay down in the valley with your sis through Christmas and New Year's, and then March I'll come for you. When we drive up out here next spring, you'll see a big new house all our very own. We may not have the Mississippi and the delta, but you're going to have your mansion at last."

She coughed and stared at her husband. "Why, John Pierson,"

she said, "I believe you really mean it this time."

"Oh, Aim," he said, hugging her as the tears welled in his eyes, "I've never been more dead-set on anything in my life. I owe you this, and I'm going to deliver."

Before she would have been skeptical. Before she would have demanded to know how in heaven's name he was going to get the money. She would have wanted to know how he could build a fine, grand house on the prairie in such a short time. And, if convinced, she would have insisted upon a say-so in how the rooms were laid out and such. But this time Amy kept her mouth shut. She did not question him on the particulars. When the time came, she boarded the train for San Antonio and the Rio Grande Valley with only a small "please don't disappointment me" plea written across her pale, pretty face.

Christmas came sunny and fair in the valley, and bronchial Amy was cheered by the second long letter John had written her. In this one he included a drawing of what the front of the dream house would look like when it was finished. Amy was impressed. John may have been the most innovatively disastrous nickel-and-dime capitalist who ever lived, but he was a draftsman and a skilled if impatient carpenter. The house he had sketched, and the one in which Bobby and I were driving thousands of nails, had, indeed, a look of grandeur as one approached it.

Looking straight at it, it was a wide, two-story Georgian mansion with stately columns and tall, shuttered windows. John wrote that he had a swarm of carpenters—the three of us—and that we were framing up the studs upon the bois d'arc piers and beams. The banker had been most generous in his financing. John even asked Amy to write back and tell him what color she wanted it painted. She replied that a "creamy Colonial White" would suit her.

Amy's health seemed to improve over the next couple of months, and the time with her sister flew by. One day in March of the new decade, John came for her in his old green DeSoto, which had replaced the red roadster. Amy could tell he was excited and straining to rein himself in. The five-hundred-mile drive home was among the happiest hours they had spent. For once, John was not in an all-fired hurry, the reason being that Bobby and I were slinging hammer and nail like fiends to finish before they arrived. Below Roy

Bean's Langtry, they even stopped at the long bridge that spans the junction of the Rio Grande and the Pecos, and had a picnic on the park benches overlooking the deep divide.

What surprised Amy as they crossed the Pecos was that John did not continue west for Alpine, but turned north toward Fort Stockton. They drove through the seat of Pecos County and continued east-north-east, the drama building for Amy, although she prayed he would stop shy of the New Mexico border. She was far enough from her sister, with whom she identified civilization, as it was.

John slowed the DeSoto west of Girvin on Highway 67, and took the gravel road to the right, past their new mailbox, a sly miniature of the house that awaited Amy, and continued out into the flats. Through the white tops of the surging sotol Amy could make out the roof of the house. As they drew closer it loomed before them.

Amy gasped.

John turned off the engine, hopped out and ran around to open her door and give her his arm. "Welcome home, Amy Dearest," said he.

"Why, John," she cried, "I haven't seen anything as grand since I was a girl back in Natchez. I love it!"

She threw herself into his arms and John, with a Confederate's flourish, lifted her easily, and carried her to the front portal.

Amy entered, enchanted, and took about ten steps before she began screaming and collapsed in a dead faint.

We rushed her to the doctor at Fort Stockton. He gave her sedatives and told John to take her home and give her plenty of bed rest and chicken soup. But Amy refused to enter the house again. John got her a room at the old Limpia Hotel in Stockton, where she remained until her sister Clara could come for her and take her back to the valley.

John followed them there and tried to see Amy. She refused him. She died two years later.

His outdoor drive-in movie never opened. It was a typical John Pierson enterprise that died a-borning, except more so because John had lost heart. He had left it in the valley. He left the Pecos and went on to other pipe dreams and other long-suffering women, each seamier and more pathetic than the one before.

But for a time the house he had built for Amy was a curiosity in the sixty thousand square miles west of the Pecos. People would even leave the highway to see it.

As I said, viewing it from the front approach, it was a wide, two-story Georgian manse. But you got a shock when you stepped inside. The rooms, downstairs and upstairs, were so shallow a bed would hardly fit lengthwise. The house wasn't any deeper than a drive-in movie screen, which was what it was at the windowless back. If you took the gravel driveway around to the rear, you saw that the back of the high, thin mansion was, indeed, the screen for the West of the Pecos Outdoor Picture Show, which night after night featured the flickering love play and cooing of barn swallows and Inca doves across its blank face.

Eventually, Uncle John went out of business and retired to Huntsville State Prison for what turned out to be a life sentence. Technically, all he got was a few years for running a bawdy house, but John became such a favorite announcer at the prison rodeos that he stayed on as a special assistant to the warden in charge of spuddle, which meant he was their PR man who went around assuming airs of importance without reason, making trifles seem important.

One day at Woodsboro, Mother and Daddy got a letter from the warden at the state prison. John Pierson was dead. He had gotten the October flu while announcing at the prison rodeo, and it had developed into pneumonia. He had scribbled a last note to my dad. It said:

> Tice, the collector who has your fiddle is John Cokinis on State Street in Chicago. He's holding it in your name. You can get it back by calling or writing him. It looks like he isn't having much luck selling it. I'm not having much luck myself. Good fortune to you and Janavee and Billy Mack and Bobby Lee and the little girl. Remember me kindly, if you can.
>
> Affectionately, John

Daddy wrote for the fiddle and got it back, in better shape than it had been before. Cokinis had kept it oiled and tuned. Now Daddy put it back in the closet to remain silent and gather dust.

I grew up, somewhat, and became a newspaperman, and found myself, seventeen years later, working in Chicago for the *Daily News*. One afternoon I looked up John Cokinis. State Street was not stately where the old Greek kept his shop. You would expect to find Maria Lott, the storefront masseuse, or the House of Crazy Tacos there. But what concertmaster in his right mind would go shopping in Cokinis's for a Stradivarius? The truth was that not many had, and that was why this John lived in the back and counted his pennies and ruefully admitted that his fiddles, which he had spent a lifetime collecting, had become a bittersweet burden.

"It is a great irony, no?" he said. "Here I have a treasure in Italian masterpieces—twelve Stradivarii, three Guarnerii, a Guadagnini, two Bergonzi—about thirty rare violins in all, worth perhaps two-hundred thousand dollars, and I can't sell them. I have to repair cheap fiddles like your father's and sell guitars to pay the rent."

He reached into the safe and brought out a fiddle case. He opened it carefully, as if it were a delicate hope chest. From a bed of faded blue velvet he lifted out the instrument and held it to the light.

"This is a Stradivarius," he said reverently. "Notice the golden yellow of the wood, the lovely grace of its lines. Very old this, and listen to it sing!"

He bowed the strings.

"You hear? The big warm tones? Unique to the master!"

"Play," I urged him.

"My concerto?"

"Yours? Of course, yours!"

"Ah," he sighed, "it has been so many years I forget Cokinis. Beethoven I know better."

He swung into the D Major concerto, but stopped.

"I am very rusty," he said impatiently. "I abuse both the work of the German and the instrument of the Italian."

I smiled, remembering the other John, and left.

15

★ ★ ★

Ma and Pa

MOTHER AND UNCLE CHARLIE

☆ DADDY FELT FORTUNATE TO HAVE COME ACROSS UNCLE CHAR-
lie after all those years. He wasn't kin. We often called the
older men we liked "Uncle," and Charlie was likable. He had been
Pa's best friend in Saudi Arabia. In fact, Charlie had been the one
who pulled strings to get my old man on a crew bound for the Persian
Gulf. They had spent four years over there pipefitting for King Saud
and his Texas oil producers, making, as Daddy put it, money hand
over fist so fast you couldn't count it. Of course most of it ended up
in the king's coffers and in the pockets of the big boys, but Daddy
and Uncle Charlie got enough to satisfy them.

Arabia was a turning point in our lives. For the first time, we
were ahead with money instead of behind. The old man had enough
to retire from the oil patch. He started him a trailer court in Seguin,
fixed it so all he had to do was sit back and collect the little rent
checks that came in month after month. No more moving across
Diddyland in search of oil. Still life was much easier, and now we
were convinced that, hell, Pa might live to be a hundred.

But there was more to it than that. After Arabia, Daddy was easier
to live with, and never again showed the violence that once simmered
beneath his surface. Mother had gotten his goat, and good. Thereafter,
he was a humbled man. The woman had won. Or so it appeared.

By the time Arabia beckoned in the 1950s, I was in college, Bobby was about to graduate from high school and Joyce was a full-bodied majorette dating a Refugio boy named Jimmy Baugh. Daddy wanted Mother to live with him in the American camp in Arabia, where he would be stationed for two-year shifts. But she had refused, claiming we needed her at home more than he did abroad. Her decision was hardly a surprise to us kids. She had always taken our side against him, so much so that we often felt sorry for him, hard as he was. When Arabia came up we urged her to go with him. Part of it was wanting them out of the way so we could romp as we pleased. But the more earnest intent was to see her follow her man and care for him, as she had vowed but which we knew she did with a great deal of personal resentment. How many times had we heard her whisper (was it confession or fabrication?) that she had married him only because her parents insisted upon it, that she remained with him only because of us. This was strangely comforting to us when Daddy was a beast, but as Bobby and I grew older, the male emerging in us began to wonder about a woman who would live with a man and not love him, a whispering mother who in one breath would turn her sons against their father, and in the other picture herself as a martyr for her children. It was quite obvious she was unhappy with him, but it's also likely that she, being a wife of the times, saw no way out of her dilemma. If she was confused, so were the children of the marriage. I remember encouraging her to leave him. On the other hand, gradually, almost unconsciously, I developed a distrust of her in the male-female regard that carried over into my relationships with future lovers and wives.

It was not a clear reversal that saw us leave her side for Daddy's. He was never considerate and kind enough to warrant that. We remained mama's boys, but with increasing awareness of the ironies. His ego and her soul were never to be balanced between them, and they hammered at the mystery of marriage upon the anvils of our hearts and heads. The only intimate thing from home Daddy ended up taking with him to the Nefud Desert was the saddle he used for a pillow. Joyce must have been going through the same tugs and pulls as her brothers, because as soon as she could, she latched onto Jimmy and planned to marry and raise her own family. From Arabia, Daddy sent a letter forbidding the marriage. After all, Joyce was still in high school and Daddy could not remember meeting Jimmy. At home we ignored him and married her off with good wishes. Daddy found himself not only a world away, but powerless in his effect on our lives. And he was away four years. We knew before he returned that he was a changed man, that each of us in our own way had broken him by denying him. This man so usually spare with his tongue let it loose in letters, sat down every Arabian night to write the most sentimental declarations of love to Mother. She was compelled to answer perhaps once a week at best. Once a month was more like it. Her tone was matter of fact, much different from his attempts at ardor.

Surely, Joyce and Bobby wrote him some. I never did, not once. By the time he got home we kids were gone, and this was just as well. He and Mother seemed to get along better when we were not there to come between them. For a time, they even seemed to enjoy one another.

It was at this stage that Uncle Charlie reentered their lives. Charlie hadn't any luck with his grubstake. He'd spent his wad on doctors and druggists trying to save his wife from cancer. This we learned later, because the two old drillers had lost touch with one another after they got back to the states. One day Daddy came home whooping and hollering. "Mama," he said, "you can blow me down if I'm lying, but guess who I saw at the pool hall awhile ago?"

She put her hands on her hips. "Well," she declared, "it has to be that big bankroller we been waitin' on to work over that pokey well on the farm and make us rich."

"Naw, woman, ye silly. I just seen a sight for sore eyes: Uncle Charlie."

"Charlie? Well, I swan! What's he doing in Seguin?"

"He's moved here. Can you beat that? We both end up in the same place after all these years."

"Lordy, Lordy," Mother said. "I'll have to call Colleen and invite them over."

"Ye cain't," the old man said. "Colleen died some years ago. Charlie's alone now, kids all grown up and gone."

"I'm sorry."

"Yeah, I feel sorry for him. He ain't the same man. Ye know he used to be such a banty rooster. Now he's eighty and feelin' poorly."

"Well, we'll just have to have him over."

"Mama, you're exactly right. That's why he's coming for supper tonight."

Their drilling days were over. But they liked to sit out on the trailer patio beneath the mesquite trees and talk big about the times they had in the oil patch. They told each other about how they told so-and-so just how the cow ate the cabbage. They relived, in hyperbole, every fistfight and blowout, every honky-tonk high and hangover, casting themselves in every telling as taciturn heroes in the frontier mold, men of few words but men of clean and decisive action.

Among others they held their tongues, out of a working man's modesty, but the deeper reason was hardly self-effacing. Behind their plain, flat exteriors were elaborate temples and ties of brotherhood, part pagan and Christian, where hunters and clansmen, knaves, knights and craftsmen—masons of construction and makers and wielders of weapons and tools outside the castle walls—were bound as fiercely free men who bartered their skill but not the secrets of their trade and union, and most certainly not the yearnings of their souls, not even to their women.

But away from the bossman and the sheriff and the little woman, relaxed in a grove, loosed by spirits and boon companions, they opened their tight mouths and spoke in tongues that harkened back to the Hebrides and Highlands. Their fathers had left their demonic woods and, armed with iron and riding horses and Greek chariots, had spread in hordes over an awed Europe and a resentful Asia, and later the American South and West. Theirs was a rich undergrowth of language, earthy and animate in its roots, thick and thorny in its limbs, seductive in its flowery flights but not dark and antagonistic to the enlightenment of mind over matter, especially when it came to practical applications. Poisonous briar became deadly arrows. They made of the ore of earth iron and steel, and put laws of the physical universe to mechanical use. My father never had the bravado and hocus-pocus of his shaman father, but in his grasp of arithmetic and his innate understanding of the static and dynamic, he was levers and gauges ahead of Grandpa.

So he and Charlie had a lot behind them they did not even know they knew until they got together as old men. They talked saga and they talked technology, in roughneck parlance. It was easy to figure out the background and origin of the roughnecks from the way they applied their tongue to the tasks and tools of their trade. They had come from the woods and farms, these long riflemen and plow-boys, and they fastened the old words to new goals and gadgets.

It was astonishing how bestial and anthropomorphic was a drilling rig. It was a tree of life harboring fish, snipe, duck's nests, black bears, monkey boards, wildcats, catheads, catlines, cat walks, mouse holes, rat holes, yellowdogs and dog houses, pigs, horseheads, jenny jacks, calf wheels, bull wheels and weevils. Besides roughnecks and roustabouts, you'd see firemen and tool pushers, even witches and Geronimos working around a rig. And sitting on the lazy bench consulting the knowledge box would be producers and rock hounds and all manner of cheaters and slack tubs. A rig was sexual. Male joints fit into female, with the help of pipe dope, and between the hot plug and the hot tube there was a lot of plugging and stabbing and swabbing and gushing. If the jerker pump slipped on a soft rope, you pulled the sucker rod, pronounced it a one-lunger peckerneck with a slack wallop, and stacked it with the dead line and wished for a nipple-up horsecock. If that didn't work, you could bail out or take the acid bottle.

Mother had heard oil talk all her life and she smiled at the stretchers and even the outright lies. Daddy hadn't been so happy in a long time, stranded as he was in a country of conservative farmers and ranchers who'd never been out of the county. So Uncle Charlie was welcome. He was, in his effect on Daddy, both antidotal and anecdotal. And Mother liked him because he was that rarity in the oil patch, an old-fashioned gentleman who did not seem uncomfort-able in the company of women. He had impeccable manners.

Tice Porterfield was a man of unswerving habit. Every afternoon just before Uncle Charlie came over Pa would go down to Baenziger's to buy something. Even if the larder was full he'd have to make the trip to complete the day. One evening when he was gone the phone rang in the trailer and Mother picked it up. To her astonishment, a man began singing:

> My wild Irish rose,
> The sweetest flower that grows,
> You may search everywhere,

But none can compare,
With my wild Irish rose . . .

Mother thought it a joke, some family friend playing a trick. She laughed and asked, "Who is this?" But whoever it was hung up. And that bothered her. Odd. But she put it out of her mind.

The next afternoon, as soon as Daddy left for Baenziger's, it happened again, just as before.

It continued through the week. It became a damned nuisance. It was not the voice of some kid. It was a man, an old man with a high, shaky voice. The words he sang and the sentiments he expressed were beautiful. Still, she decided, these were obscene phone calls, obscene in the furtive and suggestive nature of the caller, who was clearly courting her.

She hadn't wanted to tell Daddy, but finally she did. The next afternoon he stayed home from Baenziger's, and when the call came Mother answered and then handed him the receiver. He listened to the man singing while Mother slipped out to the other phone in the trailer court office and had police put a tracer on the line.

They traced the call to Uncle Charlie.

You could have knocked Mother and Daddy down with a feather. They had never suspected Charlie, not Daddy's old friend, not the Charlie of Charlie and Colleen, not the gentlemanly octogenarian widower Uncle Charlie.

Charlie confessed to the police, but Daddy refused to press charges. Instead he sent word for Uncle Charlie to come by the trailer house. He did. Charlie drove up and got out and came over and sat down with Daddy on the patio under the mesquite trees. He appeared to be quite contained. But then he began to shake and cry and ask my father's forgiveness.

"Why did ye do it, Charlie?"

"I don't know. I've always loved and respected Jennie. You both have been so good to me. I don't know why I did it. I guess I miss Colleen. I'm ashamed. I wish I were dead."

"Well," Daddy said. "A man can do some strange things. But he can right them, too. I'd appreciate it if ye'd step in the door there and apologize to Jennie. She's waitin'. That's all we ask."

And that's what Uncle Charlie did, sobbing all the time with Mother and Daddy trying to comfort him.

He was too embarrassed to come back around after that. Daddy told him to forget it and come and see them, but Charlie couldn't. It was not long afterward that his landlord found him dead in bed. He died in his sleep of a heart attack. Daddy and Mother located his kids and helped bury him.

A YEARNING FOR MARBLE

At the trailer court, Mother was admiring the glamor and get-up-and-go of the local Mary Kay cosmetic lady.

"Well," I said. "I'm sure all that's true. But don't you find that combination of piety, profit, pink Cadillac and mink a bit tacky?"

Ma looked at me hard. "Not any more than those old blue jeans and that cowboy hat you wear when you speak to the Unitarians for a measly fifty dollars."

When I went home after that, I tried to dress better and show a little more respect.

That's what I did when I got back to Dallas and went to the Mary Kay seminar at the convention center. And it worked. I looked past the Dolly Parton panache and found Glen Campbell's everyday housewife humming happily on her way to the bank. A woman of independent means was indeed a liberated woman, whether she was a Schlafly or a Steinem.

The gal behind it all, Mary Kay Ash, had to be something of a genius, a female cross between H. L. Hunt and Billy Graham meaning, of course, that there was some snake oil and pied piping thrown into her character. I wish now Mary Kay had come along a generation earlier to peddle her way into the poor White South. Gloria Steinem and Susan Sontag would have been too much too soon for the men in our family, but not for Mother or October Millstrom Ney or Aunt Arbie. And Mary Kay, I think, might have been just right when it came to making money, honey.

Being poor, our women would have perked up at a chance to make a little green and win a pink Cadillac. And being feminine in the traditional sense, they would have liked the idea of staging beauty demonstrations in the homes of neighbor ladies. In this way the husbands would not have been threatened, bless their spoiled little selves.

Of all the women in our family, October and Cousin Crystal Ball would have been the best at this kind of thing. That is why I wish Crystal Ball could have been with me at the Mary Kay awards night. In my imagination I made her a brilliant blue lady of sales, called from the crowd to be crowned a unit queen, draped in mink and adored by all upon Peter Wolf's white-trash heaven stage.

My background qualifies me to use that expression. I do so with many-spangled irony, in the same way that the "Magic of Mary Kay" set was designed. It was stunning, the most splendid tacky thing this side of the Pearly Gates. It took me back to my freckles and rickets and my trashiest dreams of what it would be like to die and go to heaven. Cousin Crystal Ball would have adored it.

You see, her life in particular was such a hillbilly hell that the only thing she could dream of as its exact opposite was a hillbilly heaven. Her husband, Burl, was a drunk and ne'er-do-well and it was fitting that he ended up tending the county dump. It was where he belonged, we used to say. The trouble was that his wife and kids had to share it with him. They lived in a shack behind the moldering mounds. Everything they had in the house was a cast-off recovered from the dump. But Crystal Ball was a fine woman, a lady in spite of all. My most vivid memory of her was the day in the dump when she put down her rake for a moment, not to rest, but to draw from her pocket a compact. She looked at herself in the mirror and rouged her cheeks and painted her pretty mouth with lipstick. Then she picked up the rake and went back to spreading refuse.

Crystal Ball had a way of turning trash into treasure. At least she found utility in things that others would not bother with. But she also saw intrinsic value in what the rest of us considered junk. Take her plastic Clorox bottles. She would fish the white ones from the dump and cut and shape them into vases and flower pots, which she sold from a stand beside the shack. She put up a sign that read: Imitation Marble Vases. 50¢ to $1. People bought them. But only, I imagine, after Crystal Ball showed them how to look at the vases. It was all in how you looked at them.

"I don't see it," I told her one day. "They looked like plastic vases."

"No, Billy," she said gently. "Squinch up your eyes until they're almost closed, and then look."

I did and it was true. They looked like marble. They looked fine and grand. "Oh, Crystal Ball," I said, "I see!"

"I've always had a yearning for marble," she said.

I too have it. That is why I squinched up my eyes and imagined that Crystal Ball was alive and well and with me at the Mary Kay gala. When you sell plastic that seems like marble you are selling make-believe like Mary Kay sells makeup. They would have understood one another. And Crystal Ball would have gotten a round of applause, the first in her life.

I think a lot about Crystal Ball and how we were raised and how things have changed.

We grew up singing hillbilly songs through our noses, and because our roots were rural we grew bored with the reality of the soil and of growing things. In the Dust Bowl nature gave us a living, but it was niggardly. Any kind of contraption that would make life easier was welcome. Nature could be improved upon. The ideal was not something organic but something artificial that could be added. We welcomed engines and chemicals into our garden. Pa preferred the tractor to the mule, the insecticide to the bug. And when the oil boom came, he left the furrow for the drilling rig. The payoff was better and quicker and it got us off the farm and out into what Aunt Arbie called the "modren" world.

Mother stopped weeding out the garden. She put away Mason jars and bought vegetables in cans. We sold the cow and bought milk in bottles. It was a marvel to us that manufacturers could make flowers and plants out of plastic and paneling out of sawdust, that they could make five-and-dime gilt look like Archimedes' gold and seguins look like silver. When our honky-tonk singers put all that glitter on their jeans and boots we thought they were pretty as peacocks. When they were wired for amplification we applauded. It both enhanced the sound and filtered out the corseness, like spreading syrup on a biscuit, or putting away your work clothes for your Sunday best. Sure. We ran away with ourselves, gooping up everything to the point where even our songs and sermons turned from salt to sugar. Salt was out anyway and refrigeration was in. Maybe it was technology, usually identified with progress, but we lost something in the exchange.

Where once we had been rustics we became rednecks. Where once we had been provincials hidebound to a time and place, we became greasy gypsies, moving back and forth across the anticlines of Texas in search of more grease. When they put metal houses on wheels and sold them as cheaply as a Ford or Chevy we cried Eureka, and used them to advantange without any idea that others might be scornful. We took our fundamentalist faith with us, transferring our letter from a small backwoods congregation to that larger, radiating laity of the radio evangelist. We mailed off our offerings to Brother Brinkley at Del Rio and received in return a genuine, simulated photograph-like portrait of Jesus Christ complete with a genuine, simulated autograph in Jesus's genuine, simulated hand. Of course, our Jew was Aryan with blue eyes and strawberry blond hair. We put him on the imitation mantel above the imitation wood fireplace in the place of honor beside the family Bible.

BOY, DID SHE FIX HIM

It was stupid, but Mother did it, the dumbest thing I can imagine. She cut off her nose to spite her face, only in this case she gave up her breast for now, and maybe her life.

The target of her spite was Daddy, and maybe a little bit of me as well. Why does pride have to be so self-destructive?

I must go back to the beginning of my parents' retreat to Seguin.

After all those years on the road to Diddy Waw Diddy, Mother wanted a permanent hometown, and she got it when Pa came back from Arabia and opened the trailer park in Seguin. That is, they were there to stay, no matter that they remained on wheels. Since all their tenants lived in trailerhouses, that's what Pa bought Ma: a tiny little silver capsule with barely enough room for two. And he parked it right in the middle of the others.

It didn't suit her.

Mother liked people, but on her own terms. She got along best with those who sought her out on her own ground and in her own time. Otherwise, she was a loner. She wanted a bigger trailer, and she wanted it on the hill of live oaks overlooking the park. It was a part of their acres anyway, and an ideal place for a home. Mother's way with Daddy was odd, to say the least. She didn't work on him the way wives usually do husbands. She seldom asked anything for herself, but when she did she wished for it aloud a time or two, and didn't speak of it again, even if it lay unfulfilled, which was usually the case. The old man was not inclined toward making others' dreams come true. His love for her brought few gifts or surprises, nor many promises. And while he committed himself to putting her up on the hill, he never said it would be in a big, new mobile home. Not only was Daddy a skinflint, he was cagey and wouldn't be confined by others' expectations. So it seemed that that was that, that Mother would never get her portable palace on the hill and Daddy would grow old with satisfaction, counting the pennies he'd never spend.

Boy, did she fix him.

When the lump developed in her breast, she felt it and guessed what it was, especially as it grew over the years. But she said nothing to anyone, not even Joyce. When finally she had no choice, and the doctor found cancer, she blamed it on the old man. "You know how Daddy is," she said. "He doesn't like for me to spend his money, and you know how expensive doctors and drugs are. I just decided to wait it out."

I had been out of the family picture for five years, mainly because my second wife, by whom I had two children, and Mother could not hide their dislike of one another. I took my own budding family and skedaddled to Detroit and Chicago for a few years, did not return to Seguin until the day Mother had a mastectomy. We forgave one another. I made it easy for her (or did I?) by bringing along a new wife.

Subsequently, I'd spent the time reestablishing family ties and plotting with Bobby and Joyce to get Ma up on the hill in her dream trailer. We waited to see if Daddy would make a generous gift to her on his own, as he did in '42 when he thought to make her well by selling his stallion for a dining room suite. When it became clear that Pa was not going to do right by her on his own, Bobby and Joyce showed up unannounced, grabbed him by the collar and said, "Come on, old man, get your hat and checkbook. We're taking you and Mother over to Repo City where you're going to buy her the longest trailerhouse they've got to put up on the hill."

He balked, but they shamed him with the prospect of her count-ing down precious little time on earth, and he went along with it, his leathery old face a study in pain as he wrote out a check for more than nine thousand dollars for the trailer of Mother's choice. My mind went back to Gladewater: Forty dollars for her first house as a wife and mother, and now, forty years later, two-hundred and twenty-five times that for this, her last house. And it wasn't much more house, to tell the truth, mostly a tinderbox of sawdust and glue sheathed in aluminum. Daddy had to anchor it in concrete to keep it from blowing off the hill.

But she was thrilled. There was nothing to do now but wait and see if the cancer returned.

A Lizard on the Blink

It was Daddy on the phone from Seguin. I held my breath. He never called. It had to be important, and it was probably bad news about Mother.

"Billy? Is this Billy?"

"Yes, Daddy, it's me."

"Who?"

"Billy! It's me. You've got 'em, Daddy. This is Billy talking to you. What's up?"

"Heh, heh, nothin's up. That's why I'm calling."

"I don't get it, Daddy. Nothing's wrong with Mother?"

"Naw, callin' for myself. I . . . ah . . . I need for you to get ye'self down here. When can ye come?"

"Soon as you need me. What's the problem?"

"Well, I can't say on the phone like this, son. We need to talk between us, you know . . . confidentially."

"Fine, Daddy. But God, you're scaring the hell of out of me. Can't you give me a clue?"

"Billy, it's nothing really, just a little something about my health that's pesterin' me, and I don't know exactly what to do about it. I don't want to bother ye mother with it, what with her medical problems. If Earl was here, I could talk with him, but he ain't. So I'm turning to you . . . "

"Don't say another word, Daddy. I think I understand. I'll be there this weekend, okay? See you Saturday after lunch."

"Billy, now keep this to ye'self about my calling. Just tell ye mother your work brought ye down this way, and you just decided to drop by, okay?"

"I see. Sure. See you Saturday."

I don't know what I thought I understood, except that Daddy was getting ready to drop something on me strictly man to man.

The week flashed past, and so did the three-hundred miles between Dallas and Seguin. That Saturday, I pulled into the driveway of their trailer on the hill, talked a while with Mother, who was flat on her back in their bedroom. She was up and about after the mastectomy, but lately she'd spent more and more days in bed. She was weak, and she looked like a ghost. But the doctors had found little to alarm them.

After a while, Daddy and I settled ourselves in chairs on the front patio beneath the mesquite. It was late in October and pleasant, the air clear and easily carrying the sounds of the earth. Bean pods lay withered and dry beneath the thorn trees, and when an armadillo poked through them after dark they rattled like vipers. It was still light, and Daddy's black cat, Cat, was having a field day with tree lizards. She had already deposited two carcasses, freshly killed but not eaten, on the porch steps, and now she was consuming a third lizard, beginning with the tip of its tail and working her way up its body as it trembled and blinked, still aware, but resigned.

Daddy had brought out the hum, even had a nip himself, so I knew we were about to get into it, whatever it was.

"Billy," he said after a while, "I cain't get a hard-on."

"Is that what you called me down to tell me?"

"Yep."

I couldn't help myself. I looked him in the old face and grinned. "Well, shit, Daddy," I said. "Don't you think it's about time? Shoot, man, only last May you turned seventy-three. A lot of men lose the lead in their pencil way before that."

He was not amused. His face reddened and he pulled himself up and slammed the folding chair together. "I was hoping ye'd take this as seriously as I do, but if ye gonna make a joke of it, let's just forget it."

"Daddy, I'm sorry," I said. "Come on. Sit down. Open your chair and sit in it. I can understand your sensitivity. If it was me with the problem, I damned sure wouldn't be joking about it."

He settled back down, gravely. I assumed the same demeanor.

"You know, it could be physical or psychological."

"Well, physically I don't feel so bad. My legs are kindy stiff and my feet get cold, even when the weather's warm, but they been doing that for years. It just seems the life's gone out of my old tool. I don't even have those morning boners anymore."

"Then it's psychological," I said.

"What's this sigh-co-logical business?"

"That it's all in your head, that you're worried about something or other and it's blocking otherwise natural impulses."

"I have natu'ally been worried about your mother . . . "

"That could be it. It could be any number of things that can be remedied. Why don't you go see Dr. Moore and tell him about it?"

"Why, shit, Billy, that's the stupidest thang I've ever heard you say. And you've come up with dillies. I don't want ever'body on the Guadalupe River to know my old pecker's limp!"

"Daddy, doctors are like priests. They're sworn to uphold the privacy inherent in a doctor-patient relationship. Besides, you know Dr. Moore's a decent man. He wouldn't put anything out like that."

"Well, one of his nurses might."

"No, don't be silly. They're not sitting up there waiting to get the goods on some old fart. You go see Dr. Moore. Set your mind to rest. Call me and tell me what he says. I'll help in any way I can, okay?"

"All right, if that's what you thank."

It turned out to be more serious than the old man imagined. He had eaten so much animal fat over the years, had smoked like a chimney so long that his pipes were clogged from his heart to his toes. His arteries were so hard he was getting little blood circulating below his waist. The doctors weren't as worried about his penis as they were his feet. Dr. Moore told him they were going to rot and fall off if he didn't submit to an operation. At his age, he had a fifty-fifty chance of surviving surgery, because it would involve replacing old pipes from his heart to his knees with new plastic ones. Daddy had spent his working life stringing pipe, and the whole idea greatly appealed to him. He went into surgery with such confidence that it all seemed a breeze. He was home in two weeks and calling me on the phone in six.

"Boy," he said, "get ye'self down here. Something's up and I want to tell ye about it."

I got down there during the Christmas holidays, bearing gifts and good cheer and finding some (Mother was doing much better), and even though it was cold and icy, Daddy and I eventually took our places on the patio, passing the bourbon between us.

"Boy," he said at last, "you should see me in the mornings."

"And what would I see if I saw you in the mornings?"

"A boner, boy, a big one as hard as you please."

"And what do you do with it, Pa?"

We heard the trailer door open behind us, and we turned to see Mother standing there in a nightgown, a grin on her face. She had heard us.

"I'll tell you what he does with it," she said, "he gets rid of it the way he always does."

"How's that, Mother?"

"He pisses it off."

She giggled and slammed the door. Pa looked at me and winked.

Things Over and Done With

One day I called Mother on the phone and said, "I've been keeping this a secret too long. Sally and I got a divorce several weeks ago. She's fine and I'm fine, but I just wanted you to know."

"Oh, Billy Mack," she said. "Don't worry about how I will take the things you do." I heard a kind of half laugh. "I'm so used to you and Bobby and your women now that nothing you could tell me would surprise me. You're my babies and I love you anyway."

She's on the last leg of her run for Diddy. The other day Dr. Moore confirmed what we've suspected for some time now. The cancer is not only in her breastbone and ribs, but spreading through her body and into her skull. She is now in the hands of Dr. Cohen, and she's in good spirits even if she does look like hell. The chemotherapy seems as ravaging as the cancer. She is bloated and hairless now, terribly thirsty, but still on the phone every day talking with Joyce and the tenants in the park. Joyce has been her mainstay. They've become so alike it's eerie.

Joyce told me something the other day that haunts me, takes me back to that fall when Daddy thought he was losing his manhood. She said that when Mother came home after her mastectomy, one night Daddy got out of his bed and went over and reached for her suggestively. Mother told him no, that sex between them was over and done with, a thing of the past. He never approached her that way again.

But that was not the end of the story. Mother complained to Joyce that every night the old reprobate went to sleep with a paper tissue wadded up in his hand, and that by morning the tissue was on the floor under the bed, full of telltale evidence. Awake, he always got up, retrieved the napkin and flushed it down the commode, thinking Mother was not privy to his secret. I wondered if all men who waste away to bed end their manhood the way they began it.

A BRIGHT KITE AND A PRAYER

DALLAS
March 13, 1979

I got word on a Tuesday that the day before Mother was rushed from the trailer in Seguin to a hospital in San Antonio, where they slit her throat and inserted tubes to ease her breathing. We thought the cancer would get her, never considered pneumonia.

Daddy and Joyce were with her. They said she came to now and then and that her condition was serious but stable, and that they would call my neighbor if she worsened. I felt awfully out of touch, what with no phone. Ma Bell, the other mother of us all, cut it off when I was in Seguin over the previous weekend. The fact that this time it was their screw-up and not mine didn't make me feel any better. I didn't have the heart to raise hell. It seemed a minor bother. I would settle come payday and AT&T would be seventy-four dollars richer. Big deal. Thank God for friends with phones they can afford.

It was the week before last that Ma went bananas. That was Dr. Cohen's word for it and he meant it affectionately. Again, it wasn't the cancer, though the lesions had been in her skull for some time, having spread from her breastbone and up her spine. Mother had forgotten to take her antidepressant pills and she got shaky and paranoiac, imagining the worst kind of calamities. She thought the people in the trailer court were fighting and she called the police out twice before Daddy realized it was all in her mind. She thought I was lying dead in my coffin in Dallas—which in a way was true—and she raised a ruckus with the old man because he didn't seem concerned about me. They dosed her up good with sedatives and took her to the local Guadalupe Valley Memorial Hospital. After a day and a night they called Daddy and told him to come after her, that she was violent and that they couldn't handle her. Dr. Moore suggested we might have to commit her. She was throwing things at the nurses and being contrary as all get-out. Daddy went down there and found her sitting at the edge of her bed, naked and defiant. He cussed out everybody and took her home. He stayed glued to her side, as affectionate, afraid and fumbling as a faithful dog. Almost dear. Now that's something we thought we'd never see. But was it worth dying for? Was Mother rational enough to catch the last irony of their marriage?

Apparently so, and she seemed to be up for it. By the time Bobby, Joyce and I got to the trailer she was calm and lucid. She had asked Daddy to give her a sponge bath and she had put on her best rose gown, lipstick and rouge. I bent over the bed and kissed her.

"You weren't dead, were you?" she said.

"Not by a long shot. I don't need to tell you what a sissy I am with the gout. But here I am, pinch me. You were just having a bad dream, imagining bad things that weren't true."

"Does it mean I'm losing my mind?" She looked at me acutely, her dark eyes gauged for the slightest suggestion of deception. We had talked about it before, when we learned the cancer had spread to her skull, and she had gotten us to promise that if her mind went we would take her off the drugs and let her die.

"Mother," I said, "Dr. Cohen and Dr. Moore both agree that it isn't the cancer that's causing you to go out of your head. It is the antidepressant that you got off of that's causing the hallucinations. We've got you back on it, in big doses, and already you're better. If you slip back over the next day or so, I'll tell you what's right about your thinking and what's wrong." I laughed. "Haven't I always done that anyway?"

She squeezed my hand. "I trust you," she said.

"Hey," I said, lying down beside her, "remember when I was a kid and having those nightmares?"

"Yes."

"And remember how you used to take me to the bathroom and wash my face and tell me that it was just bad dreams and that everything was all right?"

"Yes."

"Well, turnabout is fair play. It's my time to mother you."

"Daddy says I really put one on at the hospital," she said shyly.

I laughed. "Oh, Ma, you pulled a beaut. They'll remember you for a long time, parading bare-assed down the halls."

She giggled.

Then she grew earnest. "Billy," she said, "I wasn't completely crazy. I thought Daddy had put me in an asylum. I didn't know where I was and I kept calling for you and Bobby and Joyce but no one came. I decided that I was going to get out of there if it killed me." She sighed and wondered aloud if Dr. Moore was mad at her.

"No," I said. "He understands."

Later, when Dr. Moore telephoned from Seguin, Mother got on the line and apologized. Henry Moore is an overworked and harassed doctor in that little town, but he was sweet and made her laugh.

I left Seguin feeling better about her. Bobby and Joyce and I had stopped by to see Steve Cohen, Mother's specialist in San Antonio, and he said the spunk she had shown in the Guadalupe Hospital was the very thing that had kept her alive these past three years—six, really, if you count the first mastectomy. And he agreed with Joyce's offer to take Mother to Three Rivers where Joyce could care for her. It would relieve Joyce from making those two-hour trips back and forth, and it would give Daddy some rest. The doctor thought it would do Mother a world of good.

Our only fear was selling it to Daddy. Since their marriage, they'd not been apart except for that night he spent in jail at Altus, and the four years he was in Saudi Arabia. Oh, they'd been psychologically apart as I've made clear, had more grudges and battles than even I've mentioned, but still they'd stuck it out through the coming and going of children, grandchildren and great-grandchildren. Bobby, ever the salesman and always the stalwart when it comes to family matters, sold it to them like a preacher selling salvation. Joyce was excited. She and Jimmy would redo a room for Mother and put in an air conditioner, and we would all meet in Seguin to drive her down to Three Rivers. If she couldn't sit up all the way, we would lay her down in the back of Bobby's station wagon. Damn. The best laid plans.

But maybe, I told myself, she would surprise us and pull through again. She'd done it before. Lord knew she was tenacious as a leech. If she could read this that I wrote in my journal, perhaps she would rally. And so I wrote and sent it up like a bright kite soaring and tugging on a taut string, and wished Mother could look out her window and see it and recover and share with us one more lovely spring.

The Honey Lady

On my trips to Seguin I'd been stopping at Carrie Primm's "Help Ur Self" honey stand on the road between Zorn and Geronimo, right on the line between the Balcones Escarpment and the Blacklands. I'd bought many a bottle of Ms. Primm's wildflower honey, which complemented Mother's buttermilk biscuits and butter, but I'd never met her. None of her customers had to.

She'd thrown up a stand in front of her house alongside the road, and all you did was drive up, get out of your car, put the correct change in an old crock churn, grab you a bottle of honey off the shelf and go your merry way. If you didn't have the correct change, there was usually the makings of it in the crock, especially if there'd been customers before you. Ms. Primm didn't bother to drain the crock of the day's take until dark.

That's the way it had been, for years.

But this Sunday the stand was gone, and I stopped to find out why. I was afraid Ms. Primm had died or something. She was old. The reason I knew was because I'd seen her a time or two from a distance as she puttered about the place in a sunbonnet. Besides, I had been her customer for a long time, time enough for me to have grown a little gray myself, and settled into a sentimental habit which now was shaken by the absence of her honey.

I walked through a flock of White Leghorn hens and stepped up on her porch. "Ms. Primm," I called through the screen door.

"What'cha want?"

"Honey."

"Do ye see any out there?"

"No, ma'am."

"That's because there ain't any. I'm wore out with the honey business. Took my stand down."

"I'm sorry to hear that. I've kind of developed a taste for it." I paused, hoping she would come to the door and embody the voice from within. But she did not appear.

"Humpf," she finally said from somewhere behind the screen, "that may be, but I'm tired of fooling with it. People got to where they'd cheat. They'd take my honey but wouldn't leave me no money. Some days I'd go out there and they wouldn't be a nickel in the pot. All the honey'd be gone and nothing in its place. Here I was robbing the bees and now the public was robbing me. Sounds fair, but it was no such thing. I was gettin' stung twice!"

And with that she let out a loud cackle. If it had not been in such amusement, her laughter would have reminded me of the Wicked Witch of the West.

"Well, thank you," I said, retreating, realizing that this was all I was going to get out of her.

"No sense to come back," she shouted.

"I won't," I called back, "but thanks just the same."

I wanted to tell her how long I had been stopping there, since I was a kid in college, and I wanted to reassure her that never once had I shortchanged her. I wanted to tell her that I had often thought of her as one of the uncompromising constants in a world that had gone madly off course. I wanted to tell her that I had bounced around in my life and work, had failed at marriage and had foundered at this and that, and yet her honey had always been out there for the taking.

I wanted to tell her that the road in front of her house could change from a country lane to a highway, that the towns and cities along its way at either end could grow and change, that a generation could live and die and be born again, that luminaries like Marilyn Monroe and Elvis Presley and Janice Joplin could flare up and crash down, that Eisenhower, Kennedy, Johnson, Nixon and Ford could pass through the presidency and the country could pass through hell, but that I couldn't pass by Ms. Primm's without stopping for honey.

I wanted to tell her that everything about me might be changed, that I might be coming from a different direction in a different car with a different lady, that I might be up on my luck or down, that I might be coming or going, but that the honey pot was always there.

I wanted to tell her that it was there inviting us all to have something sweet with a clear conscience.

I wanted to tell her that it was there saying there is trust in the world, that people are okay, that they won't take something for nothing, that in the main that's how we are. That is what I wanted to tell her.

Oh, if only I had told her years before. She would have believed it then. Maybe it would have made a difference in her not giving up. Oh, if only Daddy and I had told Mother years before that we loved her, and had kept saying it, maybe she would have believed it. And maybe it would have made a difference in her not giving up.

Now it was too late. The truth was in the crock.

GOT TO SEE THE LITTLE BOY DANCE

SAN ANTONIO
March 19, 1979

It didn't sound like Mother, but Daddy swore it was true. As the ambulance came that Monday to pick her up, she scribbled a note and left it for Daddy to find. She wrote eight words: "I'll have a new home in Diddy someday."

By the following Friday I was convinced her fatalism was prophetic. For four days she had fought for each breath, her ravaged body rising and falling in a paroxysm of pain and fever as the pneumonia roared like lava in her lungs. For three nights Joyce hung by her side in Room 254 at San Antonio's Northeast Baptist Hospital. Then, Thursday night, it was my turn. I gained, in those dark hours, a new respect for Joyce. What you did, instinctively, was breathe each breath with Mother, as if to help, and of course it was emotionally and physically exhausting. Joyce had done it for three nights running, being spelled during the day by Daddy. Now, after only a single night, I was ready for Bobby to relieve me.

It had been an eerie vigil for me as Mother drifted back and forth between the conscious and subconscious. One minute she would be talking about how her skeepskin kept her from getting bed sores, and the next minute she would be back in the trailer house at

Seguin, reminding me in an impatient voice to flush the commode so Cat could drink from it. She would cry that her medicine was costing Daddy a hundred dollars a month, and then she would talk with the dead—her mother and father, Mama and Papa Harrell— though much of it was dreamy. The words came out as if from a cadaver that had been wound back up and given breath by an insistent respirator. Sometimes her words would run away from her and explode through her caked lips in bursts of air and spittle. Other times they would come out as if carved at great sacrifice from the scriptured tablets of her soul.

"Dr. Moore gave me six months to live years ago," she managed to say at one point. After that she got weaker and wobbled off into incoherence. Just about the time I thought her mind would never come back, she beckoned me close. She raised a long, shaky talon and presented it to me. "How do my nails look?"

"They look beautiful," I said. "They're a pretty orange."

"I do my nails myself," she said.

Sunrise brought a brutal Friday. Mother's fever went up, her breathing became even more labored, and her blood pressure dropped.

"I've got to see the little boy dance," she gasped, looking at me madly. "Billy wears the black hat." She sank into a semicoma.

I retreated to the waiting room, worn out with hearing her lungs heave and watching her body rise off the bed and quiver and fall. Daddy was due in from Seguin and he was late.

We worried about his driving. He thought he was a cavalier at the wheel, and, nearing eighty, he seemed to want to pair his years with miles per hour. The problem was, he handled a car in just about the way you would think.

At last he showed up, stepping stiffly from a police car in front of a wrecker that was towing his bashed-up Chevy. I ran out front.

"What's happened?"

"Had a little wreck," he said, waving the wrecker on.

The wreck involved four vehicles. He was only shaken, though his car was out of commission. And he didn't get a ticket. It wasn't his fault, he said. I couldn't believe it. I knew by hunch what he told the cop, who I was sure was young enough to be a grandson: "Hey, bub, my wife's dyin', I just ruined my car and you're sittin' out here on the highway a'askin' me stupid questions to put in your report. Why don't'che put that shit down, act like a good Scout and take me to 'er bedside?" At least the latter is what happened.

Pa and I sat in the room with Mother. She looked like she was awaiting vultures. So did he. He was gray and gaunt and sat forlornly, his horny old hands anchored like weights in his lap. He had a cut on his elbow, a bruised shoulder, a wrecked car and a dying wife, and he'd forgotten to bring his high blood pressure pills. Suddenly he belched.

"You ate a bunch of cabbage."

It came from Mother, this teasing quip, and I thought I was dreaming. She was supposed to be out, zonkers, but behind all that fever and fog, down below the cancer and pneumonia, cutting through the drugs and coming up for air, was her old wit.

"Naw, woman," he said. "Sausage."

By the time I headed for the airport to pick up Bobby, I had geared myself up again to accept her death. "I need a rest," she had said. "I am tired of breathing. It is such an effort."

"If you stop," I told her, "you're done for."

"I know," she said, "but I don't care. I'm so tired."

I looked at her and felt a great pity. The suffering had left a mark on her that I thought would never go away. For the first time, I wished she would stop breathing and die.

Bobby was with her through the night Friday and she was semi-comatose and critical. Joyce and Jimmy rested in a nearby motel. We alerted other family members and made tentative funeral arrangements.

Mother hung on Saturday, though by now she was considered comatose. All her signs were at the lowest ebb. Bobby insisted on staying with her. When I went to relieve him just before midnight, I found him trying to talk to her. He was convinced she could hear him, that the moan in her breathing, the darting of an eyebrow, was a signal, her own faint Morse code. I thought he was crazy from exhaustion. So did the nurses. We humored him and sent him to bed.

I sat and listened to Mother inhale and exhale and I grieved. I looked at her and I got angry. She was not alive. Janavee Elizabeth Harrell Porterfield was kaput. The only reason her heart beat and her lungs functioned was because of the oxygen and the fluids they pumped into her.

A big, red-faced woman, a nurse's aide, came in to adjust the bed so Mother's head would rest on her neck instead of her chest. She was so weak she couldn't hold it up. The nurse's aide tried to prop her up with pillows. Nothing worked. I took off my belt, a brown, soft swede, looped it across Mother's forehead like a headband, and buckled it to the headboard.

"It's a shame how they keep these poor things alive," the woman said. "Don't you think they ought to release her from her misery?"

I looked at Mother, upright only because of my belt.

It was 1 A.M. Sunday and Dr. Steve Cohen was home asleep, but I telephoned anyway. In essence, what I asked him was, Why continue the masquerade?

"We are doing nothing fancy," he assured me. "But we must maintain the oxygen and fluids until I am convinced the damage that has been done is irreparable. It's not likely, but she could, by some miracle, come back. But don't take heart in that. I'm speaking technically. Certainly she is most grave."

I returned to her bedside. The nurse's aide had fresh sheets. She asked me to help lift Mother a bit. I unbuckled the belt. It was soaked with her salty sweat. Now it became a holy relic to me, and I thanked Wit Odin for teaching me about the talismanic and its power. As I put my cupped hands under Mother and lifted, my left hand slipped and my fingers fell into the crack of her ass. "Billy," she scolded with a hint of amusement, "would you get your fingers out of my butt?"

The aide's jaw dropped. "Where did that come from?"

"Wow!" I said. "She's heard every word we said."

But then Mother submerged again, seemingly lifeless. I propped her head up with the belt.

Bobby showed up to spell me. I went to a cousin's house and slept.

Late Sunday morning Bobby called from the hospital. "Billy, come on over and speak to your mother."

"Bobby, you wouldn't joke about a thing like this?"

"Come quickly."

Before I entered the room, he handed me the nurses' chart. It said: "10:00 A.M. Sunday. Intermittent responsiveness to verbal stimuli—uttered 'good morning' to nurse and aware of Dr. Cohen's prescence."

We went in and Bobby touched her arm.

"Mother, look who's here. It's Billy."

She pressed against my belt, cocked open an eye and penetrated to the heart of me.

"Mother," Bobby urged, "Billy doesn't believe it. Show us a grin."

She did it. It was cockeyed and crinkled like a possum's, but it was a grin. Yes, yes, yes, yes.

DR. DISCOVERIO MEDUCI

When I got back to Dallas, I crashed. Lost track of time, slept day and night.

I experienced three kinds of sleep. The first was fitful, just this side of consciousness, where the day world was still very much with me. The second was a descent into dreams, where my consciousness remained intact but was often detached from my body in a Dalilike time-space continuum. The ultimate stage was a deep, dreamless, selfless sleep, a kind of temple sleep from which I awoke refreshed and on the mend. This latter sleep, difficult to describe since I might as well have been dead, I want to explore some other time. Now I want to tell you about a dream I had in the second sleep.

This sinister man beckoned me to a dive where people dear to me had died or disappeared. I was frightened, but felt myself being pulled there. As we waited at a table for whiskey, he produced his calling card: a worn piece of paper on which he had penciled, in a crude cursive:

DISCOVERIO MEDUCI
COLLECTOR OF DEBTS, SETTLER OF ACCOUNTS.

He dealt with me in an easy, familiar way that was unsettling because at first I did not recognize him. He was short, well past middle-age, but he gave the impression of strength and toughness. He did not look Italian like his name. He had a broad face, a handsome, straight nose and keen blue eyes. His hair was short and thick, like his body, and iron gray. He wore rough clothes, as a seaman might wear in port or a longshoreman at play. In fact, the ambience of the bar suggested a waterfront, perhaps part of a union hiring hall and hostelry where men and women are vagabonds and souls are shanghaied.

I can't remember a single word he said because I don't think he spoke in words so much as nuance. His strange name, his chilling card, his looks and gestures and grunts made me understand that he was not out to represent me against some delinquent. It was clear I was the delinquent, that I owed him something, or owed someone behind him. It was also plain that he would kill me if I did fork up whatever it was he wanted. What that was he did not say or suggest, which put me in a terrifying position. I was somewhat relieved, at last, to understand (I don't know how, exactly) that I was to buy an insurance policy on my life from him, and that he would accept it in installments dropped off at the dive. He left on a note of rugged cordiality.

I don't know why, but somehow I knew, when it came time to drop off the first of my obligations to him, to address a note of love to my mother along with a five dollar bill. That, and nothing else, was to be the installment on my obligation to him. In the dream I left at the bar many such missives over the coming years, always slipping a worn five dollar bill in the fold of the love note to Mother, which I wrote on a Big Chief note tablet. Dr. Discoverio Meduci was very exacting. If I was so much as a day late, he would have me back before him at the waterfront dive, reconsecrating his strangely sinister, strangely benign requirement of me.

I awoke from the dream, and immediately forgot it.

It was not until I went down to pick up the mail that the dream came back to haunt me. Among the bills was a letter Mother had scrawled to me just before she had been taken to the hospital in San Antonio. Her writing had become so indecipherable it often took time and code breakers at the post office to get her letters delivered. They were always the same: a small envelope containing a Big Chief page of endearments, folded around a five dollar bill. Since I left home for college I had been receiving them from her, every month without fail, and so had Bobby and Joyce, and here we were grown and with kids of our own.

Now I realized, with a shudder of regret shaking the deepest groovings of my soul, that Discoverio Meduci bore a striking resemblance to Mother's father, Daddy Harrell, not only in his appearance and manner but in his milieu of mystery—strange arrivals and sudden departures, the danger of rough ports and terminals. Why had dead Daddy Harrell merged into the shadowy eidola Discoverio Meduci?

It was to tell me Mother was dead.

I had hardly put down Mother's letter when I heard a knock at the door. It was a girl friend, the one with a phone, confirming the terrible shadow that had been cast upon my heart.

And what was more, Daddy Meduci was making it biblical that my obligation to his daughter and my mother was not about to end with her death, but really about to begin with my maturity. It was then, on that black-bordered day, that I resolved to return to this account of my journey as her son, which I had put away to molder in silent rot in a trunk, one, curiously, that Daddy Harrell had made in his rough but sturdy sea chest way.

And, just as Mother had said in her delirium, I wore the black hat to her funeral.

16

★ ★ ★

Pa

TEXAS
1979–1982

DADDY AND THE GOLD DIGGERS

SEGUIN
May 1979

☆ MOTHER HADN'T BEEN IN HER GRAVE A MONTH BEFORE SOME widow in Seguin wrote Daddy a note of admiration. That is how she put it, delicately, I thought, but the old man decided to be offended by it. At least, he decided to appear offended when he showed us the letter. "Whoever heard of such a thang?" he said. "A woman like that, a total stranger, being so nervy! Boy, I decided right then and there to stay away from her."

I laughed. "She's not going to bite you, Pa. All she wanted was to make your acquaintance. Why be so wary? All you do is sit in this trailer house watching TV."

He scoffed, said the next thing you knew she would be taking him for every red cent he had. Every cent Daddy has is always red, even when he carried silver dollars and greenbacks. I guess this was because as an Okie boy he had seen a lot of Indian head pennies. One summer, when in a torrent of Scroogelike money-counting he didn't put the red before the cent, Mother got worried about him, thought he was losing his marbles. She sent him to the chiropractor, who gave him an adjustment to relieve "pressure on the brain," and Daddy never failed to say red cent again.

"Well," I said, "if you feel that way about it you've got no problem because the next move is yours. Don't answer her letter and that
will be it. Since you've never laid eyes on her, it's no skin off your
back."

"Oh," he said, "I've seen her."

"I thought you said she was a total stranger."

"She is. But she put her address on the letter. She mentioned
that if I ever wanted to drop by, she was usually out in her yard gar-
dening. She said she always wore something red and that I couldn't
miss her."

"And?"

"I drove by one day just to see what she looked like, not because
I was interested, you understand, but just because I couldn't get it out
of my head that a woman like that could be so forward."

"And?"

"She was a looker, all right."

"And?"

"That's all. I kind of sneaked past."

"Of course," I said. "As you say, you were not interested."

"That's right. What would a woman of that age want with a man
of my age? Nothing but my money. Every red cent. That's how I figure it."

"You're probably right," I said.

"Say," he said, "would you like to drive by and take a look at
her?"

"Why not? We've got nothing better to do. Just as well play
Peeping Tom on your lady friend."

She was out in her yard, back to us, bent over pulling weeds out
of a rock bed.

"What do you thank?" Daddy said, idling past.

"I think she looks nice from behind. I wish she'd turn around."

"Oh," he said, "she's a looker for sure, even from the front."

"Certainly she keeps her place well," I said. "Pa, I'm sure she's a
nice lady."

"Now that's where you're wrong, boy. No lady would be that forward. You have to be on the lookout. Sure, her place is neat, but you
can tell she doesn't have any money, not a red cent. That's all she's
interested in that I've got."

"Then why do you keep driving by?" I said. "Bobby and Joyce told me you drove them over here, too."

He gave a sheepish little hee-hee. "Just curiosity, I guess. But shoot, I'm not interested in tha woman, don't ye know that, boy? A man my age'd be a fool."

That wasn't the end of it. He must have shown that letter to everyone who came to the trailer court. No telling how many times he conducted sightseeing tours past the poor woman's house.

Walking Mort troubles continued to plague him. A gal from one of the trailers ran up and hugged and kissed him in broad daylight. Daddy liked to have broken an arm and a leg getting away from her. Hid in his trailer house the rest of the day.

"I'd run from that woman even if she didn't have a husband," he said. "A gold digger is what she is. I could tell that when she came around the bend."

It's hell, he said, being a man and so in demand.

BEANS IS ALL HE GETS

SEGUIN
September 1979

Pa and his brothers sat on the promise of an oil strike on the farm at Little Egypt for two decades. Their wives called it a figment and made fun of their husbands' pie-in-the-sky.

I was a grown man, two years out of college and working as a journalist, when the Carter Oil Company out of Tulsa finally brought in that long-awaited well. It was an oiler, not a gasser, and it was named the Cora Moore No. 1, after Daddy's oldest sister.

The *Daily Ardmoreite* ran a story on the strike. Pa clipped it, and carried it neatly folded in his billfold the last thirty years of his life. The part of the article that impressed him was Greek to me, but after hearing him read it aloud a jillion times, I can almost quote it from memory. It said:

The Houston zones, 9,669 and 10,094 feet, made swab and flow tests of 92 barrels of 38-gravity oil in 11 hours through a 3/4 inch choke, and with all zones commingled, well pumped 73 barrels of oil and 83 barrels of load water in 24 hours. The Woodford is perforated at 9,435 to 9,576 feet and the Sycamore at 9,244 to 9,420 feet.

"Now Daddy, what does that mean?" we would say, and he would fold the clip, put it back into his wallet, lean back and say, with sublime satisfaction, that it meant what it damn well said, plain as the expression on a face: which was that that well had thick oil sands. "Thick, boy, thick!"

All he got out of it was forty or fifty dollars a month.

That was not only because oil by the barrel had gotten cheap, but because the royalties had to be divided among the heirs—which, of course, included a dozen brothers and sisters or their heirs.

There was another hitch too, which lowered production. For all its thick oil sand, the Cora Moore had a low gas ratio, which meant it needed priming to make it flow. They had to pump in a barrel of oil to get three or four back. And when you take into account how cheap oil was—$12 a barrel—you can see why the well didn't live up to her promise.

It was just enough to keep the Porterfield men dreaming. Someday, they hoped, Carter Oil would get off its duff and drill that well deeper, prime her with a big pump and get out of her all she had to give.

And, lo and behold, it's happened.

At least partly.

Last spring, about the time of Mother's death, Carter sold the lease to Chevron U.S.A. out of Denver. Chevron moved a workover rig in and dug the Cora Moore No. 1 down to 16,000 feet. She started pumping 150 barrels a day, which was supposed to put about three hundred dollars a month into Pa's pocket. My cousin, Noel, a geophysicist, figured that with a bigger pump the well could make each heir up to a thousand smackers a month.

"Well," Pa said, gulping, "I'll take the three hundred now and figger anything more is gravy."

But he and his brothers began pushing Chevron to push the Cora with the biggest pump they could find. These boys may be the longest lived Porterfields of any generation, but with Daddy at seventy-seven being among the youngest of the litter, they wanted what was coming to them now and pretty damn quick, if you please. But

Chevron, having deepened the well, wouldn't budge to anyone's timetable but its own.

Meanwhile, the first check since the workover arrived at the trailer in Seguin. Bobby and I happened to be there with the old man when he tore upon the envelope.

It was for seventeen dollars and sixteen cents. That's $17.16.

"It's $17.16!" Daddy roared. "What the shit's going on?"

"Well, Pa, read the letter that's come with it," Bobby said.

Chevron said the checks were piddling because President Jimmy Carter's crude oil windfall profit tax, which had just gone into effect, took $299.99 out of a check that would have amounted to $312.15 for each heir.

"Bad news, Pa," Bobby said, getting out his pencil and doing some figuring. "Even if they put on a bigger pump and increase production on the well, if they triple it, your part after the tax will come to $51.48."

"I know," Daddy said. "I've done figgered it in my noggin. Beans is all I'll get."

"What are you going to do?" I said.

"I'll tell ye what I'm gonna do. For the first time since the Depression, I ain't votin' Democrat. Jimmy Carter don't get my vote, that's for damn sure."

"Reagan then?"

"Nobody! They can all go to hellfire. A life's dream, gone up in taxes, just like that!"

I felt a psychic tug at my sleeve, and for a fleeting instant saw the face of Grandpa. He winked at me, and, nodding to the old man who had been his oil-crazed son, whispered, "I told him so."

SEXUS ERECTUS SENEX

SEGUIN
March 1980

"Billy, I've had me an experience a man ought not forget. I guess you'd have to get old and worn out before you really understand it, but you know what?"

"What, Pa?"

"Ye've still got to have ye sex, pitiful as it may be." Good God, I thought. Here's he's coming on seventy-eight and still chasing women. What'll I tell Bobby and Joyce? "Well, which one is it this time, Daddy? The old broad in the flower beds who's pushy with her love letters, or is that young thing that tore your clothes off your back in broad daylight?"

"Shit, son, if ye gonna make fun of me, I can damn sure snap my old jaws tighter'n Coot tha Turtle. I'm good at that, ye know. Inside my old walls a'peepin' out at ye. Feels safe in 'ere alone with yeself. But the rest of ye, and that included ye mother, confess your gabby hearts out twenty-four hours a day, even in ye damn sleep. I've listened to you all my life. Now here we come along lately and I make the mistake of acting like the rest of ye. I open my damn fool mouth and start to tell you something personal, somethin' you boys ought to know, since you follow me in the battin' order . . . "

He stopped and swore. "Yep. That's it. I've just whiffed in my last ever at bat, and they're retiring my number. So I come back to the dugout and try to tell you boys what the pitcher's throwin' and ever' thang, and ye won't listen."

"What's the pitcher's name, Pa?"

He grins satanically, showing his very white and very straight and very false teeth, and says, "Father Time." We mull that around silently, looking at the godawful green shag of the trailer, and finally, rebuked but fairly—even considering my light intent—I admit that I am up next, and that how he exits as a sexual male is just as important as how Bobby and I carry his seed after he's gone. He's still got his pride, and he can still teach us a thing or two.

And he says thank ye.

And sits there like the sphinx.

"I'm ready to listen, Pa."

"You remember back when the word got out that ye mother had cut me off, finally, feelin' as poorly as she was and ever'thang?"

I looked at him.

"And then she told Joyce she'd heard me jacking off under the covers, and they gossiped me into being a dirty old man?"

"Now Daddy—"

"Don't now daddy me. I've got ears as big as yours, Billy Mack. I took it and suffered in silence. None of ye heard my side of it. Now I want ye to understand that my side of it don't reflect ill on ye mother. I understood her turning me away. But what she and Joyce didn't take into account was my reason for comin' on to her. And that is what I need to explain to you boys, since you're gonna be in my shoes someday, if ye live long enough."

"Okay, shoot, Pa."

"I didn't try to make out with tha bedridden woman because I was a rutty old goat. I wasn't some bawdreamer. I was her husband. We had grown old together, and now she was terrible sick and not long for this world. I figured she needed some cheerin' up, some sign from me that I still cared for her as a woman, that her bein' all bald and puffed up from the chemo made no difference as far as my true feelings for her were concerned. I picked a night when we had talked real quiet-like and gentle about the thangs she wanted me to do after she died. You know, the burial and all and how she wanted me to be with you kids and all when she wasn't around. She made me swear to be easier on ye, and I said I would—which I thank I did. Don't you?"

"Oh, yes."

"After our talk, Jennie seemed to be satisfied. She was kind of perky and in good humor. So I got off my bed and went over to hers. I got down on my knees and bent over and kissed her on the lips, which gave her a start. 'Now, Daddy,' she said, 'what are you doing?'

"I told 'er I loved her and wanted to snuggle, to kindly put a seal on the last contract we'd make between us. And she said, 'Do you mean sex?' and I said yep, if she was up to it. It's a fact I felt a stirrin' in my loins and wanted one last time with her—but shit, son, she was my woman in the most precious sense. I didn't say it like I'm tellin' it to you, but I was tryin' to show her I still cared, that her bein' all bald and puffed up from chemo, and havin' her titties gone, didn't make no difference with me."

"You've already said that, Pa."

"Well, she took it the wrong way. She got offended, like I was some horny old smellsmock without any consideration for her condition, and told me no, that there'd be no more sex, which, of course, there hadn't been because of her cancer.

"It's true that during that dry spell, and it was a long one, I felt the need from time to time to relieve myself. I tried to respect ye mother's feelings and do it after she'd gone to sleep, but apparently that wadn't always the case. Now, this is a situation you and Bobby'll find yeselves in when ye get my age. I'm talkin' about the need to come. As far as I can tell, it never stops, this urge to spend yeself of ye vitals. If a prime man didn't do it, the world wouldn't go 'round. So Mother Nature sees to such as that. But when an old man does it, it's dirty, and that's a bum rap if he's a decent fella and not some pervert. That's why I couldn't get up a real head of steam at Uncle Charlie for makin' those Wild Irish Rose calls to ye mother. As a man, I understood. I didn't see Charlie as a real danger, just a nuisance. It's true that the urge gets weaker and weaker as ye age, but it's like a pilot light that never goes out if ye keep your health. It's the same thang for ye tool. The fact that it gets so soft ye wonder if you could still stick it in the woman don't make no difference. Ye've still got bullets in ye that want out. It's kindly a curse, if you want to know the truth about it. Ye know that as old and wrinkly and blinky as ye are, no woman wants to lie with ye, so ye do the best ye can, and dream and bust ye nuts like a pimply boy. Except it's a lot more pathetic. All the time I was beatin' my meat under the covers, I was pretending ye mother and I were young and naked and hot. And here she was over in the other bed, a'rollin' her old wink-a-peeps. It's sad, when ye thank about it. Jennie and I didn't always tick real good together, not even when we were young and eager to be in the traces as a team. Reckon it was an inheritance? Papa always said he and Mother were damned to *chantpleure*—"

"Yes," I said, "to sing and weep at the same time."

"Yep," he said. "Same for Jennie and me, bless her heart. I guess we done the best we could."

And that was it. A heartful was all he could say. But there was more in him, more vitals to divulge.

At dusk under the trees, mesquite beans chattered like castanets in the breeze. We sat there sipping bourbon, watching a rip of wind kick up little dust devils. They spin and skitter up the hill, passing under, over, around and right through us like mischievous children, leaving a gritty film on our shots of whiskey, brooling our ears with fleeting whispers. My mind went back a lifetime, and I thought of the foam the little red devils brewed on the mouth of Wit Odin, and of how hideously they keaked and sparpled away. Our wind sprites are more benign. We watch them hightail down the other side of the hill, dart between the rent trailers, and then rise in one last fury before spinning themselves back into the invisible but electric air that spawned them.

Pa looks at me and takes a swig of his hum. "Big Mama must be calling them to supper," he says.

The old man takes idle talk away from me by whispering the rest of his confession. He had told the hind part first; now he had to go back to the beginning. I am the afterling prince and he's the dying king, my tasking god at the lip of his grave, given to utter the last of many testimonies. Father forgive me. Make me gentle as you are strong so that I may receive your gift.

"In the beginning of manhood," he was saying, his voice growing, "and for a long time after, my pecker'd get so hard it'd fly up and whop me in the stomach, almost knockin' my breath out. It was agrum and leakin' like a woman's milky breast. It wanted its milking.

"First by any woman. Good Lord, any bawd was welcome to relieve the pressure. Then I got particular, goin' after women who really caught my eye. But then the eye gave way to fadoodle. I got all mally and fell in love, which may sound silly comin' from my mouth, and it was silly because such as that is hard for me, showin' my feelin's and being, well, being tender is the only way I know how to say it. But you know once I do a thang I do it right. At least I try to.

"It was Janavee, of course. I was in for the long haul with 'er and it was okay with me. She had me by the short hair where it hurts good. Like I used to tell you and ye brother, all a young fella's brains and half his heart are below his waist. All I could thank of was love and dancin'.

"But it didn't take long for marriage and kids and the responsibility of a family to sober me up. Along with ye mother. She was doin' a pretty good job about lettin' me know how she felt about me. Natu'ally that hurt. I'd put ever'thang I had, my name and my nature into tha woman. I loved 'er. She could barely tolerate me. But in those days word was bond. That's the way tha best people did thangs back then. It'd still work. You oughta try it sometime, Billy. You and old Bobby.

"So ye mother and I stuck it out. Day in and day out it was all right. Night in and night out it was not all right. Then it'd change, days being bad and nights good, and so forth and so on. We'd each get so deadset and stubborn in our tracks that weeks, months could go by without our realizing that we were running into one another like blind trains.

"I wasn't happy being unhappy and bein' stupid, really, making enemies of ye mate. Who wants to live thata way? A man's home oughta be relief, not the same shit ye get soon as ye stick ye head out the cave. Woman oughta feel the same safeness. And sometimes ye mother'd realize we were riding together and even sleeping next to one another in the Pullman car, and she'd try to make the best of it. And sometimes it worked. You kids saw. Yawl remember.

"But then back we'd go. She'd get so black-eyed at me I'd get hurt and then mad, lose my head in whiskey until I had to take it out on somebody. I'd get so red-eyed and mean she'd get hysterical and cry. And then moody. She'd brood for days. A'pullin' you kids to her and a'pushin' me out, a'poisonin' yawl against me. And her damned silences." He looked up at the trees and sighed, motioned for me to pass the reelpot, poured himself more hum.

"Well, shit, son, we been all through that. But, don't'che see, that was her flaw, the devil in her same as my drinkin' and rages. But she did somethin' I didn't do."

"What was that, Daddy?"

"Like I say, she spoke against me to my own children. Belittled me before my own babies. Now boy, that's a sin in any man's bible. I never did that to her with you kids. You never heard me speak of her in thata way. I protected her honor in the family same as out."

"That's true, Daddy, when you weren't teasing her . . . or beating her."

I had stunned him. He shook his white head on his wasted neck and raised it, lowering his eyes to look at me through his bifocals. His rheumy old Alice Austin chicken eyes cleared to cold blue as they leveled on me.

"It's true," I continued. "She raised her tongue against you. You raised your hand against her, and us as well. That's a pretty big statement, Daddy, pounding your wife and their mother in front of your kids. Which came first, your chicken or her egg? It hardly matters in the dark of something that extreme. You were so volatile and brutal you didn't need any help from Mother in convincing us you were an SOB."

He waited a little. Then he said, his voice husky in a frail way,

"Was my hand any crueler than that woman's tongue?"

"You could have murdered us. Man, you came close that night near Goliad. You could have ridden the stang for it, and spent the rest of your life in hell."

"How do ye not know that she murdered me? Would it surprise you if I said that the part of me yawl say I never had was once frisky and eager as a pup, and that ye mother killed it in me?"

"Daddy, do you realize what you just said?"

"What?"

"That Mother's dark spirit was stronger than your white heart, and that eventually, she was a match for the brute of your vengeance."

"Did I say that?"

"You did."

"Naw," he said, shaking his head. "You said it. I mighta meant it like you say, but I wouldn't put it like you say."

"Whatever," I said wearily, getting to my feet, "it's progress, Pa. I never thought I'd hear you admit a woman could best you. Mother was something, wasn't she? She really got under your skin. Come on, let's go to the Aumont and get some supper."

"I'll ah . . . I'll be right with ye," he said in a roaky voice. I saw he was shaky. I went in the trailer house to pee, though I didn't need to. I gave him time to compose himself before we left.

THE DEAD AND THE RESTLESS

SEGUIN
Summer 1980

Every weekday, after their eleven o'clock performance on CBS-TV, the cast of "The Young and the Restless" gather in Tice Porterfield's trailer house and practice their lines for the next day while he's trying to take his noon nap. Yep. They've been doing it for some time now, and what irritates the old man is that they don't acknowledge him. "I just sit here like a bump on a log," he says. "It looks like to me that they ought to at least thank a man for using his home and castle."

"Why don't you kick them out?" I said on the phone.

"Ah, I couldn't do that," he said. "They have enough problems with their lives as it is. Besides, I have to admit it's fun watching them. They forget their parts and ever'thang. But, boy, when they start them cameras rollin', they don't miss a beat. They've got it all down."

I sent Bobby and Joyce to check on him.

"Yawl are gonna thank I'm imagining this," he said. "But the durndest thang happened to me yesterday." He waited for a prompt.

"What was it, Daddy?" Joyce said.

"Ye mother drove up in a car. And guess who was with 'er?"

"Who, Daddy?"

"My mother."

"Alice Austin?"

"Yep. They got out of the car and walked around the trailer, talkin'. I stood in the doorway and finally they came in. But they didn't say boo. Walked right past me and sat on the couch. Talked between themselves about the family and ever'thang. Kindly surprised me. Ye know they never got along. So that pleased me, them talkin' that way."

"That's real nice, Daddy."

"But the thang that stuck in my craw was that they didn't say a thang to me, or pay me the least attention. It was like I wadn't here, and me in my own house a'sittin' here lookin' right at them. The two most important women in my life, and they wouldn't give me the time of day. Now whad'ya thank about that?"

"It doesn't sound like either of them," Joyce said, "and probably wasn't—"

"Meant to offend me. Yeah, I know. I didn't say anythang. Well, the thang that really bothered me came to me after they'd left and I was crawlin' in bed. Ye see, the notion struck me that Janavee's little old pine coffin has no lock and is only covered with dirt and grass, so I could see how she managed to dig her way out and come here. But Mother's grave is covered with concrete. Now, you tell me how that old woman clawed her way out?"

"Can't, Daddy. She couldn't. You were just imagining that."

"You mean it was just a daydream?"

"Just a silly dream."

"I reckon you're right," he said. "I knew it didn't sound reasonable. Shoot, it was only Janavee who'd come. It's funny how a man's mind can run away from him, idn't it?"

Joyce smiled and nodded. Bobby, quiet in the corner, rolled his eyes.

I told the story to Robert Bly, the old Norse poet up in Moosehead, Minnesota, and he said bullshit to our amused and condescending tolerance of Pa's delusions. "You're a fool if you think those ghosts aren't real," Bly growled. "Your father's fortunate that his mother and wife didn't speak directly to him. If he had talked to them, he would have been marked for death."

In the Spirit of a Greener, Grander Worth

SEGUIN
December 24, 1981

Christmas before last, I got my father a hat. He didn't like it. It was the right style and the right size, but the wrong color.

I took it back to Dallas and got him another one.

It didn't suit him either.

On the third try, I satisfied him. Since we lived three hundred miles apart, it was more than a bother. It took some doing, and he didn't get his Christmas hat, a felt, until April, when it was too hot to wear it.

He went ahead and wore it, sweating. "I'm wearin' this winter felt," he'd say, "because Billy thanks Christmas comes in the spring."

At least he enjoyed his joke.

Last Christmas, I got him a color drawing of three oil wells close together. The first well's casing sat in a heavy oil sand. The second well's drill stem was stuck in a dry hole. The third well, set off from the others, had been drilled at a slant and was poaching on the rich oil sand of the first well. The cutline said, "The good, the bad and the greedy."

I figured Pa would get a kick out of it, since he'd probably drilled many wells just like the three, so I had it framed. Besides, he was drawing his little income from the crude on the Okie farm, and pretending he's a real, honest-to-goodness oilman. There is a difference between an oilfield hand and an oilman. It's not the gook on your tin hat, it's royalties.

But he didn't like the drawing. Said it was full of technical inaccuracies. I told him to stick it up his . . . wall anyway.

For this Christmas I was saying to hell with it and giving him a tin of Hershey kisses, which would require him to fend off a swarm of great-grandkids.

The old man was hard to buy for because he didn't give you a clue in the kind of gifts he bought for others. This was because he didn't buy gifts, never had except for the time he got drunk and bought Mother that tacky blond dining room suite. Pa received gifts, of course, if not always happily. We humored him the way people do relics.

But don't get the wrong idea. The old man may not have given on birthdays and anniversaries, but on Christmas he made an exception. He waited until we'd all bestowed our gifts upon him, laid them at the feet of his easy chair and had watched him open each one. When he was sure everyone was rapt, he'd reach into his khakis and pull out a roll of bills.

Holding the wad up, he'd lick his thumb and peel off an Andrew Jackson while calling my name. Being the eldest I was first. I approached like a peon and accepted his largess: one worn, deflated by inflation Andy Jackson. My brother and sister followed, taking their Jacksons.

Then, if Bobby and I still had them, our spouses followed. I'd had more than a fistful along the way, and Pa didn't seem to distinguish between them. When I brought my penultimate bride to the trailer for the first time, he drew me aside and said, "Boy, are you feedin' her enough? I know closer to the bone, sweeter is the meat, but I've never seen a woman shed so many pretty pounds." He had her confused with her predecessor. Whichever, wives had to be content with an Alexander Hamilton apiece.

Lest you think Joyce as inconstant as her brothers, I should insert that her spouse was Jimmy, the same one she'd had since she was a teenager. Pa made a special exception in his case, and laid a Jackson on him.

Now it was the grandchildren's time. They came in ages and stages too. Those who were married each received a Hamilton, then stepped back to watch their spouses take an Abraham Lincoln. The mores of the younger generation were better than we'd been led to believe. At least my sister's boys' were. They were still married to their first wives, making their uncles look frivolous. Those grandchildren who were grown but not married got Lincolns. Those who were still minors got two George Washingtons.

George Washingtons did not sit well with the little rapscallions, but no one in the family dared cross Pa at the only time of year he was in a giving mood. The ritual had to continue down through the last child of the blood and altar. It ended with each great-grandchild being held up to receive one Father of Our Country from the Father of Our Clan.

It was only after this that the old Celt took the first ceremonial shot of Christmas hum, and a nibble of haggis and passed the communion down through the generations. Now that he was as elevated as a statue, and as stiff as one, he made much of this ritual of alms-giving to his brood.

Some of the youngsters made backstairs fun of his annual fit of generosity, pointing out that altogether—the grownups' take included—it wouldn't buy a good, ten-speed bicycle. But they lacked in hindsight what he lacked in foresight. They didn't consider that the old man had been handing out Christmas money to us for years, always in the same amounts, and that what now was not much of a gift was once a considerable sum to give, especially for a man like my father. It was hard enough for me to keep up with the decline of the dollar. At almost eighty, it must have been incomprehensible for him. So he lived in the past of a greener, grander worth, when a buck would buy a pig in a poke.

It was a shame that a father could give Jacksons and Hamiltons, Lincolns and Washingtons on Christmas and still be thought a Scrooge. It was the heart of the times that were niggardly, not my old man. Of course, if he had gotten off his can and tried to turn the money into presents, he would have learned that the giggles and whispers were not expressions of delight and gratitude, but ridicule. It was just as well that he hadn't.

Last Vesper

DALLAS
October 1982

When October left us that Saturday, at my place on the Eastside, I went out on the porch with everybody to bid her goodbye.

My throat was tight, my eyes were moist and I'm sure my voice wavered. I did what Daddy always did. I shifted into my lowest manly register, trying to hide the crack of emotion behind a husky rumble. October knew. I saw her glance my way as she bussed my brother, but she pretended not to notice.

Damn it, we went through this every year. She came and enchanted us for a month, visiting each of the families. Toward the end we all gathered at one of the houses, and she bewitched us with a big Halloween blast. The next morning she was off and gone again for another year. We said the same thing every time she left: "Come stay longer next time. You always leave too soon, October. Take care. We love you. Hurry back."

She said yes to everything, but we knew she would never stay as long as we wanted.

I stood there staring at her the way I had at Sophia Loren when Sophia came to Dallas some years ago. She danced with Stanley Marcus, who, blessedly short as I, buried his face in her enormous breasts. Great photo in the *Dallas Times Herald!* What magnificent creatures October and Sophia were, women at their most beautiful and most ripe, glowing with life just at the moment of its fading.

The younger men in the family preferred her younger sylphlike sisters, April, May and June, and some of the dirty old men had an eye for those torrid slatterns, July and August. I, too, remembered the girls of spring and summer, but I was wrong about them. Not even the Mermaid of Zennor could compare to October.

It was her complexity and contradiction, even her circumstance, that fascinated. She was way past the bud, past the childbearing and dumpy middle years, and yet she was not done for, not ready for the heap. Everything she shed was extraneous, and now, sleek and autumnal, vibrant with the colors and passion of a last rhapsody, she was more beautiful than she ever was, and finally whole.

We were all on the porch, all the Porterfields—save two— who've ever come and gone, the living and the dead, the yet to be, and I had to wait my turn to hug October goodbye.

Conspicuously absent was Grandpa Porterfield and Granny; Grandpa because he was afraid Granny might show up and spoil his reunion with October; Granny because she had no need to see the red bitch if Grandpa wasn't there to spy on.

Ma was up from her grave in Little Egypt, comparing her seventy-first birthday (the third one since her death) to October's one hundred and two.

Uncle Glen didn't look like he'd been down under all these years either. The old Tulsa first baseman was big and ruddy, wondering how the Yanks had fared against the Dodgers. But I noticed his hands shook, and wasn't surprised when he pulled me aside and asked if I had a shot of hum. Some things never change.

Granddaddy Harrell was husky and profane, Mama Harrell slight and polite.

Pa was stiffer that fall, moved spraddle-legged as if he was about to fall. Sometimes, I was afraid he'd outlive his sons. The grandkids towered over him. They looked down on all of us except October.

The children and grandchildren and great-grandchildren were everywhere, so many of them of every shape and size that I couldn't keep up with their names anymore. I looked at Mother. The poor squat woman had a funny look in her eye. Several kids had been born since her death and she was trying to figure out who was who.

"That's Jimbo's newest," I whispered, winking.

"Oh, I know, I know," she clucked, then blushed a bloodless, pickled green in embarrassment.

"It's all right," I said with silent lips. "No one expects you to be able to keep up."

It was the wrong thing to say. I'd made greater the gap between the living and the dead, which she'd failed to bridge to the extent that she'd hoped. She was hurt to the quick of her soul, and in her face I saw, for the first time, how terrible it had been for her up there in the forsaken tombs of Little Egypt. She was always a stranger in the house of the Porterfields, and now she pulled back from the rest of us, hung at the edge of the porch with bitter, haunted eyes. I sought her eyes out with mine, and we locked that way. I smiled with my eyes in the old way that used to win her, but she was having none of it. She gave me her black look, and was gone.

Joyce missed her. And Pa.

The old man said, "Billy, where's ye mother? I don't care what that goddamn poet says, I want to talk to her."

"You're right," I said. "This is Reunion Day. You can talk to any ghost you see, but I'm afraid I've driven Ma away."

"Wha'd you do that for?"

"I didn't mean to . . . "

Joyce stepped up. "Billy, where has Mother gone? She was here just a minute ago, at the edge of the porch. I want her to talk to little Mandy."

"She's gone back to Egypt."

"Why? Why so soon? Did someone say something to hurt her feelings? Daddy, was it you . . . ?"

Pa's mouth flapped open and his eyes narrowed. He waved his wobbly old arms in frustration and walked away mumbling.

"It was my fault," I said to Joyce. "I hurt Mother's feelings, but I didn't mean to . . . "

"Of course, you didn't," Joyce said, patting me. "I was nervous about her coming. You know, Billy, sometimes it's absolute hell, isn't it? Why do we have to go through all this Diddy Waw Diddying, this pushing and pulling, living and dying, separation and reunion and separation again, and nothing ever arrived at or settled?"

"Look at October," I said. "She knows. You can see it in her eyes."

October picked up what I said without hearing. At last she moved away from them and came to me. Joyce, understanding, backed away. October filled my being, crowded out everything else. I trembled, catching her scent and the glint in her hazel eyes. "Don't come any closer," I said, smiling, "else I'll swoon. Stay back a bit and let me look at you."

She stopped, tossing her calico mane. It fell to her shoulders in a cascade of reds, browns and golds, flecks of green and gray. She wore a light cardigan which picked up the hues in her hair, a Celtic skirt and a Scotch plaid scarf, perfect for fall football afternoons.

I remember as a boy sitting in grandstands with men who swigged from silver flasks, all of us rising to greet October as she made her rich way up the aisle to sit in the seat beside me. I remember burying my face in her woolen bosom as she reached down to hug me, breathing her dry and woody perfume, wishing I could take her away from Wit Odin and Grandpa.

Now Wit loomed as a vaporous welkin in Dallas, tall as Big Tex he billowed behind October, the god of Norseland, his visage faint but menacing as the ghost of that other cuckold, King Hamlet. He wore his original aspect, Old Man Winter, and was not inclined to give me, or any of us, recognition of our old friendship. He was of such baleful eye and icy breath that I hated the thought of him taking October away from us again. I could now agree with Grandpa in not understanding what she saw in him. But I saw she had no choice. He was primal father, fate's imprimatur. The beauty was damned.

(That is, unless she found beneath the frozen tundra of Iceland a primal mother, an Amazonian Valkyrie so much older than Odin that he must bow to her as great-of-the-greatest-grandmothers and return to her the creatures of the earth. I held out this hope for October and all humankind, and prayed the male gods would lay off and return to their sky, so that we might replenish earth for the children.)

For all October's splendidness, for all her glowing, there was sadness in her, an awareness that for now she was done for. Her last vesper had been spoken, the cold host was at her back, warning the Celts away from his ice maiden, chanting the complin and awaiting her surrender to the northern night.

He came closer, glazing autumn with ice, hovering about the porch, not fully materialized but coming into focus, ancient, hoary and helmeted, slightly uncomfortable in the warm Dallas fall. Still I shivered, for he breathed like a cold-breathed beast. I shivered and pushed him back with all my will, as sons must fathers. I turned my eyes to October for one last, deep draught of her. She came.

And . . . then . . . she . . . went.

I've since thought a good deal on October and her life. She so wanted to live grandly, on a vista comparable with the demigods, and in that she was a modern woman ahead of her time. But there are dangers in living mythologically, not the least of which is that behind the illusion of freedom, even gods and goddesses have greater ones to answer to, and on a greatly dilated time scale.

17

★ ★ ★

Not So Fast, My Dear

SOMEWHERE IN THE UNCREATION
November 1, 1982

HENRY MCMAHON PORTERFIELD: Great day, October! What in the hell kept you? I thought you'd never give up and get here.

OCTOBER NEY MILLS: It certainly was hell, Henry. And, as you can see, I did not survive it.

GRANDPA: And I am glad for that, my dear. You're none the worse for wear. I say, you are a sight for these sore old eyes, more beautiful than ever.

OCTOBER: You're not sorry to see me?

GRANDPA: I've counted the millenniums.

OCTOBER. Oh, come, Henry. It hasn't been that long.

GRANDPA: It seems forever.

OCTOBER: I did live long for a mortal. It wasn't as long as Lonnie Mareain, but, Henry, I lived to one hundred and two years.

GRANDPA: I haven't laid eyes on you for forty-five years. No, don't move. Just stand and let me feast.

OCTOBER: Henry, I'm so thrilled that you are speaking to me. I think I am going to cry. I am going to cry for the first time in my life.

GRANDPA: No, my dear. You're dead. And here you're entering eternity crying. I think you've got your lines reversed. You should have cried down there and . . .

OCTOBER: (crying) I'm so sorry I hurt you, Henry.

GRANDPA: (crying) I'm sorry I was such a sissy.

OCTOBER: (laughing) Now it's my turn, my beloved. You'll have to forgive me. I'm not quite myself.

GRANDPA: You call me your beloved?

OCTOBER: It's true.

GRANDPA: I was the lover, not the beloved.

OCTOBER: I've been both, Henry, and believe me, you do not want to be the beloved. Carson McCullers was right. It is a sentence from hell to hell.

GRANDPA: I don't understand. Are you saying your love for me—if that's what it was—was a curse?

OCTOBER: And yours for me, Henry. But not because of us, Henry, because of them. When Wit left and Alice died, I thought at last we could be alone. But it wasn't so. I hurt you and made you hate me. I suffered for it, Henry. There's nothing worse than being both the beloved and the behated.

GRANDPA: Not for once did I hate you. You get rest forever on that assurance. But if I were your beloved, how could you leave me for a total stranger?

OCTOBER: He was no stranger, Henry.

GRANDPA: You knew Suckrock before?

OCTOBER: Well, yes. I was his beloved before I was yours. You . . . Henry, you never guessed who he was?

GRANDPA: My dear, I never saw the man. All he was to me was a phantom. But he gave me more pain than any man on earth.

OCTOBER: And you to him.

GRANDPA: (He lifts an eyebrow and starts to object.)

OCTOBER: Oh, Henry, it doesn't matter now. I paid my debt to him. Let's not play tit for tat. That's past us now. We're alone! Come to me, Henry, come hold me!

They start to embrace. Offstage, they hear a nervous giggle that cataracts into maniacal laughter before the voice asserts itself and says, in devilish exultation, "Don't forget about me!"

18

★ ★ ★

Again, the Pilgrim

SEGUIN AND DALLAS
1983–1986

A Signal Day

SEGUIN
Winter 1983

It was one of those cold, stiff days, too raw and windy for flying, and I told him so. But Bobby wouldn't have it any other way. Uncle Herschel and Aunt Marguerite were down from Cement, Oklahoma, and Bobby insisted I chuck things for the weekend in Big D and drive to the trailer court in Seguin and show them how I could wing it. Pa had never seen me do it either. In fact, he was downright skeptical.

"Nobody as heavy as you are can just flap their arms and get off the ground," he reasoned.

I did feel stuffed. We had just had a big Sunday dinner. "Pa's probably right," I said, trying to beg off, but Bobby pulled me aside and said, "Billy, the only way I could get Herschel and Marguerite down here was to promise them that Daddy wouldn't take them to Corpus to see the seawall or go up in the Driscoll Tower. I told them we had something new to show them."

"You don't understand," I said. "I can't haul off and fly when I please. Everything has to be right. I have to have dreamed of flying, and—"

"Billy," Bobby said, "this may be Herschel and Marguerite's last

visit, ever. They're almost as old as Daddy is. We forget that sometimes, the way they act, still hugging and kissing like lovers. And
what've they done? They've driven more'n three hundred miles to
see you fly. You can't disappoint them."

"Bobby, I have to have that soaring feeling. I don't have it today.
I feel logy. Look at the weather! It has to be a help and not a hin-
drance. A slightly windy spring day is best, the kind that has a gentle
lift to it along the ground and a stronger current treetop."

"You sound like Icky and Sam Longmeyer."

"I know. It's strange, isn't it, that I would take up where they left
off? But I know what I'm talking about. When conditions are right, I
can ease up in stages, and let the wind carry me."

"Don't make excuses. I know you can do it if you really try.
What's the matter with you? Are you trying to make me look like a
fool? If you can't perform for the family, how're you going to take
your act on the road? When you turn pro, you're going to have to
deliver whether you feel up to it or not."

"My turning pro, as you put it, is your idea, not mine. I'm not
keen on becoming a carnival freak like Uncle Eddie."

"We're talking family here, Billy! Not some business proposition.
Will you do it for us or not? That's all I'm asking."

"Look," I said, "I'll go ahead and try it today, just for Herschel
and Marguerite, and to prove to Pa I can do it. But I can't guarantee
anything."

"Fantastic!" Bobby leaped an inch off the ground. "Here, hand
me your coat. You want your boots off?"

I stripped down to my shorts and T-shirt and started toward the
hill overlooking the rent trailers. Daddy had anchored his trailerhouse there so he could look down on his tenants. "Y'all come on," I
said, "the wind's blowing from the north. I've got to get high and
face into it, if I'm going to have any luck taking off."

"Give 'em some room," Bobby said, keeping the folks back
apiece and downwind of me. "He's going to go that way, right into
the teeth of it."

Before I gave myself to it in total concentration, I asked each of
them—Herschel, Marguerite, Daddy, Bobby and Daddy's cat, Cat—
to think of me flying, to picture it so vividly that I would pick up
their brain waves and get a boost from them.

That helped. I felt a buoyancy flowing from them. I closed my eyes and thought of lift-off. I stretched my arms out parallel with my shoulders and began to wave them, slowly at first, then faster. Pretty soon I was flapping to beat the band, my back arched, legs out straight and toes cupped toward the sky.

"My God!" screamed Aunt Marguerite, who rarely takes the Lord's name in vain. "He's a doing it! He's lifting off the ground!"

"Lordy, Lordy," Pa kept saying, "Lordy, Lordy."

Uncle Herschel yahooed and slapped his hat against his high thigh.

I was. That soaring feeling filled me like helium in a balloon. My bones felt hollow as Icky's yearned to be. But boy, was it a strain. I flapped fast enough to come off the ground a foot, then another foot. I fell back and touched the ground with a socked toe. But I squinted hard, as I do in dreams, and flapped faster and pushed myself on up until I was six, eight feet high. A waft of wind came up under me, and, just like that, I furled up and away, turning with the wind to soar above the tops of the mesquite trees. I banked into the wind, tipping starboard and came back with the wind behind me, flying over the folks, who waved.

Bobby called to me, "Go higher than the twins!"

He meant the two oaks beside Daddy's trailerhouse. They were great, gnarled giants with an expansive spread of branches. They must have been eighty feet high. I'd gone much higher psychically as a kid, but as a flapping man I've never gotten up more than sixty feet or so, and I could not top the twins. I tried until I was so tired I thought I might fall. I finally came down and slid into the hill on my belly, skinning myself on the rocks and mesquite thorns.

Still, it was a success, a signal day, and Uncle Herschel and Aunt Marguerite drove back to Cement satisfied. They said it beat the seawall and the Driscoll Tower by a mile. Daddy was proud. Yet nothing had changed. It was still the old days back in the Body of Christ. Daddy, and now Bobby, loved to show Herschel and Marguerite a good time when they came down to see us in Texas. I was happy to have been a part of it.

It was early evening. I was exhausted. I lay on the couch in the trailerhouse dozing, hearing with half an ear as Bobby talked of making a mint off me as a side attraction at air shows. Had a nightmare about being a freak. When I awoke and got ready to head back to Dallas, I told Bobby to forget about taking my act on the road.

"I'm sorry, Brother. But this is my thing, not yours or anyone else's. Besides, it's not an easy thing to live with, much less parading it around at carnivals. I can't begin to describe the pleasure I take in flying, especially on a day when I have it. But there's more to it than that. There's a darker side, which maybe I'll explain sometime."

He looked at me, affection and disappointment fighting for expression in his face. "Okay," he sighed, hanging a heavy arm across my shoulders. "I love you anyway, Billy, even if you are bound for the poor house."

NEWTON MEETS EINSTEIN

DALLAS
May 1984

For years my father's birthday fell on May 28. You could count on it like clockwork. The record said Pa was born on that date in 1902, and there was no wavering in our remembrance and celebration of his nativity. It seemed absolute, Newtonian. Time was real, continuous and circular, and there was no bull about atomistic relativity. Dates were like handles in history. Once they happened, they were set, and they would come around again just as they were, without fail. You could count on them and make plans.

That is how we did Daddy's birthday. We always met on May 28. Some of us had to come a long way, but it wasn't much of a strain. The highways would not crowd up until Memorial Day, two days hence. We were usually home by then.

But then they moved Memorial Day back to the last Monday in May, and more often than not, it fell on or next to the 28th. It became such a battle to find our way through holiday weekend traffic that we started fudging on the old man's birthday. A couple of us had had wrecks, coming close to wiping out branches of the line Pa had propagated. These close calls seemed counterproductive. We could reduce the risk by gathering early, and so we began lighting the old fart's candles the weekend before Memorial, although that was not always the case. The circumstances varied.

The result was that Daddy began experiencing some drift in his orientation. Year before that last, for instance, he called Joyce on the phone on May 11 and asked if we all were coming down the following Sunday.

"What for?" she said.

"For my birthday," he said.

"Daddy," she said, "your birthday is still three weeks away."

"Well, what's Sunday?"

"That's Mother's Day."

"Oh. Then yawl are not comin' down this weekend."

"No, Daddy. Mother is dead, you know."

"Woman, what are ye talkin' about? Natu'lly I know ye mother's dead. I don't sit around here talkin' to myself for nuthin'.'."

That last line, which he dumped on us from time to time, was his signal that he was lonesome.

That May, we were careful to notify him we would be in Seguin at the trailer on Saturday, the 21st. But when we drove up, we found him gone.

Turned out he had driven all the way to Oklahoma to visit Uncle Jim and put flowers on the grave of Aunt Esther and Mother.

"I thought yawl were not comin' until the sixth," he said in explaining his absence.

"The sixth? The sixth of what?" my sister said.

"The sixth of June."

Joyce looked at me. "What in grief is June 6?"

I went to the almanac. "The only thing I can figure is that it's D-Day, the invasion of Normandy."

"My Lord," she said. "And he wasn't even in the war."

Since the date stuck in his mind, we decided to go ahead and have his birthday at that time.

But since it was on a Wednesday, we moved it up to the weekend of the 2nd. Ought to have made everything perfectly clear.

PALLETS, SNORES AND BABY BREATHS

SEGUIN
June 1984

It was Pa's eighty-second birthday, or thereabouts, and yes, we all made it to the trailer park to wish his ornery hide more of the same in the way of longevity and filthy lucre. The oil well in Oklahoma was not the source of Daddy's fatcat years. He'd made himself what he figured was a fortune on the mobile home park.

He asked this every time we came: "How much money would you say a man would have to have before you could call him rich?"

We knew the question and we knew the answer, and each time our response was the same: "Why, shoot, Daddy. In this day and time, we'd have to say that a man would have to have at least as much money as you've got before you could call him rich."

"Yeah," he said. "You're probably right."

Then he'd chuckle to himself, shift about in his leatherette La-Z-Boy with the air of a man who had come into his own.

If there was not a ball game on TV, or some stupid sitcom or soap opera, he'd likely pull out his calculator and add up his worth. He did it every time we were there. It was for show, for surely he realized the repetition by now. He toted and bared the totals on the calculator the way we toted and bore good grades home. High marks. Blue ribbons. Gold stars. So a little geetus had come his aged way, and so he made much of it among us kids. We laughed about it, teased him about his Midas touch. What harm was there in his five-and-dime hubris? God knew he didn't throw money away. Hardly spent a nickel.

It was early in the evening. We were all blousy and bellied out from two days of beer and brisket, which brother-in-law Jimmy had barbecued on the oilfield drum. Pa was asleep in his recliner, TV blaring. The grandchildren were off on country roads burning rubber both ways while their towheads, the great-grandchildren, were piled one upon the other—sleeping puppies—on a pallet on the living room floor. A fan blew over their cotton tufts. We sat out on the patio chairs, picking meat from our teeth and wishing we had a notch or two left in the belt.

"I cain't move," Jimmy said. "If I drink one more beer, I'll bust."

Joyce was down to one hundred and eighty pounds. Lost sixty. Still, at four foot eleven, she was the best arm wrestler in the family, stronger'n her sons, who were in their late twenties. Joyce said, "Now Jimmy Baugh, you're not about to go to sleep on us with this much light left. Come on, let's take Billy down to the baseball pitching and see what we can hit."

"You bat," Jimmy said. "I'll just watch. I ain't got another swing in me."

"Are you a good batter?" I asked Joyce.

"Yeah," she said, challenging me with her green eyes. "I can out-hit Jimmy and the boys."

"I wasn't bad myself," I said, "once upon a time."

"Brother," she said, "you got yourself a match."

"Got any quarters?" Jimmy said. "We spent all ours yesterday. I whiffed ever'time. Joyce knocked the beJesus out of the balls."

"Go shake some out of Daddy's pockets," Joyce said. "He'll never know the difference."

It was one of those mechanical pitching machines. It was throwing baseballs, little hardballs as opposed to big softballs, and I stepped into the cage and watched three of the tiny things zip past me before I can get the bat off my shoulders.

"Goodness," I said. "They're fast. Small as peas. I can't even see the ball coming at me. Can we slow this thing down a notch? What is it on?"

"It's on medium," Joyce said. "You want it on slow? *You don't want it on slow, do you?*"

"Shush, Joyce. I don't want everybody in the park to think I'm some old granny that can't . . . "

"*Then you do want it on slow pitch?*"

"Just for practice, 'til I warm up."

She turned it on slow. I swung through a dollar of quarters and couldn't hit a thing.

"I can't believe it," I said, stepping back and handing her the bat. "I used to hit .400 and homers and all."

" 'Course that was slow pitch softball, wasn't it?" Joyce said.

"Well, yeah, but it's the same physics."

"Shit if it is," she said. "Anyone can hit a big, soft moon. Jimmy, turn that mother up. Turn it up to fast."

"Now, Joyce," Jimmy said. "You cain't hit it fast. Not even you can hit it fast."

"Yeah, Joyce," I said.

She put her bat down and walked over and turned the pitching machine on fast. Back at the plate, she knocked the stuffing out of almost every pitch.

I was beat. She was a middle-aged woman, weighed seventy pounds too much and on top of that she was weak from losing sixty pounds, and she was hitting like Reggie Jackson in October. I felt gout coming on. I limped with them back up the hill.

It was a hot, suffocating night and we were sweating like the pigs we were. But we loved and hated each other and the rump and romp of life, and when Pa waked and said, "How much money would you say a man would have to have before you could call him rich?" we roared and replied in unison, "At least as much money as you've got."

We filled up the floor of the trailer house with pallets. Starry, starry night. Snores and baby breaths.

KING OF THE HILL

DALLAS
Spring 1985

Word from Seguin.

The old man was in the hospital with crazy spells.

He imagined robbers were after him. Guys with guns. And that part was wrong. There was nobody. At least this is what the neighbors said, not seeing what his eyes had seen, not hearing what his ears had heard.

You know how doctors are. They have a rational, scientific explanation for everything, even the supernatural. They told Daddy that thugs from the underworld were not after him, that it was simply a case of not enough blood pumping to his brain, and he got disorientated. They called it hardening of the arteries, that old problem again, and said they couldn't do much about it at this stage in his life. He could hope the blood returns and his head clears, which it did after a couple of days.

He went home to the trailer on the hill and assumed he was out of the woods, told Bobby and Joyce they could go back to their families. They had to tell him he had another think coming, that this last spell was a turning point in his life.

The doctor said flatly he was not to drive, recommended he not be left to live alone anymore. The doc even said this to Daddy, who heard but didn't hear. Bobby and Joyce repeated it to him, as firmly as possible. It didn't take. The first thing he did when he got back to the trailer was to take his Chevy out for a spin. When he returned, he flung the car keys with marked abandon upon the kitchen table, almost hitting Joyce with them. He made much about getting the Chevy washed and waxed, wondering aloud why Bobby and Joyce kept hanging around.

How could any of us blame him? He had always been the most self-sufficient cuss, particularly crusty if he couldn't do things his way. Now, after a couple of spells, his own kids were trying to take his manhood away from him. He got up in our brother's face.

"I'm still king of this hill!" he roared.

But this time we couldn't back down. They broke him. For the first time. He growled and shook and said some terrible things. Then he cried for the fifth time in his adult life. The first had been at his mother's death, the second at Mother's close call on the Conoco Driscoll, the third when Joyce and I survived the bulls, the fourth at Mother's death, and now the fifth.

And he said weakly that he would accept it.

He knew he wasn't as sure as he was. He knew it would get worse instead of better. He went into the bathroom and dribbled a pathetic stream.

I remember placing my tiny hand in his and facing the world confidently. I think now of how deep his voice was, how big his hands and dick and hard his stream of piss—like a panther's. How rough were his whiskers, how blue the eye and forceful his swarm and smell. I think of him chinning with one arm when he was forty-eight. I think of the time he fell forty feet through a derrick before catching himself, like a glider monkey, on a girder and climbing right back up to the crown. I think of him outrunning a football star. I see him tying my Boy Scout knots and doing my high school algebra and college calculus, this Okie who went to the fourth grade when they wrote on slates. I remember Mother saying she never felt so safe as she did when Tice was on her side instead of against her. I taste his Sunday fried chicken and drink the hum and toast the implacable rectitude of his unswervingly masculine code.

With his somber approval, we turned the daily operation of the court over to trusted tenants, saw to it that his meals would be cooked and that people would watch over him from a respectable distance, and take him where he wanted. We left his car in the yard and the keys to it on his hook. You don't take everything away at once. Besides, when the doctor had told him to stop smoking cigarettes, he had.

I wrote him that hell, with our history, he and his fading brothers were lucky to be going through the decline of old age, that if he had been his half-sister Effie, his half-brothers William and Henry, or his brothers Marshall and Earl or Sister Maude, he would be dead now.

And I told him an encouraging fact I had discovered while going back through the family tree. Of the seventeen fathers who had preceded him in the male line, he was, if he forgot his older brothers, the second oldest to have lived, and this went back six hundred and twenty-three years through Texas, Oklahoma, Tennessee, New Jersey, Ireland and Scotland. The only Porterfield who had lived longer was Alexander, his great-great-great-great-great-great-great-great-grandfather who died in Scotland three hundred and ten years before, at the age of eighty-four. Alexander was heir to Duchall Castle, and is buried in the Porterfield Tombs, Kilmacolm Kirkyard, on the River Gryffe, outside Glasgow.

I closed by reminding Pa that it was time and the river, not his children, who were reducing him. The last thing I said was that I loved him. I did not know how it would be taken. Except for his confession of five years ago, he had been a man who did not speak of such things.

PA SAYS IT!

SEGUIN
Summer 1985

Daddy was on the phone pressing Bobby to come from Austin and help him pay his bills. It was the middle of July. Daddy was a month ahead on most of his accounts. Bobby saw to that. But the old man was worrying about August duns, which were hardly pressing. Bobby explained all that, but he wasn't satisfied.

"I want ye here at the trailer court this afternoon," the old man ordered. "Let's get these people paid and off my back."

"Daddy, nobody's on your back. I know your books better than you do."

"I can feel them breathin' down my neck, boy. Now git down here, ye hear?"

"I've got a full day, Daddy. It'll be dark before I get there, probably around nine."

"You mean nine in the mornin'?"

"No, Daddy. I mean nine tonight. You go on to sleep if you have to. I'll wake you with a tap on the door."

Bobby ran a mortgage company in Austin, and business was so lousy he was scratching bedrock. He had four demanding children who were in varying stages of new adulthood, and now he had a fifth who was in his second childhood. Since Mother's death, Bobby had carried the burden of dealing with Daddy because he was only an hour away by car. Well, hell, if he had been five hours away like me it would have been the same. Bobby had always been quicker on the trigger in jumping to family matters than his older brother, and so was Joyce, who at Three Rivers was more than two hours south of Seguin.

Around three in the afternoon, Bobby called from Austin to tell the old man he'd be later than nine, and for him not to wait up, that he'd spend the night and they'd get to the books the next morning.

Bobby pulled his station wagon up before Daddy's trailer on the hill about ten. In the beam of his headlights, he could see the old man's white head poking out the door.

"Boy, where ye been?"

"Daddy, I told you I'd be late."

"Shoot, boy. You must think my time is cheap, the way ye waste it. I been waitin' the whole day and half the night for ye to git here."

"Now Daddy, I always call and tell you when I'm running late. I've got business to attend to just like anybody else, but I always try to be here for you. So ease up, will you?"

"I'll ease up when the work's all done. Let's get to it. I don't want to wait until morning."

Under the circumstances, that suited Bobby fine. He sat and turned to the work at hand, figuring he'd be through in an hour or so and on the road back to Austin.

It is always a puzzle trying to piece together Daddy's papers. When the mail came, he stuffed envelopes absentmindedly into this pocket and that drawer. He did the same with rent checks, royalties from the oil well, social security, insurance and what have you. You might find $3,000 in the butter dish of the refrigerator, an obscure wastebasket full of checks that should have been cashed in 1981. And no matter in what order you put this chaos, it was not likely to suit the old man. He'd hound you with questions, as if you were not to be trusted. It was difficult to swallow, like eating tough old buzzard, and I've had but a taste of it. Bobby and Joyce had eaten whole carcasses of the bitter bird for years. But this time, after he was finished and about to leave for Austin, Bobby turned on the old man.

"Daddy," he said, "Joyce is in Three Rivers and Billy's in Dallas. But I'm within reach, and when you call I jump—"

"You said that when ye came in," the old man said.

"But I didn't get to finish," Bobby said. "What I want to say is that I have no sense at all that you appreciate a thing I do for you. In fact, as far back as I can remember, and I'm talking about when I was a kid, I don't remember ever satisfying you. I've never heard a word of encouragement or praise from you, not so much as a thank you."

"Well, I never heard such fadoodle," the old man said, staggering up from his easy chair and walking into the kitchen. He drew himself a glass of water and drank it, staring out the window.

"It's true, Daddy. Every time you've got a question about Medicare or taxes or whatever, I'm here. When you got that letter the other day from Ed McMahon saying you'd won ten million dollars, I drove fifty-three miles here just to tell you it was nothing more than a sales gimmick, and then you got mad at me instead of Ed McMahon. And so I drove fifty-three miles back to Austin with all that appreciation you showed on my mind. And you know what my conclusion was? I had to admit that I don't even know if you like me."

"Are ye out of ye mind, boy?"

"No. It's been this way all my life. You've never shown any interest or pleasure in the things I've done. Even now, you don't know my business, much less my heart. Daddy, I bet you don't even love me."

Daddy stiffened like his old mother when she thought someone might lose his head and haul off and hug her. He kept his head averted, intent on the blank window. "Shit, son," he roared, "I raised ye!"

"You raised a lot of dogs and horses, but you never told them you loved them, and they were the sorrier for it. Daddy, I don't think you've ever told anyone that. Did you ever say it to Mother? You've never said it to me. I'd like to hear you say you love me."

"What? Have ye lost ye mind?"

Bobby said the look on the old man's face was indescribable.

"Come on," Bobby said. "Out with it."

"Boy, I thank you been nippin'. Are ye drunk?"

Bobby moved up into his face. "Daddy, I need a thanks from you. We'll start with that."

Daddy set his mouth severely and closed his eyes.

"I'm not leaving until I get one," Bobby said.

"Hell, that's easy," Daddy said coldly. "I thank ye. Now git out of here. It's late. You're wastin' my time."

"I just want to hear you say you love me, just one time before we both croak. I'm gonna stay until you do."

"You leave, Bobby." Cursing, he drew more water from the tap and splashed it on his hard face and persimmon mouth.

"Not till you say it."

"Get out of here!" the old man cried. His husky voice broke, trailed off high and frail, like an ancient thing so exhausted it had no gender. All of a sudden, he turned shaking from the window and grabbed Bobby. "By damn," he managed to choke out tortuously, as if regurgitating some forbidden cud which had lain, sour and alien, upon his unruminating soul. "By damn, I love ye!"

He squeezed my brother tightly and drew him to his grizzled face, which he buried in Bobby's neck, weeping in great convulsions. They grappled with one another, hugging and crying. It was the first time Tice Porterfield had ever hugged a man. And it was the sixth time old T.C. had cried in eighty-three years, the second in the past year. At this rate, he was going to make a habit of it.

It wasn't concession, Bobby decided on the way home. It was confession.

He never spoke of love again to anyone, as far as we know.

But he seemed relieved of a great burden, and put his armor away. After that, Bobby could kiss him on the forehead on leavetaking, and the old man took it with grace.

My relationship with Daddy was different from the very beginning. Bobby and I since have talked about it. When we were boys, Daddy frightened Bobby with his unrelenting masculine code of do or die, and this was why, early on, Bobby became a hider. He didn't want the old man's hard little blue eyes and severe tongue singling him out any more than he wanted his whippings. When it came time for my brother to leave his dictionaries and crawl from under the house, he went forth bent on blending into the background of convention, running with the herd instead of ahead or behind it. And all the while he was as eccentric as any of us. I, on the other hand, almost invited my father's wrathful initiation. I knew it was what Daddy had gotten from Grandpa, and a tongue-lashing or a beating was better than nothing. It showed he cared for me, that he was correcting and preparing me to take over in his stead, toughening me for the obstacle course males had to run. He was the hardest initiator I ever had, and the more he laid it on the more confident I got. What is it that Nietzsche said? What doesn't kill me makes me stronger. I had so much ego and new skin dancing in its dazzle that I dared Daddy to flog my ass and break me. A time or two I came close to crying out in surrender, but the window on my vulnerability quickly closed, and I locked my jaw if not my tear ducts and went past him and on ahead as if I were invincible. I saw myself as a lightning rod. I strutted fire. Among male company, that is. From the beginning Mother knew my Achilles' heel, which was the fear my flash was of no account among females, of being passed over as someone dull and incidental, and it was years before I had the nerve to risk her devastating excommunication. The now whispering, now laughing all-seeing goddesses were the ones I needed to hear say they loved me. Of course, there were exceptions, women like Granny I loved to torment. But generally, for all my come-on, and swagger, I knew magical woman had me, not I her. It is still so with me, and I'm suddenly an old man.

AGAIN, THE PILGRIM

SEGUIN
July 1986

The old man was not as bound to his recliner and soap operas as we had thought. He was giving us a new worry.

It had to do with his driving, an old problem, yes, but he'd added a new wrinkle on a timeless theme. We found that he got in his Chevy and disappeared for days. Thrice, we'd found him (or other concerned parties had) miles from home, wandering about the countryside half-demented, like Lear in search of a kingdom to come.

It turned out that was precisely what he was seeking. Diddy
Waw Diddy again. After all these years of retirement, he was back on
the road, retracing the old paths and taking new ones, stopping to
ask this storekeeper and that gas attendant the same old directions:

"Diddy's just up ahead, idn't it?"

"Diddy?"

"Well, yes, you know, just a place in the road called Diddy Waw
Diddy."

"Never heard of it, friend. Now San Angelo's up ahead, but
that's a big place. This here's Eden."

"Nope. Don't need Eden, but it sounds close. I must be gettin'
warm."

"Well, sir, I don't know. Eola's the only wide spot in the road
between here'n San Angelo."

"What if I head north?"

"Eventually, you'd run into Paint Rock."

"And after that?"

The attendant went into his recitation. "Ballinger, Abilene,
Wichita Falls, the Red River and Oklahoma."

"Been to Indian Territory," Daddy said. "It's where I come from,
originally. I'm lookin' for Diddy Waw Diddy."

"As far as I can recollect, between here and the border there's,
let's see, there's a Demarton and a Dundee, and above Wichita
there's a Dan, but, boy, friend, I'd be surprised if they was a Diddy
Waw Ditty."

"Well, thank ye just the same. Reckon I'll continue west."

Something in Pa's demeanor—the attendant said later he
thought it was the look in Daddy's eye rather than his questions—
troubled the fellow, and he called the sheriff in Concho. The sheriff
radioed his deputy in Eola to watch for the old pilgrim in the faded
blue Chevy and feel him out without making a big deal out of it.
And that is how we caught up to him.

Again, we grounded him. I knew, we knew, he knew that once
we hung the keys on his hook, he'd drive off again. Haul off for
Diddy. But we couldn't treat him like a child. He had his rights.
Joyce worried about him killing himself, or worse, someone else on

the highway. But Mother had said that that would be Earl's fate, the former and not the latter, that Daddy had a different destiny. So Pa had his star regardless. And, really, all he had left were his dreams. And Diddy was the big one, the one he had followed most of his life.

"He probably thinks Ma's found Diddy, and is there waiting for him," I said.

"Naw," Bobby said. "He knows she's stalled up ahead, wondering what's keeping him."

"That's right," Joyce said, bursting into laughter. "He'll drag her all over creation all over again."

"I can just see them," Bobby said.

"Can you see us in the Terraplane with them?" Joyce said. "I don't mean now or tomorrow but someday."

"Why, of course!" Bobby said. "Three towheads bobbing in the back seat."

"Oh my God," Joyce said, tears rolling down her ruddy cheeks. "What'll I do with Jimmy? He's not a happy traveler."

"*Divorce him!*" Bobby and I cried in unison, and we all hooted and danced, chanting:

> *It's not a town*
> *It's not a city*
> *Just a place in the road*
> *Called Diddy Waw Diddy.*
>
> *Doo-waw-diddy-diddy-doom-life*
> *Doo-waw-diddy-diddy-doom-life*
>
> *Where da roof is made of pancakes*
> *And da roast duck fly by with*
> *Foik and knife.*
>
> *Doo-waw-diddy-diddy-doom-life*
> *Doo-waw-diddy-diddy-doom-life.*

19

★ ★ ★

Until Death Do Thee Part?

The span of earthly things is as a dream; but a fair welcome is given him who has reached the West.
—INSCRIPTION ON THE ROYAL TOMBS AT MEMPHIS, 3000 B.C.

PORTERFIELD CEMETERY, LITTLE EGYPT, OKLAHOMA
August 9, 1986

TICE COVEY PORTERFIELD: Move over, Mama! Make me some
room. This old man is wore out. Whew!

JANAVEE ELIZABETH HARRELL PORTERFIELD: Well, if this don't beat all
(grinning)! What took you so long, Daddy? I was beginning to
think I was going to have to rot down here all by myself.

TICE: Lord A'mighty, woman. You do look muddy and water-logged.

JENNIE: It's the cheap coffin you put me in.

TICE: It's what you wanted, the kids said.

JENNIE: Yeah, you old skinflint, (chuckling) and you were happy
enough to oblige me my last wish. But I wouldn't change it for
anything in the world. What does it matter down here? I wanted
Billy, Bobby and Joyce to get the extra money while they're still
up there. They're still up there, aren't they? You left them
ever'thing, didn't you?

TICE: Ever' dime, ever' foot of that trailer park and my part of the oil
well.

JENNIE: You're sure, Daddy? You didn't go crazy like an old coot at the
end and spend some of those CD's? *Did you get you a woman,*
Tice Porterfield?

TICE: Nupe. I had plenty of offers, but I turned all of 'um flat down. Heh. heh. I sat on nat hill and watched them CD's grow in the bank till the principle poked through the ceiling. You know what it finally amounted to?

JENNIE: Why, I can't imagine. I'm not even sure how long it's been since I've been dead? How long?

TICE: Well, you died in March of '79, and here it is August of '86. That's six years, plus nine months in '79 and eight months in '86 would make it, let's see, well that'd make it seven years and five months that I was a widower.

JENNIE: I swan, Daddy, you lived a long time without me. I knew you would, long as you had that recliner, that TV and that calculator to add up your money. How much was it, finally?

TICE: (He looks around, then whispers in her ear.)

JENNIE: My God, Daddy. That much? Well, I'm so tickled for the kids. And for us. You. You made it and watched over it. I guess it was just as well you were tight as a persimmon. I know I would have given it to them gradually, dollar by dollar, until nothing was left to leave them.

TICE: I made it for the boys to blow. I'm in my grave maybe five minutes and I'll kiss your butt here in front of God and ever'thang if Billy and Bobby don't spend it all before the flowers fade on my grave. Hell! Before they get home from the funeral. Joyce won't. Jimmy won't let her, but the boys—

JENNIE: Well, they have a good time. (She eyes his coffin and frowns.) Daddy, you haven't exactly arrived in a pine box. That coffin must have cost a pretty penny! Why, it's almost as long as our trailerhouse. Makes mine look like kitty litter. What is that's written on the side?

TICE: I don't know. I guess the kids did it. I haven't had time to get out and look. Can you read it?

JENNIE: Daddy, it says, "The Bark of Ra," and down at the foot it says, "Diddy Waw Diddy Bound." And for Heaven's sake, Daddy, it's got wheels on it! Your coffin's got radials. Why, it's the trailerhouse all over again. There's even a TV down at your feet!

TICE: You don't say. Heh, heh, those towheads, they didn't forget a thang. And look, Mama, I hadn't noticed before, but they put the old saddle under my head.

JENNIE: Well, it is nice, alright. Thoughtful. But what'd you pay for all that?

TICE: I didn't have nothin' to do with it. It was all done after I kicked the bucket.

JENNIE: How did you go?

TICE: (He looks at her with an odd expression.) Heart attack. Had one in the trailer. But the killer was the one you and Mother brought on at the hospital. You know, it hit me just after yawl talked to me and put the hex on me.

JENNIE: Well, we wondered if we'd gotten through to you. All we wanted was for you to come on down.

TICE: (Raising a wicked eyebrow) Was that because you missed me?

JENNIE: (Laughing) Well, your mother misses you, since you're dead ringers for one another. Old Alice'll be glad to hear you've arrived. I wanted you down here because I was afraid you'd live so long you'd leave the kids nothing. You know, I always put the kids first.

TICE: Woman, you don't have to rub it in my face, not after all these years, and please not here in the grave. I was hopin' for better things.

JENNIE: Boy, you got another think coming.

TICE: Why, what's it like?

JENNIE: (She whispers in his ear.)

TICE: (Face falling) *The same old thang!* Ah, come on, woman! It's gotta be better than that. I'm talking about Heaven, not Hell. Ain't we in Heaven?

JENNIE: More like in between, as far as I can tell. Even your pious old mother doesn't seem to know any more about it than I do, and you know how long she's been down here. It's still a big mystery exactly where we are and where we're going and what's it all about. Looks like we got a long way to go.

TICE: (Brightening) You don't say. Sounds like Diddy Waw Diddy all over again, so I guess the kids were right in outfitting my rig like this. Little woman, we may have to do some traveling after I rest a hundred years or so. I am tuckered out. A catnap of a century or so would do me a world of good. Which reminds me. Billy told me the damndest thing before I died. He said some professor he knew had done a study of Diddy Waw Diddy, and had concluded that it was not only nigger heaven, but nigger hell! Can you beat that?

JENNIE: I'm going to beat you if you don't stop saying nigger. I know Billy didn't put it that way. You can't get away with that here.

TICE: It had got that way up there too. Sorry. Anyway, Billy said a town named Diddy Waw Diddy had actually existed in Texas. I guess it was the one place we missed. Billy said it was somewhere between Richmond and Rosenberg in Fort Bend County. Can you imagine? A white man a'lookin' his whole life for black folks' heaven or hell or whatever, and not knowin' it?

JENNIE: White, black, technicolor, it's all the same. I'm not sure Diddy even exists. God knows we never found it in life. This may be it, the grave the best and the worst.

TICE: Woman, Diddy's got to exist, or it wouldn't have the tug on people the way it does. Gravity doesn't pull at us for nothing. It's a'fightin' the magnetic attraction of Diddyland. That's how I figure it.

JENNIE: I wish it was true, too, Daddy. But there's nothing down here to suggest—

TICE: Where've you been, woman?

JENNIE: You mean since I was dead? Well, I been to Seguin twice to spook you, and I went to that family reunion in Dallas where Billy Mack made me so mad I left early—

TICE: And that's it?

JENNIE: Well . . . I've been so fascinated listening to the weeping and wailing and whispering of the dead around me that I haven't—

TICE: . . . that you haven't hit Purgatory Road. Shoot, woman, don't disappoint the family name. We're moving soon as I get my bearings. I ain't about to molder in my grave. If Diddy Waw Diddy's out there, we'll go look for it, and by God, we just might find it.

JENNIE: Oh, shoot, Daddy. It makes me tired just thinking about it.

TICE: Well, we'll abide here awhile, like we did in Seguin. Catch our breath. And then we'll head west toward the setting sun.

JENNIE: Daddy, it's already set on us.

TICE: Do you know what time it is? I left Billy my Rolex.

JENNIE: Time? It doesn't mean anything down here.

TICE: Well, since we got a TV, let's pass it by catching up on the

soaps. I'm way behind on "The Young and the Restless." I wonder if they thought to put a plug in this coffin?

JENNIE: I'd rather listen to the neighbors. Listen, Daddy . . . Hear all
that moaning and groaning and regret? It never ceases.

TICE: What channels do they have down here?

JENNIE: Good Lord, Daddy. The plug's been pulled. Period.

TICE: No way, woman. We're bound for glory.

20

★ ★ ★

A Cautious Ba

☆ AND WHAT OF DOODY MAREAIN AND HIS MOTHER AND THEIR date with Osiris?

Sorry. Not this time. I'm still pretty much in the dark about that. This'll scare Doody away for a while anyway. He said it was a sin for the living to get too close to the dead. Every time he said it I had to laugh to myself, because in that case Doody was blacker than a tar baby. If black is sin. White works just as fair, polar bear. They are poles so apart they've backed up into each other. But I'm hopeful, attentive for word of Doody.

You know what I would like to report. I dream it often, but how can I say it's true? It could be a fiction like this that has been my life, a delusion, a conceit of ego, or worse, a conceit of spirit. How can I separate it when it slides so easily into my days? After it has me, I can say that in the drowse of October afternoons, when half fires in the hearth and half dreams drug and memories are as long as an old man's teeth, Doody returns. His Ba flits about the edges of my conscious, beckoning. My little blackbird joins his, and he leads me into the underworld, as he led me in my youth to the tombs. I go far enough to see him past Osiris and become a bony-like man again. I see him wade into the Field of Reeds and find the Great Lake in the Field of Offerings where the great gods sit. He turns and waves, and I respond. But I must turn back. Already I've gone too far. I wing my way back home, carving in my mind a prayer to Osiris on Doody's behalf. May his calamities be at an end. May the great gods give him the Tree of Eternal Life. May his white bread never decay, his red beer never stale. And may he take his pure seat in the bow of the Bark of Ra, and may they row forever from the East to the West.

★ ★ ★

Diddy Waw Diddy
or Ditty Waw Ditty

(Brazoria, Texas)

The significance of the name given by Black residents of the area lies somewhere between heaven and hell. One explanation is that it was a conception of heaven, a place of no work or worry for "man or beast," thought up by nineteenth-century slaves. Diddy Waw Diddy wasn't nearly so stern and formal as the white folks' heaven, however. Another version claims Diddy Waw Diddy was the last depot stop on the railroad to hell. Youngsters who did not walk the straight and narrow were told by elders that they were headed for Diddy Waw Diddy if they didn't mend their ways.

—*1001 Texas Place Names,*
Fred Tarpley, University of Texas Press, 1980

diddy-wah-diddy *n.* also *doo-wah-diddy* Also sp. *diddie wa diddie* old-fash.
Used as a substitute for a word or name one does not want to use; hence as the name of an imaginary place, often conceived of as fabulous and far-off.
1929 in 1983 Taft Blues Lyric Poetry 30 (Black), Then I got: put out of church Because I talk: about diddie wa diddie too much. **1942** Amer. Mercury 55.223.91 **Harlem NYC** (Black), I'd walk clear to Diddy-Wah-Diddy to get a chance to speak to a pretty lil' ground-

angel like that. Ibid. 94, Diddy-wah-Diddy—a far place, a measure of distance. (2) a suburb of Hell, built since way before Hell wasn't no bigger than Baltimore. The folks in Hell go there for a big time. **1960** Williams Walk Egypt 114 **GA,** It (a radio program called Ozark Jubilee) was as real to him as Diddy-Wah-Diddy was to a Negro child, Diddy-Wah-Diddy where the roofs were made of pancakes and roast ducks flew by with knives and forks in their backs, quacking, "Sweet, sweet, come eat." **1981** NADS Letters, Southern Illinois (white) has Doo-Wah-Diddy as a similar imaginary place . . . It is often used as a thingamabob word for a place; it occurs in teasing answers to questions about location and so on. No longer current. Ibid., in my Mississippi childhood there was a song on the Grand Ole Opry (then strictly white) with the lines: "It ain't a town and it ain't a city,/ It's just a little place called Doo-Wah-Diddy." This, like Diddy-Wah-Diddy, seems to have been a Land of Cockaigne, especially of sexual license. **1988** DARE file **csWI,** Phil Harris popularized a song called "That's What I Like About the South" (DARE Ed: Words and music by Andy Razaf, c1944) that had these lines: "Let me tell ya' 'bout a place called Doo-Wah-Diddy/ It ain't a town and it ain't a city/ But it's awful nice and it's awful pretty/ and that's what I like about the South."

—*DICTIONARY OF AMERICAN REGIONAL ENGLISH*, VOL. II D-H;
FREDERIC G. CASSIDY, ED.,
Belknap Press of Harvard University Press,
Cambridge, Massachusetts, and London, England, 1991

Glossary

Agathokakological—good and evil
agruw—to frighten, to make someone shudder
beek—to bask in sun or before a fire
bellibone—pretty girl
cockshut—dusk, when the roosters retire
chantpleure—sing a sad song
devilshine—act like the devil
fadoodle, flapdoodle—talk nonsense
faffle—to blow hard; so much gust
fellowfeeling—empathy, sympathy
flag-fallen—out of work and on the bum
hoddypeak—a dunce
hum—spirited alcoholic drink
liripoop—a tassel on a graduate's mortarboard; an over-educated lout
mally—silly in love
mubblefubbles—the blues
roaky—hoarse and incomprehensible
smellsmock—a dirty old man
snapsauce, snapsaucer—stolen soup; a food sneak
spuddle—hot air and bullshit
swerk or swerked—to trouble, or be troubled
sloom or sloomy—to make sleepy or be sleepy
tear cat—a ranting show-off or cry baby
wheeple—a whistle or fart that falls flat
xenodochial—being friendly and open to strangers

Copyright Acknowledgments

Billy Porterfield's Labor

HE HAS WRITTEN FOR NEWSPAPERS, MAGAZINES, RADIO AND TELEVISION. He has been a reporter for the *New Braunfels Zeitung*, where he was fired for covering in English a city council meeting conducted in German. He went on to report for the *Houston Chronicle*, the *Detroit Free Press*, and the *Chicago Daily News*. He was a columnist for the *Dallas Times Herald* before he was fired by telephone. He had a radio show in Dallas before he was fired. And he was with KERA-TV-Radio, the Dallas Public Broadcasting station, from 1969 to 1978, where he became executive producer and news director before he was fired by telephone. He was fired as a columnist for the *Plano Courier*. He has not yet been fired as a columnist for the *Austin American-Statesman*. *Diddy Waw Diddy* is his seventh book and the only good one, so don't bother with the others, which were starter logs for the great hearth fire that is *Diddy*. His other titles include *LBJ Country*, *A Loose Herd of Texans* and *Texas Rhapsody*. Porterfield's prizes include the 1963 Ernie Pyle Memorial Award from Scripps-Howard, two Stanley Walker Awards for distinguished writing from the Texas Institute of Letters (TIL), the 1967 Dobie-Paisano Fellowship from the TIL, a gold medal from the Atlanta Film Festival and the George Peabody Award for broadcasting, given by the University of Georgia.